The Politics of the Female Body in Contemporary Turkey

Gender and Islam Series

Series Editors
Professor Nadia Al-Bagdadi, *Central European University, Hungary*
Professor Randi Deguilhem, *National Institute of Scientific Research (CNRS), France*
Professor Bettina Dennerlein, *University of Zurich, Switzerland*

Advisory Board
Madawi Al-Rasheed, *Middle East Centre, London School of Economics, UK*
Kathryn Babayan, *University of Michigan, USA*
Jocelyne Cesari, *Berkley Center, Georgetown University, USA, and University of Birmingham, UK*
Dawn Chatty, *University of Oxford, UK*
Nadia El Cheikh, *American University of Beirut, Lebanon*
Hoda Elsadda, *Cairo University, Egypt*
Ratna Ghosh, *McGill University, Canada*
Suad Joseph, *UC Davis, USA*

Published and Forthcoming Titles
Queer Muslims in Europe: Sexuality, Religion and Migration in Belgium,
Wim Peumans
Mainstreaming the Headscarf: Islamist Politics and Women in the Turkish Media,
Ezra Ozcan
Masculinities and Displacement in the Middle East: Syrian Refugees in Egypt,
Magdalena Suerbaum
Sex and Desire in Muslim Cultures: Beyond Norms and Transgression from the Abbasids to the Present Day, Aymon Kreil, Lucia Sorbera and Serena Tolino (Eds)
The Politics of the Female Body in Contemporary Turkey: Reproduction, Maternity, Sexuality, Hilal Alkan, Ayşe Dayı, Sezin Topçu and Betül Yarar (Eds)

The Politics of the Female Body in Contemporary Turkey

Reproduction, Maternity, Sexuality

Edited by Hilal Alkan, Ayşe Dayı,
Sezin Topçu and Betül Yarar

I.B. TAURIS

LONDON • NEW YORK • OXFORD • NEW DELHI • SYDNEY

I.B. TAURIS
Bloomsbury Publishing Plc
50 Bedford Square, London, WC1B 3DP, UK
1385 Broadway, New York, NY 10018, USA
29 Earlsfort Terrace, Dublin 2, Ireland

BLOOMSBURY, I.B. TAURIS and the I.B. Tauris logo are trademarks of
Bloomsbury Publishing Plc

First published in Great Britain 2021
This paperback edition published 2023

Series design by Adriana Brioso
Cover image © Untitled by Serpil Odabaşı, 2019

A catalogue record for this book is available from the British Library.

A catalog record for this book is available from the Library of Congress.

ISBN: HB: 978-0-7556-1740-1
         PB: 978-0-7556-4274-8
         ePDF: 978-0-7556-1742-5
         eBook: 978-0-7556-1741-8

Series: Gender and Islam

Typeset by Integra Software Solutions Pvt.,Ltd

To find out more about our authors and books visit www.bloomsbury.com
and sign up for our newsletters.

To all women who were subjected to sexual and reproductive violence and to the feminists whose dedication has given us our rights.

Contents

Illustrations

Figures

Tables

Contributors and Editors

Hilal Alkan is Research Fellow at Leibniz Zentrum Moderner Orient, Berlin. She works on migration, care ethics and informal welfare provision, with a particular focus on gender. Her most recent publications include 'The Gift of Hospitality: (Un) welcoming Syrian Migrants in Turkey' (2021) and 'Syrian Migration and Logics of Alterity in an Istanbul Neighbourhood' (2020). She has co-edited *Urban Neighbourhood Formations: Boundaries, Narrations, Intimacies* (Routledge, 2020).

Ayşe Dayı is a feminist activist scholar and meditation teacher. Her areas of expertise are women's sexual and reproductive health care and rights, medicalization of reproductive health, transnational feminism, neoliberal globalization and health policy. She has published on the legacy of the US Women's Health Movement and autonomous feminist clinics, foetal personhood and women's bodily integrity, and on the effects of the neoliberal health restructuring and conservativism on eroding women's sexual and reproductive rights in Turkey. At the time of the preparation of this manuscript, she was an Academy in Exile Fellow at the Margherita von Brentano Center in Freie University, Berlin. Currently, she is the Founder and Director of *Orca Dreams: Platform for Mindful Living*.

Selen Göbelez is a PhD candidate of social anthropology at *Ecole des hautes etudes en sciences sociales* (EHESS, Marseille) with a thesis on the women's narratives of childbirth in contemporary Turkey. Her research interests focus on gender studies, medical anthropology and social movements. In addition to her academic work, Selen is a *doula* and an activist for women's reproductive health rights, who also worked previously as an independent researcher, translator, editor and writer with a field experience in Cambodia, Jamaica and Sri Lanka besides Turkey.

Burcu Kalpaklıoğlu is a PhD candidate at the University of Amsterdam in the Department of Anthropology. Her research interests focus on Islamic jurisprudential discourses on marriage and family, Islamic feminism and politics of gender in contemporary Turkey.

Eylem Karakaya, MSc in Obstetrics and Gynecology Nursing, is a sexual health educator and activist based in Istanbul, Turkey. Eylem has been developing educational modules for seventeen years and providing trainings on sexual and reproductive health and gender equality for children, adolescents, parents and educators in schools, colleges, municipalities, the private sector, the Ministry of Education, Ministry of Family and Social Policies, and for NGOs. She also coordinates projects and conducts research in the areas of women's rights and sexual and reproductive rights. Her latest publication is 'Fertility Characteristics and Related Factors Impacting on Syrian Refugee Women Living in Istanbul'.

Azer Kılıç is Assistant Professor in the Department of Sociology at Istanbul Bilgi University. She holds a PhD from the International Max Planck Research School on the Social and Political Constitution of the Economy, Cologne. She has published in the fields of gender, social policy, interest representation and reproductive technologies, in journals such as *Economy and Society, Social Science & Medicine*, and *Social Policy & Administration.*

Şafak Kılıçtepe is Assistant Professor in the Department of Anthropology at Kırşehir Ahi Evran University. Her interests include science and society studies, reproduction and reproductive technologies, anthropological demography, nation-state, gender, race, ethnicity and identity. Her PhD dissertation titled 'Reproductive Technologies, Pronatalism and Ethnicity: An Ethnography of Situated Reproduction in Turkey' (2019) investigates how the relationship among assisted reproductive technologies, political Islam and changing ethnic-minority status shapes the experiences, strategies and negotiations of infertile Sunni Kurdish women in Turkey. She is one of the coordinators of STS Turkey, which is the Turkish Scholarly Network for Science and Technology Studies.

Burcu Mutlu is an independent researcher. Her research interests focus on assisted reproductive technologies (namely gamete donation and embryonic sex selection); biopolitics of biotechnologies; feminist studies of family, kinship and gender; transnational reproduction; and feminist science and technology studies. Her recent publications include: 'Gizleyerek Aile Olmak: Yurtdışında Yasaklı Biyoteknolojilerle Çare Arayışları' [Making Families in Secrecy: Seeking Forbidden Biotechnologies as Last Resort Abroad] (2018), and 'Morally Accounting for Sex Selection Online in Turkey' (2017).

Nurhak Polat is Postdoctoral Research Fellow in the Department of Anthropology and Cultural Research at the University of Bremen, Germany. She completed her dissertation in European Ethnology at Humboldt University in Berlin. Her research and teaching interests are medical anthropology, science and technology studies, digital technologies and authoritarianism. She currently works on the intersection of authoritarianisms, digital technologies and data politics. Her book in German is *Umkämpfte Wege der Reproduktion: Kinderwunschökonomien, Aktivismus und sozialer Wandel in der Türkei* (2018). Her most recent publications: 'Negotiating masculinities: reproductive technologies, biosocial exclusion and men's engagements in Turkey' (2020) and 'Koronavirüs normalliği, viral izler ve dijital otoriterleşme' (2020).

Seda Saluk is Postdoctoral Research Fellow in the Department of Women's and Gender Studies at the University of Michigan, Ann Arbor. Her research interests focus on medical anthropology, feminist science and technology studies, and Middle

East studies. She has published on politics and technologies of public health and reproduction in modern Turkey. Her most recent article is 'Türkiye'de Üreme Sağlığı ve Kürtaj Tartışmaları' (Reproductive Health and Abortion Debates in Turkey) (2020).

Esra Sarıoğlu is a researcher at the Center for the History of Emotions at Max Planck Institute for Human Development, Berlin. She works at the intersection of feminist theory, sociology of emotions and globalization studies. Her work on gender appeared in *Gender, Work & Organization*, *Women's Studies International Forum*, and *Kadın/ Woman 2000*.

Sezin Topçu is a sociologist of science, technology and medicine. She is a senior researcher at the French National Research Center (CNRS), and a lecturer at *Ecole des Hautes Etudes en Sciences Sociales* (Ehess, Paris). Her current research tackles the dynamics of medicalization of the female body and the related controversies in France and Turkey. Since 2016, she has been the principal investigator of the international research project '(Over)medicalization of Childbirth as a Public Problem: Material Trajectories, Public Controversies and Institutional Changes' (ANR *Hypmedpro*). In 2019, she coordinated a special journal issue on the same theme for *Health, Risk & Society* (vol. 21, issue 3–4), in collaboration with Patrick Brown, Ilana Löwy and Kirstie Coxon.

Didem Ünal is a postdoctoral researcher at the Religion, Conflict and Dialogue Research Center at the Faculty of Theology of University of Helsinki. Her research interests focus on gender politics in contemporary Turkey, Muslim women and politics of Islamic veiling in Western diasporic contexts, Muslim feminism, everyday Islam and Muslim fashion. Her recent publications appeared in various academic journals such as *Women's Studies International Forum, Journal of Women, Politics and Policy, European Journal of Women's Studies* and *Politics & Gender.*

Betül Yarar is a professor and working as a senior researcher at the University of Bremen. Before, she has done various research projects concerning different aspects of gender and body politics. The most recent one is her study that she has conducted as a Phillipp Schwartz Fellow of Alexander Von Humboldt Foundation at the same University with the title 'Neoliberal-Neoconservative Biopolitics of AKP and Counter-Strategies of Women's Movement(s) in Turkey'. She has also given courses on gender, violence and body politics in various countries. In respect to her experience as an exiled scholar, since 2019, she has engaged in exile studies. Her most recent publication appeared in *New Perspectives on Turkey, 2020.*

Acknowledgements

This book is an enlarged outcome of the international symposium 'Neoliberal-Authoritarian Modes of Governing the Female Body: Health, Reproduction and Sexuality in Turkey' held at the Bremen University on 5–6 April 2018. We are grateful for the support of the host institution, EHESS-Paris and the French National Research Agency, that co-financed the symposium through the ANR Hypmedpro Research Project. We have also benefitted from the logistic and financial support of the Leibniz Zentrum Moderner Orient, Berlin, the Alexander von Humboldt Stiftung, the Academy in Exile, and Margherita-von-Brentano Zentrum at the Freie Universität, Berlin.

With diligence and kindness, Ruth Mas created miracles in language editing. Nico Putz and Jona Vantard put incredible effort in getting the bibliographies in order, and Svenja Becherer assisted us during the lengthy final process.

The illustration on the cover is created by the wonderful artist Serpil Odabaşı, who understood our concerns and wishes and transformed them into a unique and beautiful work of feminist art.

We are lucky to have worked with Sophie Rudland and Yasmin Garcha as our editors at I.B. Tauris, and we are greatly indebted to our series editor Nadia Al-Bagdadi for her trust in the project.

Introduction

Changing Regimes of Governing Women's Bodies in Contemporary Turkey

Hilal Alkan, Ayşe Dayı, Sezin Topçu and Betül Yarar

In *The Second Sex*, Simone de Beauvoir wrote: 'to be present in the world implies strictly that there exists a body which is at once a material thing in the world and a point of view towards the world' (Beauvoir 1949 [1982]: 39). Female bodies have, following her analysis, constantly been spaces lived or experienced by women, and entities gazed at or encountered by others, with the latter largely shaping the former. They have in this respect been privileged sites of male control and domination throughout history.

This edited volume illustrates and examines the various ways in which neoliberal modes of governing women's bodies come together with religious, conservative and authoritarian measures in contemporary Turkey. Focusing on the fields of reproduction, maternity and sexuality where political and gendered power exerted on women have been the most significant, our ambition is to propose a feminist intervention into the domain of increasingly hegemonic and naturalized discourses on the female body that come to the surface in medical establishments, court-rooms and public discussions. At the same time, this volume is an inventory of women's responses to desired, attempted or executed actions on their bodies. Hence, this volume is a diverse account of politics of the body-in-the-making during the first two decades of the twenty-first century in Turkey.

Like in many other nation-states, since its inception, 'citizenship in the modern Turkish nation-state is inextricably linked to gender, sexuality, and reproduction' (Miller 2007: 348). Situating bodies as the 'microphysical domain of power' (Zengin 2016), a 'politics of intimacy' (Korkman 2016) has always been a major element of Turkish biopolitics, that links demographics to nation-building and economic development. However, until the last two decades, politics of the body has been understudied as part of the feminist scholarship. Seminal works like Şirin Tekeli's (1995), Yeşim Arat's (2000), Deniz Kandiyoti's (1987; 1988) and Nükhet Sirman's (1995), reflecting the spirit of the time they were written, critically analysed modernization discourses, and highlighted juridical processes, issues of representation and familial relations as the core realms of gendered operations of power and accompanying dissidence. More recent scholarship builds on their analysis and takes it further to examine the close relationship between the political investments in the body and the gendering practices of the Turkish state (see for example: Parla 2001, 2020; Kogacioglu 2004; Korkman 2015; Ozyegin 2015; Sehlikoglu 2015; Scalco 2016; Zengin 2016; Güzel 2018). In parallel, political commentaries and public debates that concern with intimate relations, interventions on the body and reproductive and sexual capacities are also on the rise. A state-level 'masculinist restoration' (Kandiyoti 2013) project targets women's bodies through gender-based violence, intimidating public discourse, impunity for perpetrators, and with softer measures like interpellation and persuasion. This happens at a time of neoliberal restructuring/destructuring, a rising paternalist authoritarianism and increasing power of conservative politics. The chapters in this volume offer a fresh view into the politics of the body under these conditions in contemporary Turkey.

Convergences of neoliberalism, authoritarianism and conservatism

Governing women's bodies with religious, patriarchal or economic concerns is certainly not a novelty, yet new forms and modalities are emerging and older canons are being transformed under the global sway of expanding neoliberal policies, rising authoritarianism(s) and evolving conservatism(s). From the 'illiberal democracies' of Eastern Europe (Grzebalska and Pető 2018) to the United States, from India to the United Kingdom (Phipps 2014), as well as in Turkey, women experience previously unimaginable (self-)control over their bodies, while at the same time being subjected to equally unimaginable interventions both inside and outside their skins. While their reproductive capacities are, as ever, approached as a matter of national and communal interest, their bodies are intimately surveilled and transgressed upon by the new technologies that carry these interests to the microscopic hair of their uterus or to the molecular cocktails of drugs and treatments running in their veins. Most of this certainly has to do with the expansion of the market-oriented rationality that is commonly called neoliberalism, which operates at times, as in Turkey, in conjunction with pronatalist policies and in other contexts with population control.

The authors in this collection approach neoliberalism with the joint use of Marxist and Foucauldian perspectives, with inspiration from Wendy Brown (2005; 2006; 2018). Approached as such, neoliberalism has been hegemonic for the last three decades in most parts of the world, with its varying consequences on welfare regimes, that have resulted from the imposition of austerity measures, and the restructuring of health systems. While these developments have had important implications for all gender and sexual identities (see for example the analysis of neo-patriarchy in Campbell 2014), they have affected women in specific ways via increasing commercialization of women's access to reproductive health care, as well as the increasing medicalization and commodification of the female body, and of pregnancy and motherhood itself (Duden 1993; Rapp 1999; Topçu and Brown 2019). Since their onset in the 1980s, the biopolitical and the bioeconomic dimensions of governmentality have been the distinctive and determining features of all neoliberal rationalities and regimes. The expansion of IVF and egg markets, the commodification of pregnancy and motherhood through surrogacy, and the privatization of gynaecological and obstetrical care are some illustrative cases among many (for feminist analyses of these developments, see: Franklin 2006; Cooper 2008; Walby and Cooper 2008; Inhorn 2012; Lafontaine 2014). While each of these areas include varying levels of surveillance and control on women, conservative and authoritarian forms of government, which have become the norm in an important number of neoliberal settings (as in the United States, Hungary, Turkey and India), directly assault women's bodies, their health and their sexuality; and legitimize this assault with patriarchal notions of religious morality. The Turkish case, without being unique, offers a privileged laboratory for an in-depth analysis of these transformations.

Although the book is mainly contextualized by Turkey's neoliberal years, which spans from the 1980s, it particularly focuses on the period after 2002, when the AKP (Justice and Development Party) has been in power. After its initial 'reformist' period, which lasted from 2002 to 2008, the AKP's political tendency shifted from being a neoconservative party with some liberal views, to one of authoritarian conservatism (Bruff 2016; Bruff and Tansel 2018; Yarar 2020). The party's brand of authoritarian conservatism has involved the increasing centralization and personalization of power, which has culminated in a presidential system that holds power over the Parliament (Kaygusuz 2018), and has accentuated Turkish nationalism with strong references to Sunni Islam. Mobilizing religious values and discourses has been increasingly crucial to the AKP's elaboration of a 'new regime' (geared towards the foundation of a 'New Turkey') out of a very specific synthesis of neoconservatism, neoliberalism and authoritarianism.

Within this new setting, the offensive drive of pronatalist forces has become the main issue that has led to renewed and sometimes paradoxical discourses, practices and regulations about reproductive rights, family/gender policies and the administration of women's sexuality (Özbay, Terzioğlu and Yasin 2011; Acar and Altunok 2013; Korkman 2016; Yarar 2020). Accordingly, starting from the second half of the 2000s, the central role of women in reproductive and domestic work has been reaffirmed via the government promotion of family values and religious discourses. Yet, this has contradictorily encouraged women's reinsertion into the labour market, albeit mostly on a part-time and precarious basis. Abortion was reopened to political and religious debate for the first time, since its legalization in 1983. Thanks to strong feminist resistance, the allowed time-period for abortion was not decreased and neither was the procedure banned. However, due to neoliberal measures and the conservative pressure put on medical providers and institutions, abortion services have become inaccessible to women in public hospitals and they are being pushed towards private care (O'Neil 2017). With the restructuring of health care, there has also been a decrease in the availability of birth control methods and family planning counselling (Dayı 2019; Saluk, in this volume).

In terms of the interactive effects between neoliberal mechanisms and conservative discourses and policies in Turkey, we are also able to cite the regulations that were placed on assisted reproductive technologies (ARTs) and on C-section interventions. IVF interventions benefitted from insurance coverage, but the expanding restrictions on access to these services provoked new social and economic inequalities, as well as new types of discrimination against unmarried or same-sex couples (Gürtin 2011; Göknar 2015). Surrogacies, egg and sperm donation and sex selection are formally forbidden, but they continue to be practised in adjusted forms (Mutlu 2017; Mutlu, in this volume). The abuse of caesarean births was raised as an issue by public authorities themselves for pronatalist reasons (Frank and Çelik 2017), but private hospitals, where the boom is the most significant, are still only subject to 'loose' regulations (Topçu, in this volume).

Sexuality, the control of which lies at the heart of all citizenship frameworks (Miller 2007), has also become a matter of large-scale public debate in the past decade. Invoking the tradition of the Republic that links the nation's well-being to the chastity and virtue of women (Kandiyoti 1988), the debates have evolved at different levels. First, there has been an increasing tendency to sexualize women's clothing while scrutinizing their public behaviour. The drastic outcomes of the circulation of such discourses have found expression in misogynist vigilante violence directed against women in urban public spaces or media (Sarıoğlu, in this volume). Second, there have been widespread discussions on who is entitled to have a sexually active life that specifically target university students and those engaged in extramarital relationships. Third, legal jurisdiction on sexual crimes has come under scrutiny and amendments that would justify criminal offenses have been proposed. Fourth, Kurdish women's bodies and the intimate spaces they inhabit came under unprecedented attack – often verging on sexual violence – during the military operations against Kurdish cities in 2015–16 (Üstündağ 2015; Alkan 2018). Last but not the least, different sexual identities have been increasingly policed and trans-and-homosexual communities have been marginalized even further.

Between control and resistance

While this book was in its final preparation phase in the summer of 2020, the Council of Europe Convention on Preventing and Combating Violence Against Women and Domestic Violence, famously known as the Istanbul Convention, has come under assault. One after the other, significant male figures of the AKP made declarations against the Convention, which was signed and ratified by Turkey in 2011, in a Council of Europe meeting in Istanbul under the hospices of an earlier AKP government. They expressed their discomfort with the Convention on two grounds: first, its prerogative against discrimination based on sexual orientation and gender identities in the application of legal tools; second, the presumed threat it has posed on the unity of family in Turkey (Akçabay 2020; İlkkaracan 2020). Their discourses made clear how much, in their eyes, women's bodies and wellbeing were considered dispensable for the sake of keeping male-dominated families intact. In juxtaposition, even government-supported women's groups objected to the proposal and a wide goal-oriented coalition was formed.

While the primacy of the family and women's inclusion in the citizenship framework as reproducers of the nation constitute the baseline, the neoliberal, authoritarian and conservative ways of governing the conduct, bodies, reproductive rights and sexuality of women constitute hybrid regimes. They converge in many cases yet appear to be irreconcilable and entirely antagonistic in many others. The analysis of recent modes of governing women's bodies becomes even more complicated when one considers the fact that these policies have had differential impacts on subjects of diverse ethnic, cultural, sexual identities, and for women in different social, economic and political positions. Women respond to these modes of governing in equally diverse ways. They often bargain and strategize to calibrate their own desires with the situations in which they find themselves (Kılıçtepe, in this volume; Polat, in this volume). They also resist subordination and refuse to obey the attempts to sexualize and regulate their behaviour (Sarıoğlu, in this volume; Göbelez, in this volume). They try to find a middle path between religious doctrines and the wellbeing of their fellow women as well as their own (Kalpaklıoğlu, in this volume). Finally, they also relentlessly resist, create their own political discourses and claim their bodies and agency. In short, what we discuss in this edition is not a unidirectional hegemonic governance but a politics of the body made up of many voices and actors that interact under conditions specific to contemporary Turkey.

One significant element of these conditions is the increasing prominence of religion in public and government discourses. Debates on topics ranging from criminal law to pregnancy attire have all become arenas where different interpretations of the Islamic doctrine and more secular arguments are positioned against each other so as to further the control of women's bodies. However, the main focus of this edited volume is not Islam; the different types of diagnosis we propose for the Turkish case regarding the changing regimes of female body governance do not *de facto* take Islamization as the central interpretation frame, either. Some of the chapters in this volume explore how Islamic references, embedded within conservative discourses, interact with the neoliberal market discourses and implementations, which leads to the (attempted) control of women's bodies and sexuality in contemporary Turkey. They also illustrate different positions within self-identified Muslim circles (Ünal, in this volume; Yarar, in this volume). This book elaborates on the ways religion appears in the changing governmental technologies of Turkey as a potent source of legitimization, while resisting the popular urge to discuss the issues at hand as a matter of Islamization. The contributions, especially those in the final section, provide a nuanced understanding of these developments. In that sense the arguments in this compilation confirm Frank and Çelik's (2017: 201) argument that 'policy positions [in Turkey]… cannot be explained merely by the Islamic versus secular divide'. Instead there is a continuity in targeting women's bodies and reproduction 'to promote population growth and to deepen control over the population' (2017: 213) throughout the Republican era, albeit with the employment of slightly changing discursive strategies.

This volume brings together diligent ethnographic inquiry and discourse analysis. The contributors offer a close-up view of how female bodies are targeted by government policies and market forces – a task undertaken by doctors, nurses, midwives, bureaucrats, journalists, lawmakers and, literally, men on the street. Strategies of governance also span a wide range, from outright violence to compassionate compelling, from threats of abandonment to celebrations of conformity. The tools used are as varied as possible: fatwa booklets, lancets, syringes, lit cigarettes, computer screens, databases, journals and social media clicks accompany better-known surveillance apparatuses of the state. Each chapter presents a different constellation of these actors, techniques and technologies with detailed accounts from the field.

In sum, this book is about bodies and the ways they are shaped and manipulated, and have become reproductive, barren, desirable, vulnerable and disposable. However, as the title suggests it is not about all bodies in the time-space of contemporary Turkey, and not even the bodies of all women. Its scope is limited to heterosexual cisgender women, that is, women who were born with female genitalia and self-identify as women at the time research was conducted. The inclusion of the experience of trans and lesbian women would have broadened the horizon of the book and enriched the debates. The present focus is more incidental than deliberate. Despite much effort, we could not guarantee a recent and previously unpublished contribution from the very few scholars who work on these topics in the Turkish context. However our contributors benefit a lot from the analysis of the encounters of transgressive bodies with the state, as they provide crystallizations of the state's tactile power (Zengin 2016), the questions of intimate sovereignties (Zengin 2019) and construction of femininity as the disqualifier for male citizenship (Başaran 2014). As much as the male/female divide, that brings together the medical and the legal, is key to biopolitics in Turkey and all around the world (Miller 2007: 351), the category of women as the object of regulations, interventions and legal sanctity is built with reference to the bodies that transgress this divide. Hence, although this is a collection on cisgender female body politics, the contributions reflect the awareness that the technologies and fantasies that address and shape these bodies are in continuation with the ones that non-binary, transgender and non-heterosexual bodies encounter, often more violently. We are also proud that the chapters presented herein bring to the fore the voices of women from different classes and ethnicities in their encounters with neoliberal and neoconservative governmentalities of today and their varied responses to these forces.

Overview of chapters

The book is organized in three parts in order to explore and illustrate three domains of bodily politics: reproduction, maternity and sexuality. The chapters in the first part focus on the marketization of reproduction and the questions of morality that accompany this process. The first chapter, entitled 'Neoliberal Health Restructuring, Rising Conservatism and Reproductive Rights in Turkey: Continuities and Changes in Rights Violations', provides a broad yet brief description of the neoliberal mechanisms and neoconservative pressures on women's sexuality and reproduction, and their rights specifically in relation to neoliberal restructuring of healthcare with its market, bureaucratic and conservative arms. Using their focus group data from five cities, Ayşe Dayı and Eylem Karakaya investigate sexual and reproductive rights violations in contemporary Turkey in the areas of abortion, birth control, birth and routine gynaecological care. Given the restructuring of healthcare in 2003 by the AKP and the rise of neoconservatism, which has at its centre pronatalist and at times misogynist discourses, policies and implementations, the authors focus on rights violations. They first identify the continuities in rights violations, like judgemental care, the lack of adequate information, gynaecological violence during gynaecological exams, birth and abortion care. Second, they provide examples of the augmentation of existing rights violations, such as the newer forms of the invasion of privacy produced by the digitalization of health data, and the increasing difficulties of being a single, lesbian or a refugee woman in the system. Finally, they look into the newly emerging violations created by neoliberal policies and conservative pressures, such as decreased access to contraceptives and abortion care, and decreased access to sexual and reproductive counselling.

The second chapter of this section, 'Crafting Moral Agency in Transnational Egg Donation: The Case of Turkish Egg Donors', by Burcu Mutlu, addresses the disguised reproductive travels of young Turkish women 'donating' their eggs for money in neighbouring, Turkish-speaking Northern Cyprus. Based on her observations of and interviews with egg donors who visit a Northern Cypriot fertility clinic (after the 2010 Turkish ban on gamete donation abroad), Mutlu examines how these young women actively participate in transnational egg donation as a new (clandestine) realm of financial opportunity, and, thus, how their eggs become disembodied, mobile and exchangeable. She argues that Turkish egg donors are not only pragmatic and entrepreneurial but are also moral agents and not simply passive objects of commodification. Attending to the experiences of Turkish egg donors, this chapter aims to shed light on the forms of bodily (re)productivity of women in the twenty-first-century global bioeconomy.

Continuing on the theme of ARTs as emerging markets and sites for the negotiation of gender, sexuality and moralities, Nurhak Polat's chapter is entitled 'Fantastic Microscopic Hair of Uterus': Navigating Reproductive Trajectories, Biomedical Bodies and Renegotiation of Heterosexual Femininities and Masculinities. It brings us specifically into the gender work that is reproduced in a neoliberal-authoritarian context, and enabled with the emerging biocapitalist sites of ARTs. The chapter captures how heterosexual middle-class women and men navigate their reproductive journeys in Turkey in assisted reproduction clinics. Given the fact that the treatments are coded as predominantly female terrains, Polat argues that the reproductive trajectories related to infertility are marked by complex gender work situated in the morally contested biomedical space of ARTs, which became sites of bargaining with the patriarchal gender and kinship order, and with the policies and public moralities of the biomedical sciences.

'Feeling Like a "Misfit": Kurdish Women's Entangled Reproductive Experiences in Turkey' by Şafak Kılıçtepe is the last chapter of the first section. Here, Kılıçtepe analyses the kinds of reproductive experiences that emerge from the gendered and ethnic subjectivity of Kurdish women and the positions they hold within their communities and in the nation. She contextualizes the historical details surrounding the reproductive experiences of Kurdish women within the intersecting systems of family/community and nation. Kılıçtepe's chapter is particularly illustrative of the conflicting and overlapping claims of different authorities on women's bodies. The entanglements she explores touch upon Turkey's ongoing suppression of Kurdish identity and culture, while at the same time point to the patriarchal notions that position women as the reproductive safeguards of the nation, i.e. the Kurdish nation, as opposed to the Turkish nation. In that sense, Kurdish women navigate through two competing patriarchal systems – the patriarchal system of the nation state and the patriarchy nested in their community – while negotiating their own desires and the suffering they undergo to become mothers.

The second part of the volume explores how the neoliberal and neoconservative transformation of the healthcare sector interacts with biomedical power to impact women's bodies and their maternal experiences. In her chapter titled 'Banning Caesareans or "Selling" Choice? The Paradoxical Regulation of Caesarean Section Epidemics and the Maternal Body in Turkey', Sezin Topçu explores the diverse and sometimes unexpected fallouts of the recent regulatory measures targeting caesarean 'abuse' in the public and the private sectors. She analyses the ways C-section procedures – whose routinized use was problematized as a public health problem by WHO already in 1985 and has since then been denounced as a form of violence and disrespect against women – have contributed to new justifications that are positioned at the centre of neoliberal and conservative concerns and policies during the past years. Utilizing ethnographic observations, Topçu shows in particular that the 'caesarean law' of 2012 in Turkey, which was meant to regulate a problem that was mostly produced in the private sector, has rather served to place public hospitals under greater pressure of profitability and performance, while the private sector took benefit from these developments in order to better promote C-sections as women's 'choice'. Women, women's demands and women's needs for a safe, empowering birth experience have been mostly pushed aside in this framework.

Seda Saluk, in her chapter 'Monitoring Pregnancies: The Politics and Ethics of Reproductive Health Surveillance in Turkey', scrutinizes another key development of the recent health reforms and regulations in Turkey aiming to govern women and their maternity: the monitoring of pregnant bodies via electronic health records, software systems and centralized databases. While the Turkish Ministry of Health and the World Health Organization have celebrated the rise and circulation of new surveillance mechanisms, the implementation of these mechanisms has profound impact on the ground. Seda Saluk probes this process in contemporary urban Turkey through her investigation of the controversial reproductive health surveillance program GEBLIZ (Pregnancy Monitoring System). She examines the introduction, implementation and impact of this program in public health policies and practices related to the pregnant body. The chapter argues that these new technologies of reproduction are predicated upon not only regulating women's bodies and sexualities but also reshaping their labour and care practices. New surveillance mechanisms thus operate as a particular mode of reproductive governance in today's Turkey.

In order to reorganize maternity in neoliberal and in conservative-pronatalist frameworks, more radical or 'extreme' reproductive technologies have entered the scene in Turkey during the past years as well. Elective egg freezing, legalized in 2013, is one of them. In her chapter entitled 'Egg-freezing Narratives of Women: Between Medicalization and Marketization', Azer Kılıç tackles the reasons and ways women make use of this new technology. She reveals the socio-economic perspectives on three major aspects of women's experiences of egg freezing. First, women do not decide to freeze their eggs in order to better focus on their future career goals, as suggested in Western mainstream media. Rather their decisions to freeze their eggs are shaped by their (past) experiences of education and work. Second, while egg freezing initially appears at odds with moral norms, such as the need to preserve the hymen as an indicator of virginity, Kılıç shows that virgin women who opt for egg freezing medicalize and redefine virginity, and medical markets offer various remedies to alleviate women's concerns in this area. Third, egg-freezing women explain their behaviour with risk management and self-investment. With the introduction of the concepts of individualization of risk and responsibility, and emphasizing medicalization and market forces, Kılıç's chapter continues the debate introduced by the first section on the negotiation of morality, gender and sexuality by women in the ART sites that are evolving.

In the final chapter of this section, 'Tactics of Women Up against Obstetrical Violence and the Medicalization of Childbirth in Turkey', Selen Göbelez looks into women's experiences in birth and operation rooms. Complementing Topçu's analysis of the over-medicalization of childbirth, Göbelez documents the violence inherent in this process. The intimate accounts of her interlocutors describe how women feel disrespected, humiliated and intimidated, how much unnecessary physical pain they have to endure and also how they strategically manoeuvre and resist their subordination during one of the most significant events of their lives.

In the final part of the book, our contributors explore different examples and corresponding dimensions of the ways in which women's bodies and sexualities are governed and controlled through moralizing discourses and/or the use of symbolic or physical violence. This adds to the discussion of obstetrical violence in the previous sections of the book. In this way, this volume highlights the various types of violence against women, all of which have risen exponentially and became more public in the last decades in Turkey. In the first chapter of this section, 'Misogynist Body Politics under the AKP Rule in Contemporary Turkey', Esra Sarıoğlu focuses on vigilante violence directed against women with reference to moral norms (mainly concerning female sexuality) in public places in the past few years. She illustrates the link between these events that increasingly take place in the urban centres of the country, and the hegemonic discourse on proper womanhood. Sarıoğlu argues that these violent acts differ from the more common forms of violence to which women are subjected under patriarchal social systems – like domestic violence or partner violence – because the most recent perpetrators are men who attack women they don't know in public. Sarıoğlu argues that certain women are chosen as targets because of the ways they are seen as insubordinate to hegemonic femininities with their appearance. Hence she approaches these attacks not as singular violent acts but as the reaching out of a governmental logic that targets female bodies by sexualizing them, only to then humiliate and punish them.

Betül Yarar's chapter 'Disciplining Pious Female Bodies/Sexualities in the Authoritarian Times of Turkey: An Analysis of Public Moral Discourses on *Süslümans*' introduces another form of violence, i.e. symbolic violence, which is directed by religious authorities taking place in the media towards the women who identify themselves as Muslim and pious, who wear headscarves and who follow certain religious restrictions. These women, who act not only as religious subjects but also with class motivations, are called Süslüman in social and mainstream media. The concept of Süslüman signifies a critique that targets these women's performances of religious identity and symbols within the scope of Islamic fashion. Yarar's analysis of discourses on the concept of Süslüman delineate recently widening social tensions that seem to be emerging along the lines of class, ethnicity and age among conservatives that extend beyond the classical opposition between 'Islamists' and 'Laicists'. Yarar argues that these tense and conflicting sociological dynamics, which have aroused simultaneously under the impact of neoliberalism, might lead to new social cracks existing within the social basis of the new power block. Yet, it is the power block that attempts to appeal to widening anger among religious conservatives against the new age performances of young pious women. These also partly explain the populist sensitivities to which the AKP government and its authoritarian regime appeal.

Moving from social media debates to everyday negotiations and deliberations of religious norms, Burcu Kalpaklıoğlu's chapter entitled 'Guiding the Female Body through the *Alo Fetva* Hotline: The Female Preachers' Fatwas on Religious Marriage, Religious Divorce and Sexual Life' focuses on the intimate encounters between female state-employed preachers who work in the hotline of the Directorate of Religious Affairs and women who seek religious guidance in their personal lives. The chapter sheds light on the ways preachers negotiate their clients' needs, religious norms and the government's stance on the subject of female sexuality. It illustrates how norms of proper femininity and female sexuality are not completely fixed, but are flexible and open to different interpretations by preachers. On the other hand, it also underlines the desire of religious conservative authorities to control and regulate femininities with the use of newly invented governance techniques. These are the techniques through which 'improper' femininities are made targets of intervention, this time not by violence but by compassionate preaching and counselling.

In the final chapter of the section and of the volume, 'Positioning the Critical Pious Self vis-à-vis Authoritarian Populist Body Politics: Limits of Feminist Dissent in Pious Women Columnists' Narratives in Turkey', Didem Ünal looks into the commentaries of pious women columnists on key moments of feminist mobilization between 2010 and 2020. Ünal applies frame analysis to these narratives to dissect the factors that lead to a cleavage between these otherwise pro-feminist columnists and feminist political agents. Her analysis emphasizes the borderland position of these writers particularly on the issues that relate to reproduction and sexuality. Hence, what they debate is, once again, the politics of the body.

With all these rich discussions on women's sexuality, reproduction and motherhood, this edited volume explores how women navigate through the neoliberal, neoconservative, religious and authoritarian discourses and policies in contemporary Turkey. Looking into how gender and sexuality are incorporated into neoliberal projects also provides insight into understanding the alliance of the latter with conservatism. We firmly believe that these experiences resonate in many other global contexts undergoing a similar trajectory, and the chapters provide ample data and conceptual tools for comparison.

References

Acar, F. and G. Altunok (2013), 'The "Politics of Intimate" at the Intersection of Neo-Liberalism and Neo-Conservatism in Contemporary Turkey', *Women's Studies International Forum*, 41: 14–23.

Akçabay, F. C. (2020), 'Bir garip imza hikayesi: İstanbul Sözleşmesi', *Gazete Duvar*, 5 July. Available online: https://www.gazeteduvar.com.tr/konuk-yazar/2020/07/05/bir-garip-imza-hikayesi-istanbul-sozlesmesi/ (accessed 6 October 2020).

Alkan, H. (2018), 'The Sexual Politics of War: Reading the Kurdish Conflict Through Images of Women', *Les Cahiers du CEDREF. Centre d'enseignement, d'études et de recherches pour les études féministes*, 22: 68–92.

Arat, Y. (2000), 'Gender and Citizenship in Turkey', in S. Joseph (ed.), *Gender and Citizenship in the Middle East*, 275–86, New York: Syracuse University Press.

Başaran, O. (2014), '"You Are Like a Virus" Dangerous Bodies and Military Medical Authority in Turkey', *Gender & Society*, 28 (4): 562–82.

Beauvoir, S. de (1982), *The Second Sex*, Harmondsworth: Penguin (original publication: 1949, *Le Deuxième Sexe*, Paris: Éditions Gallimard).

Brown, W. (2005), 'Neo-liberalism and the End of Liberal Democracy', in *Edgework: Critical Essays on Knowledge and Politics*, 37–60, Princeton: Princeton University Press.

Brown, W. (2006), 'American Nightmare: Neoliberalism, Neoconservatism and De-democratization', *Political Theory*, 34 (6): 690–714.

Brown, W. (2018), 'Neoliberalism's Frankenstein: Authoritarian Freedom in Twenty-First Century "Democracies"', *Critical Times*, 1 (1): 60–79.

Bruff, I. (2016), 'Neoliberalism and Authoritarianism', in S. Springer, K. Birch and J. MacLeavy (eds), *The Handbook of Neoliberalism*, 107–17, New York: Routledge.

Bruff, I. and C.B. Tansel (2018), 'Authoritarian Neoliberalism: Trajectories of Knowledge Production and Praxis', *Globalizations*, 16 (3): 233–44.

Campbell, B. (2014), 'After Neoliberalism: The Need for a Gender Revolution', *Soundings*, 56 (Spring): 10–26 (17).

Cooper, M. (2008), *Life as Surplus: Biotechnology and Capitalism in the Neoliberal Era*, Seattle: University of Washington Press.

Dayı, A. (2019), 'Neoliberal Health Restructuring, Neoconservatism and the Limits of Law: Erosion of Reproductive Rights in Turkey', *Health and Human Rights Journal*, 21 (2): 57–68.

Duden, B. (1993), *Disembodying Women. Perspectives on Pregnancy and the Unborn*, Cambridge: Harvard University Press.

Frank, A. and A.B. Çelik (2017), 'Beyond Islamic versus Secular Framing: A Critical Analysis of Reproductive Rights Debates in Turkey', *Journal of Middle East Women's Studies*, 13 (2): 195–218.

Franklin, S. (2006), 'Embryonic Economies. The Double Reproductive Value of Stem Cells', *Biosocieties*, 1: 71–90.

Göknar, M. D. (2015), *Achieving Procreation. Childlessness and IVF in Turkey*, New York, Oxford: Berghahn.

Grzebalska, W. and A. Pető (2018), 'The Gendered Modus Operandi of the Illiberal Transformation in Hungary and Poland', *Women's Studies International Forum*, 68: 164–72.

Gürtin, Z. (2011) 'Banning Reproductive Travel: Turkey's ART Legislation and Third-party Assisted Reproduction', *Reproductive Biomedicine and Society Online*, 23 (5): 555–64.

Güzel, H. (2018), 'Pain as Performance: Re-virginisation in Turkey', *Medical Humanities*, 44 (2): 89–95.

İlkkaracan, P. (2020), 'The Istanbul Convention Debate: What Has Changed in a Decade?', *5Harfliler*, 15 August. Available online: https://www.5harfliler.com/pinar-ilkkaracan-istanbul-convention/ (accessed 6 October 2020).

Inhorn, M.C. (2012), 'Globalization and Gametes: Reproductive Tourism, Islamic Bioethics, and Middle Eastern Modernity', in M. Knecht, M. Klotz and S. Beck (eds), *Reproductive Technologies as Global Form: Ethnographies of Knowledge, Practices, and Transnational Encounters*, Berlin: Campus Verlag.

Kandiyoti, D. (1987), 'Emancipated but Unliberated? Reflections on the Turkish Case', *Feminist Studies*, 13 (2): 317–38.

Kandiyoti, D. (1988), 'Bargaining with Patriarchy', *Gender & Society*, 2 (3): 274–90.

Kandiyoti, D. (2013), 'Fear and Fury: Women and Post-revolutionary Violence', *Open Democracy*, 10 January. Available online: https://www.opendemocracy.net/en/5050/fear-and-fury-women-and-post-revolutionary-violence/ (accessed 10 November 2020).

Kaygusuz, Ö. (2018), 'Authoritarian Neoliberalism and Regime Security in Turkey: Moving to an "Exceptional State" under AKP', *South European Society and Politics*, 23 (2): 281–302.

Kogacioglu, D. (2004), 'The Tradition Effect: Framing Honor Crimes in Turkey', *Differences: A Journal of Feminist Cultural Studies*, 15 (2): 119–51.

Korkman, Z. K. (2015), 'Blessing Neoliberalism: Economy, Family, and the Occult in Millennial Turkey', *Journal of the Ottoman and Turkish Studies Association*, 2 (2): 335–57.

Korkman, Z. K. (2016), 'Politics of Intimacy in Turkey: A Distraction from 'Real' Politics?', *Journal of Middle East Women's Studies*, 12 (1): 112–21.

Lafontaine, C. (2014), *Le corps-marché. La marchandisation de la vie humaine à l'ère de la bioéconomie*, Paris: Seuil.

Miller, R. A. (2007), 'Rights, Reproduction, Sexuality, and Citizenship in the Ottoman Empire and Turkey', *Signs: Journal of Women in Culture and Society*, 32 (2): 347–73.

Mutlu, B. (2017), 'Morally Accounting for Sex Selection Online in Turkey', *Biosocieties*, 12 (4): 543–67

O'Neil, M. L. (2017), 'Abortion Services at Hospitals in Istanbul', *The European Journal of Contraception and Reproductive Health Care*, 22 (2): 88–93.

Özbay, C., A. Terzioğlu and Y. Yasin, eds (2011), *Neoliberalizm ve Mahremiyet. Türkiye'de Beden, Sağlık ve Cinsellik*, Istanbul: Metis.

Ozyegin, G. (2015), *New Desires, New Selves: Sex, Love and Piety among Turkish Youth*, New York: New York University Press.

Parla, A. (2001), 'The" honor" of the State: Virginity Examinations in Turkey', *Feminist studies*, 27 (1): 65–88.

Parla, A. (2020), 'Revisiting 'honor' through Migrant Vulnerabilities in Turkey', *History and Anthropology*, 31 (1): 84–104.

Phipps, A. (2014), *The Politics of the Body: Gender in a Neoliberal and Neoconservative Age*, Cambridge: Polity Press.

Rapp, R. (1999), *Testing Women, Testing the Fetus. The Social Impact of Amniocentesis in America*, New York: Routledge.

Scalco, P. (2016), 'The Politics of Chastity: Marriageability and Reproductive Rights in Turkey', *Social Anthropology*, 24 (3): 324–37.

Sehlikoglu, S. (2015), 'Intimate Publics, Public Intimacies: Natural Limits, Creation and the Culture of Mahremiyet in Turkey', *The Cambridge Journal of Anthropology*, 33 (2): 77–89.

Sirman, N. (1995), 'Friend of Foe? Forging Alliances with Other Women in a Village of Western Turkey', in Ş. Tekeli (ed.), *Women in Modern Turkish Society: A Reader*, London: Zed Books.

Tekeli, Ş., ed. (1995), *Women in Modern Turkish Society: A Reader*, London: Zed Books.

Topçu, S. and P. Brown (2019), 'The Impact of Technology on Pregnancy and Childbirth: Creating and Managing Obstetrical Risk in Different Cultural and Socio-economic Contexts', *Health, Risk & Society*, 21(3/4): 89–99.

Üstündağ, N. (2015), 'Ekin Wan'ın bedeninde ifşa olan devlet ya da kadınlar sıra bizde [The state exposed in the body of Ekin Wan, or women it's now our turn]', Evrensel, 23 August.

Walby, C. and M. Cooper (2008), 'The Biopolitics of Reproduction: Post-Fordist Biotechnology and Women's Clinical Labour', *Australian Feminist Studies*, 23 (55): 57–73.

Yarar, B. (2020), 'Neoliberal-neoconservative Feminism(s) in Turkey: Politics of Female Bodies/Subjectivities and the Justice and Development Party's Turn to Authoritarianism', *New Perspectives on Turkey*, 63: 113–37.

Zengin, A. (2016), 'Violent Intimacies: Tactile State Power, Sex/Gender Transgression, and the Politics of Touch in Contemporary Turkey', *Journal of Middle East Women's Studies*, 12 (2): 225–45.

Zengin, A. (2019), 'The Afterlife of Gender: Sovereignty, Intimacy and Muslim Funerals of Transgender People in Turkey', *Cultural Anthropology*, 34 (1): 78–102.

Part One

Governing the reproductive body: Emerging markets and contested moralities

1

Neoliberal Health Restructuring, Rising Conservatism and Reproductive Rights in Turkey: Continuities and Changes in Rights Violations

Ayşe Dayı and Eylem Karakaya

Neoliberal health restructuring in Turkey

In the latest stage of neoliberalism, termed *the debt economy* by Maurice Lazzarato (2012), finance dominates every sector of the economy and society, from housing, education and health, to public services. Through mechanisms such as privatization and the imposition by banks and rating and investment agencies of interest rates, and of 'appropriate rates' for unemployment wages, pensions, public services and the rates of public debt for governments and municipalities, the public sector (including the welfare state) is completely dismantled, privatized, public debt is created and the role of the state is turned into a regulator of services that is itself bound to credit and debt mechanisms.

Lazzarato (2012: 10) writes that 'the neoliberal power bloc cannot and does not want to "regulate" the excesses of finance but seeks to follow through on a program it has been fantasizing since the 1970s: reduce wages to a minimum, cut social services so that the Welfare State is made to serve its new "beneficiaries" – business and the rich – and privatize everything'. Assaults on welfare systems include the restructuring of healthcare. This is seen in the latest case of Greece (Europe Solidarity Declaration 2013) as well as in the global emergence of a 'health reform epidemic' (Klein 1993), or, in World Bank discourse, of Health Sector Reforms (HSRs). These are reforms undertaken in the late 1980s to early 1990s in 'developing' countries such as Brazil, Mexico, South Korea and Taiwan, always under the rationale of a 'healthcare crisis' and framed in terms of efficiency and cost while the public sector is denigrated as corrupt and inefficient, and markets are seen as a panacea to many problems (Ağartan 2012). The AKP's 'Health Transformation Program', launched in Turkey in 2003, also outlined an agenda to 'improve governance, efficiency, user and provider satisfaction, and the long-term fiscal sustainability of the healthcare system', and is part of this global neoliberal trend. As in these other geographies, the latest Turkish health reform also originated in the late 1980s and took shape within the Ministry of Health as a result of reports prepared by public health academics from Harvard and Johns Hopkins and in consultation with World Bank advisers (Keyder 2007).

Turkish health reform shares many of the characteristics of neoliberal global health reforms such as financial reform, managerial reform, changes in service provision, decentralization and the quantification of services over quality of care in the name of 'cost reduction' and 'efficiency'. Changes in healthcare provision and financing, which specifically relate to sexual and reproductive health, include the closing down of the AÇSAP (Mother-Child Health and Family Planning) Directory that had specialized in reproductive health provision in primary care, the introduction of the 'family physicians system' the implementation of a performance system for healthcare that comprises abortion, prenatal follow-ups, births and the digitalization of health data.

In the new system, former 'health centres' (*sağlık ocağı*) and AÇSAP centres were replaced with family health centres (FHC) and 'community health centres' (*toplum sağlık merkezi*) at the primary level. Family physicians, the intended 'gatekeepers' of the system, would provide preventative care and refer patients to a secondary level for specialized care. Different from the previous system, the family physician system brought on a form of semi-privatized care, which added to the ongoing privatization of care. The family physicians work as contract workers who contract midwives and nurses for a period of two years, with their wages based on the capitation set by the socio-economic development of their region. The salaries of physicians, midwives and nurses are subject to performance criteria and can be cut by up to 20 per cent when they fail to reach their targets. Instead of serving a geographic area (as previously done), FHCs serve the population who register under them. Physicians compete with one another to keep their clientele and to keep patients that have less chronic problems.

Rise of neoconservatism and sexual-reproductive rights

Alongside neoliberal policies, there has also been a rise in neoconservatism under the AKP regime. Initially calling itself a moderate Islamic regime, the social policies of the AKP can be best described as 'an amalgam of neoliberalism with social conservatism' (Buğra and Keyder 2006: 3) and have at their centre, anti-women, and at times misogynist discourses, policies and implementations that reposition women in familial roles thereby overturning decades of gain by feminist movements in Turkey towards the recognition of women as individuals and citizens in their own right (Acar and Altunok 2013). In the realm of sexual and reproductive health, these anti-women discourses and policies include the reigniting of the abortion debate with signals to change the existing law on abortion, and the promotion of a pronatalist policy.

During the March 8 celebrations in 2008, then–Prime Minister Erdoğan announced the government's plans to introduce financial incentives for births, which, from 2009 onwards, quickly turned into a formulation of three children per family (i.e. per women). The initial sign of this shift of policy – from the anti-natalist stance upheld since the 1960s, to a pronatalist one – can be found in the government's attempt in 2003 to re-draft the Law on the Rights of the Disabled, to bring restrictions to abortions conducted after ten weeks, that had been previously allowed for the medical reason of foetal disability (Acar and Altunok 2013). Due to objections by women's organizations, medical associations and media, the proposed article was removed from the draft. Yet in May 2012, Erdoğan made a statement during the closing session of the Parliamentarians' Conference of the UNFPA in Istanbul, saying that abortion was mass murder (referencing the killing of thirty-four Kurdish citizens in Uludere for which his government had been critiqued). He later included caesarean section procedures as murders, declaring both to be 'secret plots designed to stall Turkey's economic growth and a conspiracy to wipe the Turkish nation from the world stage' (Hürriyet Daily News 2012).

Erdoğan's remarks on abortion were met with criticism from opposition parties and his own Minister of Family and Social Policy, and elicited a strong reaction from the feminist movement in Turkey who under the slogan 'abortion is a right and a woman's decision', organized protests in multiple cities. The 'Abortion Is a Right and a Woman's Decision Platform' was formed and the status of abortion care began to be monitored via research done by Mor Çatı-Purple Roof Women's Shelter (2015) and Kadir Has University (2016). All of these efforts were successful in preventing a change in the abortion law. However, as seen in this chapter too, the neoconservative discourse and pressure from state officials, combined with the neoliberal mechanisms of assigning low performance points for abortion procedures, led to a serious decline in abortion services in Turkey.

In previous articles (Dayı and Karakaya 2018; Dayı 2019), we discussed in detail the effects of neoliberal health restructuring and conservatism on women's sexual and reproductive care and rights from the perspective of FHC workers. We showed how neoliberal mechanisms (i.e. the dismantling of the public through market and bureaucratic mechanisms) and conservative pressure on providers led to: (1) the indebtedness of women through out-of-pocket payments for private contraceptive and abortion care; (2) the indebtedness of physicians, nurses and midwives to the state through salary cuts from missed performance targets (and the use of fraud to avoid missed targets); (3) a reduction in the quality of existing reproductive care (such as prenatal follow-ups) and (4) a reduction in access to reproductive care itself (namely contraception, sexual and reproductive counselling, and abortion). Dayi (2019) discusses how neoliberal mechanisms used in tandem with conservative discourse can erode, as in Turkey, the right to abortion and contraception without changing the abortion law or official policies on contraception themselves.

In this chapter, using women's own narratives, we investigate sexual and reproductive rights violations in contemporary Turkey, in the areas of abortion, birth control, birth and routine gynaecological care. We specifically focus on: (a) the continuities in rights violations (prior to health restructuring), (b) the augmentation of certain rights violations that accompanied this neoliberal health restructuring that is coupled with conservative discourse and policies (including the new pronatalist policy) and (c) the new rights violations that came into being as a result of neoliberal policies and conservative pressure. In doing so, we aim to contribute to existing literature on feminist political economy, especially in terms of the research and activism that transnationally connect neoliberal health restructuring and women's sexual and reproductive care and rights. We aim to make visible the direct and indirect effects of neoliberal reforms that are used in conjunction with conservative pressures on these rights and on women's bodies, the topic of this edited collection. Even though lesbian women's invisibility in gynaecological care emerged as a topic as brought up by one self-identified lesbian participant and by the Family Health Center staff, our sample is predominantly composed of heterosexual ciswomen. Thus, the paper is on the rights violations of mainly heterosexual ciswomen, with implications for lesbian, bisexual and trans individuals who utilize gynaecological care, sexual counselling, birth control and abortion as needed. While reproductive politics is a sexual-gender-class-race-ethnicity based issue and has been analysed as such in the feminist literature, a newer trend added to the analysis is that of queering reproduction. This is seen in the attempts to queer bioethics (Richie 2016) and to queer abortion, the latter of which emerges directly from the movement side, in working of LGBTI+ and feminist movements as in the United States (Thomsen and Tacchera Morrison 2020) and Argentina (Sutton and Borland 2018) for example, to widen the definition of abortion – which is seen typically as a heterosexual and feminist and not LGBTI+ movement issue – to include lesbian and bisexual women and trans men as possible users of abortion care alongside heterosexual women and to bring LGBTI+ and feminist movements together in reproductive rights struggles. These, we believe are hopeful emergences. Future work on neoliberalism and women's sexual and reproductive rights in Turkey could take up heterosexual and LGBTI+ people's access to services and rights together, engage with queer theory and present a more holistic picture then does our present study at the moment. Before discussing our methodology and findings, a brief section on sexual and reproductive health rights in Turkey will help to better contextualize the findings.

Sexual and reproductive rights in Turkey

Sexual and reproductive rights in Turkey, especially those that relate to gynaecological, contraception and abortion care, and sexual-reproductive counselling, which are the main focus of this chapter, are protected through the laws on contraception and abortion (law on population planning and related laws and regulations), the constitutional right to healthcare, through regulations on patient rights and through international aggrements, such as the International Conference on Population and Development (ICPD) Programme of Action, UN Sustainable Development Goals: SDGs, and the Convention on the Elimination of All Forms of Discrimination against Women: CEDAW, to all of which Turkey is a signatory.

The history of reproductive law in Turkey follows a trajectory that parallels global trends, dating back to the late nineteenth century, the period of modernization in the Ottoman Empire, when abortion moved from the religious to legal domain and became codified in law under the 1858 Criminal Law. As in Europe and in the United States, pronatalist laws and policies were prioritized in the aftermath of wars and during the formation of the nation-state (late Ottoman period to early years of the Turkish Republic). This was followed by the legalization of contraception and therapeutic abortions in 1965, which was parallel to the international shift in population policies whereby population growth was seen as a hindrance to economic development. As a result of the global feminist debates on abortion that reached Turkey, the lobbying efforts of the Turkish Medical Association, the Turkish Family Planning Association and the Turkish Gynaecological Association, and the publicizing of public health studies that revealed the effects of unsafe abortions on women (including maternal mortality), abortion on demand (up to ten weeks of pregnancy) was legalized in 1983 with the revision of the 1965 'Law on Population Planning'. The law requires the written consent of the husband of a married woman seeking an abortion, and parental consent from minors. According to the regulations in place, in addition to obstetrician-gynaecologists (ob-gyns), the general practitioners who receive training can also perform abortions under the supervision of an ob-gyn. In the case of rape, women can obtain abortions up to twenty weeks.

As discussed in a previous article by Dayı (2019), and more in depth in Erkaya Balsoy's (2015) and Akşit's (2010) works, reproductive law in Turkey has been introduced and framed in the context of a population planning approach which instrumentalizes women's bodies and sexuality. The actual name of the law legalizing both contraception and abortion is the 'Law on Population Planning', where, while the individual right to determine the number and spacing of children is recognized, the state is defined as the agent responsible of taking necessary steps to 'provide education and the implementation of population planning'. While this population control agenda continued as the governing legal framework, the years 1965–2009 saw more of a family planning approach, which evolved in the 1990s (at least in reproductive policies) to include a 'women's rights' approach. This was due to Turkey's support for the international documents that emphasized women's sexual and reproductive rights as human rights, which included the International Conference on Population and Development (ICPD) Programme of Action, UN Sustainable Development Goals (SDGs) and the Convention on the Elimination of All Forms of Discrimination against Women (CEDAW), that Turkey ratified in 1985. For each of these agreements there is a monitoring and reporting procedure that the Turkish state needs to complete periodically, and each is monitored by independent women's organizations and platforms in Turkey that produce shadow reports.

Under the ICPD Programme of Action, states are expected to take all necessary measures to secure access to healthcare, including sexual and reproductive healthcare, and to take into consideration gender equality and women's autonomy in decision making in sexual and reproductive health matters when developing reproductive health programs and population-related programs. The UN Sustainable Development Goal on gender equality (Goal 5.6) also includes stipulations for the granting of universal access to sexual and reproductive care, including abortion access, stating that governments should not limit access to abortion on cultural or religious grounds. Additionally, CEDAW requires governments to attain gender equality in healthcare, including in family planning services (art. 12) and to secure adequate access for rural women on family planning counselling and methods (art. 14(b)). In CEDAW General Recommendation no. 35, the denial or delay of safe abortions and the forced continuation of pregnancy are considered gender-based violence (Item 18).

In terms of constitutional protections, sexual and reproductive rights are protected under the right to health, which includes the right to access healthcare and the right to bodily integrity to bodily integrity (Item 17), through the regulation on patient rights and the bioethics agreement that was signed by Turkey in 2003 (Law no: 5013).

Methodology

We collected data for our study, which is a feminist research-advocacy project, in 2014 and 2015 from Family Health Centre (FHC) workers and women receiving reproductive care from public and private sectors in five cities: Istanbul, İzmir, Van, Diyarbakır and Gaziantep. These cities reflect the geographical variations in reproductive healthcare access that are found in the Turkish Population and Health Survey conducted every five years (TNSA, 2013). Maintaining this geographical diversity, we chose cities where we had connections to women's organizations and to medical associations that helped us recruit participants. We completed 313 surveys with women (aged 18–45) in four of these cities; 103 surveys in Diyarbakir and Antep with reproductive health personnel who worked in the public sector at the primary and secondary levels; and 19 focus groups with women (aged 18–45), and 9 focus groups and 3 individual interviews with FHC personnel in all cities except in Van. The personnel were from 12 FHCs and one AÇSAP centre. All interviews were transcribed verbatim and analysed using a grounded theory approach.

The mean age in our focus groups was 35.5 for women and 36.6 for health personnel. In terms of marital status, there were more single women (53.6 per cent) than married women in our focus groups. The health personnel who participated in surveys and in focus groups were mainly female health workers (77.7 per cent for surveys and 85.7 per cent for focus groups), with the majority being nurses or midwives (75.7 per cent of health workers in surveys and 81.8 per cent of health workers in focus groups). The results discussed here are mainly from focus groups with women who receive care from public and private institutions, and the occasional support from the data from FHC workers.

Findings and discussion

In her dissertation research on the legacy of the US Women's Health Movement and the meaning and experience of reproductive empowerment for women who received gynaecological, birth control and abortion services from autonomous feminist clinics, Dayı (2009) found that for women empowerment meant safety, and humane and dignified care. Safety referred to both physical and emotional safety, where physical safety meant being safe from anti-abortion violence, having access to safe birth control methods and safe abortions, and emotional safety denoted being in a space where one did not feel vulnerable, judged or directed/cajoled into decisions, and where one received safe, non-judgemental, and non-directive care.

The second dimension of empowerment, humane treatment, meant receiving dignified, egalitarian, individualized and holistic care. Dignified care referred mainly to care that reveals basic respect for women as humans, by being informed about services (where the information is given in an interactive way and nonmedical language), having enough time and not feeling turned into numbers as happens in mass-produced service settings.

Non-judgemental care

In this research, we found echoes of the above-mentioned dimensions of empowerment in women's narratives about gynaecological exams, birth control methods, abortion care and birth. Since the sexual activity of unmarried women is subject to more scrutiny in patriarchal cultures, including that of Turkey, it is not surprising that in our research, the experiences of young single women in the ob-gyn world of Turkey were that of being judged by the medical staff (general practitioners in FHC, ob-gyns in public hospitals, nurses and nurse-midwives in both settings) for utilizing gynaecological (services, including routine gynaecological care, birth control and abortion care). The main indicator of this was the doctors' discomfort in asking women directly about the status of their sexual activity. Either because of their own discomfort, and/or assuming, perhaps, that the woman would be embarrassed, most doctors asked women whether they were married or single in order to ascertain their sexual activity.

> Mavi: A gynaecological exam is problematic for me. Uhmm, I mean, I have only gone three times in my life. I do have routine tests but those are in the community centre not at the gynaecologist's. For example, I had a yeast infection and went [to the gynaecologist] and there they asked me if I was married. No, I am not. Why is the question 'are you sexually active?' this difficult? I mean, going to a gynaecologist in a public hospital is even more problematic. I think the private hospitals might be better about this.
> Interviewer: So you feel uncomfortable because of the way they ask the question?
> Mavi: The way it's asked, I mean, you feel judged. You feel conflicted about whether to tell the truth or not.
>
> (Mavi,[1] single woman, age 29, İzmir)

> I am 33 years old and my periods are pretty regular. In the last 3-4 months, they were irregular. I started bleeding every 15 days. I did not want to go to the doctor when it first happened. It happened once and maybe it was stress. Then it happened a second time, and I said ok, if it happens the third time, I'll go for sure. I don't want to go, 'cause I don't want to explain myself to anyone... Don't want to face stupid questions.
>
> (Yasmin, single woman, age 33, Antep)

Whatever were the doctors' motivations for asking the question in this way, for single women, this conveyed a judgement about premarital sex which then made it harder to talk about their gynaecological needs, that included diagnostic gynaecological exams, as well as discussing and obtaining birth control and abortion.

A participant voiced her discontent over judgements about divorced women who in Turkey are also suspected of being promiscuous (now that they had 'lost' their virginity). These women thus might have the same worries about being judged by others as they are going to an ob-gyn as do the never-married single women did.

I am divorced and I moved here to escape the attitudes in Mardin. Here, most people know me as single [never married]. I went to a gynaecologist here, for example, for a Bartholin cyst – 'So... you are divorced?' – this is also an ugly attitude.

(Gülten, single, age 37, Antep)

For single (never married women), whose sexual activity is not thoroughly discussed, there is also the problem of the gynaecological exam, and whether the doctor will do a pelvic exam or use an external ultrasound to protect the hymen (and, thus, their 'virginity'). Women call this an 'examination from below' (meaning from inside -*alttan muayene* in Turkish) vs. 'examination from above' (meaning from outside- *üstten muayene* in Turkish). If a woman was assumed to be a virgin (because she answered she was single and not married and did not explicitly discuss her sexual activity), some doctors were reluctant to do a proper pelvic exam, which would be crucial for the prescription of birth control and/or for the diagnosis of sexually transmitted infections and cancerous growths, etc.

Interviewer: Can the single women go to the gynaecologist for birth control here in Antep?
Nilgün: No, they can't go. Cause they would have to examine from below, and how would they possibly do that? [All women laugh at this remark].

(Nilgün, married woman, age 30, Antep)

A lesbian woman recounted her experience with her FHC doctor who held a heteronormative understanding of virginity, and did not see a reason for, or was reluctant to perform a pelvic exam.

Zehra: I had asked my family doctor about the Pap smear test, cervical cancer, which age range has more risks etc. Then the topic of virginity came up and I told them that I was gay. They replied that this would stay between us. So, setting this aside, I told them that I am sexually active, and they still imagined my sexuality as if it were based on penetration. I couldn't have them do a pap smear for 6 years. [They were] not going to do it. Not going to insert that speculum there.
Interviewer: So, what is the wording that they used to deny the test?
Zehra: I guess they were seeing it as if one were still a virgin.

(Zehra, single woman, age 29, İzmir)

This shows that, alongside single women, lesbian women in Turkey also face judgements (about their sexuality) and that both are invisible in a (public) system that has not adjusted to their specific gynaecological needs.

This judgemental behaviour of medical staff towards single women and lesbians is not caused by the neoliberal restructuring of healthcare. However, given the climate of increased conservatism, when doctors feel pressured not to perform abortions and even sometimes to not talk about birth control to all women, the sexuality of single, lesbian, poor and minority (e.g. Kurdish women, Syrian and other migrant women) will come under more scrutiny. We heard from single and poor women in our study that if they have the means, they prefer to go to private hospitals and private ob-gyns, to obtain birth control and abortions and to receive non-judgemental care with more information and time per patient. This means they will pay out of pocket and go into debt, instead of utilizing public services, which is their right to do.

Being informed

In Dayı's (2009) doctoral research, for women, being informed was an indication of dignified care. In Turkey, the right of women to proper information about their health and illness, and about any procedures, methods and side effects, and having their decisions be respected is protected under patient rights and through international agreements such as the ICPD and the Beijing Platform for Action.

Item 15 of the Regulation on Patient Rights (no: 23420) states that 'a patient has the right to request and obtain, in writing or orally, all information about his or her health, the medical procedures to be performed on him or her, the benefits and possible side effects of these procedures, alternative treatment options, the results of rejecting a treatment, and the course of the illness and its results'. Item 18 states that 'the information is given, if needed, through the help of translators, in a way that is legible to the patient, using medical terms as little as possible, in a clear way (so as to dissolve a patient's hesitations or doubts), politely, and in accordance with the psychological state of the patient'.

In our research, we found that women were not properly informed about a diagnosis, about birth control methods, or about the procedures they underwent (e.g. gynaecological exams, abortions, sterilizations, and procedures during birth).

> I was taking the birth control pill and was smoking. So, I asked the gynaecologist (at the public hospital) if that was a problem. She told me, as she took her purse from the hanger, that I was like a ticking bomb and could die any moment. I asked what she meant. She said if you smoke, you should not take it.
>
> (Şule, single woman, age 39, İstanbul)

> Interviewer: Why was it an IUD and not something else?
> Dilem: They did not give me the pill 'cause of my age. I was 45-46 then.
> Interviewer: They did not discuss alternatives with you, but just.
> Dilem: I said that, I asked if there were other methods… they said this was the best.
>
> (Dilem, married woman, age 49, Istanbul)

> Once they were going to take a smear test at the public hospital. Without any prior information, I got on the examination table. They asked, 'When is the last time you had sexual intercourse?', I said that it was yesterday. They said, 'Then we can't take it'. There was no information provided. They should have asked that before. That was my first smear. Smear tests were new then.
>
> (Izabella, married woman, age 35, İzmir)

Young women who were having their first gynaecological exam were not informed either:

> Two years ago, I went to the emergency service of the University Hospital. Uhmm... I had used the morning-after pill, Norlevo. I had used Premen before and had no problem but with Norlevo, this was the first time. My body started to react if I was pregnant. I was nauseated, and revolted by food and some substances. My head was spinning. Since I couldn't deal with it any more, I went to emergency care at night... I was kept there till 5 am. In the end, I was sent for a gynaecological exam. There was a female doctor and her nurse, another woman. This was my first time on the gynaecological table and I was already in a tough spot, but there was no explanation nor any attempt to make me feel better. I thought I was relaxed but I tensed up without realizing it. She scolded me 'Enough now, don't tense up!' I left there crying. She put the speculum inside and turned and turned... That was how I experienced it and felt about it. I will never go back to the public hospital. After this, I made up my mind that if I do have to go again, I will get private care.
>
> (Zeynep, single woman, age 30, İzmir 1)

Women were also not informed about their problem or about the type of treatment that would be applied:

> Diren: I mean you don't receive any information. You don't know. They look at you as if you need an exam then send you off. There is no communication. You don't get much information from either the nurse or the doctor. So, it's as if they don't attend to you one on one.
> Nesibe: Sometimes the doctor treats you on their own and doesn't say 'This is your illness'.
>
> (Diren, married woman, age 36, Diyarbakir Nesibe, no demographic info, Diyarbakır)

And despite the fact that patient rights regulations state that the information needs to be given in a non-medical way and via translators if needed, we found that illiterate women, Syrian women (due to lack of sufficient translators) and Kurdish women (due to not being able to communicate in their mother tongue) could not exercise this right fully:

> Nesibe: On my paper they wrote 'curettage'. But, I can't read or write. When I asked someone to read it, they told me 'You don't have a husband. Why would you have a curettage?'
> Interviewer: But curettage is not only for abortion. It also means cleaning the womb.
> Nesibe: But it didn't state the reason of the curettage there, and when I had someone read it they said 'Abla [sister], you had an abortion? Were you pregnant?'
>
> (Nesibe, no demographic info, Diyarbakır)

Havva: There is the issue of language. Already there is no proper information, and when they do so, they use medical terms and no one understands. If I look at this from the doctor's perspective, there is limited time and various pressures, like you have to see so many patients in so much time. Maybe that's the reason, but we need to find a solution for that too.
Interviewer: As for the language, so it can be Kurdish or Arabic...
Havva: I mean in Antep, it's hard to find people who don't know Turkish, but if your mother tongue is Kurdish, it is not possible for you to master Turkish. You can communicate but understanding is a different thing. My husband is Kurdish and he says that he thinks in Kurdish and translates what he thinks into Turkish when he talks. For these women it is more difficult. How do you talk about medical things?
Interviewer: Aren't there doctors who speak Kurdish?
Havva: I am sure they exist. But, there is this policy that it is a forbidden language. They can't communicate with the patient in Antep's public hospital. Maybe in a small place [Interviewer: like in a family physician centre] they will be forced to speak it out of necessity. Otherwise they won't be able to provide care.

(Havva, married woman, age 55, Antep)

Even more worrisome are the cases of procedures that are conducted without the consent of women, including sterilizations without their consent and denying them access to sterilization in the Southeast of Turkey, all of which are violation of the right to informed consent (Item 24 of the regulation on patient rights) and to bodily integrity, thus double the violations of patient rights and the constitutional right to bodily integrity.

Mary: In the second exam, I said that I would like to have a smear test, and she said 'I am taking it right now'. I could feel that she was doing it.
Interviewer: So she was taking it [the Pap-smear] without informing you?
Mary: So, she did not tell me what she was doing. Like, now I will do this in this way... I mean, some people are hesitant to talk, to discuss their problem, their sexual problems. I am the reverse. As if the doctor and I had reversed roles. I told her very clearly. She did not ask me anything in order to expand on this. After I had the smear experience too, I was disturbed. I don't want to continue with the same doctor.

(Mary, married woman, age 30, İstanbul)

Misafir: They hospitalized my mom when we were in the village. They took her for an emergency operation. They got the signature from my father. They removed her ovaries because of a cist. They sent them a message one day before telling them to come and what the cost was etc.
Ayten: (this is) sterilization.
Interviewer: Which hospital is this?
Misafir: This is in the public one. Then, my mom goes to the private hospital. They research and find out that her ovaries had been removed. My mom went into menopause, she was sick. It was a very bad situation.

Ayten: My mom had tubal ligation at the age 32 after giving birth to me.
Interviewer: Voluntarily?
Ayten: No. The bleeding would not stop and her ovaries were damaged. Because my dad is a health worker and works in the same hospital, they explained to him 'Brother, you have 7 children, if we don't operate now she will come back in 2 weeks'. She did not have early menopause. But if you don't treat it properly, it can lead to early menopause.

(Nesibe, no demographic info, Diyarbakır)
(Ayten, single woman, age 44, Diyarbakır)

Xece: Perhaps because she had had enough children and did not want to give birth again, my mom went to the hospital and said she did not want any more children. She fills out all the procedures paperwork. My grandma goes to the doctor and talks to them, and says 'My daughter has a heart condition. If something happens to her I will sue you'. Then, without listening to my mom, the doctor tears up the papers, and says, 'I won't perform your operation', and sends her home.
Interviewer: So the doctor goes with your grandma's words…
Xece: But the doctor should have asked my mom. Though, if she had asked her, I wouldn't have been born.

(Xece, single woman, age 27, Diyarbakır)

Mesudeyn: For Syrian people, it's a different system. I went to uhh public hospital, because we couldn't go to private doctors, it's sooo crowded and if you sit and wait, sometimes you forget why I came here. I am not sick, I want to go home [laughs]. So I checked with the doctor but the problem is uhh we need translators because of the language barrier so doctors. The doctor didn't speak uhh English. I speak Arabic. The doctor does not speak any Arabic or English or Kurdish, I know three languages. But he had to speak in Turkish and it's very difficult to find a translator come with you and explain. If I become sick again, I will never go to hospital because I'll feel nervous.
Interviewer: There's no translator at all or…?
Mesudeyn: No no, no no, there is translator at hospital but the number of translators are very limited, you have to wait to you the turn to see the doctor and then you have to wait your turn to have a translator with you and wait and wait and wait.

(Mesudeyn, married woman, Syrian, age 33, Antep)

With regard to the preceding violations of consent and bodily integrity in sterilization procedures, Gürkan Sert (2013) writes that the clause in the Law on Population Planning that requires the husband's consent for abortions and sterilizations is a violation of women's bodily integrity since it disenables her from making an autonomous decision on her body. We agree with him. Furthermore, we believe that the lack of informed consent, where consent would mean taking the time to explain to a woman in a manner she would understand, and aside from emergencies, asking her and not the husband or another family member, and respecting her decision, is a class-based phenomena in healthcare in general and reproductive care in particular. However, the lack of informed consent and the performance of sterilizations become even more problematic, when the women involved are not only poor but also Kurdish, as in this case, who have previously suspected the AÇSAP's campaign in the late 1990s to distribute free birth control in the East and Southeast as the State's attempt to sterilize them (Suzuki Him and Gündüz Hoşgör 2015).

These violations of the right to proper information and to informed consent did not start with the neoliberal restructuring of healthcare. They existed beforehand and continue up to our current time with the new health system. Now Syrian women are included in previously existing vulnerable groups. With the neoliberal restructuring of healthcare, a new rights violation has been added to these: the violation of women's right to sexual and reproductive counselling, which is called *family planning consultation* in the Turkish health system. The neoliberal restructuring of healthcare brought about performance measures for both hospital and Family Health Centre (FHC) workers. In FHCs, physicians, nurses, and nurse-midwives are subject to performance measures in areas such as the rates of medical referral, child vaccinations and prenatal and infant follow-up care, and they can lose up to 20 per cent of their salary if they do not meet their targets. Nonetheless, they are not evaluated for this is together: family planning counseling not family planning, counseling or the supplying of contraception, which includes the insertion of IUDs. Performance measures and the digitalization of health data, which is another new measure of the health reform discussed in more detail in Saluk's chapter in this volume, have culminated in both the quantification (over the quality) of care and, ironically, the lack of efficiency for the staff, whose workload has increased by the added paperwork and computer work. It is mainly the nurses and nurse-midwives who perform the labour of gathering and entering the data into the computer. In our surveys 86.4 per cent of health providers stated that their workload had grown since the healthcare reform.

As discussed in more detail in a previous paper (Dayi 2019), we found that performance measures, together with the increased workload caused by digitalization and the extra work required by performance measures, affected sexual and reproductive care by decreasing the quality of reproductive care that was provided, and decreasing the type of care that is excluded from performance measures. For example, the nurses and midwives we interviewed stated that they were unable to find time to offer sexual and reproductive counselling and that, due to the lack of training and work overload, they were not willing to insert IUDs. They also mentioned the lack of proper space for such counselling:

Leyla: We need to explain how condoms are used. But we don't have space to do it. We talk to her in the corridor, here and there...
Interviewer: Do you have a model for showing how to put on the condom?
Çiçek: No. We don't explain that much. It would be even useful to tell her what to do in case the condom breaks. There are those who have no information about that. Ooops it broke, so they say there is nothing to do and they don't do anything. So, at minimum, we can raise awareness about that but then the doctor has a visitor in their room or a patient or a drug representative. There is always someone there. There is no counselling room. We try to talk with the patient discretely in the corridor. And, she says 'I have to go, have something to do'.
(Çiçek, age 40, Nurse, FHC in Diyarbakır)
(Leyla, age 26, Nurse-Midwife, FHC in Diyarbakır)

The quote above touches upon the new differentiation amongst the FHCs that was brought with neoliberal reforms. Under the new system, FHCs are divided into four categories (A, B, C and D), with only A and B having an additional room with an ob-gyn table. Having a general practitioner trained in intrauterine device (IUD) insertion can change a centre's status from a C or a D to a B. However, since it is the physicians who in this system are brought into the role of entrepreneurs and managers, and are responsible for renting the space, the type of the centre will be based on their decision and financial responsibility. According to a report by UNFPA Turkey (2016) on access to family planning services and contraception, this differentiation has led to inequality in access to care, which we predict is related to decreases in IUD insertions and possibly in spaces where sexual-reproductive counselling can take place, as mentioned in the preceding quote.

The right to privacy

In terms of the right to privacy, what continues from before is the violation of women's privacy during gynaecological consultations with the doctor, gynaecological exams, prenatal check-ups, cervical exams to determine stage of birth and during birth itself. Women told us stories about the doctor's doors left open after the consultation began, unrelated health personnel peeking in to ask something of the doctor or of the nurses during gynaecological exams, conducting ultrasounds in spaces separated only by folding screens, women giving birth lined up and waiting to be checked for dilation one after the other, multiple patients in the same room awaiting exams or being prepared for an exam, and medical students and assistants who were brought to the gynaecological exam without previous consent of the woman being examined. All of these had taken place in public hospitals.

> The only disturbing thing for me and for other patients, was that the student assistants enter with the doctor. We had talked about this with the people in the waiting room. I had been disturbed by this. After the gynaecologist entered, they did not ask for permission for the students to enter. Privacy was not considered then.
>
> (Zeynep, married woman, age 42, Antep)

Interviewer: Were you alone when you entered the exam room or were there others there?
Rojda: No I was alone. But they were taking two patients at the same time. I entered when she exited. The one after me, they took while I was inside.
Interviewer: Did you have your exam in a separate section or?
Rojda: Separate.
Interviewer: The other patient heard what you were saying and you heard her. How did you feel in such a place?
Rojda: I mean, I did not feel comfortable. 'Cause I could hear her and she could hear me. The doctor was doing the exam very fast. I don't think I was able to

talk much about my complaint. And they did not understand much 'cause they were as if 'let me examine this so that I can move on to the next patient'. I did not understand anything about what they said. They said to come back but I did not go back 'cause I have not had a chance.

(Rojda, married woman, age 28, Diyarbakır)

For example, for so many women to be grouped together in the same place in a birth hospital, I think that is disgusting treatment. I mean, I lived it (as a child) with my mother. Many women, I mean to see that as a child – it was 13 years ago, at the birth of my last sibling – it was traumatic for me. You pass women one by one, all lying there ready to give birth and you are shocked.

(Çilek, single woman age 25, Antep)

I mean, we went to the public hospital, and they took us to the birthing ward. There, women are lined up lying on stretchers next to each other. Sometimes there's a curtain between them, sometimes not. They all scream, cry. The ones passing by, nurses, or the birthing ward doctor, they all insert their fingers. What? Why? To check dilation, how many centimetres. Ask first, ask permission – make her comfortable. I had taken my aunt there 'cause I was working there, and I was ashamed to be working at a place like that.

(Mary, married woman, age 30, İstanbul)

Azra: I had gone 3 years ago. For an abortion. To the birth hospital. It was a 3 month pregnancy. They told me your baby is dead – had died in my belly. There was no caring there, and everyone saw everyone when they were examining a woman.
Interviewer: So, they took you to the birthing ward for an abortion?
Azra: Yes.
Interviewer: Were there curtains?
Azra: One had curtains. The others did not.

(Azra, married woman, age 31, Antep)

In terms of privacy, in addition to these continuing violations of privacy, there were new violations of women's privacy in the sharing of her pregnancy results with her partners or family. In the community health centres (*sağlık ocağı*) that were in place before being transformed into FHCs, the staff was still responsible for prenatal follow-ups and vaccinations. However, when performance measures were brought to these follow-ups with the added risk of salary (and job) loss for not reaching set targets, FHC personnel insisted on reaching all women of reproductive age registered to them, especially pregnant women. This included calling or texting the phone numbers they had in their files. The introduction of the digitalization of health data and media reporting of some of these cases of invasions of privacy are discussed in detail in Saluk's chapter in this collection. In our research, we also found evidence of such invasions, including the giving of test results in person to the father (prior to the reform) and sending the result of a woman's gynaecological blood test to her husband (after the reform).

Ebru: I had finished high school and had a cold. I was in bed and the community centre was located on the ground floor of our building. My dad and I went and they did tests and gave me a prescription and sent me back home. Then my dad went to get the lab results and the results said I was pregnant. Then my dad said, 'Ebru, what is this?' I said, 'I don't know'. He tells my mom to come and ask me.
Interviewer: Oh my god, this is terrible. He could have killed you if he were a different man.
Ebru: Then my mom came and asked me... She said, 'I know this isn't possible, but what does this mean?' I said, 'I don't know... It is nothing'. Then my dad goes back and they tell him it's the wrong results. If I saw things the way I do today, I would have sued them. My parents did nothing. The case was closed after that.

(Ebru, no demographic info, Diyarbakır)

I don't know about that but it happened to a close friend of mine. It was a difficult time for her. She wasn't pregnant but her menstruation was not regular and she was afraid of the blood test. 'Cause a couple of weeks prior one of our friends had gone through it. She was married. A gynaecological test she had done was texted to her husband. So my friend was afraid that the blood test results would go to her family. Every time she took a urine test, it was positive. And, she was sure that she was pregnant... In the university hospital, a similar thing happened a couple of years ago. Another university student had a gynaecological exam and the family was informed by a message. We saw it in the public hospital too. We see it in public hospitals.

(Mavi, single woman, age 29, İzmir)

These are serious violations of women's rights, which could lead to violence against women, including death by the family members of single women, and prevent a woman from making a decision about her pregnancy independently of her husband or family. She might be forced to abort or to keep a pregnancy that she does not want. In this way, these new violations that are enabled through the neoliberal bureaucratic mechanisms of surveillance of women's bodies go against the right to privacy and to safety and to bodily integrity. As Saluk in this volume argues, these mechanisms also result in the surveillance of the work of nurses and midwives, thus the female labour force of the FHCs.

Gynaecological violence

In our research, we found that there is widespread violence against women, which we call here as 'gynaecological violence'. This ranges from the mistreatment of women, disrespectful behaviour towards them and verbal abuse in the form of demeaning remarks, insults and scolding, to physical violence (slapping the woman's belly, utilizing the speculum in a very harsh way inside the vagina during an exam, etc.).

I had all of my births [in Gaziantep] as C-sections and I was knocked out in all of them, so I did not see anything. I thought there was very little attention in the after-care. For example, they tried to make me stand up after the birth to get the bladder working. I couldn't get up and fainted. I remember the nurse pulling my ear and saying come on… I was half-awake but I remember that my ear was pulled.

(Zeynep, married woman, age 42, Antep)

Kübra: For whatever reason, both the doctors and the secretaries are like that… you ask about something and by the second question they are telling you to go away. I mean, they take your signature, you leave, but you come back to ask a second question and they scold you.

(Kübra, married woman, age 34, Antep)

Müjgan: I witnessed something when my aunt went to give birth. A woman was giving birth right next to her and I don't know if it was a nurse or the doctor, but she slapped the woman. They were yelling at her. It was many years ago. [Interviewer: Here in Antep?] No, in Diyarbakir.

(Müjgan, single woman, age 31, Antep)

Rojda: We hear a lot of violence directed against women from nurses during birth, insults etc. Like, they say that 'It was ok when you lay under your husband and now you scream when you have the contractions'. Our daughters in law talk about these things. They really offended them then.
Beritan: Or they ask you, for example, 'Why do you have so many children?' As if they were the birth registry. They bring the woman to these conflicting situations. None of your business!
Interviewer: So, this type of talk still exists, huh?
Beritan: Yes, yes.
Çiçek: Yes, especially in public hospitals. In the private ones, they are a bit more careful.

(Rojda, married woman, age 28, Diyarbakır)
(Çiçek, married woman, age 37, Diyarbakır)
(Beritan, single woman, age 30, Diyarbakır)

I had gone to the public [hospital] once, for a yeast infection. I had a smear test done. Then I was disgusted cause I had an infection there. So I thought it's easier to go to the public [one] where I was. It was a woman gynaecologist. She took two tools in her hands [speculum]. I said, 'That is too wide'. She said 'Aah, didn't you give birth vaginally?' I said, 'I had C-sections and these look too wide to me and I am quite scared'. She was in a hurry and wanted me to sit in the exam chair. She put it inside, and the way she did it made me tense up involuntarily. She told me 'Why do you tense up?' and slaps my belly. I told her, 'Look, I am in pain, and you put this in very roughly'… Then she had it in and she moved it back and forth, and said, 'Ok, you can get up'. She was in a hurry.

(Firuze, married woman, age 38, Izmir 1)

Izabella: For example I had an acquaintance. Her contractions began. She went to the hospital. It's the public hospital, and people go in and out of the room. She said that she was disturbed by all this. They then tell her to leave, and that people are not fond of your thing [meaning vagina], and they sent her out.
Interviewer: Is this the health personnel?
Izabella: No, the doctor.

(İzabella, married woman, age 35, İzmir)

Izabella: I had it (an IUD) placed 10 years ago. And they made a huge deal when I wanted to remove it before its (expiration) date. They said, 'You are harming the state's property. You have it placed for 10 years and then, take it out in 5'. I was really humiliated then. I am afraid now to go have it removed.
Interviewer: This was at the community centre?
Izabella: Yes.

(İzabella, married woman, age 35, İzmir)

These experiences of rights violations (in terms of mistreatment, verbal and physical abuse, including the denial of care) are ongoing from before the reform of healthcare to our current time. It is sad for all of us, as feminist scholars, practitioners, activists and as women, to know that this abusive and violent patriarchal behaviour within the medical system by both male and female providers towards mainly poor (and young) women who utilize the public sector has not changed over the years. It shows how women's right to dignified care (as discussed in Dayı's dissertation, and as protected in Turkey by both patient rights and in international agreements) is not respected. Item 39 of the regulations on patient rights is called 'Respect for Humane Values and Visit' and states that all health personnel should treat patients, their relatives, and visitors in a polite, friendly, compassionate way, and provide appropriate information on the time of the procedures, on how and why they will be performed, and explain the reasons for any wait period. The experiences of violence described above are clear violations of the humane treatment of patients.

In addition to these continuing violations, we witnessed new forms of gynaecological violence that were the result of the neoliberal restructuring of healthcare and conservative pressures. As will be discussed in the next section, the decrease in access to low-cost birth control and abortion services in the public sector (contraception in FHCs, and abortion in public hospitals) leads to women having to decide to change the form of contraception, pay out of pocket in order to access contraception and abortions from the private sector, and experience unintended pregnancies as a result of a lack of contraception (and abortion). In CEDAW General Recommendation no. 35, the denial or delay of safe abortions and forced continuation of pregnancy are considered gender-based violence (Item 18), with which we agree. Denial of abortions is also against the Law on Population Planning which still upholds the provision of abortion on demand up to ten weeks of pregnancy.

In our research, we also had a few examples of women being told that they would only be allowed 4 C-Sections.

Kübra: On the right to have children, after the third child, at the 4th, they ask you at the hospital, how many children you had.
Nilgün: And there is this, for example, if we had C-sections, they say that we have only 4 chances. Is that true? Wherever I went to the doctor, they said that the C-section limit is 4.

(Kübra, married woman, age 34, Antep)
(Nilgün, married woman, age 30, Antep)

We also heard from women who were denied C-sections, whose ob-gyn insisted on vaginal births instead. This might be a response to the pressures on ob-gyn's who work in public hospitals through the new 'C-section law', as described in more detail by Topçu in this volume.

Meryem: In birth for example, there wasn't a choice. Now they push everyone to have a normal birth. They don't take you to have a C-sections unless there is a risk. I lived this with my daughter. I was in pain for 5 hrs. They didn't take me to have a C-section. At 3 a.m. in the night, my daughter's heart was stopping, so they hurried me to have a C-Section. So, I didn't have the right to choose.
Interviewer: When did you give birth?
Meryem: 3 years ago.

(Meryem, married woman, age 44, Diyarbakır)

The right to (accessible) contraception and abortion for all women

As mentioned briefly before on the discussion of sexual-reproductive counselling, in our research, we witnessed a decrease in the provision of IUDs due to the exclusion of birth control provision (including the provision of condoms, pills, injections and IUDs) from performance measures, the lack of proper training in IUD insertion and removal, and the lack of time due to an increased workload (i.e. of the follow-ups required by performance measures, and the digitalization of this data). In addition to these neoliberal market measures (of efficiency, performance, etc.) that were bureaucratically introduced (in the form of increased paperwork and computer work), another bureaucratic mechanism that we found impeded women's access to contraception were periodic problems in the supply of contraceptive methods to FHCs by the city health ministries. In all of the cities where we conducted our research, women and providers mentioned the periodic irregularity of supply. The result is the violation of women's right to free contraception at the primary level, which leaves women with the option of paying out of pocket (and getting into debt), or changing to another contraceptive method available at the FHC or a hospital nearby, or continuing an unwanted pregnancy.

Fatma: Last year, we had nothing for four months except for the injection.
Anonymous: Most of the time, the ministry buys, it but it doesn't come to us, and just waits there. The municipality doesn't inform us. There is a waiting. It's a two-way problem. Eighty to ninety per cent of the problem emanates from the ministry.

Interviewer: Okay, so when there is nothing, and the woman comes and asks for a method, what do you do?

Ayşe: They become pregnant. Because, you know, the pill in the pharmacy costs 18 lira. They can't buy it. They can only buy as much as they can afford from the pharmacy, otherwise they become pregnant.

> (Fatma (female), age 29, Nurse)
> (Ayşe (female), age 37, Nurse-Midwife anonymous (male),
> age 43, Physician, A-type FHC, Diyarbakir)

There are those who get pregnant. There was no pill available for a while, for example, and we saw many women who got pregnant and gave birth to their umpteenth child.

> (Habibe (female), age 42, Physician, B-type FHC, İzmir)

Zehra: In 2008, there was a community health centre below us, and nurses from there said that women could access condoms and pills from the centres. But, a bit later, they had run out of emergency pills or birth control pills.

Elif: The nurse in my family health centre told me that she fits IUDs, but that her physician does not know. Told me she can fit one for me, but I know they don't provide condoms anymore.

> (Zehra, single woman, age 29, İzmir) (Elif, married woman, age 30, İzmir)

Interviewer: Is the IUD placed in FHCs here?

Havva: In some, but not all.

Interviewer: How about injected contraceptives or condoms?

Havva: That might change according to the location of the centre. Some do have it but some say they have problems getting them and they push the limits of their budget and have their unit buy them... They say at meetings that they have a lot difficulty when the supplies are finished.

> (Havva, married woman, age 55, Antep)

In our focus groups, we asked both providers and women about the availability of abortion and birth control in their cities since the healthcare reform. We were surprised to learn that not only most of the women but also most of the health providers were confused about the legal status of abortion. Some thought it was banned while others were not sure whether the legal time limit had been shortened. This showed us that the conservative discourse that started with Erdoğan's remarks in 2012, that 'abortion is murder', was successful in muddying the waters and creating confusion about the legal status of abortion, as well as putting pressure on providers, without actually changing the law. The decrease in abortions in public hospitals throughout Turkey was documented by Kadir Has University in a recent survey of state hospitals and of state teaching-hospitals. Our findings also showed that abortion has become more difficult in public hospitals in recent years due to refusals to provide the service and due to the requests by providers made of pregnant woman that they obtain her husband's or parents' consent:

If we can collect money, we send the women [we work with] to private hospitals. When there is no husband, the public ones reject them anyway. In the private, there is resistance as well. I have been doing this job [working at a women's shelter] for seven years. For the last three years, we have had serious difficulties about this [accessing abortion]. The number of kids we give up [for adoption] to protection services is too many. There are many pregnant women coming to us, ending their pregnancies, and returning home. They have no other way of hiding their pregnancies. Why couldn't you abort? 'I had no money'. But, this is a public service. But, if it's recorded in her social security, anyone can access it and now they inform the husbands, and parents, by text message… So, she has no other option.

(Elif, married woman, age 30, İzmir)

Meryem: In public hospitals now, they don't do it [abortions] if there is no problem [medical necessity].
Zeynep: I went and said, 'I do not want this pregnancy', when I went to the birthing hospitals. They said, 'Go bring your husband, he signs, and we do it'… And I was scared.

(Meryem, married woman, age 44, Diyarbakır)
(Zeynep, single woman, age 20, Diyarbakır)

As discussed previously, single women already find it difficult to obtain gynaecological care, birth control and abortions in Turkey, especially in the public sector. Igde et al. point to how the legal restriction of abortion provision to ob-gyns and to general practitioners who work under the supervision of ob-gyns contributes to urban–rural inequalities in access to abortion since rural areas lack ob-gyns. Given the climate of conservative and patriarchal care, where some providers do not feel comfortable talking to or treating single women, these new conservative pressures, together with the existing limitations of the law itself, will disproportionately affect poor women, young single women, and rural women, who will be forced to pay out of pocket for contraceptive and abortion care, to seek unsafe abortions, or to carry unwanted pregnancies to term.

Under the ICPD Programme of Action, states are expected to take all necessary measures to secure access to healthcare, including sexual and reproductive healthcare. The UN Sustainable Development Goal on gender equality (Goal 5.6) also includes stipulations for the granting of universal access to sexual and reproductive care, including abortion access, stating that governments should not limit access to abortion on cultural or religious grounds. And CEDAW requires governments to attain gender equality in healthcare, including family planning services (art. 12) and to secure adequate access for rural women on family planning counselling and methods (art. 14(b)). The decrease in access to contraception and abortion in Turkey through neoliberal and conservative measures reflects a violation of all these rights, imprisoning the women in her body for unwanted pregnancies, which, as said above, is a form of gender-based (gynaecological) violence.

Conclusion

In this chapter, focusing on women's experiences of gynaecological visits, birth control and abortion care and birth in the public system (in hospitals and FHCs), we discussed the state of sexual and reproductive rights in contemporary Turkey. We found that (young) single and lesbian women are not visible in the reproductive scene, that their sexuality is not accepted and thus accommodated for, especially in the public health system. While this is not a new situation, we expect that it might worsen in the increasingly conservative climate of Turkey, which includes increased pressures to health providers, on birth control and abortion counselling and provision.

We discussed existing violations on the right to be properly informed, including in non-medical language and in one's mother tongue with the provision of translation as needed, a problem which disadvantages women who are illiterate, and belong to minority groups (i.e. Kurdish women and Syrian migrant women). The decrease in the access to sexual and reproductive counselling was a new rights violation in this area that was brought by the health restructuring and conservative pressures and policies (e.g. pronatalist policy). It was through the exclusion of counselling in performance measures, increased workload (and thus less time and willingness to provide counselling) and lack of space that led to nurse and nurse-midwives' inability to continue this service.

And, while there were already serious problems with the right to privacy and gynaecological violence, new rights violations were added to these such as sending women's gynaecological information to husbands or fathers, and the decreased access to birth control methods in FHCs and abortion services in public hospitals.

We discussed how the present state of sexual and reproductive rights reveal multiple violations of constitutional rights to healthcare and to bodily integrity and violations of patient rights to non-judgemental, dignified care where one receives proper information, gives informed consent and is guaranteed privacy and confidentiality. We emphasized that in addition to these internal documents, Turkey's commitments to international agreements such as the ICPD, UN SDGs and CEDAW are also violated through failing to guarantee women's access to sexual and reproductive rights and increasing the already existing gap among women in accessing this care. With the decrease of birth control and abortion services in the public sphere, more women are forced to switch to pharmacies, private hospitals and private ob-gyns for obtaining contraceptives and abortions. This means the poor and young single women will have to pay out of pocket and/or will carry out unwanted pregnancies when they cannot afford private care. This is a double violation of her right to (free or low-cost) public reproductive care and to her bodily integrity. The switch from the public to private sector in contraceptive care (especially with respect to tubal ligations, the pill and condoms) and the dominance of the private sector in providing abortion care (62 per cent of all abortions) are noted in the latest Turkish National Health Survey (TNSA, 2013). The dangers of lowering public health spending and the implementation of privatization without securing affordable costs for women's healthcare are also mentioned in the Beijing Platform for Action, Paragraph 91 which reads:

In many countries, especially developing countries, in particular the least developed countries, a decrease in public health spending and, in some cases, structural adjustment, contribute to the deterioration of public health systems. In addition, privatization of health-care systems without appropriate guarantees of universal access to affordable health care further reduces health-care availability. This situation not only directly affects the health of girls and women, but also places disproportionate responsibilities on women, whose multiple roles, including their roles within the family and the community, are often not acknowledged; hence they do not receive the necessary social, psychological and economic support.

(Beijing Declaration and Platform for Action – The Fourth World Conference on Women 1995)

Although many of the rights discussed in this chapter are protected by international agreements, which are monitored both by the state (that periodically submits reports on the targets) and by independent women's organizations and platforms in Turkey (that produce shadow reports), the rise of neoconservatism and the authoritarian turn are creating obstacles for these independent feminist monitoring efforts as well. A 2019 Policy Position Paper by the Beijing+25 Women's Platform Turkey discusses the alarming state, and worsening of gender inequality in the country in every area (from education, labour and health, to migration and politics), while displaying the increasingly conservative and authoritarian measures that are eroding existing women's rights in Turkey through direct government actions (Beijing+25 Women's Platform – Turkey 2019). This includes: the abolishment of the State Ministry on Women and Family, the relocation of issues regarding gender equality and women and girls under the Ministry of Work, Family and Social Security; the arresting of twenty-eight female co-mayors who were elected to cities with Kurdish populations; the shutting down (under the State of Emergency Measures) of 370 civil society organizations – including eleven women's organizations and forty-three women's centres in municipalities – and the banning of all activities of the LGBTQI+ organizations for two years until April 2019. We can add here the most recent 8th of March women's March in Istanbul, which the government tried to ban and the police raided.

The Policy Paper states that shrinking democratic spaces for feminist action include at the global level constraints put on international monitoring appeal bodies on gender equality. It states that although there still are international monitoring appeal bodies on gender equality and human rights, such as CEDAW, GREVIO or HR Committee (Human Rights Committee), it is actually difficult to consider them as fully independent bodies, since it is the state/parties that nominate and elect these experts. In Turkey, this was experienced most recently in 2019, when the Turkish government did not nominate and elect Professor Feride Acar (the previous President of the Committee and the candidate of women's organizations) for the GREVIO Committee that monitors the Istanbul Convention on Action Against Violence Against Women and Against Domestic Violence. The Beijing+25 Platform further reports that the only intergovernmental entity, the UN Commission on the Status of Women (CSW), where governments meet every March in New York, and make decisions on women's rights and gender equality policies globally, has closed its doors to women's NGOs during the recent years. And, as in many places including the United States and Turkey, governments increasingly establish their own NGOs (i.e. GONGOs, the governmental NGOs) and pretend to work with civil society. The report finishes with a call for a new decentralized international independent body for women and women's NGOs that will both conduct a truly independent monitoring of gender inequality and respond in meaningful ways to urgent needs. This state of affairs from the women's NGO scene adds to the macro-level of neoliberal health policies and reproductive rights. It reminds us that for the true protection of women's sexual and reproductive rights in Turkey and elsewhere, it is important to be aware of the neoliberal restructuring of healthcare as it is situated within neoliberal globalization – *the debt economy* as Lazaratto calls it – with its neoconservative and authoritarian arms, in order to be able to formulate meaningful local and global feminist responses to it.

Acknowledgement

We would like to thank our co-researcher and colleague Brigitte Marti for introducing us to the literature on the debt economy and helping problematize the connection of the debt economy to reproductive and sexual rights. Our research in Turkey was partially funded by the Raoul Wallenberg Institute in Turkey whom we would like to thank as well.

Note

1   All names used are pseudonyms that the women chose for themselves.

References

Acar, F. and G. Altunok (2013), 'The "Politics of Intimate" at the Intersection of Neo-Liberalism and Neo-Conservatism in Contemporary Turkey', *Women's Studies International Forum*, 41: 14–23.

Ağartan, T. (2012), 'Gender and Health Sector Reform: Policies, Actions, and Effects', in S. Dedeoğlu and A. Y. Elveren (eds), *Gender and Society in Turkey: The Impact of Neoliberal Policies, Political Islam and EU Accession*, 155–72, New York: I.B. Tauris.

Akşit, E. E. (2010), 'Geç Osmanlı ve Cumhuriyet Dönemlerinde Nüfus Kontrolü Yaklaşımları', *Toplum ve Bilim*, 117: 179–97.

Artıran İğde, F., R. Gül, M. İğde and M. Yalçın (2008), 'Abortion in Turkey: Women in Rural Areas and the Law', *The British Journal of General Practice*, 550 (58): 370–3.

Beijing Declaration and Platform for Action – the Fourth World Conference on Women (1995), Available online: https://www.un.org/en/events/pastevents/pdfs/Beijing_Declaration_and_Platform_for_Action.pdf

Beijing+25 Women's Platform – Turkey (2019), *Policy Paper by Beijing+25 Women's Platform Turkey*. Available online: https://www.kadinininsanhaklari.org/wp-content/uploads/2019/11/Beijing25_eng_web.pdf

Biyoloji ve tıbbın uygulanması bakımından insan hakları ve İnsan Haysiyetinin korunması sözleşmesi: İnsan hakları ve biyotıp sözleşmesinin onaylanmasının uygun bulunduğuna dair kanun (2013), *Kanun No: 5013.* Available online: https://www.tbmm.gov.tr/kanunlar/k5013.html

Buğra, A. and Ç. Keyder (2006), 'The Turkish Welfare Regime in Transition', *Journal of European Social Policy,* 16 (3): 211–28.

CEDAW: Convention on the Elimination of All Forms of Discrimination against Women (1979), Available online: https://www.un.org/womenwatch/daw/cedaw/

Dayı, A. (2009), 'From Power to Safety and Respect: The Changing Meaning of Empowerment in Women's Reproductive Health Care in the US', *Fe Dergi,* 1 (2): 55–70.

Dayı, A. (2019), 'Neoliberal Health Restructuring, Neoconservatism and the Limits of Law: Erosion of Reproductive Rights in Turkey', *Health and Human Rights Journal,* 21 (2): 57–68.

Dayı, A. and E. Karakaya (2018), 'Transforming the Gendered Regime Through Reproductive Politics: Neoliberal Health Restructuring, the Debt Economy and Reproductive Rights in Turkey', in A. Kian and B. Turkmen (eds), *Les Cahiers Du Cedref: Transformations of the Gender Regime in Turkey 22,* 158–92. Available online: https://journals.openedition.org/cedref/1150

Erkaya Balsoy, G. (2015), *Kahraman Doktor İhtiyar Acuzeye Karşı: Geç Osmanlı Doğum Politikaları,* İstanbul: Can Sanat Yayınları.

Europe Solidarity Delegation (2013), 'Greece on the Frontline of Austerity (April 2013)'. Available online: http://greecesolidarity.org/wp-content/uploads/2013/11/Greece-on-the-frontline-of-Austerity-Europe-1smallpdf-com.pdf (accessed 12 November 2020).

General Recommendation No. 35 on Gender-Based Violence against Women, Updating General Recommendation No. 19. Available online: https://www.ohchr.org/EN/HRBodies/CEDAW/Pages/GR35.aspx

Hacettepe University Institute of Population Studies (2014), '2013 Turkey Demographic and Health Survey', Hacettepe University Institute of Population Studies, T.R. Ministry of Development and TÜBİTAK, Ankara, Turkey. Available online: http://www.hips.hacettepe.edu.tr/eng/tdhs13/report/TDHS_2013_main.report.pdf

Hürriyet Daily News (2012), 'Abortion Is "murder," Says Turkey's PM', 26 May. Available online: https://www.hurriyetdailynews.com/abortion-is-murder-says-turkeys-pm-21665 (accessed 12 November 2020).

Kadir Has University Gender and Women's Studies Research Center (2016), *Legal but Not Necessarily Available: Abortion Services at State Hospitals in Turkey.* Available online: https://gender.khas.edu.tr/sites/gender.khas.edu.tr/files/inline-files/Abortion%20English.pdf

Klein, R. (1993), 'Health Care Reform: The Global Search for Utopia', *British Medical Journal,* 307 (752).

Lazzarato, M. (2012), *The Making of the Indebted Man',* trans. J. D. Jordan, Amsterdam: Semiotext(e).

Mor Çatı (2015), 'Kürtaj yapıyor musunuz? Hayır yapmıyoruz', 3 February. Available online: https://morcati.org.tr/izleme-raporlari/371-kamu-hastaneleri-ku-rtaj-uygulamalari-arastirma-raporu/

Richie, C. (2016), 'Lessons from Queer Bioethics: A Response to Timothy F. Murphy', *Bioethics,* 30 (5): 365–71.

Sert, G. (2013), *Üreme Haklarının Yasal Temelleri ve Etik Değerlendirme,* İstanbul: İnsan Kaynağını Geliştirme Vakfı.

Sutton, B. and E. Borlan (2018), 'Queering Abortion Rights: Notes from Argentina', *Culture, Health, & Sexuality*, 20 (12): 1378–93.

Suzuki Him, M. and A. Gündüz Hoşgör (2015), 'An Implication of Health Sector Reform for Disadvantaged Women's Struggle for Birth Control: A Case of Kurdish Rural–Urban Migrant Women in Van, Turkey', *Health Care for Women International*, 36 (9): 969–87.

Thomsen, C. and G. Tacchera Morrison (2020), 'Abortion as Gender Transgression: Reproductive Justice, Queer Theory, and Anti–Crisis Pregnancy Center Activism', *Signs: Journal of Women in Culture and Society*, 45 (3): 703–30.

UNFPA (2016), *Aile Planlaması Hizmetleri ve Kontraseptif Yeterliliği Ulusal İstişare Çalıştayı Raporu*, Ankara: Birleşmiş Milletler Nüfus Fonu.

2

Crafting moral agency in transnational egg donation: The case of Turkish egg donors

Burcu Mutlu

It was a hot sunny afternoon in mid-July 2015 in a Northern Cypriot clinic. Twenty-one-year-old Ülkü[1] was resting in an air-conditioned recovery room after undergoing her second OPU (the English abbreviation for 'Oocyte Picking Up' is used in the clinic) operation, during which her eggs were removed from her hormonally stimulated ovaries through a vaginal surgery under general anaesthesia. When I entered the room, she was sitting up in the bed, wrapped in a hospital gown, with an intravenous (IV) drip attached to her right arm. I was able to talk with Ülkü for an hour before the nurse came in to ask Ülkü to get dressed and be ready for the ride to the airport by the clinic's private chauffeur.

Over the past year or so, Ülkü has been travelling from Turkey to Northern Cyprus to donate her eggs in exchange for money since she was recruited as an egg donor by a sending clinic (these Turkish clinics send egg donors as well as fertility patients to Northern Cypriot clinics) in Istanbul through her aunt's ex-co-worker (probably working by commission as an egg donor broker). The egg donor payments ranged between 700 and 850 euros per retrieval in 2015. Ülkü told me that she started donating her eggs because she had credit card debts and wanted to save money for her university education. She was unemployed since she had recently quitted her minimum-waged retail salesperson job. In fact, she humorously told me how it all started with a misunderstanding that occurred during a Facebook chat with her aunt's friend. At some point, when this person asked if Ülkü, as a young unmarried woman, was not a virgin because only non-virgins could 'do this egg business'. She found this question suspicious and did not understand how being a virgin or not was relevant to the egg-packing business. When the aunt asked her friend how (non)virginity mattered for egg-packing, the reply was that 'It is women eggs, not chicken eggs! These are the eggs you give away with blood in every (menstrual) cycle'.

This chapter explores the experiences of Turkish egg donors who embody the 'supply side' of transnational egg donation between Turkey and Northern Cyprus, which constitutes a growing segment of global reproductive market. Based on observing egg donors' visits to a Northern Cypriot IVF clinic and conducting interviews with them,[2] I will examine how young Turkish women like Ülkü are actively engaging in egg donation as a new (clandestine) realm of financial opportunity as their eggs become disembodied, mobile and exchangeable. I argue that reproductive 'bioavailability' (Cohen 2007) of Turkish egg donors, extending beyond straightforward economic rationality, entails complex moral deliberations and cultural practices of valuation in and beyond the clinic. This chapter reveals how Turkish egg donors legitimize providing eggs as a reasonable way of making money despite its legally and morally stigmatized status in Turkey. They do so, while at the same time performing a virtuous identity as a young woman through the enactment of various strategies including wearing a headscarf and undergoing hymenoplasty, among others.

In Turkey, hegemonic notions of masculinity and femininity are 'closely tied to heteroreproductive sexuality and thus to the processes, desires, and practices of family making and the state's investments in this intimate domain' (Zengin 2016: 228). Within this dominant gender/sexual culture, women's social position and recognition are intimately related (and reduced) to their sexual and reproductive capacities and the domain of family through the governing discourses of chastity, fertility, domesticity and moral purity (Zengin 2016).

Women are thus expected to control and discipline their bodies in compliance of complex workings of this value system (Kogacioglu 2004; Zengin 2011, 2016; Ozyegin 2015; Sehlikoglu 2016). So, what happens when women use their reproductive capacities for others within the commercial-medical context of transnational egg donation that unsettles dominant feminine norms of heteroreproductive sexuality in Turkey? This chapter follows this question by examining the ways in which these women make sense of their egg donations as a legitimate way of making money in relation to gender norms and ideologies, and the increased sense of social and economic insecurity at a larger scale. As these young women purposefully navigate their ambiguous sexual and reproductive subjectivities within the realities of their lives and in relation to gender norms and expectations for 'good womanhood' in contemporary Turkey, they also expect to govern potential (health-related and other) risks involved in egg donation through practices of self-care as responsible 'good donors'.

In her classic article examining the gendered scientific accounts of reproductive biology, Emily Martin (1991) explains how human reproductive systems are often depicted in the United States (and beyond) as factories to produce valuable substances, namely eggs and sperm. A woman's monthly cycle is described as being designed not only to produce eggs, but also to prepare a proper environment for them to be fertilized and developed into potential babies. Martin notes, if the female cycle is seen as a productive enterprise, menstruation must be understood as a failure 'making products of no use, not to specification, unsalable, wasted, scrap' (1991: 486). Similarly, in egg donation, eggs are often conceptualized as 'too precious to waste', adding the possibility of exchange of eggs as a third option to Martin's framework.

Most donors I interviewed insisted that they were donating eggs that otherwise would be 'given away' or 'wasted' with their period since they did not need them for the time being. Instead, by donating their eggs, which would be monthly replenished, they were helping other women in need of eggs while also making money for themselves. Yet, eggs are precious to the donors themselves in that they should not 'waste' their eggs by irresponsibly donating in a way that would put their own fertility and future maternity in danger. Hence, their eggs transform from 'waste' into 'resource' 'as the primary generator of wealth, agency and value' (Franklin and Lock 2003: 7) in global reproductive bioeconomy.

New biotechnologies have now made available a new, molecular level (cells, molecules, genomes and genes) of intervention in, manipulation and governance of life itself beyond the classical Foucauldian biopolitical poles of the 'individual' and the 'population' (Helmreich 2008:464). Egg donation as a form of contemporary bioeconomics of life itself capitalizes the reproductive capacities of the woman's body at the molecular level, generating new biological entities (e.g. donated eggs), new subjectivities (e.g. egg donors and donated egg recipients) and new sources of value creation (e.g. economic, health and ethical values). However, value is 'not inherent in biological materialities' themselves; it is instead constituted and managed through 'the social practices and processes of valuation' (Birch 2017: 460–462). For example, Rene Almeling (2009), writing on the egg agencies and sperm banks in the United States, investigates how 'the social process of assigning value to the human body varies based on the sex and gender of the body being commodified' (39). She concludes that eggs and sperm are 'differently valued' since they are 'produced by differently sexed bodies' (2011: 10).

Linking value to labour, feminist scholars have further pointed to how some women's bodies (as egg donors and/or surrogates) become 'bioavailable' and 'biodesirable' to others, thus forming a global reproductive labour market and (re)producing transnational inequalities and vulnerabilities (Nahman 2008; Waldby and Cooper 2008; Whittaker and Speier 2010; Pande 2010, 2020; Bergmann 2010; Gupta 2012; Kroløkke 2014). As these scholars highlight, eggs tend to travel from younger, less affluent eastern and southern egg donors to older, more affluent northern and western recipient women (and men). However, although some '[s]cholars typically invoke victimhood when the bodies of third world women are their focus' (Pande 2010: 293), others call for study of these women's multiple and complex engagements with reproductive technologies. For example, Michal Nahman (2008) rejects seeing Romanian egg donors as '*passive objects* at the mercy of global capitalism, bioenterprise and the desires of other ova recipients' instead she argues that 'they are actively engaging in selling eggs' (67). She underlines: 'Ova donors are differently positioned to one another, in terms of their relationship to the state, power, the global economy and ova recipients' (2008: 68).

Following Nahman, I here analyse how Turkish egg donors negotiate their engagements in egg donation not only economically but also socially and morally as gendered beings. This chapter also expands the scope of the emerging academic literature on infertility and IVF in Turkey (Polat 2012, 2020; Gürtin 2012a, 2012b; Demircioğlu-Göknar 2015; Açıksöz 2016; Kılıçtepe 2019) by exploring the transnational dimension of assisted reproduction in Turkey in relation to its moral and bioeconomic aspects. The focus will be shifted from conventional IVF using one's own gametes to egg donation and from infertile couples to egg donors as the essential, yet largely invisible, actors of technologized, commodified and globalized reproduction. By doing so, it aims to shed light on the forms of women's bodily (re)productivity in the twenty-first-century global bioeconomy, which is not free from the risks, contradictions and complexities.

Transnational reproduction between Turkey and Northern Cyprus

The misunderstanding exhibited by Ülkü in the opening story strikingly, yet unsurprisingly, reveals the invisibility and unfamiliarity of egg donation to Turkish people, even young women such as Ülkü who may be potential egg donors. It is striking but unsurprising due to the disguised nature of this 'egg business' in Turkey, owing to the legally and morally problematic status of gamete donation in the country.

In Turkey, since its inception in the late 1980s, IVF has been legally accessible only to married heterosexual couples to create a child using their own gametes. All forms of third-party reproduction (namely sperm, egg and embryo donation as well as surrogacy) are strictly prohibited (no matter one is married or not). In Turkey, as procreation is expected and socially accepted within a heteronormative system of marriage, the ban on gamete donation reproduces this ideal on the ideological grounds of preventing the intrusion of a third party in heteronormative reproduction, marriage and family, thus protecting the lineage (*nesep*) – and especially patrilineage – of offspring. This ban reflects a 'harmony between secular legislation and [Sunni Islamic] religious opinion' (Gürtin 2012a: 286). For example, the Turkish state's principal religious authority, the Presidency of Religious Affairs (*Diyanet İşleri Başkanlığı*), in its public opinions (*fetva*), denounces IVF as a form of adultery (*zina*) if it is practised outside the parameters of marriage with third-party intrusion; and it is not only the case of sperm donation, but also of egg donation and surrogacy (Dörtkardeş 2015).

In 2010, the Turkish government, ruled by the Justice and Development Party (JDP), went further by forbidding reproductive travels abroad for donor gametes (Gürtin 2011). Interestingly, this ban was enforced by the same government that has initiated a pronatalist agenda in Turkey especially over the last decade, configured at the seemingly paradoxical intersection of neoliberalism and neoconservatism (Yazıcı 2012; Acar and Altunok 2013; Korkman 2015). Rather than being a biopolitical paradox, this anti-natalist ban on the use of third-party gametes complies with the JDP's stratified and selectively pronatalist political rhetoric and policies that quantitatively promote larger families, and by extension a larger population, and national economy, while qualitatively praising a (Turkish nationalist and Sunni Islamic) patriarchal heteronormative family at the expense of gender equality.

Despite the 2010 Turkish legislation, increasing numbers of Turkish citizens, including egg donors, continue to cross national borders to engage in donor conception (predominantly egg donation), although now more covertly. These disguised travels not only make it harder to apply the 2010 ban, but also enable the legitimacy of the ban and hence the Turkish state's symbolic power to remain unchallenged in the public sphere. Meanwhile, in Northern Cyprus, which has been hosting many of these disguised travels from Turkey, the number of IVF clinics has doubled (around 14 now) (Güler 2018) since both the 2010 Turkish ban and the 2009 Turkish Cypriot ban against providing gamete donation to Turkish citizens.[3] It is thanks to complex and covert medical and professional business arrangements that have formed between clinics and doctors in Turkey and Northern Cyprus since early 2000s.

This increase in the number of the Northern Cypriot IVF clinics in the post-2010 ban period might make sense in the light of recent neoliberal socio-economic transformations that have turned the island into an investment arena for Turkish capital (Bozkurt 2014), including the Turkish IVF industry. It is worth noting here 'the role of tourism in [the] normalization process of contested and colonized spaces' (Gonzalez 2013, cited by Ram 2015: 28), like Northern Cyprus, which is occupied by military force. Tourism, Vernadette Gonzalez claims, can help to justify militarism, while the latter becomes a platform through which tourism is sustained (cited by Ram 2015: 28). Through infrastructures of militarism and tourism (including medical tourism), Northern Cyprus has emerged as Turkey's political and ethical grey zone, an offshore site where what is illegal in Turkey can be practised. What began as gambling tourism when casinos were banned in Turkey in 1996 was followed by 'tube-baby tourism', as it is popularly called in the media since it is conceived as a variant of the wider trend of medical tourism, over the last decade.

The Turkish-speaking northern part of Cyprus, which has been politically separate since 1974 from the Greek-speaking south (the Republic of Cyprus), emerged as a self-proclaimed independent state (the Turkish Republic of Northern Cyprus [TRNC]) in 1983, but this autonomy is recognized only by Turkey which has assigned itself 'a paternal protectorate' of Northern Cyprus (Bryant and Yakinthou 2012: 17). Although the relationship Turkey and Northern Cyprus has been defined by 'various degrees of dependency over time', 'the perceived familial nature' of this relationship often expressed via the 'motherland-babyland' metaphor and recently via the 'siblings' (read brothers) metaphor (Bilge 2015) 'creates ambiguity in this particular relation of domination and authority, and also makes it difficult to regulate' (Bryant and Yakinthou 2012: 18). Since the early 2000s, 'tube baby tourism' (including egg donation) between the two countries has been embedded in these complicated relations of familial dependency. Northern Cyprus has thus emerged as an attractive destination for 'reproductive tourism', joining the competitive fertility market in the region, along with other countries such as the Republic of Cyprus (southern part of divided Cyprus), Israel, Dubai and Lebanon (Inhorn et al. 2017). This chapter will reveal how expectations, desires and economies are (re)configured in and through transnational egg donation between Turkey and Northern Cyprus, which requires the reproductive assistance and bioavailability of young Turkish women as egg donors.

Research setting and methodological reflections

Egg donors go through a series of embodied medical procedures for about a month. These involve hormonal stimulation (over the course of approximately ten days, in order to produce multiple eggs) and OPU surgery (to vaginally remove eggs under general anaesthesia), with the potential side effects and complications of both (such as ovarian hyperstimulation, abdominal pain and bloating, cysts on the ovaries, vaginal bleeding, injection-site bruising, post-operative nausea, and vomiting after general anaesthesia). In accordance with the egg donors' menstrual cycles and hormonal

Table 2.1 Biographical information on participants

#	AGE	ORIGIN	PLACE OF RESIDENCE	EDUCATION	OCCUPATION	MARITAL STATUS	CHILDREN	DURATION OF RECRUITMENT
1	23	Turkey	Turkey	University graduate	Journalist (unemployed)	Single	0	5 years (approx. 20 times)
2	23	Turkey	Turkey	University student	Student (unemployed)	Single	0	1 year (4 times)
3	21	Turkey	Turkey	High school graduate	Salesperson (unemployed)	Single	0	1–1.5 years (multiple times)
4	23	Turkey	Turkey	High School graduate	Customer service in bars (employed)	Single	0	2 years (7 or 8 times)
5	27	Turkey	Turkey	University graduate	Accountant (employed)	Single	0	3 years (multiple times)
6	22	Turkey	Northern Cyprus (11 years)	University dropout	Accountant (employed)	Single	0	2 months
7	28	Bulgaria	Northern Cyprus (8–9 years)	High school graduate	Accountant (unemployed)	Married	2	2 years (3 or 4 times)
8	25	Turkmenistan	Northern Cyprus (8 months)	University Student	Student and service sector (unemployed)	Married	1	A few months (multiple time)
9	22	Turkey	Turkey	University student	Student (unemployed)	Single	0	First time
10	27	Turkey	Turkey	University dropout	Salesperson (employed)	Single	0	1 year (5 or 6 times)
11	23	Turkey	Turkey	Open university student or graduate	Cinema cashier (employed)	Engaged	0	2 years (3–4 months apart)
12	22	Turkey	Turkey	High school dropout	Multiple service sector jobs (unemployed)	Single (divorced)	1	1.5 years (multiple times)
13	25	Turkey	Northern Cyprus (8–9 years)	University student	Student (unemployed)	Single (divorced)	1	1.5 years (multiple times)
14	21	Turkey	Northern Cyprus (8–9 years)	High school graduate	(Unemployed)	Single	0	6 months (approx. 3 times)

injection protocols, their flight to Northern Cyprus for the OPU is planned and booked in advance by the clinic.

Like Ülkü, egg donors are recruited by the clinics through a word-of-mouth strategy; public advertisement is not used. Most egg donors told me that they were asked to consider donating eggs by 'friends' who were also donating eggs and/or working by commission as egg donor brokers, either directly for the Northern Cypriot clinics or indirectly for sending clinics in Turkey. When young women travel from Turkey to the island to donate eggs, they usually arrive by plane in the morning and leave in the late afternoon or early evening that same day. Their flights are paid by the clinics. During their short visit, they are transported by the clinic's private chauffeur between the airport and the clinic.

Through a contingent personal connection, I gained initial access to a Northern Cypriot IVF clinic, which I will call Clinic Delta throughout this chapter. I conducted fieldwork in this clinic[4] between November 2014 and January 2016. At Clinic Delta, I closely tracked the arrival dates of egg donors to the clinic for the OPU operation. All of my interviews with donors were conducted in the private recovery room (with one exception, occurring in the backyard) during their period of rest following the OPU operation. I interviewed fourteen egg donors (two were sisters) in all. They were between twenty-one and twenty-eight years of age.[5] While nine of fourteen egg donors were living in Turkey and travelled to Northern Cyprus to donate eggs, the others were living in Northern Cyprus. Nine were never married and had no children. Two were married, one with two children, and the other with one child. Two were divorced with one child. They were at least high school graduates (except one high school dropout). Only five of them were working (mostly in the service sector) at the time of interview (For details, see Table 2.1).

Crafting a new financial landscape

For almost all women in my study, the primary motivation for donating eggs was financial. Their reasons for earning money through egg donation ranged widely and included: paying off credit card debts or personal (or family) bank loans, getting a supplement to their income, recently being unemployed, being a full-time university student, saving money for their own university education, buying a house for a mother (divorced with no financial means), purchasing an iPhone for themselves or a sister ('if she gets into university'), going on vacation with a boyfriend in a luxury hotel or buying an expensive first-anniversary gift for a boyfriend, or saving money for hymen reconstruction before getting married.

As the post-1980 Turkish society has gone through a transformation from state-controlled capitalism to a privatized and liberal market economy within the context of neoliberal globalization, political Islam and Turkey's accession to the European Union, new ideals of entrepreneurial self, individual autonomy and self-realization have emerged (Ozyegin 2015: 1–3). In the 2000s, with the rise of finance and credit markets as part of the country's neoliberal transformation under the consequent JDP governments, credit-reliant consumption and welfare (accompanied by the mushrooming of shopping malls across Turkey) have increased, creating simultaneously new forms of socio-economic vulnerability (especially for lower and middle classes) (Kus 2016: 42–3).

In their pursuit of means to deal with such socio-economic vulnerabilities, the gender-biased structure of the Turkish labour market makes egg donation a reasonable way of making money for these young women, despite its informal and stigmatized status in Turkey. As I have mentioned before, although the egg donors I talked to were at least high school graduates, only five of them were working at the time of interview. In Turkey, women largely work in the informal sector and get employed in the service sector, labour-intensive and unskilled manufacturing jobs and agriculture (KEIG 2013: 14). Although the rate of the female labour participation increases by education, employed women earn lower wages in comparison to their male counterparts (KEIG 2013: 14–15). Social policies in Turkey are still based on the ideal of a male breadwinner family, rendering women dependent on male family members (father or husband) for social security and contributing to their exclusion from the labour market (Buğra and Yakut-Çakar 2010). This system especially puts divorced women in an economically and socially vulnerable position (Özar and Yakut-Çakar 2013). Furthermore, student life is expensive especially in big cities like Istanbul (with limited public housing and funding, expensive public transportation and higher costs of living).

Within this social, political and economic context, donating eggs might be a reasonable way to make money, but it is still highly informal and morally stigmatizing. Turkish egg donors are engaged in a 'stigmatized form of [reproductive] labor' (Pande 2010: 293), which, in their eyes, tends to be associated by others with organ trafficking, selling one's own child, sex outside marriage, committing a sinful act and harming one's health and fertility. However, studies on stigma which 'assume a self-determining, autonomous individual with choices and a mass society that allows for privacy' (Riessman 2000: 113) tend to overlook issues of power and inequality and their relations to stigma (Gregg 2011: 73). Instead, as Margaret Lock and Patricia Kaufert write on pragmatic agency, 'for by force of the circumstances of their lives, women have always had to learn how they may best use what is available to them' (1998: 2). In neoliberal capitalism, individuals are also encouraged to become entrepreneurs of themselves by best using what is available to them (Rose 1999). While considering how to do so, however, Turkish egg donors are not only pragmatic and entrepreneurial but also moral agents as will be further discussed.

Crafting moral selves as egg donors

To manage stigma associated with egg donation, these young women therefore strategically and discursively moralize egg donation and thus create meaningful and moralized subject positions for themselves as egg donors, through enactment of various intersecting justifications and realizations: morally differentiating egg donation from other ways of making money, constructing moral façades, separating egg donation from the label of 'job', distancing themselves from the label of 'mother' and developing an ethic of self-care to reject the idea that egg donors are disposable.

They deploy these strategies to make sense of and socio-morally navigate their medico-commercial reproductivity in relation to dominant feminine norms and ideals of 'heteroreproductive sexuality' (Zengin 2016).

Donating eggs as a better way of making money

As a 25-year-old university student, divorced with a child (who lives with the father) and living in Northern Cyprus for almost a decade with her mother and siblings since her parents' divorce, Nalan started donating her eggs after she spent the money that her father had sent for her monthly tuition payment on other things. She had since become a serial donor and had helped her younger sister get recruited as an egg donor so they could together contribute to the family income and also keep up their expensive (*sosyete* in her words) lifestyle. I interviewed Nalan and her 21-year-old sister together on an April day in 2015 when her sister was undergoing OPU for her third or fourth donation since the summer and Nalan was accompanying her sister. Nalan had started donating eggs in the first year of the university approximately one and a half years ago. After a year break (she did not say the reason for the break), she started donating her eggs again along with her sister.

Nalan morally accounted for their financial motivation this way:

> It is difficult to be a student. You pay rent, fuel for your car, tuition fees, food etc. I pay 300 [English] sterlings for an unfurnished apartment. And 1800 Turkish liras monthly payment of my tuition fee – which changes according to fluctuations in euro [...] Money my father sends to us is not enough. What else can I do? Should I sell weed or what? God forbid! This is the easiest way to make money for now![...] I also consider this as a 'good deed' (*hayır işi*) (religiously and socially altruistic) if your family does not have money or if you go through financially bad times. I know that there are those who pay tuition fees by doing this. It is better than 'going astray' (*kötü yola düşmek*), lying under men. At least I am selling my eggs as an honorable woman (*namusumla satıyorum*).

Like Nalan, some egg donors created moral boundaries to construct a sense of self-worth by interpreting differences between morally better and morally worse ways of making money (similar to Indian surrogates, Pande 2010). For them, donating eggs is also a better way of making money than the (rhetorical or not) alternatives of selling sex, drug dealing or low-paying service work since it enables them to help others to have children. This way, the discourse of 'helping others' emerges in the egg donors' accounts as an altruistic justification for egg donation. Even one egg donor referred to the altruistic side of egg donation as something that she could not find in working as a salesperson. While she was donating eggs in return for money, she was also helping other people, which made her 'peaceful and happy'.

During our interview, Ülkü also expressed the altruistic side of donating eggs:

> I see it as [doing] a good deed. For people who cannot have children. I really think about it this way. Okay, I come here for money! But, my heart [pointing to the left

side of her chest] is comfortable. Why? Because couples are waiting in hope to have children. Maybe even some are now gratefully praying for me. I think this way. I do not think it is sinful (*günah*), this or that. Even if we think it is sinful, we are committing many sinful acts anyway.

As I have mentioned before, 21-year-old Ülkü started donating her eggs because she had credit card debts and wanted to save money for her university education since she had recently quitted her minimum-waged salesperson job. At the time of interview, she was undergoing her second OPU operation. As her aunt's friend told her when she heard about egg donation for the first time, 'these are the eggs you give away with blood in every cycle'. As her eggs transform from 'waste' into 'resource', detaching self from body parts enabled Ülkü to morally legitimize selling eggs (whether sinful or not in the eyes of others). She, like other egg donors, described herself as providing substance with which *other* women could become mothers; motherhood, in her view, was about gestating and care-giving – what egg-recipient women would do, as will be discussed in detail later.

However, it is worth noting that the discourse of mutual gain seemed to be first used strategically by intermediary friends and/or the clinics in recruiting egg donors to alleviate their concerns and to convince them, and only then was it embraced by egg donors themselves to justify their act of donating eggs. Although I did not observe in person any recruitment meetings between a potential egg donor and her intermediary friend, or between a potential egg donor and the clinic staff, I got the impression from the accounts of egg donors that intermediary friends and/or the clinical staff tended to introduce and explain egg donation to potential egg donors by using the discourse of mutual gain in a strategically moralized way. This reflects in some ways 'the organization of the market' that 'influences processes of valuation' (Almeling 2011: 10) through the circulation of the legitimizing discourses. As 23-year-old Ilke, who has been donating her eggs for five years, emphasized, however, the real motivation is always financial: 'Even if I say I am doing a good deed, I would be fooling myself, my real motivation is always money. My own benefit overrides other's [benefit]. When I read other people's [Internet] posts saying that it is a good deed, I do not believe them. This [egg donation] could not be done just as a good deed.'

Moral façades of good womanhood

Perceived stigma and consequent secrecy around egg donation becomes related not only to the moral status of selling eggs, but also to the moral status of young women selling their eggs. Although Ülkü thought that she was not doing anything wrong, she was careful about to whom she disclosed her egg donation. She explained it: 'If this (donating eggs) would be somehow known to people, my nonvirginity would also be known!' since egg donation requires the woman's eggs to be surgically removed from her ovaries through the vagina. So, what is at risk here for some of these women is not just their health but also their reputation and social appearance.

The majority of the egg donors that I interviewed were single women. So, they were trying to manage stigma associated not only with egg donation but also with the non-virginity of an unmarried woman since, in Turkey, women's sexual and reproductive capacities are expected to be confined within the bounds of heteronormative marriage. Gul Ozyegin's concept of 'virginal façade' (2015) is helpful to understand how single women construct a virginal façade to craft moral selves as women who provide viable eggs to other women. The notion of virginal façades, as Ozyegin writes, helps 'to capture the dynamic nature of putting on appearances, pretensions, and creating or permitting silences that enable young women to accommodate their own desires and negotiate the often conflicting expectations of parents, men, and peers' (2015: 68).

Similarly, the desexualization of unmarried women under the social category of 'unmarried/virgin girl' is utilized by Turkish egg donors as 'virginal façade' to keep their egg donation as a secret from others and thus to maintain a moral façade of good womanhood. At the same time, hiding egg donation helps them to hide their nonvirgin status and maintain their reputation and social appearance, that is, their 'gender proficiency' (Paxson 2004). 'Gender proficiency entails a kind of moral relationship with the body – one's own as well as others' bodies', depending on 'one's age, social position, marital status, and with whom one is interacting' (Paxson 2004: 17). Ülkü even told me that she was planning to undergo a virginal repair surgery (hymenoplasty) in Clinic Delta so as to become 'marriageable'. The clinic offers this surgery as a service that costs about the same as she earns in a cycle of donating her eggs. So, she would have to sell her eggs to be able to afford virginity repair surgery. Although Ülkü was the only one among my interviewees who was seriously considering having this surgery, I found her case illustrative of how hymenoplasty serves a material-symbolic form of virginal façade to assert her gender proficiency as a virtuous woman.

There were also a few divorcees among the egg donors I talked to. In their case, it is not the non-virginity of an unmarried woman, yet it is the assumed sexual promiscuity of divorced (and widowed women) in Turkey, which might be morally counteracted by women to demonstrate their proficiency as a virtuous woman. For example, Banu, a 22-year-old divorcee whose non-virginity was incontrovertibly established, turned to wearing a headscarf to create a moral façade to hide her egg donation. Banu left high school, got married at seventeen and had a daughter. After her divorce, she worked at different jobs, all in the informal sector, including selling textiles at local open market bazaars, known as high-society bazaar (*sosyete pazarı*). As a young divorced woman, she said she had to 'dress less femininely and wear no make-up' to 'fit in' the local bazaars' male-dominated working environment. She told me she almost 'forgot to feel like a woman' (implying also the social constraints of being a divorcee). That's why egg donation was tempting to Banu, not only for financial reasons, but also owing to the desire 'to feel like a woman again'. Now, she could dress up like a woman.

Banu, after starting to donate eggs, began to wear a headscarf. She explained the reason for veiling as her way of 'closing the (moral) gap', referring to egg donation. It might be also a moral façade that enables her to realize (pious) cross-border social mobility as a divorced woman, who regained her sense of femininity with egg donation (by dressing up like a woman, in her view). She saw egg donation as religiously wrong, but still kept doing it because she did not regard herself strictly religious enough to totally reject it; otherwise, she would be hypocritical. She also added, whispering to me, that she did not wear the headscarf when she came to Northern Cyprus because she was told that the clinics did not want the veiled egg donors, maybe implying the morally confusing image of veiled (pious) women, selling eggs.

'It is not a job!'

Although these young women started donating eggs out of financial necessity, it was not always an easy decision to make for the majority of them. However, once they were involved in egg donation, many became serial donors (even a few became egg donor brokers who recruited egg donors by commission). Even though many had been donating eggs for months or even years, they were not willing to define egg donation as a 'job'. Similarly, Rene Almeling (2011) found that the egg donors in the United States are encouraged by the egg agencies to see egg donation as an altruistic act rather than as a professional job, by enforcing cultural norms of caring motherhood to distance egg donation from economic exchange.

As a 22-year-old university student at the private university with full scholarship, living with her mother (teacher) and sister working in a low-paid job, Ceren no longer wanted to ask her mother for money. She had worked in a number of service sector jobs since high school, including as a waitress and masseuse. Although she was aware of the health risks involved in egg donation, she was also aware that she could not afford a healthy life and take care of herself as a university student who did not have much extracurricular time for a regular part-time job. So, egg donation was a better (financial) option available to her. However, like others, Ceren as a first-time egg donor also tended to define egg donation as a temporary financial solution rather than a job, which she would not prefer to do in her 30s, projecting for herself a better career trajectory (social mobility) in the future: 'It would be sad if I would still have to rely on this [egg donation] for money in my 30s, meaning that I would not able to achieve anything in my [professional] life by then.'

Many women described donating eggs as a way of making 'easy money' in comparison to full-time, yet low-paid, jobs available to them. Yet, for the very same reason, it is not seen by many egg donors as a 'real job' that requires a full-time working schedule and regular payment. Additionally, whereas a regular job would be continual and paid on a monthly basis (and hopefully had social security rights), due to the health risks involved in egg donation, they were advised to donate eggs not every month, but rather once in two or three months. For this reason, the money that they gained from donating eggs was twice higher than the minimum average wage in Turkey,[6] but egg donors mostly had to rely on that money for two or three months (if they would follow the advice of not donating eggs every month). Furthermore, many knew that they would do it only until the age of 30 at most because of the clinics' preference for younger donors, as well as due to their own health concerns and life plans (e.g. marriage, having a child or having a better and more secure job). Donating eggs thus appears as the best available option for these young women to make quick money.

However, for a few women, it might be 'easy money', but was never 'blessed' (*bereketli*) (one that brings abundance, if the flow of which is facilitated by pious and moral action, Korkman 2015: 337); it was easily and carelessly spendable unlike the money one gained from a full-time job. Ülkü had a similar understanding of egg donation. In her view, her donation money went easily away compared to the money she used to gain as a salesperson working on her feet all day and dealing with diverse people. She believed that it might be because that she gained her donation money without much labour (*emek*) or it was not inherently blessed, yet easily spendable. When I asked her why she thought no labour was involved in egg donation, she replied: 'Yes, there is some labor in this too. But [in this] you do not work like other people for 30 days and get paid [monthly]. Otherwise, to come here [Cyprus] is hard. I am also going to Istanbul [from her hometown in Turkey], and taking hormonal injections for 10 days and then going to Istanbul again.' Then, when I asked her again if she still did not see it as a job despite all these efforts involved in egg donation, she tended to say no by explaining what a 'real job' meant to her: 'involving more labor, working for hours a day, and hesitating to spend even 10 liras out of your salary because you got so tired to gain it.' She added: '[with egg donation] easy come, easy go' (*haydan gelen huya gider*). For the time being, Ülkü was trying to make her donation money blessed and therefore abundant by purchasing gold coins and wishing to buy a house later with her savings as a long-term investment.

In these accounts, blessed money implies that it is not just the amount of money but the means of acquiring it that makes it differently valuable, useful and fruitful, as a personal (and also family and household) spending money. As they pursue and preserve egg donation as a new realm of financial opportunity, these women attribute an agentive force to the money itself to justify new financial strategies as well as expenses. In other words, cultural concepts of value and '[n]otions about the nature of money that govern proper and improper modes of exchange shape actors' sense of themselves and the world around them' (Gamburd 2004: 170). In Ülkü's view, money earned by hard work is blessed whereas money earned 'easily' through egg donation has an inherent tendency to be unfruitful, which does get spent easily and quickly (e.g. on shopping), as she acknowledges.

Similarly, for Banu, a 22-year-old divorcee, egg donation failed to bring in blessed money, but for a totally different reason than Ülkü. For Banu, donating eggs was a 'sin'. When her all savings were stolen by the man whom she was planning to marry and to start a new life with by taking custody of her daughter from her ex-husband, she thought his theft might be a warning to her from God. Yet, despite her ambivalence, she kept donating eggs because she believed that donating eggs, as a divorced woman, was morally better than other ways of making money. While egg donors are helping other women to become mothers in exchange for money, they are not only differentiating egg donation from the label of 'job', but also distancing themselves from the label of 'mother', given gendered social and biopolitical expectations and pressures on women to be 'good mothers' and 'good citizens' in Turkey.

De-kinning

Gamete donation is anonymous at Clinic Delta (and possibly at most of other Northern Cypriot clinics too) and donors are not given any information if their donations result in children. Regardless of whether they knew that offspring actually existed, egg donors tend to 'de-kin' (Fonseca 2011) themselves from offspring that would be conceived with their donated eggs, as another way of legitimizing their involvement in stigmatized egg donation market. De-kinning refers to the ways in which egg donors define themselves as 'not mothers' (similar to the egg donors in the US context, Almeling 2011) by describing motherhood as being about gestating and care-giving (what egg-recipient women would do) rather than contributing reproductive biosubstances; such as the eggs they otherwise would 'waste' with their period and that keep producing every month. Perhaps, from their perspective, they were never kinned in the first place. By downplaying their genetic contribution, egg donors not only distance themselves from the label of mother as a moralizing strategy, but also contribute to the stabilization of the (heteronormative reproductive) Turkish family model through the erasure of their role as a third party in reproduction.

Furthermore, for many egg donors that I interviewed in Clinic Delta, since there is no 'living being' (a child) in the case of egg donation, they did not feel like they were giving their child away (i.e. contrasting egg donation to giving up a child for adoption). Following a similar logic, many egg donors found surrogacy daunting. Referring to the popular appearances of surrogacy in the media, especially in popular Turkish television series such as *Bebeğim* (My Baby) and *Kaderimin Yazıldığı Gün* (The Day My Destiny is Written), many women described surrogacy as a form of adoption, like 'giving your own child away', because there is 'a real child' in surrogacy while 'it is more like a bean-size thing you are giving away, not a real child, in egg donation', in one donor's words. Here, it is not just size that matters but the nature of the substance: unrealized (in the case of donating eggs) versus realized potential (in the case of surrogacy and adoption).

Moreover, some egg donors also emphasized that care is more important than genes in making a parental connection between adults and children. Twenty-two-year-old Ceren, as a first-time egg donor, put it this way: 'This is a totally biological thing. Eggs are just taken. The important thing is care (*emek*), always the emotional side. And this is what the [recipient] mother would do. It is up to her to achieve motherhood or not.' When I asked her about surrogacy, she replied:

> I cannot do surrogacy. It is totally a different thing. In this [egg donation], as I said, I do not care about genes. I do not see genes as what belongs to me or what makes who I am. I look at my father, my mother, my grandparents. I do not think that it is genes that hold us together. Of course, our nose looks similar in some way, or other parts of the body, but nothing more.

Ceren emphasized that what holds a family together is not genes but care. When I asked her if she would consider receiving eggs if she needed to in the future, she replied she would prefer to receive eggs from a family member, for example, from her sister. Likewise, she would like to consider giving her eggs for free only to her sister. I asked her to further elaborate on how genes matter in this case for her. She replied that this way there would be 'no surprise' by referring to a lesser degree of the genetic risk of disease in terms of family history.

So, egg donors were also mindful of the possibility that they might be in need of donor eggs for themselves in the future. As a result, they not only contributed to the supply side of egg donation, but also envisioned themselves on the demand side as the potential recipients of donor eggs in the future; two women even mentioned that they would consider using donor sperm to have a child if they did not find the right person to marry and have a child with. This potentially shifting positionality of egg donors not only complicates the victimized image of donors and their reproductive bodies as bioavailable to other (recipient) women, but also helps them to adopt the altruistic discourse of 'helping other women' by imagining themselves in recipient women's position. Through their familiarity with IVF clinics in Northern Cyprus, these women could be integrated into the gamete donation market as recipients by using their credit cards and/or bank loans, which had led many of them into this business in the first place.

Ethic of self-care

Eggs are precious to the donors themselves in that they should not 'waste' their eggs by irresponsibly donating in a way that would put their own fertility (and future maternity) in danger. They were urged to donate once in two or three months by the clinic in a more paternalistic tone not only for the health-related concerns but also possibly for being kept from shuttling among the different clinics to donate their eggs where a national egg donor registry and monitoring system did not exist. Egg donors therefore did not see themselves as disposable by often emphasizing how they thought of and took care of their health and future fertility by not donating every month.

As long as they were told by the clinic that their egg quality and quantity were okay – and thus, that they were not undermining their own chances to have children of their own one day – Turkish egg donors tended not to be much concerned about donating their eggs – even when they believed that donating eggs might cause premature menopause. Twenty-three-year-old Aleyna, who saw donating eggs as an acceptable way of making money in times of financial difficulties and as a means of helping people, also viewed it negatively due to the potential risk of premature menopause. Yet, she downplayed this risk by adopting the following medical and maternal logic: 'If a woman enters menopause at age 45, an egg donor might enter menopause earlier at age 40. Even if this is the case, it would not matter so much to me because I am willing to have a child until 30, not in my 40s.'

Many expressed concern about their future fertility since they were aware of the condition of their egg donor friends who were suffering from low ovarian reserves, not to mention the fertility patients in need of donor eggs whom they were helping. For example, 22-year-old Ceren was aware of the health risks involved from a friend who took a break after one year of donating her eggs to reduce the potential risks of egg donation on her own ovarian reserve. Ceren also heard a story about an egg donor who had been hospitalized following the OPU probably due to her allergic reaction to anaesthesia. Yet, this story did not concern her because this woman got the medical care she needed and her medical expenses were covered by the clinic. So, she believed that even if something bad would happen to her, she would be taken care of. She also knew that she was not allergic to narcosis since she had gone under anaesthesia before. Despite the health risks involved, Ceren thought that she would be taking better care of herself with money earned from egg donation, because she was already living on limited financial resources and eating poorly as a full-time university student at the private university with full scholarship.

Even when egg donors suffered from any of these side effects, they believed that their health would be okay as long as they did not have any long-term effects such as unusual irregularities in their menstruation cycles following the OPU. On the other hand, some women asserted that egg donation was *good* for their health since it put them under routine medical care of the clinic which needed them for their eggs. A few women even had their first gynaecological controls with their egg donations.

Although some egg donors believed that the clinics would protect their health and future fertility since they knew that the clinics needed donor eggs as much as they needed money, others underlined the fact that egg donation was a business from which the clinics were making profits by emphasizing that egg donors should think about and take care of themselves and their own health, and be 'conscious' (*bilinçli*) and self-responsible. In their view, this is how one would become a 'good' donor. For example, 27-year-old Kezban, who has been an egg donor for three years and recently an egg donor broker, emphasized that she was not donating every month not only to let her body rest but also not to ask frequently for days off from work for the clinic visits. Yet, she felt 'consciously' 'responsible' not only for her own health as a woman and for her work as an accountant; but also for the recipient couples and the clinic as an egg donor:

> Previously, many more [eggs] were taken (*çıkıyordu*), 19–20 eggs. At the beginning, even 35 or so were taken. It [the number] always changes. It changes due to stress. When you are stressed, fewer can be taken. If you do not eat well or do not take care of yourself. It is like pregnancy; if you do not eat, it affects the baby. It is like that. They [eggs] are like that. They might turn out like chicken eggs, which are empty, only covered with the shell. It is like that. For this reason, you should be careful. Even if the doctors do not say it, since I am aware of that, I take care of myself.

Conclusion

In his comprehensive review article on social studies of biocapital, Stefan Helmreich poses this question: 'What if we asked not what happens to biology when it is capitalized, but asked whether capital must be the sign under which all of today's encounters of the economic with the biological must travel?' (2008: 474). As medical anthropologists and sociologists have shown, the commodification of the human body is not a generic or uniform social process; instead, it can be expected to vary and be shaped by cultural norms, moral values and social inequalities (Cohen 2007; Almeling 2011). Similarly, this chapter has examined how the reproductive capacities of the woman's body are commodified at the cellular level, generating not only novel forms of economies and exchange relations, but also new biological entities such as donated eggs and new subjectivities such as egg donors.

Focusing on transnational egg donation from the perspective of Turkish egg donors as its essential yet largely invisible reproductive actors, I have demonstrated that these young women are not only pragmatic and entrepreneurial but also moral agents, rather than being simply passive objects of commodification. As they participate in egg donation as a stigmatized form of reproductive labour, they morally account for their donations to craft moral subject positions for themselves as women, while at the same time hoping to be able to govern potential (health-related as well as economic and moral) risks involved in egg donation by acting as self-caring and responsible good donors. In other words, for these young women, egg donation retains both moral and economic value.

Notes

1 All names are pseudonyms.

2 This chapter is based upon ethnographic research I conducted between November 2014 and January 2016. Primarily centred at a Northern Cypriot IVF clinic, I interviewed married Turkish couples seeking gamete donation and/or sex selection; medical experts from Turkish and Turkish-Cypriot clinics; and Turkish egg donors. My doctoral research was funded by the (American) National Science Foundation Doctoral Dissertation Research Improvement Grant (# 1456130).

3 The first Northern Cypriot regulation regarding IVF was introduced in 2002. Amendments were made to the 2002 regulation, respectively, in 2006, 2009 and 2016. In 2009, the Northern Cypriot government, bowing to political pressure from Turkey, banned its nation's IVF clinics from providing gamete donation to Turkish citizens. The Northern Cypriot restriction was soon followed by the Turkish 2010 ban on gamete donation abroad. After I completed my fieldwork, a new regulation on IVF came into force in June 2016 in Northern Cyprus, which makes no mention of restricting gamete donation to Turkish citizens.

4 To ensure anonymity and confidentiality, I remain purposely vague in describing Clinic Delta, omitting information about how long it has been operating, how many patients it serves each year and so forth.

5 According to the 2006 Northern Cypriot IVF regulation, egg donors were allowed to donate only once a year and their age was required to be not less than 20 and not more than 32. The 2009 regulation, however, did not include any information regarding egg donors. The 2016 regulation allows egg donors to donate three times per year at most and their age should be between 20 and 35. There are also other requirements for egg donors such as body mass index; physical, psychological and genetic health; having two healthy ovaries; XX-chromosomal sex.

6 In 2005, monthly gross minimum wage was around 1,270 Turkish liras in Turkey and around 1,700 Turkish liras in Northern Cyprus.

References

Acar, F. and G. Altunok (2013), 'The "Politics of Intimate" at the Intersection of Neo-Liberalism and Neo-Conservatism in Contemporary Turkey', *Women's Studies International Forum*, 41 (1): 14–23.

Açıksöz, S. C. (2016), 'In Vitro Nationalism: Masculinity, Disability, and Assisted Reproduction in War-torn Turkey', in G. Ozyegin (ed.), *Gender and Sexuality in Muslim Cultures*, 35–52, New York: Routledge.

Almeling, R. (2009), 'Gender and the Value of Bodily Goods: Commodification in Egg and Sperm Donation', *Law and Contemporary Problems*, 72 (3): 37–58. Available at: https://scholarship.law.duke.edu/lcp/vol72/iss3/4 (accessed December 15, 2019).

Almeling, R. (2011), *Sex Cells: The Medical Market for Eggs and Sperm*, Berkeley, CA: University of California Press.

Bergmann, S. (2010), 'Resemblance That Matters: On Transnational Anonymized Egg Donation in Two European IVF Clinics', in M. Knecht, M. Klotz and S. Beck (eds), *Reproductive Technologies as Global Form: Ethnographies of Knowledge, Practices, and Transnational Encounters*, 331–56, Frankfurt: Campus Verlag.

Bilge, Ö. (2015), 'KKTC'nin Yeni Lideri Akıncı: Biz Hep Yavru mu Kalalım? (TRNC's new Leader Akıncı: Should we always stay a baby?)', *Hürriyet*, 27 April. Available online: http://www.hurriyet.com.tr/dunya/kktcnin-yeni-lideri-akinci-biz-hep-yavru-mu-kalalim-28850482 (accessed 14 December, 2019).

Birch, K. (2017), 'Rethinking Value in the Bio-Economy: Finance, Assetization, and The Management of Value', *Science, Technology, & Human Values*, 42 (3): 460–90.

Bozkurt, U. (2014), 'Turkey: From the "Motherland" to the "IMF of Northern Cyprus"?' *The Cyprus Review*, 26 (1): 83–105.

Bryant, R. and C. Yakinthou (2012), *Cypriot Perceptions of Turkey*, Istanbul: TESEV.

Buğra, A. and B. Yakut-Çakar (2010), 'Structural Change, the Social Policy Environment and Female Employment in Turkey', *Development and Change*, 41 (3): 517–38.

Cohen, L. (2007), 'Operability, Bioavailability, and Exception', in A. Ong and S. J. Collier (eds), *Global Assemblages: Technology, Politics, and Ethics as Anthropological Problems*, 79–90, Malden, MA: Blackwell.

Demircioğlu-Göknar, M. (2015), *Achieving Procreation: Childlessness and IVF in Turkey*, New York and Oxford: Berghahn Books.

Dörtkardeş, İ. (2015), 'Diyanetten Fetva: Taşıyıcı Annelik Yöntemi Zina Unsurları Taşır [Diyanet's Fatwa: Surrogacy contains elements of adultery]', *Hürriyet*, 22 March. Available online: http://www.hurriyet.com.tr/gundem/diyanetten-fetva-tasiyici-annelik-yontemi-zina-unsurlari-tasir-28520975 (accessed 12 December 2019).

Fonseca, C. (2011), 'The De-Kinning of Birthmothers: Reflections on Maternity and Being Human', *Vibrant: Virtual Brazilian Anthropology*, 8 (2): 307–39.

Franklin, S. and M. Lock (2003), 'Animation and Cessation: The Remaking of Life and Death', in S. Franklin and M. Lock (eds), *Remaking Life and Death: Toward an Anthropology of the Biosciences*, 3–22, School for Advanced Research Press.

Gamburd, M. R. (2004), 'Money at Burns Like Oil: A Sri Lankan Cultural Logic of Morality and Agency', *Ethnology*, 43 (2): 167–84.

Gonzalez, V. (2013), *Securing Paradise: Tourism and Militarism in Hawai and the Philippines*, Durham: Duke University Press.

Gregg, J. L. (2011), 'An Unanticipated Source of Hope: Stigma and Cervical Cancer in Brazil', *Medical Anthropology Quarterly*, 25 (1): 70–84.

Güler, A. (2018), '1 Yılda %80'i Yabancı 1754 Tüp Bebek (1,754 Tube baby [cycles] in one year, 80 % of which is for foreigners)', *Yeni Düzen*, 18 June. Available online: http://www.yeniduzen.com/1-yilda-80i-yabanci-1754-tup-bebek-103642h.htm (accessed 14 December 2019).

Gupta, J. A. (2012), 'Reproductive Biocrossings: Indian Egg Donors and Surrogates in the Globalized Fertility Market', *International Journal of Feminist Approaches to Bioethics*, 5 (1): 25–51.

Gürtin, Z. (2011), 'Banning Reproductive Travel: Turkey's ART Legislation and Third-Party Assisted Reproduction', *Reproductive BioMedicine Online*, 23 (5): 555–64.

Gürtin, Z. (2012a), 'Assisted Reproduction in Secular Turkey: Regulation, Rhetoric, and the Role of Religion', in M. Inhorn and S. Tremayne (eds), *Islam and Assisted Reproductive Technologies: Sunni and Shia Perspectives*, 285–312, Oxford and New York: Berghahn.

Gürtin, Z. (2012b), 'Practitioners as Interface Agents between the Local and the Global: The Localization of IVF in Turkey', in M. Knecht, M. Klotz and S. Beck (eds), *Reproductive Technologies as Global Form: Ethnographies of Knowledge, Practices, and Transnational Encounters*, 81–110, Frankfurt: Campus Verlag.

Helmreich, S. (2008), 'Species of Biocapital', *Science as Culture*, 17 (4): 463–78.

Inhorn, M. C., D. Birenbaum-Carmeli, S. Tremayne and Z. B. Gürtin (2017), 'Assisted Reproduction and Middle East Kinship: A Regional and Religious Comparison', *Reproductive Biomedicine & Society Online*, 4: 41–51.

KEIG (2013), 'Women's Labor and Employment in Turkey: Problem Areas and Policy Suggestions II', Available online: http://www.keig.org/wp-content/uploads/2016/03/keig-policy-report-2013.pdf (accessed 14 December 2019).

Kılıçtepe, Ş. (2019), 'Reproductive Technologies, Pronatalism and Ethnicity: an Ethnography of Situated Reproduction in Turkey', unpublished PhD diss., Indiana University Bloomington.

Kus, B. (2016), 'Financial Citizenship and The Hidden Crisis of The Working Class in The "New Turkey"', *Middle East Report*, 278: 40–8.

Kogacioglu, D. (2004), 'The Tradition Effect: Framing Honor Crimes in Turkey', *Differences: A Journal of Feminist Cultural Studies*, 15 (2): 119–51.

Korkman, Z. K. (2015), 'Blessing Neoliberalism: Economy, Family, and The Occult in Millennial Turkey', *Journal of the Ottoman and Turkish Studies Association*, 2 (2): 335–57.

Kroløkke, C. (2014), 'West Is Best: Affective Assemblages and Spanish Oocytes', *European Journal of Women's Studies*, 21 (1): 57–71.

Lock, M. and P. A. Kaufert, eds (1998), *Pragmatic Women and Body Politics*, Cambridge, UK: Cambridge University Press.

Martin, E. (1991), 'The Egg and the Sperm: How Science Has Constructed a Romance Based on Stereotypical Male-Female Roles', *Signs*, 16 (3): 485–501.

Nahman, M. (2008), 'Nodes of Desire: Romanian Egg-Sellers, "Dignity" and Feminist Alliances in Transnational Ova Exchanges', *European Journal of Women's Studies*, 15 (2): 65–82.

Özar, Ş. and B. Yakut-Çakar (2013), 'Unfolding the Invisibility of Women without Men in The Case of Turkey', *Women's Studies International Forum*, 41 (1): 24–34.

Ozyegin, G. (2015), *New Desires, New Selves: Sex, Love, and Piety among Turkish Youth*, New York and London: New York University Press.

Pande, A. (2010), '"At Least I Am Not Sleeping with Anyone": Resisting the Stigma of Commercial Surrogacy in India', *Feminist Studies*, 36 (2): 292–313.

Pande, A. (2020), 'Visa Stamps for Injections: Traveling Biolabor and South African Egg Provision', *Gender & Society*, 34 (4): 573–96.

Paxson, H. (2004), *Making Modern Mothers: Ethics and Family Planning in Urban Greece*, Berkeley: University of California Press.

Polat, N. (2012), 'Concerned Groups in the Field of Reproductive Technologies: A Turkish Case Study', in M. Knecht, M. Klotz and S. Beck (eds), *Reproductive Technologies as Global Form: Ethnographies of Knowledge, Practices, and Transnational Encounters*, 197–227, Frankfurt: Campus Verlag.

Polat, N. (2020), 'Negotiating Masculinities: Reproductive Technologies, Biosocial Exclusion and Men's Engagements in Turkey', *NORMA: International Journal for Masculinity Studies*, 15 (3–4): 267–82.

Ram, M. (2015), 'Colonial Conquests and the Politics of Normalization: The Case of the Golan Heights and Northern Cyprus', *Political Geography*, 47: 21–32.

Riessman, C. K. (2000), 'Stigma and Everyday Resistance Practices: Childless Women in South India', *Gender and Society*, 14 (1): 111–35.

Rose, N. (1999), *Governing the Soul: The Shaping of the Private Self*, London: Free Association Books.

Sehlikoglu, S. (2016), 'Exercising in Comfort: Islamicate Culture of Mahremiyet in Everyday Istanbul', *Journal of Middle East Women's Studies*, 12 (2): 143–65.

Waldby, C. and M. Cooper (2008), 'The Biopolitics of Reproduction: Post-Fordist Biotechnology and Women's Clinical Labour', *Australian Feminist Studies*, 23 (55): 57–73.

Whittaker, A. and A. Speier (2010), '"Cycling Overseas": Care, Commodification, and Stratification in Cross-Border Reproductive Travel', *Medical Anthropology*, 29 (4): 363–83.

Yazıcı, B. (2012), 'The Return to the Family: Welfare, State, and Politics of the Family in Turkey', *Anthropological Quarterly*, 85 (1): 103–40.

Zengin, A. (2011), *İktidarın Mahremiyeti: İstanbul'da Hayat Kadınları, Seks İşçiliği ve Şiddet* (Intimacy of power: Prostitutes, sex work, and violence in Istanbul), Istanbul: Metis.

Zengin, A. (2016), 'Violent Intimacies: Tactile State Power, Sex/Gender Transgression, and the Politics of Touch in Contemporary Turkey', *Journal of Middle East Women's Studies*, 12 (2): 225–45.

3

'Fantastic microscopic hair of uterus': Navigating reproductive trajectories, biomedical bodies and renegotiation of heterosexual femininities and masculinities

Nurhak Polat

First, it may have something to do with the man and the sperm; second, and most fundamentally, with the woman's eggs; and third, with the woman's womb. Most problems occur in the case of women in the uterus. The inside of the womb can be imagined as the black box in an airplane. It receives, and then closes and makes the decision. Well, the microscopic hairs (which propel the ovum towards the uterus) in my wife's uterus are fantastic. So, when the doctor injected the fertilized egg, I listened carefully; the uterus closed immediately... the microscopic hair of other women are about one centimeter long. In comparison, those of my wife are longer than one centimeter. The inside of the womb is very clean. It [the embryo] can implant and nourish very well. (Serkan, business manager man, early fifties)

This was my first interview at their home with the Durmazes, a middle-class couple in an upscale district of Istanbul. Actually, we were talking about how wanting a child turned into a troubled and long journey for the couple that they navigated for over twelve years of marriage. At the very beginning, they couldn't imagine that they would be able to navigate through ten rounds of fertility treatments, as they say, 'even going so far with an egg donation' abroad as 'last resort'[1] before adoption. Giving the blame to preconceived notions of the womanhood and manhood, both complained about being somehow 'obsessed' with having 'success' more than having a biological and genetic related child. For 38-year-old Pelin it 'felt like wanting to prove: I'm also a woman'. They explained to me on that afternoon in 2010, that they felt challenged to journeying 'properly' as a couple, especially by facing highly gendered and ambivalent imperatives imposed on them by the reproductive treatments. In the middle of our conversation, Serkan went into the other room and appeared a little later with a folder that contained Excel sheet tables of weekly hormonal fluctuations and examination results such as the number of oocytes retrieved, fertilized and transferred. They walked me through the folder demonstrating how they had navigated the socio-technical arrangements of repro-medicine. It seemed to be an experience of 'a fight to success', where 'her anatomy has changed' because of being 'pumped full of a bunch of hormones'.

Serkan, quite proficient about the medical and biological aspects of in/fertility, informs me that he is barely targeted by medicine as 'the patient', especially since he is not the 'cause' of the couple's infertility. Yet, his role in this journey is one of providing support and being present as his wife gets treated. His comment on his wife's body and her uterus with its fantastic microscopic hairs is atypical. It also reflects very well the clinical gaze on reproductive bodies – especially on women's bodies both as a source and as trouble for 'achieving procreation' – even if, as Serkan said, it might include the men's bodies and reproductive cells. It demonstrates how journeying – at least in most cases – is constituted and experienced as a 'battle' in woman's body – on a truly microscopic and hormonal level.

This chapter analyses this and similar cases I came across during my fieldwork in Turkey. Drawing upon praxiographic approaches to assisted reproductive technologies (ARTs) as possible technologies of and for gender (Thompson 2005; Franklin 2013), it aims to capture how heterosexual middle-class women and men navigate their reproductive journeys; how they are entangled and engaged with the reproductive treatments and how this process led them to transform the meanings of procreation, bodies and gender. At the intersection between clinics and everyday life practices, I focus on situated renegotiations of 'gender work' (Barnes 2014) performed in particular situations. To discuss the changing meanings and constructions of femininities and masculinities, I'm particularly interested in the ways how they incorporate and challenge the preconceived gender roles during and after the treatments that seem to be considered as a matter of participation and exclusion, and by fluctuating between active and passive modes of caring, responsibility and accountability.

I draw on my research from 2009 and 2013 in three private fertility clinics in the wealthier and politically diverse middle-class neighbourhoods of Istanbul as well as on an Internet platform. By doing so, I also present ethnographic material with a demographic and socio-political diversity of different ages, ethnicities, religious or secular and political identities and socioeconomic background of people – even though it can be only partially representative for the contemporary social and political complexity in the country. It shows that ARTs – publicly known as *tüp tebek tedavisi* – present a morally contested biomedical space for trajectories of governing bodies and navigating reproductive paths. In the specific Turkish case of the neoliberal-authoritarian and patriarchal turn under the AKP (Justice and Development Party) government, this transformed over the last two decades to a site for bargaining on body politics, gender, kinship and the policies and public moralities towards biomedical sciences (Mutlu 2011; Gürtin 2012; Demircioğlu 2015; Açıksöz 2015; Polat 2018).[2]

In what follows, I first analyse how women's bodies are constructed as troublesome bodies to be treated in the specific context of reproductive medicine – which is coded as a predominantly female terrain. Thus, I then turn to the men's role, which is often considered as being 'privileged excluded' in the reproductive journey. I argue that the reproductive trajectories related to infertility and ARTs are marked by a complex gender work; however, its renegotiations stay tied to the medical and heteronormative matrix of femininities and masculinities, parenting and family.

Perspectives on gendered reproductive trajectories

Repro-medicine facilitates and is utilized by couples like Durmazes[3] 'as a path (to) parenting in the context of multiple institutional sites, each promoting hegemonic family customs in distinctive ways' (Jennings 2010: 216). It also shapes the socio-moral practices and meanings of 'having one's own children' and being a 'proper' (gendered) member in a heteronormative, pronatalist-patriarchal society that is experienced as 'a fertile society' and argued that it codes some reproductive biographies and bodies as 'deficient', 'deviant' or requiring to be 'fixed medically'. Which bodies are subject to technological 'fixing' or perceive these as blessing or curse depends on how technologies engender new gender work. As an important number of feminist ethnographic studies suggest, it is embedded and might be re-negotiated in different contexts, settings and situations, in fact, at the moment that these occur (Rapp 1987; Lock and Kaufert 1998; Thompson 2005; Knecht and Hess 2008). I draw upon the insights offered by Mol's praxiography (2002) to capture events in heterogeneous configuration as well as on the locally variable, situated disparate moralities, broader negotiations, and contradictions (Mol 2008). This makes it possible to study, both in singular and in local situations, how body politics, different logics of care and treatment, embodied cultures and materialities operate together and between clinics and everyday lives.

Thus, I build on the feminist critique focusing on reproductive medicine suggested that gender is not only 'ontologically choreographed' (Thompson 2005) by the clinical procedures. Rather, women – and also men – do act over ontologically choreographed gender that is enacted biologically and socially in clinics as well as in their daily medicalized bodily practices (Knecht and Hess 2008; Inhorn 2012b; Barnes 2014). To be more precise, gender – in the sense that Butler (1993) theorizes the term – is performative in this context. It is a matter of doing, as well as how bodies matter within a 'matrix of gender relations' that is not 'singular' or 'acts in a singular and deterministic way to produce a subject as its effect'. Rather, gender performativity, as Butler put it, is 'always a reiteration of a norm or set of norms, and to the extent that it acquires an act-like status in the present, it conceals or dissimulates the conventions of which it is a repetition' (Butler 1993: 12). In this sense, we need to look how cultural constructedness, material-physical and discursive practices, not as necessarily oppositional operations, come together in gender work. In practice, as Thompson suggests in her ethnographic research in US clinics, this choreography brings a 'hyperconventional' context into being, including the broader, conventional and 'highly scripted roles and stereotypes' of sexuality, gender, kinship and family. It results in women and men mostly trying 'harder than ever to perform and norm gender' (Thompson 2005: 118) and to navigate their reproductive journey, either by reflecting or contrasting with what is considered as 'appropriate'.

Following Sarah Franklin, ARTs are utilized as 'technologies of gender'. Therefore, it is important to ask to what extent these technologies are utilized for 'identity repair' or for 'the arrangement of successful conjugality' (Franklin 2013: 154). In addition, one can also ask how women might utilize them to acquire more reproductive control, knowledge over their own bodies and resources in marital relations. The answer to these questions requires a discussion on gender work, as Barnes describes, that entails mentally and emotionally processing how personal ideas about gender fit in or clash with ubiquitous cultural ideas of gender. '[It] requires digging deep, reconsidering personal values, and weighing the social and economic benefits and costs of conforming to society's expectations or going against the grain' (Barnes 2014: 6). Thus, reproductive paths, as they disclosed to me, include different discursive practices, analogies and narratives that replicate hyperconventional gender roles 'in the carefully monitored, arduously clinical, and heteronormative context of IVF, where patients are highly conscious of their dependence on the medical staff assisting them in their pursuit of an elusive goal' (Franklin 2013: 234). They also include tensions and negotiations over the preconceived gender notions, roles and attitudes towards reproductive biographies of couples, highly gendered perceptions of taking care of treatments and visibility/invisibility during the treatments. In this context, gender seems to be referring primary to womanhood.[4] Women's bodies are more likely considered as troublesome bodies to be treated than are men's bodies. On the contrary, men are largely 'missing' (Culley, Hudson, and Lohan 2013), and their role is often constituted as 'peripheral' (Barnes 2014) and (re-)negotiated out of a biosocially privileged excludedness from the woman's reproductive journey (Polat 2020). In this chapter, I will analyse how women and men employ differently gender work and navigate their journey within the socio-technical arrangements of ARTs.

Journeying 'properly' within the socio-technical assemblages

Seen as a 'helping hand' (Franklin 1997), these technologies do not only offer the proper pathways to have one's own, desired, genetically related child. In dealing with them couples are often confronted with various decisions and justification constraints, and grapple with social and medical values, religious convictions as well as socio-economic, body, sexuality and health-related calculus. More importantly, they bring the moral and the political into the everyday intimate lives of couples. Whether secular or religiously oriented urban middle-class individuals and medical consumers, most of the couples I've met in the clinics and an online platform emphasized fertility treatments metaphorically as a 'journey', 'adventure' (*macera*) and 'path' (*yol*). Simpson and Hampshire notice that the metaphor of journeying is associated with the idea of people taking new roles in the biomedical terrain 'in which frameworks of meaning are typically partial, contradictory and emergent' (2015: 13). They act as 'moral pioneers' (Rapp 1987) in navigating and managing their own ways into a socio-technical 'assemblage' (Ong and Collier 2005). This includes clinical practices, people and substances, things, discourses, regulations, moralities and locally situated knowledge (Knecht, Klotz and Beck 2012). Today, as socio-economic inequalities widen and patriarchal pressure grows, the online platforms and spaces play a crucial role in navigating and negotiating individual paths into the socio-technical arrangements (Speier 2011; Polat 2012). Journeying implies 'the lived entanglement – of local biologies, social relations, politics, and culture' (Lock and Nguyen 2006: 2). It requires a substantial bodily and emotional commitment as well as embeddedness in the changing social, political, legal and ethical aspects of what makes ARTs contextually doable. It is primarily asked, what counts as 'legitimate' child making. At other times, it challenges social norms related to practices of procreation, family and kin making within both secular and religious Euro-American and non-Euro-American societies across the Middle East (Thompson 2005; Kahn 2006; Inhorn 2012a). Further, this journey is closely related to 'everyday makings of heteronormativity and heterosexuality' (Sehlikoglu and Karioris 2019), gendered public intimacies and in/visibilities of reproductive bodies in Turkey – as elsewhere. As already mentioned, I followed an intersectional and praxiographic perspective to capture the different doings, practices and actors that are involved in the highly gendered, heteronormative worlds of reproductive technologies. In what follows, I would like to give some information regarding the methodological background of my fieldwork.

Methodical background

My own journey into this assemblage, as a social anthropologist, started in 2008 as I started to work at a multi-sited and *longue durée* research project in Berlin, Germany.[5] In order to study the different practices within what we called socio-technical arrangements, I moved between various sites: clinics, online platforms for self-help (like *www.cocukistiyorum.com*)[6] and the everyday life of women and couples. I conducted interviews (in some cases recurring) with couples, doctors and medical experts, policy makers and concerned group activists and did participant observation in different settings.

Over a period of several years, I conducted field research in three private clinics, two of them located in the Eastern districts of Istanbul and one in a Western, wealthier one. On my first visit, Dr Kaplan, a clinician specialized in Germany, introduced me to his fertility hospital by using the German phrase *Selbsthilfe*, 'as self-help-like atmosphere'. He meant a particular clinical philosophy that offers only *tüp bebek* (test tube) treatment 'tailored' to individual needs, and caring for broader social components, socio-psychological experiences and intimate worries of their clients. The other two clinics were the fertility units within the private hospitals. They were thus able to offer this atmosphere only to a certain extent. Nevertheless, they share similar views of the treatments and also of the people going through them. The director of the second clinic put it that way: the patients would search for 'the best (treatment) available on the market' and be willing to 'fight till the last egg and sperm'. What all three have in common is that they serve a both rural and urban financially prosperous middle class and also the less well-off couples that come from different parts of the country and take the subsidies from the state health insurance agency (SGK – Social Security Institution). They have also put a particular focus on high-tech and invasive methods. During my fieldwork, they usually performed most frequently ICSI ('micro-injection' by which a single sperm cell is injected directly into the egg under the microscope) than the conventional IVF, in some cases also PGD (preimplantation genetic diagnosis) to maximize the chances for pregnancy and so-called 'baby-take-home-rate'.

I recurrently spent several days in the clinics by 'hanging around' in waiting and operation rooms, including in the laboratories. I interviewed couples seeking treatment and doctors and shadowed the medical staff through all possible steps and procedures. I participated in medical counselling as well as medical procedures such as egg retrieval, cell processing and the final embryo transfer, as long as my presence was 'socionaturalized up' (Thompson 2005: 83). To penetrate ethnographically into the paternalist walls of such self-help-like clinics was challenging, especially considering the neoliberal market conditions. In this choreography, since my role as an anthropologist was not defined or included always into the whole scene, my presence appeared sometimes as disturbing for clinical privacy and had to be negotiated over and over again.

For the purposes of this chapter, I will introduce ethnographic data and vignettes from my clinical field site and also interviews with couples from a wide variety of backgrounds, views, biosocial and reproductive health experiences. At the end of my fieldwork, I conducted more than forty interviews and informal conversations with women and men. Most of those I spoke to were urban middle class, yet I also interviewed less well-off couples seeking treatment in the private, rather than state, sector. More than half of them already had several treatments and could get cost coverage by the SGK up to three cycles – with a co-payment and additional charges – in a private clinic. Some of them were private payer. All of them were between twenty-five and fifty-three years of age and Turkish citizens. Some of them expressed themselves as conservative Sunni-Muslims, whereas others as modern, secular Kemalist-Republicans. A comparatively small number of women and men were from political, religious and ethnic minorities – such as feminists, leftists, Alevis or ethnic non-Turkish.

Troublesome reproductive bodies, booming IVF and neoliberal-authoritarian policies

Over the past two decades, reproductive medicine became a moral venue for the struggles of co-existing ideas of social order and moralities (Polat 2018). Various pronatalistic interests are operating on the macro and micro levels of bodily experiences of reproduction, which are embedded in a nexus of biopolitics, clinical and regulatory spheres and techniques. They involve both pathologizing and normalizing processes. The booming economy of ARTs, especially after the 2000s in Turkey, has played an important role in this regard. While the number of registered fertility centres at the beginning of my research was 120, it has steadily increased to 148 by 2016.[7] The number of treatment cycles was approximately 40,000 treatments per year. Since 2005, the costs of three treatments are covered by SGK. The lobby by an alliance of clinics, the pharmaceutical industry, medical and patient associations and organizations has been effective to integrate infertility 'as a disease' and medical condition into the state health insurance.

Promoted as a *tüp bebek cenneti* (test-tube baby paradise), the Turkish market continues to be 'dedicated' to producing and sustaining 'the heteronormative reproductive unit' (Gürtin 2016: 40). It codes ARTs as *meşru* (legitimate) and *makbul* (proper) ways of procreation, of being parents and reproductive selves/citizens (Mutlu 2011; Açıksöz 2015; Demircioğlu 2015). *Tüp bebek* is considered as largely normalized; however, it is restricted to heterosexual married couples. Sunni-Muslim bioethical values prevail in regulations. The 'repro-national' character, as Gürtin put it, has distinguished itself very long time 'in a hybrid state, with its precarious relations between secular principles and Sunni morality', a form of 'patriarchal pronatalism' promoting and funding ARTs but only within strict 'conjugal confines', justified with reference not only to religious but also to moral, social and scientific rhetoric (Gürtin 2016: 40). The so-called 'third-party donation' of sperm, eggs, embryos and also surrogacy have always been prohibited. These are considered as non-normative means that require – as most of my interviewees put it – 'going so far' and overcoming personal moral boundaries as well as societal taboos and conceptualizations of gender identities and family. Even as these means are a less visible part of 'child-wish-economy' (Polat 2018), every year approximately 5,000 women, men and couples make their journey abroad for third-party donations and carry out a sort of moral work at two levels on boundaries of reproduction, family, sexuality, gender, and medicine. The first level concerns the complex biomedical regimes and the second the local worlds and normative surroundings in which women and men live, experience and navigate their own path. This, I would argue, is extended gender work within specific reproductive regimes.

As elsewhere, ARTs are constantly related to 'heterobionormative' (Leighton 2013) assumptions in Turkey. This fixes reproduction, kinship and family to women's bodies, especially by the ways of putting women's bodies to the centre of the fertility treatments. Scholars have demonstrated how ARTs have contributed to the everyday and bodily makings and navigating of heteronormativity, heterosexuality and gender identities (Mutlu 2011; Gürtin 2012; Polat 2012, 2018; Demircioğlu 2015; Açıksöz 2015). They have also illustrated how ARTs relate to and challenge heteronormative moral-cultural order. Especially during the authoritarian turn of AKP in Turkey, these technologies have embedded into the politics of governing reproductive bodies and put the womb at the centre of 'the new restructuring of family, society and state relations' (Mutluer 2019: 113).

The current AKP government interferes more aggressively than ever into the private and intimate life of its citizens. Several researchers have pointed to the dramatic political transformations that merged the oppressive neoconservative politics of intimacy and neoliberal-authoritarian biopolitical agenda in AKP policies. Acar and Altunok (2013) emphasized that 'reproductive governance' (Morgan and Roberts 2012) of AKP style aims to operate as a guardian of 'politics of the intimate'. It employs and promotes more offensive Sunni-Islamic 'moral-cultural order' (Acar and Altunok 2013: 18), 'familialism' (Korkman 2016) and a new mode of 'patriarchal pronatalism' (Gürtin 2016). Current reproductive politics relies deliberately on a selective-pronatalist, 'nationalist, Islamist and patriarchal moral regime of truth' (Özgüler and Yarar 2017: 144). In this context, ARTs have been employed for mediating certain kind of public intimacies (*mahremiyet*) 'through creating borders, normalcies, and privileges' (Sehlikoglu 2015: 235); by promoting hegemonic gender ideologies, repressive heteronormativity and (hetero)normative public intimacies, they also push specific '*yeni milli* (new national) values' (Mutluer 2019: 113) of AKP's distinctive authoritarianism.

Since my fieldwork, and more so after 2011, beginning with the AKP's third term in government, authoritarian governance targets every single aspect of the life of every single citizen, and attempts to control and monitor the reproductive decisions and paths within and outside of the national borders (following the AKP's attempt to ban the third-party donation abroad in 2010, and also abortion). Defining what counts as *meşru* and *makbul* ways became direct tools for biopolitical transformations related to reproductive decisions, rights and concerns of sexuality.[8] Reproductive issues, bodies and rights are at the centre of a different, more polarizing and selective pronatalism, as the discourse 'three children' targets the ethnic-Turkish, Sunni-Muslim, heterosexual-married majority (Mutlu et al. 2018).[9] Moreover, the diversity of reproductive experiences – such as for third-party donations, surrogacy, including those of non-reproducing, unmarried couples/singles or LGBT – is made invisible.

As I have analysed elsewhere, the reproductive trajectories and journeys are embedded in this particular climate (Polat 2018). To navigate through highly gendered, locally situated 'moral worlds' (Kleinman 1992; Inhorn 2003) of ARTs, many women and men I met in the clinics and on the internet do different bodily gendered works. In the following, I illustrate how ARTs provide a specific terrain where men and women get in touch with new, unfamiliar embodied experiences. Rather than focusing on the governing power of medical science and patriarchal imperatives, I'm interested in the practices of gendered negotiations in this specific field and within a specific context: rising neoliberal-neoconservative authoritarianism in Turkey. Let me stress that I am up against the cultural narratives of biopower, patriarchy and gender as omnipotent. Doing this is challenging, especially while observing the hegemonic codes, gender scripts and prevalent gender asymmetries on a daily basis and in all routines – within and beyond the institutional, clinical and biographic settings. ARTs might be the emerging, flexible tools, as well argued by other scholars already, for women and men in negotiating and navigating through the arrangements within the biomedical and patriarchal gender regimes. From the praxeographic perspectives, a precise focus on the individual practices and ways of navigations can be analytically fruitful in analysing how gender does work and is made to work by different actors, authorities and institutions within the larger gendered constellations. I aim to capture the moments and situations that raise the question of how gender arrangements become problematic in this particular repro-medical field that is constituted stereotypically speaking 'as a female terrain'.

Gender in absence and presence in the journey

It is generally known that infertility and reproduction are frequently associated almost exclusively with women. Despite their focus on woman's body, for involving practices with various consequences for conjugal relations, a research on ARTs raises interesting questions about the role of men, or of their absence, as much as on the ways in which gender roles and identities are interactively produced throughout reproductive journeys, which are still informed by gendered contradictions and asymmetries. Totally 'pissed off', Şebnem complained, 'this starts and ends with you' and continued, 'the problem is Kadir's, but Kadir is never there'. In contrast, she 'got the full program' which forced a new 'tempo' in her life and a 'totally different lifestyle':

> Don't forget the pills, don't forget the vitamins, don't forget this, don't forget that'. You take so many hormones, so many medications, get so many injections, organize your life around that. It's your body riddled, penetrated and suffers and it's you who is going through a whole emotional and hormonal instability. [...] For men it is simple, really I mean, there is almost totally absence of men that we are talking about here... my arms, abdomen and even bottom were completely punctured, my husband just had to masturbate. That is it how it felt.
>
> (Thirty-year-old woman, self-employed, Istanbul)

Şebnem considers herself informed by feminist and critical leftist politics, which have played a crucial role in her life, including on sexual and reproductive decisions. She always felt herself in conflict with the patriarchal-normative societal order and with the idea of leading what she called a 'petite bourgeois *(küçük burjuva)* family lifestyle'. A life with children, as a small family, seemed to both her and her husband to be a way of losing control and autonomy in their lives. 'Completely unconcerned about not being able to get pregnant', due to several abortions in earlier relations, they had been convinced they 'would be able to have children, if and when they wanted to'. Her medical check was fine, but in his mid-thirties Kadir had a medical issue called varicoceles, and the number and quality of his sperm were significantly limited. They 'laughed to death about silly sperms' when they got the test results and made jokes like: 'Instead of penetrating into darkness [towards the egg], they wander stupidly towards light [towards the outer labia]'. They did not take the diagnosis seriously, yet they knew that 'the biological clock was ticking'. That's when they turned to IVF, she realized that there is 'the absence of the present husband' *(var da yok koca)*. She could only hope and expect her husband to be at least emotionally and socially part of the process. She blames the asymmetrical medical procedures that should have communicated much better than her doctors did. Although she – like her husband – didn't care a lot about having children, once started, she had to put her body under permanent surveillance and manage treatment, everyday life and marital relations.

It was similar for Emel; the treatments felt like her own private issue. In the beginning, the 37-year-old woman and her five-year younger husband had to 'have sex by recipe' *(reçete üzerine berabere olmak)*. She was the one whose body was involved, who got tested and who 'calculated everything and every scenario of *what if*'. On the contrary, her husband found his own ways of not engaging so much with the treatment. I didn't meet him, but I was told by Emel that he would not differentiate himself from other men: 'of course, a man considers himself healthy in this matter and does not want to see anything lacking in himself'. Against 'all the masculine stuff', she tried to show him how he could engage as a man without feeling ashamed and less manly. In their case, the struggle started with convincing him to go to a spermiogram – sperm analysis for investigating the level of male fertility – and continued with persuading him to engage actively and responsibly in treatment. Women like Emel and Şebnem feel challenged by the fact that their bodies were usually subjected to the medical treatments and considered as the bodies-to-treat, whereas men could be just absent, as their presence is mostly expected for giving a sperm sample. As I analysed elsewhere, there is a strong narrative that enables men to resort to being a drifting, ghostly male figure, somehow avoiding being present, 'as outsiders', as 'being reduced to a sperm provider' or 'structurally excluded by the nature of the treatments' (Polat 2020). Women consider themselves to be forced into a position of 'taking the direction' (*reji*). Such negotiations demonstrate, in the view of female interlocutors, 'how men release themselves from a commitment to child issues', while women pursue the imperative of an activist mode in their individual and family reproduction biographies. Their bodily stories are interwoven with highly gendered biomedical choreographies.

Micro-gender work at a lab

Indeed, there is kind of gendered negotiation that takes place at the microbiological level at a lab. Performed as a 'gamete interaction' at a lab, as van der Ploeg put it (2004), biomedically assisted procreation merges the female and male bodies into a hybrid, 'couples' body'. As the gametes, sperm and egg interact, the body boundaries blur. However, women's bodies are constituted as the target and the site at the same time. My observations in all three clinics demonstrated that a kind of micro-gender works facilitate a smooth passage between bodies, and also natural, technical, social and political orders (Latour 2005; Thompson 2005).

    In the clinics, I was told by different doctors that 'creating a body-like atmosphere in the laboratory is the key' or 'you have to build via high-tech an artificial uterus', suitable for egg, sperm and embryo. Such discourses associate not only a displacement of the bodily functions and 'failure', but also mark that the laboratory and clinics are places where the boundaries between the natural and the cultural are negotiated and reassembled. As a female doctor put it, ARTs give 'a little assistance to procreation'. The cultural images of reproductive body parts easily pass through the clinical doors and overlap, on a daily basis, with biomedical constructions of sperm as 'penetrator' and egg as receiver to conceive (cf. Martin 1991). ICSI conveys the perception that 'only one single sperm is enough', as said by different medical and non-medical actors in all three clinics.[10] Into the bargain, men's bodies are mostly 'choreographed as ejaculatory extensions of their partners' (Thompson 2005: 128) and male infertility is treated as a pathology to be cured not necessarily in a male body, but instead in a Petri dish and via the work of the female body. On the contrary, the woman's body – especially the womb (*rahim*) – is classified in most cases beforehand as the problem to be 'fixed'. *Rahim* was occasionally referred to as 'field' (*tarla*) – like in the patriarchal monogenetic beliefs of conception known as 'seed and soil' theory, which subsists of a combination of the biomedical and cultural models in Turkey and also in different parts of the Middle East (Delaney 1991; Culley, Hudson, and Van Rooij 2009). Unlike Serkan who imagined his wife's uterus as a well-functioning black box, Feyza, a 38-year-old Sunni-Muslim woman, adopted the discourse I occasionally heard during my fieldwork: 'if *tarla* is not suitable, you can give what you want, it will not hold.'

    During treatments, the woman is rendered into multiple body parts, such as eggs, fallopian tubes and uterus. Moreover, there is also an unstable hormonal body that is permanently under the clinical and laboratory monitoring by numbers, medical values and norms. Watching egg collections and embryo transfers made me think that there is something more than technical and medical in working on bodies and reproductive cells. Extracting eggs out of women's bodies and 'transferring them back' is not a routine, even not in the perfectly choreographed medical scenes. The woman lies at the operating table, half-anaesthetized; a female psychologist stands besides her to support her emotionally. Next to the doctor, who uses a special, thin needle to ultrasound the vagina, there are two assistants, one next to the monitor and the other closer to him, holding a petri dish, into which the doctor puts the retrieved eggs. Not surprisingly, the women I met in different clinics were aware of such fragmentation. Nonetheless, they didn't always comply with bodily fragmentations. They rather often dealt with them strategically. Some of them resisted by cutting out the microbiological routine in the clinics. For example, before leaving the operation room after the egg collection, Perrin, a 28-year-old woman, asked the embryologist to 'take care of her Perişs'. By giving her eggs a cute short name, she framed them as whole part of herself and anticipated them as her future babies. Every one of them was seen as 'gold egg' (*altın yumurta*), as a 'preliminary stage of life's creation'. However, treatments were about to generate 'usable substances to fertilize.' Often, doctors and couples were pleased with the large number of oocytes. Berna, one of the women, for example, was shocked and proud, even though she had to suffer from pain for days with a swollen stomach, because '33 eggs were collected' from her. To her this meant an extremely successful treatment, although she complained about suffering, physically and mentally. Because of the side effects of hormones, her ovaries became stimulated to grow multiple eggs to maturity. She suffered from ovarian hyperstimulation syndrome in which her ovaries became swollen and caused bloating and abdominal pain. She said that this 'ultra-high number' of eggs caused a frenzy and a stir when she came out of the operating room 'half awake, half unconscious' and was lying there with other women waiting with, on their bellies, a note indicating the number of eggs that had been retrieved from them. Afterwards she realized that women around her had 'maximum seven eggs or so'. She suggested to her husband not to tell anyone. Otherwise, they could be touched by the 'evil eye' (*nazar*). Here there are very flexible and practical opinions from both sides, as all are concerned with 'achieving the desired result'.

Heroic struggles?

Aynur, a young woman from the wealthy middle class of Istanbul, who didn't feel rushed to get married and have children, suffered from endometriosis, an oestrogen-dependent, mostly painful inflammatory disease that causes infertility. Treatment in this case generally had poor outcomes. Her 'permanently failing body', as she felt, 'is not even able to produce eggs with the help of medication'. It didn't react to the heaviest hormone preparations, despite having the maximum dose of medication in each treatment. Her hormone levels merely increased or decreased drastically. Was this a crisis of her femininity? No. But still 'an endless battle, only for a fertile egg', she said. When I met her in 2009, she had already tried everything she could within the last seven years.

Many marital, sexual and social problems followed; not to mention socio-psychological 'breakdowns' and 'traumas', she suffered under severe physical complications in every treatment, which 'never led to anything'. The challenge for her was 'starting all over again'. She described her experiences with treatments as a moral journey:

> The things you experience are not normal. It is a highly sensitive subject. There are hormones, emotions at work, families and society involved... you can't just reduce that. You experience much more than the individual child wish. You have to pay attention to many things, to learn, organize, think and so on.
>
> (In her mid-thirties, unemployed at the time of her treatments)

This replicates a common and familiar portrayal when women report on their reproductive path. It implies the bodily work and moral and social engagement which bear significant challenges for women in becoming familiar with the biomedical procedures and knowledge. This quote is taken from a conversation where Aynur states clearly that it is 'much more comprehensive than the individual desire to have a child'. There was the 'know-it-all society', a 'fertile society' that exerted ferocious pressure, arbitrarily and brutally, on the wounds where it hurt the most. Navigating also meant to her, like to many, to learn to cope appropriately with everything; with hormones as much as emotions, sexuality as much as socio-psychical 'ups and downs'. This required keeping an eye on the norms of the society, as well as active learning, decision making, 'being an expert on her own'. This included also 'taking action' (Becker 2000) and engaging proactively within the moral and socio-political world of ARTs. To be able to do this, many years ago Aynur turned to an online community of people, mostly heterosexual women and couples who are active participants in internet discussions. Talking and sharing the problems with others helped her to reconsider her experiences with medical and societal conditions, and with the 'female issues'. Moreover, it was a kind of taking action, attempting to embody the ideal of the informed, active patient/consumer in the neoliberal healthcare sector. This enabled her to navigate 'the complex knot' in a more informed, practical and emotional way, she argued. She wrote and told her story publicly, and so altruistically rendered her own 'expertise' available for others.

Thinking through this complex knot, one can argue that there is new 'patriarchal bargaining' (Lorber 1989) in this specific field. ARTs as technologies of gender facilitate and challenge gender works of women and men. They are utilized by women like Aynur strategically in acquiring more reproductive control and taking action in order to shape one's own knowledge practices, gender work, to help other people to do so, and to intervene much more broadly in policies, local moral worlds and regimes of reproductive governance. As a means for renegotiating gender works, it extends, however, the power exerted on bodies, for governing the bodies to govern, and the gendered paths to navigate into both socio-technical arrangements and (hetero) normative society. All this goes hand in hand with the normative glorification of reproductive trajectories as 'heroic battles' in making modern would-be-mothers, parents and patients/consumers (Paxson 2004; Polat 2018). Of course, medicalized and mediated journeys, as such, offer a particular sociotechnical framework to men and women, of heroically performing and renegotiating their gender identities and their sense of femininity and masculinity (cf. Hinton and Miller 2013; Inhorn and Wentzell 2011). The following vignettes exemplify changing marital and gender relations on the basis of embodied and biosocial experiences of infertility and *tüp bebek*.

Men's doings – from a position of privileged excludedness

Most of the men emphasized having 'men specific issues with that' (*erkeğe özgü zorluklar*) and that they wouldn't know 'how to be part of it as a man'. They reoriented themselves pragmatically against the feelings of being lost, disorientation and challenge caused by being what anthropologists called 'second sex' (Inhorn et al. 2009; Culley, Hudson, and Lohan 2013). The main discourse in my field on men caring for reproductive health was that men are 'helping out the wife with it'. To navigate the reproductive journeys without being stigmatized and excluded, they felt themselves to be forced to challenge and transform the ascribed masculine ways of being and acting. As Ozyegin put it in a different context, men I talked to were willing 'to actively disinherit traditional masculinity and pursue self-consciously unpatriarchal selves' (Ozyegin 2018: 246).

I accompanied Mehmet and Bediha Kirac, a couple in their early thirties, to their consultation. Mehmet and his wife have been married for over six years and came to Istanbul for ICSI treatment from a nearby city. Bediha is a housewife, Mehmet works in a private company, with limited educational background and low-income. 'We are modest people', Mehmet mentioned, who have little opportunities and social resources for access to the medical treatments. It was their second cycle of a treatment for which they chose to proceed in a private clinic where they believed they would be provided a better and more effective treatment. Like many others, they made a sacrifice to be able to cover the costs, back then in 2012 approximately 2,000 to 4,000 Turkish lira, which was covered only partially by the state insurance of SGK. During the consultation Bediha was relatively quiet, whereas Mehmet spoke often for her, and as 'we'. The counsellor spoke directly to Bediha and told her 'step by step' what she had to do, what she had to pay special attention to and how she should inject the medication herself. Laughing, Bediha said that her husband would do the shots and also schedule the treatment, dosage and other things. The counsellor explained to him exactly how to take the exact dosage of hormones. In all the treatments they have had so far, he has acted not only as a responsible 'patient', but also as the caring husband who took care of everything he could. After all, as he said to me later, it seemed to be one possible 'way for a man to do something in return for the great stress and strain Bediha is going through'. Both infertility and IVF induced in him 'a new level of intimate relations' he shares with his wife, especially deep compassion, emotional attachment and care. He would 'take care of a lot of things, even after the long workday trying to do something for the household if necessary, laundry, cleaning, cooking, depending on what is actually needed. [...] sometimes I should be as funny as a barrel of monkeys to cheer her up' (*yani ben de şebeklik yapmaya devam edicem moralini düzelticem*). He was willing to sacrifice much more, other than 'gambling with his wife's wellbeing and health or disturbing the happiness' and 'peaceful life together as a couple'. As a religious person, he would act in a manner consistent with his religious belief and resignation (*tevekkül*) that the things will turn out for the best, 'if Allah wants it to be'.

After a few days of this conversation with Kiracs, I met Belcans, a newly married, well-educated, working couple, in the same clinic. The Belcans were quite different from Kiracs, not only in their attitudes towards family planning, couple life and privacy, but also in their lifestyle. They wouldn't necessarily let in Allah's will or wait for it to work by itself and by nature. We were sitting in a small private room, where Perrin, in her early thirties, had been brought after the embryo transfer. At the beginning of our conversation, her husband Can, an urban, white-collar man, seemed a little uncomfortable with me asking questions, so he let me understand that they choose a private clinic – and not a public hospital – because of provision of better clinical privacy and good medical care. Can would like to start 'directly with a *tüp bebek*', because of low sperm counts. He described himself as 'a little bit, like, a realist man' who would take the numbers into account and attempt to make use of the 'technically most efficient' service they can possibly get and afford. Like many other couples I met, they also decided for an 'outstanding' clinic within the private reproductive healthcare sector felt like a 'jungle' which might offer 'patient-centred', 'scientifically professional' and 'best efficient techniques and equipment'. Perrin was sceptical. Since the problem is low sperm count and not the so-called female factor, such as uterine anomalies preventing pregnancy, she said, 'the conception might occur the normal way'. ICSI would 'fast-track' it. After the first clinical consultation they decided for ICSI by which a single sperm cell is injected directly into the egg under the microscope. The job will be 'done' by the embryologist in the laboratory, both the doctors and the couples stated repeatedly. There was something very intriguing in this discourse. 'What is happening on the microscopic level', as both referred, seems to be about renegotiating the gender roles and gender work done by themselves. Moreover, there were contradictory changes as to one's role and seeing oneself as 'an assemblage of body parts' (Becker 2000: 26).

The vignette of Pelin and Serkan that I introduced at the beginning of this chapter exemplified that women and men rethink of themselves, and see their reproductive and other capabilities, from different angles. They felt forced to find ways, as Pelin put it, for 'flexible adjustments to the medical techniques, to bodily and hormonal problems that might occur in time and coping with the idea that it is not just a little assistance, at all'. Positioning themselves as responsible and informed medical consumers, they said to me that they 'proceeded by assessing the risks' (*risk ölçerek gittik yani*). For Pelin, it often felt like her eggs and womb had failed over and over again. Even recognizing that it's not an individual failure, it turned into 'a fight to success' against her body, which was governed, surveilled and managed by an extended complex of medicine. Her husband Serkan took mostly over the role of a navigator, hoping to find a way out of a perceived exclusion and feelings of being 'lost, helpless'. His self-perception (as a caring husband and as a man who wanted to be the father of a biological child) collided with that, when he said that he would do 'this whole shit because she wanted to have her own child so badly'. Again, during the struggle for having an own (biologically related) child, her body was 'changed' and 'pumped full of a bunch of hormones'. It 'felt like a battle for womanhood' and 'not giving up' was a decisive hallmark. By moving from one treatment to the next, like medical nomads, they considered every possible way as 'embodied, calculative consumers' in the highly 'promissory' repro-medical regimes (Thompson 2005) and even became, as Serkan explained, 'expert on the illegal ways' of 'getting a child', from egg donation, surrogacy to abroad adoption. Whether religious, fatalistic or secular impulses, some couples had more moral questions as to how far they would go for a biological child than others. On the other hand, after each treatment most of the people I met in clinics and online forums felt all the more the pressure to 'do everything possible', to 'always go one step further'. That resulted in the case of the Durmazes, in a 'doom loop'. In dealing with infertility, their moral limits became more elastic, regarding what is 'doable' or not. After the adoption, the couple felt 'a little ashamed' and complained about the exaggeration of having own child and of 'genetic ties'. Annoyed, Serkan also criticized the 'money making machine with child-wish':

> It is a sign that the typical merchant mentality governing Turkey currently is mirroring everywhere, right. It cannot be true; it's like selling the chocolates, biscuits or buying anything.[11]

As Franklin pointed out, 'once inside this topsy-turvy world', couples face 'not a simple process of steps leading to potential success – it is a confusing and stressful world of disjointed temporalities, jangled emotions, difficult decisions, unfamiliar procedures, medical jargon, and metabolic chaos' (Franklin 2013: 7). Likewise, their assumptions about infertility, a 'genetically related child', and parenthood vary, as do their perceptions of masculinity and femininity.

Conclusion: Renegotiation of heterosexual femininities and masculinities

As this volume invites us to rethink the governing of women's bodies, gender identities and reproductive experiences in contemporary Turkey, the ethnographic vignettes I presented in this chapter provide an insight into renegotiations of new, medical practices in relation to femininities and masculinities in Turkey's expanding ART market. They highlight that women are not merely subject to the monitoring and governing of their bodies, lives and social-conjugal relations (Throsby 2010). Instead, they demonstrate far more dynamic 'patriarchal paradoxes' (Faircloth and Gürtin 2017), and the pragmatic ways of coping and defying the biomedical choreography. Reproductive trajectories related to infertility are marked by a complex gender work as contextually situated in the intersection of medical discourses and clinical practices, gender regimes, politics of care and visibility, and biopolitics. Following this line, I began this chapter by considering ARTs as a lens to analyse the negotiated gender works at various levels. Ethnographic and praxeographically collected material aimed to show that this occurs and is bargained for on the clinical and microscopic level, in bodily engagements and in conjugal relations. I traced the many ambiguities, variations and contradictions in this particular medical terrain, predominantly constructed 'as a female terrain'.

My aim was to capture the practices and situations that destabilize our views of gender arrangements, without ignoring the hegemonic codes and asymmetries in the daily routines within and beyond the institutional, clinical and biographic settings. The infertility and fertility treatments are not exceptional and extreme conditions, as usually imagined; rather, they intertwine with the ideas of what is thought of as 'normalcy' (Becker 2000). However, the public and individual narratives tend to frame this normalcy with a kind of 'heroic struggle for a child' that takes place in women's bodies. Notice that this framing is neither cultural nor nationally unique. Rather, it typifies how reproductive bodies, biomedical practices, patriarchal pronatalisms, promissory and monopolistic markets and neoliberal healthcare logics are tied up into a patriarchal and negotiated mixture. By trying to sketch out some of the trajectories of governing bodies and navigating reproductive paths from a praxiographic perspective in Turkey, I find Butler's performative 'mattering' of bodies and gender identities very suggestive. Following her, I suggest that we should look into practices, events and power relations regarding how and where bodies matter and gender works are done. In the clinics, women's and men's bodies, and by the extension femininities and masculinities, are portrayed through the bodily fragmentation. In the case of men, the preconceived masculine positions – as being 'privileged excludeds' – have been the virtually defining signifier for male negotiations. Whether in clinics or in social or conjugal relations, this shapes mens own embodied and/or non-embodied journey into the ARTs. In confrontation with pronatalist ideas and hegemonic reproductive norms, they often felt to rearrange and renegotiate their own gender work (see also Polat 2020).

It was beyond the scope of this chapter to examine how the particular challenges, disorientations and fuzziness of the body boundaries lead to further biopolitical changes with regard to the reproductive governance of women's and men's bodies. By talking about a 'complex knot', women like Aynur phrase the socio-technical arrangements that weave and build up on preconceived, hegemonic gender notions, the neoliberal imperative to navigate reproductive trajectories and moral obligations. Women – and heterosexual couples – pursue very different ways of navigation in the complex reproductive regimes and position themselves as self-reflexive subjects 'intimately connected with, critical of, informed about, and committed to the technologies' (Thompson 2005: 16). They act proactively, anticipating and promoting changes rather than simply being patronized by medicine or patriarchal reproductive regimes in their gender work on their bodies, in their everyday lives, as well as in the clinical and social environments. The individual practices at the intersection between clinics, social contexts and political changes in contemporary Turkey illustrate that the reproductive trajectories are made more than just to a bodily, social and clinical management. They are anchored in the discursive matrix of (hetero)normativity about reproduction, motherhood and fatherhood, family and gender. Thus, they demonstrate situated renegotiations of heteronormative gender work, of both heterosexual women and men, that remains attached to the preconceived ideas of family as a normative (biological) unit and of parenting.

Notes

1   Since ARTs with egg and sperm donation are prohibited, at the time of my fieldwork, approximately 5,000 couples per year went to Cyprus or to other countries within the transnational 'repro-scape' (Inhorn 2012a; Knecht, Klotz, and Beck 2012) for reproductive treatments. In the Turkish case, Cyprus is often considered as a medical backyard to elude the national laws that specifically prohibit third-party donations.

2   I would like to thank the editors and Meghana Joshi for critical comments during the writing of various drafts. My gratitude goes to the men and women who spoke to me about their most intimate experiences with infertility and reproductive medicine. Also to the clinics, and doctors and activists who provided me access.

3   All names have been changed to pseudonyms and other identifying features are disguised to protect the confidentiality of research participants.

4   Men's bodies are largely 'ignored', as Rosenfeld and Faircloth argued in both the clinical contexts and social scientific analyses of medicalization (2006: 1). Scholars demonstrated that it is similar in the case of social-scientific research on ARTs (for a discussion see Inhorn et al. 2009).

5   It was the project 'Kinship as Representation of Social Order and Practice', in Collaborative Research Cluster (SFB 640) 'Changing Representations of Social Order' at the Humboldt University, Berlin, which was funded by the German Research Foundation (DFG). We comparatively investigated, from 2004 to 2013, local and national modes of using and appropriating IVF/ICSI in Turkey, Great Britain and Germany and traced practices, reproductive biographies and emerging experiences within the globally and transnationally entangled realm of reproductive medicine. I also had access to the data of the project for my analyses, i.e. a total of over 100 interviews that were conducted in Turkey over a period of about 10 years. I would like to thank my colleagues Michi Knecht, Stefan Beck and Maren Heibges. Some material and cases are already published in previous publications (see Knecht et al. 2011; Polat 2012, 2018, 2020).

6   *www.cocukistiyorum.com* has been run since 2002 by ÇİDER (*Çocuk İstiyorum Derneği – Association 'I Want a Child'*), the Turkish NGO for and by involuntarily childless people. I conducted research approximately for two years on this platform to understand the role of such platforms within the growing reproductive market in Turkey.

7   See http://www.saglik.gov.tr/TR/Genel. In 2015, according to ESHRE (European Society of Human Reproduction and Embryology) there were 1,343 fertility clinics in 38 European countries; 849,811 cycles of treatments were performed per year. There are no reliable figures from Turkey. In 2008, Turkey reported 43,928 cycles yearly and 98 per cent per ICSI (http://www.eshre.eu/).

8   By attempting to ban the cross-border third-party donation in 2010 the government made, for example, 'a move to readjust' (*ayar cekmek*) to contra bonos mores and therefore take action against the violation of national law, as Ministry of Health representative Irfan Şencan put it at the time. Contrary to earlier assumptions (Baykal 2008; Gürtin-Broadbent 2011), this does not demonstrate solely symbolic, rather an authoritarian, turning point in biopolitics and reproductive governance.

9   In a speech in Uşak, Recep Tayyip Erdoğan addressed the women and told them 'Children are a blessing' *(bereket)* and pleaded for 'at least three children per family'. Since then, a discourse has established itself on the hypothetical decline in the birth

rate and the degeneration of the family as a cultural value (http://arsiv.ntvmsnbc.
com/news, 10.03.2008, accessed 13 April 2011). This kind of pronatalism is highly
selective; the political agenda set by AKP primarily addresses certain population
groups and heterosexual families. Not only non-heterosexual partners and singles,
but also Kurds, non-Muslims and others, are excluded.

10 It is more likely the result of both ICSI and TESE, a testicular operation to extract
sperm from the testicles. It helps to relocate one's own masculinity from a stigmatized
situation into the scientific and medical contexts. Especially, ICSI as a technical
procedure of direct intracytoplasmic sperm injection contributed to decouple the
cultural link between masculinity and virility.

11 In Turkish: *Şu anda Türkiye'yi yöneten tipik tüccar zihniyetinin her yere yansımasıdır
bu tamam mı böyle çikolata satar gibi, bisküvi satar gibi böyle.*

References

Acar, F. and G. Altunok (2013), 'The "politics of intimate" at the Intersection of Neoliberalism and Neo-conservatism in Contemporary Turkey', *Women's Studies
International Forum*, 41 (1): 14–23.

Açıksöz, S. C. (2015), 'In Vitro Nationalism: Masculinity, Disability, and Assisted
Reproduction in War-Torn Turkey', in G. Ozyegin (ed.), *Gender and Sexuality in
Muslim Cultures*, 19–36, London and New York: Routledge.

Barnes, L. W. (2014), *Conceiving Masculinity: Male Infertility, Medicine, and Identity*,
Philadelphia: Temple University Press.

Baykal, B. E. A. (2008), 'Opinions of Infertile Turkish Women on Gamete Donation and
Gestational Surrogacy', *Fertil. Steril*, 89 (4): 817–22.

Becker, G. (2000), *The Elusive Embryo: How Women and Men Approach New Reproductive
Technologies*, Berkeley and London: University of California Press.

Butler, J. (1993), *Bodies that Matter: On the Discursive Limits of 'Sex'*, New York: Routledge.

Culley, L., N. Hudson and F. Van Rooij, eds (2009), *Marginalized Reproduction: Ethnicity,
Infertility and Reproductive Technologies*, London and Sterling, VA: Routledge.

Culley, L., N. Hudson and M. Lohan (2013), 'Where are all the men? The Marginalization
of Men in Social Scientific Research on Infertility', *Reproductive BioMedicine Online*, 27
(3): 225–35.

Delaney, C. (1991), *The Seed and the Soil: Gender and Cosmology in Turkish Village Society*,
Berkeley: University of California Press.

Demircioğlu, M. (2015), *Achieving Procreation: Childlessness and IVF in Turkey*, New York
and Oxford: Berghahn.

Faircloth, C. and Z. B. Gürtin (2017), 'Fertile Connections: Thinking across Assisted
Reproductive Technologies and Parenting Culture Studies', *Sociology*, 52 (5): 983–1000.

Franklin, S. (1997), *Embodied Progress: A Cultural Account of Assisted Conception*,
London: Routledge.

Franklin, S. (2013), *Biological Relations: IVF, Stem Cells, and the Future of Kinship*,
Durham and London: Duke University Press.

Gürtin, Z. B. (2012), 'Assisted Reproduction in Secular Turkey: Regulation, Rhetoric,
and the Role of Religion', in, M. C. Inhorn and S. Tremayne (eds) *Islam and Assisted
Reproductive Technologies: Sunni and Shia Perspectives*, 285–311, New York and
Oxford: Berghahn.

Gürtin, Z. B. (2016), 'Patriarchal Pronatalism: Islam, Secularism and the Conjugal Confines of Turkey's IVF Boom', *Reproductive BioMedicine and Society Online*, 2: 39–46.

Gürtin-Broadbent, Z. (2011), 'Banning Reproductive Travel: Turkey's ART Legislation and Third-Party Assisted Reproduction', *Reprod Biomed Online*, 23 (5): 555–64.

Hinton, L. and T. Miller (2013), 'Mapping Men's Anticipations and Experiences in the Reproductive Realm: (In)fertility Journeys', *Reproductive BioMedicine Online*, 27 (3): 244–52.

Inhorn, M. C. (2003), *Local Babies, Global Science: Gender, Religion, and In Vitro Fertilization in Egypt*, New York and London: Routledge.

Inhorn, M. C. (2012a), 'Globalization and Gametes: Reproductive "Tourism," Islamic Bioethics, and Middle Eastern Modernity', in M. Knecht, M. Klotz and S. Beck (eds), *Reproductive Technologies as Global Form. Ethnographies of Knowledge, Practices, and Transnational Encounters*, 229–54, Frankfurt am Main and New York: Campus.

Inhorn, M. C. (2012b), *The New Arab Man: Emergent Masculinities, Technologies, and Islam in the Middle East*, Princeton and New Jersey: Princeton University Press.

Inhorn, M. C. and E. A. Wentzell (2011), 'Embodying Emergent Masculinities: Men Engaging with Reproductive and Sexual Health Technologies in the Middle East and Mexico', *American Ethnologist*, 38 (4): 801–15.

Inhorn, M. C., T. Tjørnhøj-Thomsen, H. Goldberg and M. l. C. Mosegaard, eds (2009), *Reconceiving the Second Sex: Men, Masculinity, and Reproduction*, New York and Oxford: Berghahn.

Jennings, P. K. (2010), 'God Had Something Else in Mind': Family, Religion, and Infertility', *Journal of Contemporary Ethnography*, 39 (2): 215–37.

Kahn, S. M. (2006), 'Making Technology Familiar: Orthodox Jews and Infertility Support, Advice, and Inspiration', *Culture, Medicine and Psychiatry*, 30 (4): 467–80.

Kleinman, A. (1992), 'Local Worlds of Suffering: An Interpersonal Focus for Ethnographies of Illness Experience', *Qualitative Health Research*, 2 (2): 127–34.

Knecht, M. and S. Hess (2008), 'Reflexive Medikalisierung im Feld Moderner Reproduktionstechnologien. Zum Aktiven Einsatz von Wissensressourcen in Gendertheoretischer Perspektive', in N. Langleiter, E. Timm and M. Haibl (eds), *Wissen und Geschlecht*, 169–94, Vienna: Department of European Ethnology of University of Vienna.

Knecht, M., M. Klotz, N. Polat and S. Beck (2011), 'Erweiterte Fallstudien zu Verwandtschaft und Reproduktionstechnologien: Potentiale einer Ethnographie von Normalisierungsprozessen', *Zeitschrift für Volkskunde*, 107 (1): 21–48.

Knecht, M., M. Klotz and S. Beck, eds (2012), *Reproductive Technologies as Global Form. Ethnographies of Knowledge, Practices, and Transnational Encounters*, Frankfurt am Main and New York: Campus.

Korkman, Z. (2016), 'Politics of Intimacy in Turkey: A Distraction from "real" Politics?' *Journal of Middle East Women's Studies*, 12 (1): 112–21.

Latour, B. (2005), *Reassembling the Social: An Introduction to Actor-Network-Theory*, Oxford and New York: Oxford University Press.

Leighton, K. (2013), 'To Criticize the Right to Know We Must Question the Value of Genetic Relatedness', *The American Journal of Bioethics*, 13 (5): 54–6.

Lock, M. and P. Kaufert, eds (1998), *Pragmatic Women and Body Politics*, Cambridge: Cambridge University Press.

Lock, M. and V. Nguyen (2006), *An Anthropology of Biomedicine an Introduction*, Chichester: Wiley-Blackwell.

Lorber, J. (1989), 'Choice, Gift, or Patriarchal Bargain? Women's Consent to in vitro Fertilization in Male Infertility', *Hypatia*, 4 (3): 23–36.

Martin, E. (1991), 'The Egg and the Sperm: How Science Has Constructed a Romance Based on Stereotypical Male-Female Roles', *Signs*, 16 (3): 485–501.

Mol, A. (2002), *The Body Multiple: Ontology in Medical Practice*, Durham, NC and London: Duke University Press.

Mol, A. (2008), *The Logic of Care: Health and the Problem of Patient Choice*, London: Routledge.

Morgan, L. M. and E. F. S. Roberts (2012), 'Reproductive Governance in Latin America', *Anthropology and Medicine*, 19 (2): 241–54.

Mutlu, B. (2011), 'Türkiye'de 'Üremeye Yardımcı' Teknolojiler: Kadınların Tüp Bebek Anlatıları', in C. Özbay, A. Terzioğlu and Y. Yasin (eds), *Neoliberalizm ve Mahremiyet: Türkiye'de Beden, Sağlık ve Cinsellik*, 73–93, İstanbul: Metis Yayınları.

Mutlu, B., N. Şen, N. Erten, N. Polat, S. Saluk and Ş Kılıçtepe (2018), 'Cinsellik, Üreme/ Doğurganlık ve Sağlık Politikaları Üzerine Bir Sohbet', *Feminist Yaklaşımlar*, 34–5: 122–54.

Mutluer, N. (2019), 'The Intersectionality of Gender, Sexuality, and Religion: Novelties and Continuities in Turkey during the AKP Era', *Southeast European and Black Sea Studies*, 19 (1): 99–118.

Ong, A. and S. J. Collier, eds (2005), *Global Assemblages: Technology, Politics, and Ethics as Anthropological Problems*, Malden, MA: Blackwell.

Özgüler, C. and B. Yarar (2017), 'Neoliberal Body Politics: Feminist Resistance and the Abortion Law in Turkey', in W. Harcourt (ed.), *Bodies in Resistance: Gender and Sexual Politics in the Age of Neoliberalism*, 133–61, London: Palgrave Macmillan.

Ozyegin, G. (2018), 'Rethinking Patriarchy through Unpatriarchal Male Desires', in J. W. Messerschmidt, P. Y. Martin, M. A. Messner and R. Connell (eds), *Gender Reckonings: New Social Theory and Research*, 233–53, New York: New York University Press.

Paxson, H. (2004), *Making Modern Mothers: Ethics and Family Planning in Urban Greece*, Berkeley, Los Angeles and London: University of California Press.

Polat, N. (2012), 'Concerned Groups in the Field of Reproductive Technologies: A Turkish Case Study', in M. Knecht, M. Klotz and S. Beck (eds), *Reproductive Technologies as Global Form. Ethnographies of Knowledge, Practices, and Transnational Encounters*, 197–226, Frankfurt am Main and New York: Campus.

Polat, N. (2018), *Umkämpfte Wege der Reproduktion: Kinderwunschökonomien, Aktivismus und sozialer Wandel in der Türkei*, Bielefeld: transcript Verlag.

Polat, N. (2020), 'Negotiating Masculinities: Reproductive Technologies, Biosocial Exclusion and Men's Engagements in Turkey', *NORMA – International Journal for Masculinity Studies*, 15 (3–4): 267–82.

Rapp, R. (1987), 'Moral Pioneers: Women, Men and Fetuses on a Frontier of Reproductive Technology', *Women and Health*, 13 (1–2): 101–16.

Rosenfeld, D. and C. Faircloth, eds (2006), *Medicalized Masculinities*, Philadelphia: Temple University Press.

Sehlikoglu, S. (2015), 'The daring Mahrem: Changing Dynamics of Public Sexuality in Turkey', in G. Ozyegin (ed.), *Gender and Sexuality in Muslim Cultures*, 235–52, London and New York: Routledge.

Sehlikoglu, S. and F. G. Karioris, eds (2019), *The Everyday Makings of Heteronormativity: Cross-Cultural Explorations of Sex, Gender, and Sexuality*, London: Lexington Books.

Simpson, B. and K. Hampshire, eds (2015), *Assisted Reproductive Technologies in the Third Phase: Global Encounters and Emerging Moral Worlds*, New York and Oxford: Berghahn.

Speier, A. R. (2011), 'Brokers, Consumers and the Internet: How North American Consumers Navigate Their Infertility Journeys', *Reproductive BioMedicine Online*, 23 (5): 592–9.

Thompson, C. (2005), *Making Parents. The Ontological Choreography of Reproductive Technologies*, Cambridge, MA and London: The MIT Press.

Throsby, K. (2010), 'Doing what comes naturally … ': Negotiating Normality in Accounts of IVF-Failure', in L. Reed and P. Saukko (eds), *Governing the Female Body: Gender, Health, and Networks of Power*, 233–53, New York: SUNY Press.

Van Der Ploeg, I. (2004), 'Only Angels Can Do without Skin': On Reproductive Technology's Hybrids and the Politics of Body Boundaries', *Body and Society*, 10 (2–3): 153–81.

4

Feeling like a 'Misfit': Kurdish women's entangled reproductive experiences in Turkey

Şafak Kılıçtepe

It was a sunny afternoon when I met Hatun in the windowless hospital room lit by phosphorescent lighting. Hatun was alone when I knocked on her door to ask if I could talk to her about her experiences with the *in vitro* fertilization (IVF) process. She was resting in the room after her embryo transfer. Hatun welcomed me to the room warmly, but did not let me record her voice. She was doing IVF secretly and did not feel comfortable having her voice recorded 'in case anyone has access to my recordings', she mentioned.

Hatun is a 26-year-old Kurdish woman. She comes from Bitlis, an eastern province of Turkey, to Diyarbakır to get IVF treatment. She had a five-year-old daughter whom she had, in her words, 'in natural ways' [*doğal yollarla*]. She was 'treated' as an infertile individual in her immediate circle as she was not able to conceive after she had had her daughter. Hatun cried when she told me about how much pressure she received from both her husband's family and her daughter to have another baby. Her daughter continually pressured her to have a sibling because all of the other children her age whom she knew had siblings. Hatun's mother-in-law kept telling her that 'others' daughters-in-law lined their children up [*milletin gelini çocuklarını sıraya dizmiş*], suggesting that other married women kept giving birth, whereas Hatun did not. Her husband's family looked down on her because she could not bear more children. Hatun explained:

> For example, my husband's brother's wife got pregnant. She kept telling me that she was going to give birth to the family's successor [to a baby boy, that is] by holding her belly. She later had a stillbirth. You know, it was Allah's justice. It is not only her, but some other women did the same to me.

Due to these pressures, Hatun and her husband were seeking for infertility treatment all over Turkey for years. Hatun, in fact, did not care that she had only one daughter. Indeed, she was worried about giving birth to another child, but the extent of the pressure to have another baby (and a boy) was so strong that she had to undergo IVF treatment, even secretly. She was concerned about giving birth to another child as a

Kurdish woman at a time when military operations were taking place in the eastern and south-eastern regions of Turkey. She stated:

> It makes me worry about bringing another child into this world because I am thinking what if there is a war in Turkey. I would definitely not think about having another child and going through IVF again if my daughter did not want a sibling and if there were not so much pressure from my family and immediate surrounding. It seems like Turkey is going into a war.

Hatun's anxieties about her reproduction show how local and national patriarchal systems, as well as sociopolitical contexts, create competing subjectivities for Kurdish women. Within such convergent contexts, women have to develop (new) ways to navigate these systems. This chapter draws from my long-term doctoral dissertation research on Kurdish women's reproduction.[1] My dissertation explored how the relationship between assisted reproductive technologies (ARTs), political Islam and changing ethnic-minority status shapes the experiences, strategies and negotiations of infertile Sunni Kurdish women in Turkey. The dissertation research consisted of a systematic ethnographic study, which was continually carried out for seventeen months between 2016 and 2017, in addition to four and a half months of preliminary research between 2012 and 2014. Exploring the meanings of, and experiences with, biological reproduction and its relation to social, cultural and politically fertile terrains and establishing a politics of belonging requires strategic and supporting methodological tools. Therefore, I adopted a multi-sited ethnography, a methodological approach first portrayed by George Marcus (1995), which moves from its traditional single-sited location to multiple geographic ones. I collected data by way of three complementary approaches: (1) participant observation, (2) personal conversations and structured interviews, and (3) in-depth interviews with semi-structured questions. I conducted seventeen months of multi-sited research in the socioculturally diverse capital Ankara for five months and the Kurdish-populated metropolitan city Diyarbakır for twelve months.

Through the example of women's narratives and my own participant observation within and outside of medical institutions in Ankara and Diyarbakır, this chapter analyses the kinds of reproductive experiences emerging from Kurdish women's positions as gendered and ethnic subjects within their communities and in the nation. In this chapter, I contextualize Kurdish women's reproductive experiences within the intersecting systems of family/community and nation by providing historical details.

Being an infertile Kurdish woman and feeling like a 'misfit'

Hatun, as a female member of her ethnic Kurdish group, was expected to give birth, ideally, to more than one child. Yet, the stability of her local environment was shaken to the extent that she worried about having another one. To provide context, the time when I met Hatun was right after the abandonment of the Peace Process [*Barış Süreci*] between the Turkish state and the PKK (Kurdish Workers' Party [Kurdish: Partiya

Karkeren Kurdistan]. More than a thirty-year-long armed conflict between the Turkish military and PKK in eastern and south-eastern Turkey has polarized the society into Turkish and Kurdish ethnic camps. In 2009, a process called the Kurdish Opening [*Açılım*], which in 2013 evolved into the Peace Process, was commenced and advocated by the ruling government Justice and Development Party (in Turkish: *Adalet ve Kalkınma Partisi* [AKP]).[2] In so doing, the AKP aimed to improve democratic practices and increase security by ending the long-lasting war between the Turkish state and the PKK. This led to a cease-fire between the PKK and the Turkish army in 2013, which lasted two years, until 2015. My Kurdish informants living in the Kurdish-populated south-eastern city of Diyarbakır defined the Peace Process as 'the most peaceful time' of their lives. However, the war restarted in July 2015 and moved into the cities, leading to the loss of many lives throughout Turkey and to the destruction of large areas within Kurdish-populated provinces.[3]

Hatun, like my many other informants living in the south-eastern Diyarbakır city, interpreted all these developments and the armed conflict transmitted from rural to the cities as signs of war. Both the military operations and the potential war in Turkey put them in vulnerable positions that they have to navigate when it comes to reproduction. On the concept of vulnerability, Judith Butler states:

> In a way, we all live with this particular kind of vulnerability, a vulnerability to the other that is part of bodily life, a vulnerability to a sudden address from elsewhere that we cannot pre-empt. This vulnerability, however, becomes highly exacerbated under certain social and political conditions, especially those in which violence is a way of life and the means to secure self-defense are limited. (Butler 2004: 29)

Butler suggests that individuals live within different degrees of vulnerabilities. These vulnerabilities, according to her, are ways of living. However, some individuals are more vulnerable than others depending on their situatedness within their social and political conditions. Kurdish women's reproductive experiences are situated in the changing political environment and social context that they live in. Hence, their reproduction depends on the degree of their vulnerabilities within their ethnic group and in the nation. The way Hatun felt about the political conditions of the region in which she lived and the possibility of war illustrates how national developments intersect with the reproductive experiences of women living in patriarchal systems. For some, the conflict was part of their reproductive experience and 'a way of life' in Butler's words, as in Hatun's case. Hatun was worried about giving birth if a war broke out since she could potentially lose everything, including her children with whom she was emotionally and materially invested. During the time when the armed conflict moved into cities, for Hatun and others having similar concerns, being an ideal Kurdish woman who bears more than one child would mean being a woman who could protect their un/born child(ren). These various meanings were deeply attached to the region where they dwelled and where the operations were taking place.

Yet, in Hatun's case, the expectations of her daughter and community from Hatun outweighed how she felt about having another child. Validating her position as a mother and a Kurdish woman depended on giving birth to another; thus, she had to seek for solutions to be able to conceive again. Seeking IVF treatment, Hatun had been in several hospitals known for their infertility treatments in cities such as Istanbul, Ankara and İzmir, in western Turkey. Having tried options in such big metropolises in western Turkey, Hatun and her husband decided to seek out IVF treatment in Diyarbakır. This was for two reasons. First, Diyarbakır was a closer destination for her and her husband in comparison with the big metropolises in western Turkey. Because people in her surrounding saw IVF as *zina* [adultery] and equated it with having someone else's child, they were secretly undergoing treatment. Thus, the closer destination allowed them to be relatively free from the pressure of fabricating stories for their family when they travelled outside of Bitlis. Second, despite its political turmoil, Hatun saw Diyarbakır as a home away from home since it was a Kurdish-populated city, which hosts peoples, languages and cultural codes that she was familiar with. At some point during our interview, Hatun stated how exhausted she was and expressed her feeling of being on the verge of giving up the search for further solutions if this IVF did not produce a positive outcome because, she said:

> I am tired of being seen as something, how to say [*nasıl desem*], like a misfit (*uymayan*) everywhere I go. In my hometown (*memlekette*), I am a *kısır* [infertile]. Somewhere else, I get discriminated against. I am exhausted [*tükendim*] from all of this… For example, a doctor in Istanbul refused to examine me because I am Kurdish, but another doctor did his best for me although he was Turkish. I went to GATA[4] in Ankara for infertility treatment. The doctor looked at my veil and at me. I was wearing a black topcoat. He looked at my ID and saw that I am Kurdish.[5] He then began insulting me. He was presumably asking me why my mother gave birth to seven children. But, another guy in the room, who had a tattoo of Atatürk, got upset with the doctor for insulting me. I mean, not everybody is the same.

Hatun's feeling of being a 'misfit' is created by the intersectionality of her identities as a woman and a Kurd in Turkey. As a citizen of Turkey, Hatun wanted to get the best treatment for her infertility in western Turkey, where IVF treatments are well developed and widespread. However, her decision to have the treatment in the western part of Turkey has had various consequences for her as a Kurdish woman, such as being humiliated by doctors. Her hope of having a baby in order to legitimize her position as a mother and as a woman in her ethnic group was accompanied by the feeling of being a 'misfit' by her experiences in the medical institutions of western Turkey. While the doctor at the military hospital in Ankara saw Hatun as being overly fertile, within her community she was perceived as infertile despite the fact that she already had a daughter and was only twenty-six years old. Being the wife of the eldest son and having no son who could continue her husband's lineage increased the pressure to get pregnant that she was put under. Women who became pregnant in her family and surrounding community performed an identity of ideal womanhood that she supposedly did not have as a woman. On the other hand, as she travelled to medical institutions across the country for IVF treatments, she met different doctors who treated her in different ways in accordance with how they racialized her veil, hometown and her Kurdish accent. All these factors contributed to her feeling of being a 'misfit'.

As in the above example, racial categorizations could emerge via regional associations. For instance, Murat Ergin (2014) and Cenk Saraçoğlu (2010) elucidate how racial categorization works through location, specifically in Turkey. They explain that being from south-eastern Turkey, especially from certain cities in the region, evokes particular kinds of deviant images in recipients' minds, such as being untrustworthy, *kıro* (mannerless, rude *in* Turkish), uneducated, separatist and disharmonious. This was similar to the case of the doctor at GATA. The doctor at GATA looked at Hatun's veil, and then her ID card indicating that she was from Bitlis, a Kurdish-populated city, and this, in large part, determined how he treated her. Hatun was at GATA to be examined for her infertility, yet she was insulted, in her words, because of her veil and her ethnic identity that was associated with high birth rates. The specific markers of Hatun's identity, such as the veil and her hometown Bitlis, situated Hatun as 'the Other' within the medical institution.

Michel Foucault and Paul Rabinow argue that the technology of power is a means of managing and controlling the population (Foucault 1978, 2003; Rabinow 2005). Knowledge and perceptions about and performances of ideal citizenship are some of the fundamental ways of shaping reproductive experiences. Hospital settings are the places where historically situated knowledge, power relations and gendered practices and performances can best be observed (van der Geest and Finkler 2004). The infertility unit that Hatun visited was a state institution and the doctors and employees were employees of the State. Thus, it is possible to see how State power works through doctors and the interactions between doctors and patients. Hatun's experience at the GATA was the consequence of the constructed relationship between dress codes and traditional, religious and modern ways of life.

To put this in historical context, the projects of Turkish secularization and modernization, which are the grounds that Kemalist thought rests on, aimed at transforming Muslim Ottoman subjects into secular Turkish citizens.[6] Ayse Gül Altınay (2004:6) describes Turkey's state-making process as a gendered cultural revolution: 'a revolution whose discursive power is derived from nationalism and is enabled by modern apparatuses of power.' It is a patriarchal kind of power. For instance, in her detailed study, Carol Delaney (1995) illustrates how the Turkish state is considered as the *father* and the land as the *mother*. More precisely, due to their symbolic association with soil, women are seen as the field where national identity is played out. Delaney states:

> The land was owned by the state and imagined both as the vast amorphous expanse of state patrimony and as the small areas of the earth one was reared on. But in either case, *Anavatan* (Motherland) was a generalized medium of nurture, under the control of the state but without specific borders of identity. (Delaney 1995:179)

Nira Yuval-Davis argues that the position of women 'has been one of the important mechanisms in which ethnic and national projects signified—inwardly and outwardly—their move towards modernization' (Yuval-Davis 1997: 60). Women, in the nation-state-making process, are seen as instruments used in the service of the state, the responsible enhancers and bearers of an ethnically defined Turkish race. Deniz Kandiyoti (2004: vii), furthermore, describes the *new* women's status in the nation-state as 'modern-yet modest'. Historically, ideal womanhood is associated with being virtuous, modern and fertile as well as with giving birth to Turkish children and raising them to be loyal to the nation (Atakav 2007; White 2011).

The project of making women secular and modern (Yuval-Davis 1997; Altan-Olcay 2009) considered the veil as the ultimate impediment in creating a modernist and secularist Turkish nation-state because of its ties to political Islam. For this, the veil had to be removed from public domains (Cindoğlu and Zencirci 2008). Thus, the traditional headscarf was initially banned for women working at public institutions because of the dress codes that were issued after the 1980 coup. In the 1980s and 1990s, headscarf legislation prohibited individuals from wearing a headscarf from primary education to higher education. In Hatun's incident, the doctor interpreted the veil as a form of femininity that had religious bases, which had no place within the imagined nation-state at the time. However, what the veil represented in public realms started changing with the AKP government. After coming to power in 2002, the AKP managed to remove the headscarf ban in 2008. With the AKP government in charge, devotion (religious and otherwise) has become a significant element for citizenship in the imagined nation-state.

The ruling 'conservative–democratic' government of the AKP, since 2002, favoured new forms of bodily images in public spaces, such as men wearing the same Recep Tayyip Erdoğan-style moustache and women wearing their headscarves in specific ways. Cenk Saraçoğlu (2010) discusses that the AKP aimed to generate identification between the party and the nation by appointing individuals described as devout Muslims to ministries and to bureaucratic positions. In a similar vein, but in the French context, Mayanthi L. Fernando (2014) shows that government institutions in France and its employees entail the role of reflecting and refracting the new subjectivities created by a nation-state's ideologies. In other words, government institutions are representations of racialized categories and of what has been racialized, within which a compatible subject is being crafted and displayed within the institutions by political powers. Thus, Hatun's experience with the veil was indeed the result of such nationalist gendering in public spaces, as well as of the history of the veil as a bodily representation of womanhood before the AKP came to power.

Hatun's statement about the doctor who perceived her as a member of a so-called over-fertile group indicated the biopolitics at work that is specific to Kurds living in Turkey. The birth rate of Kurds has historically been a sociopolitical concern for different political actors in Turkey. The Kurds' relatively high birth rates compared to other groups' living in Turkey are seen as a threat for the unity of the nation-state, which is primarily defined by its ethnic 'Turkishness' and Turkish language.[7] For instance, in the 1930s, Zeynel Abidin Özmen – a prominent politician – prepared a report in the 1930s called *Siyah Rapor* (the Black Report). The so-called Black Report claimed that the Kurdish population's growth was a problem for the Turkish nation and suggested that the solution to the 'problem' was assimilation (Dündar 2012). The report's recommended process of assimilation included prohibiting the use of the Kurdish language in state institutions, encouraging Turkish men to marry Kurdish women and taking Kurdish children and raising them away from their families (Dündar

2012). Later, in the 1990s, the concern with Kurdish population growth was officially regarded as a 'security problem', which led to the publication of a 1996 report titled 'Problems and Suggested Solutions' (*Sorunlar ve Çözüm Önerileri*). The stigmatization of Kurds' birth rates has, thus, historically ethnicized Kurds and positioned them as the ethnic Other in Turkey.

Hatun faced the double burden that stems from the nationalist and secular-modernist imaginaries of the nation-state. Here, facing the doctor's offenses, Hatun felt that she was being punished and disciplined due to her mismatch with a citizenry ideal. Hatun's reproductive context illustrates that ideas about racialized ethnicity, combined with ideas about what dress codes represent, create 'misfit' subjects. Michal Nahman articulates how idealized representations of the nation and national bodies are brought into and by the discourse about reproductive experiences in Israel. Nahman (2006: 200) argues that 'scientific and national agendas co-produce one another... the statements, images and practices themselves are technologies of racism'. In a similar vein, I argue that ideal citizen imaginings reproduce ethnicized reproductive contexts that are specific to Kurdish women living in Turkey. In what follows, I continue illustrating how these imaginings interact with the lived experiences of Kurdish women as they experience feelings of disempowerment, disenfranchisement and ways of belonging both within and outside of medical institutions. Questioning this unveils the ways in which women define themselves within their reproductive context and make sense of their belonging within their own groups and within the nation. In this sense, Hatun's story of her experience with reproductive technologies is significant because the story encapsulates how an individual's reproduction might be shaped when they represent neither the ideals of citizenship (including languages, regions and dress codes) of the imagined nation-state (Anderson 2006) nor the ideal of womanhood within their own cultural group.

Patriarchal systems meet language

Historically in Turkey, language is seen as one of the signifiers of the nation-state wherein the Turkish language represented belonging to a 'superior race' as well as to a 'western' identity (Kirişci and Winrow 1997; Altınay 2004; Yeğen 2004; Maksudyan 2005). This belief led to the proposal of the Sun Language Theory (Turkish: *Güneş Dil Teorisi*) that suggests that all languages were descended from one proto-Turkish ancient language; thus, their roots could substantially be traced back to Turkic (language family) roots. Attempts to prove the superiority of the Turkish language, i.e. belonging to the superior race, justified the initiatives of banning citizens from speaking in languages other than Turkish in public arenas, which in turn led to the stigmatization of the Kurdish language and the Kurdish accent. Such stigmatization has disadvantaged women speaking Kurdish when receiving medical services and when encountering and interacting with non-Kurdish citizens using the same medical services, as this section shows. Ongoing stigmatization continues to affect the distribution of resources, ultimately limiting access to those resources.

Navigating patriarchal systems through the systems

Hatun spoke to me in broken Turkish and with a heavy Kurdish accent; this was a way of speaking that not only shaped her reproductive experiences, but also guided her in how she chose to speak to her own daughter. She admired the fact that I spoke Turkish with no Kurdish accent despite the fact that I am Kurdish as well.[8] Hatun was enthusiastic about educating her daughter in all matters so to prepare a better future for her in Turkey. Therefore, she did not speak to her daughter in Kurdish so that her daughter would be better assimilated and would not speak Turkish with a Kurdish accent in school. This was a concern for many of my Kurdish informants since the nation-state ideology defines ideal citizens by their ethnicity and by the degree to which they are integrated into Turkishness (Zeyneloğlu, Sirkeci, and Civelek 2016). The history has produced a hierarchical structure in which speaking fluent Turkish has become not only a racialized category, but provides social capital as well. Within this context, those who do not speak the language properly are held at a disadvantage, which explains why some Kurdish women like Hatun did not teach their children Kurdish.

To further explain, some of my informants mentioned that there were two main challenges that women faced when they needed to see a doctor. First, it was the language that became a barrier. Women who did not speak Turkish could not adequately express themselves within medical institutions. Some doctors refused to examine non-Turkish speakers – like in Hatun's experience in Istanbul – or did not examine them properly. Second, it was the nested oppressive societal system. Some of my informants were not permitted to leave the house without being accompanied by their husbands or someone (generally, a man) from the household. Since men often worked during the day or worked outside of the city due to the lack of job availability in the region,[9] it was a challenge for these women to go to the hospital. It was seen as inappropriate when a woman without any children wanted to leave the house; to do so would be considered as bringing shame upon the men of the house. Thus, having a child would strengthen women's position both within and outside of the family. Women's mobility would relatively increase after having a child. They even become more respected with a child, especially after having a male child.

Both of the barriers mentioned indicate how Kurdish women's health intersects with the way women negotiate their positions as Kurdish women in the nesting patriarchal system and in the narrow construction of the ideal citizen. There are various kinds of negotiations, which result in different subjectivities. For example, Zehra, one of my interlocutors, illustrates how she used both barriers in order to create mobilization for herself and her children. Zehra was a 30-year-old woman with three children. She married her husband at the age of eighteen to escape her father's never-ending oppression of her. Marriage, for her, was going to bring her some freedom. Yet, Zehra did not encounter a different treatment from her husband than from her father. Zehra explained:

> I married my husband to escape from my father's torment [*eziyet*]. My father was too mean and oppressive. He would not let us (Zehra and her sisters) even look out the window. So I decided to get married to my husband. But I jumped out of the frying pan into the fire [*yağmurdan kaçarken doluya tutuldum*]. My husband

did not let me leave the house by myself until after Sidar [her oldest son] was born. The worst part was that my husband was not in the house either. There was no one to take me to the hospital, and I would sometimes go to the doctor secretly since I had to. Thank God [*Allah'a şükür*] I speak Turkish… So, I wanted to teach Sidar housework and equality [*eşitliği*] so he does not do to his wife in the future what his father does to me. Sidar is a great help [*Sidar benim elim ayağım*].

After Sidar's birth, Zehra gained the freedom to go from one place to another. By having children, she both complied with and resisted the patriarchal system, which positions women as the bearers of a male lineage and keeps them in their private confines. Being grateful for having Sidar, Zehra was also happy that she spoke Turkish, the official language, which helped her when going to see a doctor. She always talked to her children in Turkish so that they would learn the language before beginning school. Jeroen Smith and Ayşe Gündüz-Hoşgör (2003) explain that non-Turkish parents in Turkey 'prefer to speak Turkish at home to teach their children the country's official language, because they believe that this may increase their children's upward mobility', as this is also related to formal education being conducted in Turkish. In a similar vein, for Zehra, language was a significant tool to get access to socio-economic capital like education and medical services. These types of capital are shaped by an ethnic-nationalist patriarchal system that does not welcome non-Turkish speakers and demands that its members be assimilated into Turkishness.

To put it differently, giving birth and raising her children in a particular way are the strategies that Zehra developed to deal with the two oppressive systems in which she lived in. Zehra strived for both the ideal womanhood in her ethnic group and ideal citizenship in the nation. She had to develop different strategies in 'perfecting' herself and her children in order to respond to the ideals. For instance, teaching her children Turkish as their primary language was a way to increase her children's upward mobility. Her children would not have to go through the same struggles as Zehra did if they spoke the language without a Kurdish accent, which would become their social capital. Zehra resisted accordingly, and attempted to change the system by educating Sidar about housework and equality, and encouraging him to be successful in school. Zehra's reproductive context illustrates the intersectionality of women's positions within ethnic patriarchal and ethnic-nationalist systems. In what follows, I will illustrate the bodily consequences for women when they do not speak the official language of the nation-state.

Ethic-nationalist patriarchy makes infertile bodies

I met Fatma at the infertility clinic. When I asked her about how she interpreted the concept of citizenship, she voiced how language functioned within and beyond medical settings. She stated:

Everyone who is under the Turkish flag is a citizen. However, not everyone is a citizen on the same level. They [the State] do not care about this place [eastern Turkey]; they [the State] do not see this place. If you are Kurdish, you are a citizen too, but you have to endure so many difficulties… I remember that doctors did not treat us when we went to the hospital because we spoke Kurdish. (Diyarbakır, Interview, December 2016)

Fatma's account is significant in laying out the additional afflictions that infertile Kurdish women have due to their ethnicized positionality, which substantiates their feelings of being a 'misfit'. For Fatma, being a Kurdish woman would cause her to 'endure so many difficulties'. That is to say, Fatma faced the consequences of speaking Kurdish at an early age. She had spoken only Kurdish until she started going to school. Once enrolled, she started learning Turkish, which she described as a painful process for her, as the teacher beat her and other students when they spoke Kurdish. Also, because her family lived in a politically volatile place, the teacher did not regularly come to the school in her village. 'Teachers were scared of the events that's why they [teachers] either refused to come to the village or did not come on a regular basis,' she said.[10] Later, Fatma and her family had to move to Diyarbakır before she finished her primary school education due to village evacuations in the 1990s.[11] They left the village with hardly any belongings and moved into a one-room apartment in Bağlar, Diyarbakır, without any furniture. There, they had been sleeping on the bare floor when Fatma and her sister got sick. Her mother took them to a health clinic [*sağlık ocağı*], but the doctor refused to treat them since they spoke Kurdish. Fatma wondered if she had become infertile due to all the difficulty she and her family had gone through during that time.

For Fatma, her reproductive body was disrupted by her ethnic positionality within the Turkish nation-state, the conflict between the state and the PKK, and the violence stemming from state officials like teachers and medical employees. Her comment about the association between her infertility and the trauma of being Kurdish in the midst of ethnic conflict shows how she also embodied the conflict. Fatma illustrates how a politically violent past shaped her current reproductive anxieties and her reproductive narrative. Accordingly, Hatun's narrative about her reproductive anxieties stemmed from the current state of the violence at the time in the eastern region of Turkey. Although political conflict was part of both Hatun's and Fatma's reproductive experiences, their experiences are differently situated within their respective sociopolitical context. Hatun was considered infertile in her family, although she had a daughter. On the contrary, Fatma was not able to conceive at all. The capacity to give birth defined both Fatma's and Hatun's womanhood in their communities, yet to different degrees. Fatma's reproductive body is a constant reminder for her about the political conflict, and how her body is inseparable from the conflict as she could not conceive. Fatma's account shows that some individuals', such as Fatma's, reproductive bodies are more vulnerable than those who were not exposed to the political conflict.

Using Butler's argument, I suggest that it was Fatma's ethnicized identity that positioned her as a vulnerable subject in the context of the Turkish nation-state. Her body, which represented a certain ethnic identity located in a specific geographic region, needed to be relocated for security reasons. Village evacuations have had lifelong effects on individuals like Fatma, whose life was seen as disposable. Similarly, due to the language that Fatma spoke, the doctors from whom she sought medical help regarded her life as invaluable. Fatma's struggles to learn the language, her experiences with being relocated and with the medical services defined in large part how she perceived her body and her childlessness. In other words, her infertility was the fault of an ethnically defined nationalist patriarchal system.

Language that silences

Fatma's story elucidates how language capital might shape individuals' reproductive experiences within, outside and beyond medical institutions. While Fatma's narrative about language reveals the impact of nation-state formation and the history of ethnic conflict on the citizens, it also exemplifies how the treatment of Kurdish women is also shaped by the employees of medical institutions. Medical institutions are the spaces where the technologies of power take place. In addition to employees, the interactions among the patients within the medical institutions reveal the relational aspects of an ethnically centred patriarchal nation.

One of the striking details about the women's health hospital in Ankara was the silence of Kurdish women who travelled from eastern and south-eastern Turkey to Ankara for their childlessness. They would be silent both in the waiting room where the patients were waiting for their turns to see doctors, and in the hospital rooms where they stayed after the egg retrieval or embryo transfer. The rooms at the hospital were not private. They contained two beds so that patients would have to share the room with another patient. Even though in these rooms I was able to listen to most of the women who defined themselves as Turkish, Kurdish women preferred to be left alone and did not want to participate in my study. My encounter with Figen, one of my informants in Ankara, exemplifies why this might be the case.

I met Figen, an ethnic Turk, at the state hospital in Ankara. We had a long conversation about her experiences with infertility, particularly in regard to how these experiences shaped her identity as a woman and as a proud Turkish citizen. Figen emphasized that she loved her country and the harmony that the AKP government had brought to the country. Figen was referring to the harmonious synthesis of Islam and Turkishness. Yet, when referring to another woman's comment at the hospital in Ankara about how she got angry when she heard some women speaking Kurdish in public, Figen said, 'I, too, think that the best language is Turkish. Why do they speak Kurdish, *ayıp yani* [it is a shame]? We have our beautiful Turkish! I do not understand them.' She continued:

I hate Kurds... You should be extra careful with the mouths where two languages come out, as Atatürk said... No one likes them (Kurds) where I am from.

Figen's blunt statement about why she hates Kurds illustrates my previous point about stigmatization and might explain why most Kurdish patients at the state hospital in Ankara did not want to talk with me and why they were silent during their stay in the hospital rooms. Their accent would give away their identity, which could bring them discomfort. For example, Saliha, a Kurdish woman, who was seeking IVF treatment in a private clinic in Diyarbakır, told me:

> They find Kurds wicked. They hate us. We are always worried that they despise us when we talk to Turks because of our broken Turkish. The new generation does not teach their kids Kurdish so that their kids are not despised.

Saliha's perception of how Turkish people think about Kurds is supported by the views expressed by Figen who saw the Turkish language as a superior language and associated speaking the language with such things as being loyal to one's country, being in harmony with others and not being separatist. All these are related to the historical processes and developments about the imaginings of the nation-state, which have led to ongoing stigmatizations, thus putting Kurdish women in more *vulnerable* situations when they seek infertility treatment (Butler 2004).

One of the consequences of the formation of an imagined Turkish nation-state that is defined by Turkish language is the 'Citizen, speak Turkish! (Turkish: *Vatandaş Türkçe konuş!*)' campaigns, which historically ground Figen's comment. The campaign became one of several historical attempts to build the imagined nation-state (Cagaptay 2004; Anderson 2006). It was initiated by law students and supported by the government throughout the 1930s to designate Turkish as the superior language, and to diminish all other languages in the public sphere. Showing that the policing of language and the cultural ideologies that supported them were mutually constituted, during the 1920s and 1930s some municipalities applied fines for those who did not speak Turkish in public (Aslan 2007). This practice continued into the 1980s when the Law 2932 outlawed the use of Kurdish in public, which remained official from 1983 to 1991. Attempts to canonize the Turkish language within the nation also ethnicized and racialized the members of non-Turkish speakers, including Kurds, and those who speak the Turkish language with an accent. Therefore, language has become the condition for being a proper citizen of Turkey, and a social capital. Knowing Turkish and speaking it fluently has become the essential criterion for citizenship (Maksudyan 2007). In other words, one deserves to be Turkish only if they are able to speak the language (sometimes, properly).[12]

Saliha's account illustrates how this dynamic affects Kurdish women in different ways and on different levels. Although Kurdish women in Ankara were silent, women at the hospital in Diyarbakır were willing to talk to me. Like Saliha, women in Diyarbakır were willing to talk about how speaking Turkish with a Kurdish accent would put them in disadvantaged positions when traveling outside of south-eastern Turkey. In this sense, speaking Turkish with a Kurdish accent has positioned Kurdish women as 'misfits' within the context of the national categories of the ideal citizen. On the other hand, one of the ways in which Kurdish women dealt with negative associations due to their ethnic identity within medical settings was through silence. I argue that although Kurdish women's wide use of reproductive technologies serves as a way to claim their citizenship rights, they are compelled to remain silent and to be subordinate within the medical system in order to avoid being subjected to anti-Kurdish discrimination.

Conclusion

For members belonging to ethnic groups other than Turkish, speaking Turkish and speaking the language with no accent become a means to negotiate the discrimination arising from the way the language is spoken as well as having access to resources in the same way as others, like Figen, who are defined as ideal citizens. However, there is a wide range of experiences with, and efforts to, speak the language properly, and this range shapes women's reproductive experiences within and outside of medical institutions. For example, Hatun became a 'misfit' while seeking infertility treatment since she had to deal with not fitting in to the ideal of womanhood for her ethnic group as well as not conforming to the elements that define proper citizens of the Turkish nation, such as ethnicity and dress codes. In addition, Fatma saw language as one of the problems that led to her infertility. The fact that her body being was afflicted by infertility represented the effects of the conflict between the Turkish state and the PKK. On the other hand, Figen became a proud citizen due to how her dispositions harmonized with these elements. As the above reproductive contexts show, it is both Kurdish and Turkish women who enact the elements defining the ideal citizen, albeit within a different range of possibility. Women's positions as reproducers of the nation and lineage lead Kurdish women to respond to the elements defining citizenship and womanhood. Due to their ethnic position, Kurdish women's responses could turn into different struggles and methods of resistance as they try to *achieve procreation* (Göknar 2015). While Hatun's and Fatma's feelings of disempowerment and disenfranchisement are the results of the nation-state-making that have led to their struggles within and outside of medical institutions, Zehra's resistance toward her patriarchal structure through Sidar proves that negotiation and the navigating of different systems are part of ethnicized women's everyday lives. In this sense, the stratification existent within the reproductive experiences of the groups emerged as the result of individuals' ethnicities, cultures and their negotiations of these within and outside of medical institutions. While my Kurdish interlocutors developed ways to negotiate their ethnicized identities within the imagined nation-state, their ethnic identity has remained essential to the way their access to reproductive resources and experiences with reproduction are stratified.

In her assisted reproduction study in the Andes, Elizabeth F. S. Roberts argues, 'Ecuadorian IVF participants are involved in an "ontological choreography... assembling people and things to bring into existence new kinds of people and things... Like all reproductive endeavours, IVF entailed not only making children but also making and reinforcing relations among adults, and between adults and God"' (Roberts 2012: 6). In the context of reproductive technologies, I argue that IVF-related reproductive endeavours generate relations between the citizens' situated reproductive contexts and the elements defining the ethnically defined patriarchal nation-state, such as language and dress codes. Thus, it is this relation that contributes to infertile Kurdish women's sense of belonging to their ethnic group as women and mothers and to the nation. This relationship is also dispersed in Kurdish women's everyday lives and is reflected in their narratives about their reproduction. As these relationalities are part of their being, Kurdish women have to navigate the elements of the imagined nation-state in their everyday lives in order to validate their identities as women, mothers and citizens.

Notes

1   A number of organizations and institutions have provided generous financial support for my dissertation project. I would like to thank and acknowledge the support provided by the Social Science Research Council Mellon International Dissertation Research Fellowship, the National Science Foundation Doctoral Dissertation Research Fellowship, Indiana University's Center for Research on Race and Ethnicity in Society Graduate Student Research Award, and Mellon's Innovating International Research, Teaching and Collaboration Graduate Dissertation Fellowship. I would also like to thank to the book editors, and my friends Sevsem Cicek Okay and Sami Atassi for their precious comments, feedback and edits that helped me tremendously in crafting this chapter.

2   The Justice and Development Party (AKP) describes the party's agenda as 'conservative–democratic', and has been in power in Turkey since 2002.

3   Authorities ordered curfews for an indefinite time, with most lasting for months, for security reasons. Large areas of the majority of Kurdish cities, including Diyarbakır, Şırnak, Nusaybin and Yüksekova, were demolished. According to a United Nations Human Rights Office report (2017), the operations in south-east Turkey between July 2015 and December 2016 affected more than thirty towns and neighbourhoods. It is also estimated that between 355,000 and 500,000 people, mostly of Kurdish origin, were displaced.

4   The hospital's name was changed from *Gülhane Askeri Tıp Akademisi* [Gülhane Military Medical Academy, GATA] to Gülhane Eğitim ve Araştırma Hastane*si* [*Gülhane Training and Research Hospital*] in August 2016 (Habertürk 2016).

5   ID cards in Turkey used to indicate the person's place of birth. Hatun was from Bitlis, a province in eastern Turkey, whose inhabitants are mostly Kurdish. Thus, this positioned Hatun as Kurdish in the eyes of the doctor.

6   The Kemalist regime represents the very ideology of Mustafa Kemal Atatürk and his founding cadre.

7   In contemporary Turkey, according to the Turkish Statistical Institute's data in 2018, the top ten provinces out of eighty-one with the highest birth rates are Kurdish-populated provinces. The average total fertility rate within these cities is estimated at 3.4 (Tüik 2018).

8   It is important to mention here that I am not a fluent speaker of Kurdish. As my informants did, my parents communicated with us (their children) in Turkish so we would not have difficult experiences with our school's teachers and throughout our lives.

9   South-eastern Turkey has the highest unemployment rate in Turkey (DrDataStats 2019).

10   By this, she referred to the violent conflict and clashes between the PKK and Turkish state.

11   Village evacuations happened in the 1990s as a result of the conflict between the PKK and the Turkish state (which started in 1984). According to the Turkish government's

estimates, 3,236 settlements had been cleared in south-eastern Turkey, forcibly displacing 362,915 people (Göçek 2008: 45).

12   For this, one of my informants, whose name is Hatice, told me, 'as a Kurdish woman who does not speak Turkish properly [meaning with an accent], you do not even have the right to work. Almost all the places [in Istanbul] that I applied to work in told me that they can't hire me because I have an accent.' Murat Ergin (2014) also comments on the effects of the stigmatization of the Kurdish language and its speakers on the job opportunities for Kurds who have accents.

References

Altan-Olcay, Ö. (2009), 'Gendered Projects of National Identity Formation: The Case of Turkey', *National Identities*, 11 (2): 165–86.

Altınay, A. G. (2004), *The Myth of the Military-Nation: Militarism, Gender, and Education in Turkey*, London: Palgrave Macmillan.

Anderson, B. (2006), *Imagined Communities: Reflections on the Origin and Spread of Nationalism, Revised Edition*, London and New York: Verso.

Aslan, S. (2007), '"Citizen, Speak Turkish!": A Nation in the Making', *Nationalism and Ethnic Politics*, 13 (2): 245–72.

Atakav, A. E. (2007), 'Mona Lisa in Veils: Cultural Identity, Politics, Religion and Feminism in Turkey', *Feminist Theology*, 16 (1): 11–20.

Butler, J. (2004), *Precarious Life: The Powers of Mourning and Violence*, London and New York: Verso.

Cagaptay, S. (2004), 'Race, Assimilation and Kemalism: Turkish Nationalism and the Minorities in the 1930s', *Middle Eastern Studies*, 40 (3): 86–101.

Cindoğlu, D. and G. Zencirci (2008), 'The Headscarf in Turkey in the Public and State Spheres', *Middle Eastern Studies*, 44 (5): 791–806.

Delaney, C. (1995), 'Father State, Motherland, and the Birth of Modern Turkey', in S. J. Yanagisako and C. L. Delaney (eds), *Naturalizing Power: Essays in Feminist Cultural Analysis*, 177–200, New York: Routledge.

DrDataStats (2019), 'Türkiye Bölgelere Göre İşsizlik Oranları (2017 ve 2018 Yılları)', 21 April. Available online: https://www.drdatastats.com/turkiye-bolgelere-gore-issizlik-oranlari-2017-ve-2018-yillari/ (accessed 2 May 2019).

Dündar, F. (2012), 'Abidin Özmen'in "Siyah Raporu" Vesilesiyle Kürt Nüfus Artışı Sorunu', *Toplumsal Tarih*, 226: 76–82.

Ergin, M. (2014), 'The Racialization of Kurdish Identity in Turkey', *Ethnic and Racial Studies*, 37 (2): 322–41.

Fernando, M. L. (2014), *The Republic Unsettled: Muslim French and the Contradictions of Secularism*, Durham: Duke University Press.

Foucault, M. (1978), *The History of Sexuality Vol. 1*, New York: Random House.

Foucault, M. (2003), *'Society Must Be Defended': Lectures at the Collège de France, 1975–76*, New York: Picador.

Geest, S. van der and K. Finkler (2004), 'Hospital Ethnography: Introduction', *Social Science & Medicine*, 59 (10): 1995–2001.

Göçek, F. M. (2008), 'Through a Glass Darkly: Consequences of a Politicized Past in Contemporary Turkey', *The Annals of the American Academy of Political and Social Science*, 617: 88–106.

Göknar, M. (2015), *Achieving Procreation: Childlessness and IVF in Turkey*, New York: Berghahn Books.

Habertürk (2016), 'Ankara GATA'nın ismi değişti', 29 August. Available online: https://www.haberturk.com/gundem/haber/1288317-ankara-gatanin-ismi-degisti (accessed 18 April 2019).

Kandiyoti, D. (2004), 'Identity and Its Discontents', *DOSSIER 26 A Collection of Articles*, 45.

Kirişci, K. and G. M. Winrow (1997), *The Kurdish Question and Turkey: An Example of a Trans-State Ethnic Conflict*, Hove: Psychology Press.

Maksudyan, N. (2005), 'The Turkish Review of Anthropology and the Racist Face of Turkish Nationalism', *Cultural Dynamics*, 17 (3): 291–322.

Maksudyan, N. (2007), *Türklüğü ölçmek: bilimkurgusal antropoloji ve Türk milliyetçiliğinin ırkçı çehresi; 1925-1939*, 2. Baskı, İstanbul: Metis.

Marcus, G. E. (1995), 'Ethnography in/of the World System: The Emergence of Multi-Sited Ethnography', *Annual Review of Anthropology*, 24 (1): 95–117.

Nahman, M. (2006), 'Materializing Israeliness: Difference and Mixture in Transnational ova Donation', *Science as Culture*, 15 (3): 199–213.

Rabinow, P. (2005), 'Artificiality and Enlightenment: From Sociobiology to Biosociality', in J. X. Inda (ed.), *Anthropologies of Modernity*, 179–93, Hoboken: Blackwell Publishing.

Roberts, E. F. S. (2012), *God's Laboratory: Assisted Reproduction in the Andes*, Berkeley: University of California Press.

Saraçoğlu, C. (2010), *Kurds of Modern Turkey: Migration, Neoliberalism and Exclusion in Turkish Society*, London: I.B. Tauris.

Smith, J. and A. Gündüz-Hoşgör (2003), 'Linguistic Capital: Language as a Socio-Economic Resource among Kurdish and Arabic Women in Turkey', *Ethnic and Racial Studies*, 26 (5): 829–53.

Tüik (2018), Türkiye İstatistik Kurumu Basın Bülteni. Available online: http://www.turkstat.gov.tr/PreHaberBultenleri.do?id=27589 (accessed 2 May 2019).

White, J. B. (2011), *Islamist Mobilization in Turkey: A Study in Vernacular Politics*, Washington: University of Washington Press.

Yeğen, M. (2004), 'Citizenship and Ethnicity in Turkey', *Middle Eastern Studies*, 40 (6): 51–66.

Yuval-Davis, N. (1997), 'Women, Citizenship and Difference', *Feminist Review*, 57 (October): 4–27.

Zeyneloğlu, S., I. Sirkeci and Y. Civelek (2016), 'Language Shift among Kurds in Turkey: A Spatial and Demographic Analysis', *Kurdish Studies*, 4 (1): 25–50.

Part Two

Governing the maternal body: Between biomedical power and neoliberal healthcare

5

Banning caesareans or selling 'Choice'?: The paradoxical regulation of caesarean section epidemics and the maternal body in Turkey

Sezin Topçu

Introduction

With the highest acceleration rate among member countries, Turkey is the OECD champion when it comes to caesarean sections (CSs). In 2012, the Anglosphere press reported it as the first country in the world to ban elective C-sections in order to stop the national CS epidemic.[1] The expression 'caesarean epidemic' refers to contexts in which the use of CSs has become too high to be medically justified. The number of countries around the world affected by the normalization of CSs (Brazil, the United States, China, Mexico, etc.) is increasing to such an extent that international organizations such as the World Health Organisation and the International Federation of Gynecology and Obstetrics have intensified their calls for a halt on the globalization of the problem (World Health Organisation 2015; Visser et al. 2018). The many reasons for CS normalization have been tackled in depth in the social sciences literature (Diniz and Chacham 2004; Mc Callum 2005; Roberts 2012; Morris 2013; Wolf 2018). Analysts have shown that CS epidemic is often the tip of an iceberg: it is one manifestation of a systemic problem, namely the over-medicalization of the maternal body and the 'fordization' of the childbirth process through the routinization of medical interventions whose benefits and (iatrogenic) risks are not always evaluated, studied or recognized objectively (Sarda 2011; Maffi 2015; Topçu and Brown 2019). The arguments put forward for this over-medicalization are birth safety and the standardization and rationalization of maternal care. However, ecofeminists, natural birth activists and critical birth ethnographers have argued that it can also be seen as the by-product of a patriarchal society in which women and their bodies are controlled by medical experts in the name of science, modernity, capitalist profit or pronatalist conservatism (Jordan 1978; Odent 1992; Davis-Floyd and Sargent 1997; Gaskin 2008; Kitzinger 2015).

Most countries with a 'CS epidemic' have been quick to implement state measures to regulate the problem, but these have not always been effective (Mc Callum 2005; Diniz et al. 2018; Wolf 2018). Their policymakers have sometimes been forced to admit that the problem is *beyond* their control or, more simply, that the rates *do not* reduce despite the measures undertaken. Turkey is one of these countries. In 2012, its Justice and Development Party (Adalet ve Kalkınma Partisi – AKP) government introduced what was presented in the media as a 'C-section ban'. This was preceded by an unexpected and provocative polemic from the then prime minister, Recep Tayyip Erdoğan, who, in May 2012, claimed that 'Both caesarean births and abortions are murder'.[2] At a time when the government was accelerating its pronatalist offensive, Erdoğan said CS delivery was not only a hidden family planning tool that prevented women from having more than three children (in Turkey, the medical norm of 'once a caesarean always a caesarean' is valid, and quite often a tubal ligation is carried out during the third birth procedure because medical organizations consider more than three CSs to be risky) but also a conspiracy tool against the Nation and the rise of a 'strong', 'young', 'populated' Turkey. In response to Erdoğan's criticisms, the government promptly modified the existing law which dated back to 1957, stipulating that 'C-sections should be carried out for medical reasons only', and Turkey's Ministry of Health declared that doctors who abused CSs would be sanctioned. This legal modification (2012) was called the 'caesarean law' by the media. The Ministry of Health also added, however, that a woman's anxiety about giving birth was considered a medical reason and therefore justified a CS. In economic terms, the sanction was quickly made concrete through the government's decision to reduce the level of its approved public health insurance cover for CSs, and through the reduction of performance points attributed to CS births (CS was lowered to the category of basic operations, like appendicitis). An organizational benchmarking process was also implemented in 2012, whereby the monthly CS data from each maternity hospital were reported to the Ministry of Health. When the CS polemic emerged (2012), the national CS rate was 48 per cent. Despite the 'ban' and the regulatory measures put in place, however, the CS rates continued to rise, from 48 per cent in 2012 to 50.4 per cent in 2013, 51.1 per cent in 2014 and 53.1 per cent in 2015, 2016 and 2017 (Ministry of Health of Turkey 2018: 80).

In 2016, the debate around why the rates had continued to increase despite the new law was opened up to the public in the national press. Among the many reasons put forward, medico-legal issues were considered the biggest factor by the public authorities and professional organizations. The latter complained that obstetrician-gynaecologists (OGs) did not have sufficient protection against legal action in cases of a medical accident. Other contributing factors included the woman's 'preference' for a CS or their anxiety about a vaginal birth, the absence of alternatives for managing birth pain such as epidural anaesthesia and the inadequacy of midwifery training. In February 2017, the public was informed that scientific commissions would be set up by the government to monitor hospitals with the highest CS rates and to train medical teams that 'do not know' how to supervise vaginal births.[3] Positive encouragement mechanisms were also envisaged for doctors with low CS rates. In January 2017, a ministerial commission published the names of approximately 150 OGs practising in (both public and private) hospitals in Istanbul who had 'appreciably low' CS rates, especially for primary births, and who were to receive awards (Ministry of Health of Turkey 2017: 116–28). At the end of 2017, the Ministry of Health announced that a new CS law was being drafted that would, in particular, protect OGs.[4]

Methodology

In this chapter, I would like to propose an ethnographic contribution to this debate. I designed my research with the aim of understanding the impact of the 'ban' and its associated regulations on obstetric practice in public and private maternity hospitals from a comparative perspective. The first stage of my research (2014–15) consisted of long-term observations in two hospitals – one public (Public Hospital #1), one private (Private Hospital #1) – in an average-size city in Turkey's Marmara region (population = 140K). I observed a total of twenty deliveries (both vaginal and CS in both hospitals) and conducted extensive interviews with OGs, midwives and mothers. During the research period, the maternity service team at Public Hospital #1 comprised three OGs and six midwives, and its annual birth rate was approximately 1,200. The maternity service team at Private Hospital #1 was much smaller, with two OGs, two midwives and one nurse, and its annual birth rate was approximately 500. Private Hospital #1 is a 'standard' one with an agreement with the social health insurance system (*Sosyal Güvenlik Kurumu* – SGK), which implies that public-insured patients can receive medical care there with some extra payment. In case of a convention with the SGK, which became widespread with the recent health reforms, the rate of extra payment to be charged to publicly insured patients should be declared and, in theory, they can't exceed 200 per cent of the SGK contribution. This was the rate declared by Private Hospital #1.

The second stage of my research (2015–16) consisted of *following* the work of six OGs who, in addition to their obstetric practice, were engaged in the evaluation and regulation of CS norms and practices. Two of them were members of the TJOD (the Turkish Society of Gynecology and Obstetrics), two were a member of the TTB (the Turkish Medical Association) and two were regular members of scientific or advisory bodies set up by the Ministry of Health on issues relating to CSs and childbirth. These OGs worked in four different settings in Istanbul: a long-established private practice (the OG in charge of the practice also worked in some prestigious public and private hospitals); a newly established private practice that promoted alternative birthing methods (the OG who had founded it also practised in a few luxury private hospitals where he rented birthing rooms for his clients); a large public university hospital (Public Hospital #2) that specializes in gynaecology, obstetrics and paediatrics and deals with a large number of high-risk pregnancies; and a luxury private hospital (Private Hospital #2). The maternity service team at Public (University) Hospital #2 comprised ten OGs, ten intern doctors and thirty midwives and nurses. Its birth rate in 2016 was approximately 7,600. The maternity service team at Private Hospital #2 in 2016 comprised seven OGs, one intern doctor and four midwives (who worked as both nurses and birth assistants). Its birth record in 2016 was 1,050 (see Table 5.1).

In addition to the in-depth interviews I recorded with these OGs, who all had a high public profile, I carried out interviews with those who worked alongside them (midwives, nurses, students). Finally, I observed the antenatal courses offered by Public Hospital #2 in Istanbul. Because such courses were rare in Turkey until only recently, many women attended these courses even though they were not necessarily going to give birth at that university hospital. The midwives who led these courses

Table 5.1 Brief presentation of hospitals that were subject to the study. These data were collected during field research. They correspond to the period 2014–15 for the Public Hospital #1 and Private Hospital #1; the period 2015–16 as to what concerns Public Hospital #2 and Private Hospital #2

	Public Hospital #1	Private Hospital #1	Public Hospital #2	Private Hospital #2
Location	Marmara region	Marmara region	Istanbul (Anatolian region)	Istanbul (European region)
Number of births per year	1,200	500	7,600	
Volume of medical personnel	3 OGS, 6 midwives, 3 intern midwives	2 OGs, 3 midwives/nurse	10 OGs, 10 intern doctors, 30 midwives/nurses	7 OGs, 1 intern doctor, 4 midwives/nurses
Convention with SGK?	Public	Yes	Public	Yes
Rate of extra payment to be charged to publicly insured patients	–	200%	–	Unknown

had never supervised a birth themselves but were perfectly qualified to train and support women and couples in preparation for vaginal, non-intervention and even orgasmic births.[5]

I have already described elsewhere the technocratic nature of obstetric care provided in the public and private hospitals where I conducted my research. I have highlighted, in particular, the absence of alternatives to over-medicalization in these hospitals for both CS and vaginal deliveries (Topçu 2019). During my field research, in the name of safety, vaginal births were organized and managed in a highly medicalized way (enema and oxytocin induction were widespread, women were continuously attached to monitoring devices, episiotomies were performed very frequently, etc.). Such an 'aggressive management' of vaginal birth (Diniz et al. 2018), with interchangeable cuts either 'above' or 'below' (Diniz and Chacham 2004), constituted an obstacle to the woman's autonomy during childbirth. I have argued that it also helped to promote CS as a better alternative to vaginal birth. Indeed, vaginal birth is commonly called 'normal birth' in Turkish, but in the last decades, it has been mostly managed as an abnormal and high-risk event requiring many medical interventions (Cindoğlu and Sayan-Cengiz 2010).

I have also underlined the fact that CS delivery became a medical 'culture' among many OGs and even midwives. This 'culture' developed as a consequence of many factors: the health professionals' lack of confidence in women's capacity to give birth in an autonomous way; midwives' loss of skills as well as OGs' *lack* of skills (given the fact that their training was focused more on producing surgeons than accoucheurs); the positive professional and social representations of the CS as a modern, safe, painless birthing method (most of the midwives' and OGs' children had been born by CS); and the advantages that CSs offered practitioners in terms of saving time (it is a faster procedure) and/or organizing hospital space (especially in the private hospitals). My field research also revealed the importance of medico-legal risks in orienting the OGs towards CS delivery, although this risk appeared to be mostly indirect or hypothetical as far as their personal experience was concerned. Of the fifteen OGs I interviewed, only one told me that he had faced legal action because of a birth procedure accident. When asked, 'Have you ever faced legal action because of a vaginal birth complication?' the others responded that they had not but that some of their colleagues had. Some mentioned the recent, highly publicized cerebral palsy case, which resulted in a record compensation payout (of 2.5 million YTL) following a ruling that the OG in question had opted for a CS too late despite alarming signs of foetal distress (Arman 2015). This case helped the participants explain why OGs were often reluctant to go down the 'risky route' of vaginal birth. Some criticized the fact that a birth complication had never been defined in Turkey and that the boundaries between a medical error and a medical complication had never been made clear. They also blamed the 'CS law', which they saw as just a tool to transform Turkey into a 'little America' without the necessary insurance infrastructure in place for OGs. Some also pointed the finger at the 2004 Turkish Criminal Code law[6] claiming that it had led to a normalization of legal action against OGs and that the OG community had therefore developed a self-defence reflex by systematizing CSs.

In this chapter, I propose to go beyond an explanation of the *causes* of CS epidemics. The totality of the above-mentioned cultural, political, juridical, professional and gendered elements has contributed, and continues to contribute, to its expansion. I propose rather to tackle one simple question. What impact did the 'caesarean law' have in the public and the private sectors? To answer this question, I will explore two closely related questions. To what extent have the recent regulations on CS epidemics contributed or not contributed to bringing it under control? And what do all these changes tell us about the new economy and politics of the maternal body in contemporary Turkey?

Turkey's Health Transformation Program, the public/private sector dichotomy and the CS controversy

The CS delivery rate in Turkey almost quadrupled in the space of nearly two decades (13.9 per cent in 1998, 21.2 per cent in 2003, 36.7 per cent in 2008, 53.1 per cent in 2016). The rapid rise in CS rates during the 2000s was closely related to a contemporaneous boom in the private hospital sector, which recorded the higher CS birth rate (70.5 per cent in 2016). While the public hospital sector saw only a relatively modest growth (from 774 hospitals to 879) between 2002 and 2017, the number of private hospitals more than doubled (from 271 to 571) (Ministry of Health of Turkey 2018: 113). The public procurement of healthcare services from the private sector, the resurgence in public healthcare expenditures, the indulgent provisions for extra billing by private healthcare providers and the investment subsidies allowed such important growth in the private hospital sector and bolstered both global funds investments and chain formation by some large hospital groups (Eren Vural 2017: 276–7). Medical tourism also took off during these two decades, with its popularity increasing in parallel with the boom in luxury private hospitals being built in the big cities (Omay and Cengiz 2013). On the overall, health expenditures expanded. While they corresponded to 5.5 per cent of GDP in 2000, the rate reached 6.7 per cent in 2011 (World Bank 2018). Relevantly healthcare became a consumption good and patients' or clients' satisfaction became a priority concern for the AKP government(s). The highest acceleration rate of demands for medical care was recorded in the private sector. Between 2002 and 2017, while the annual volume of patient registrations in the public sector was multiplied by 3.2 (from nearly 110 million to nearly 354 million), it was multiplied by 12.7 in the private sector (from nearly 6 million to around 72 million) (Ministry of Health of Turkey 2018: 161). Out-of-pocket expenditures were multiplied by 5 (Turkish Medical Association 2018a: 11). These changes came about as a result of Turkey's so-called Health Transformation Program (HTP) (2004–12). HTP was launched thanks to program loans from the World Bank. It should be considered as one of the key pillars in the AKP's strong 'neoliberal turn' since 2002 (Acar and Altunok 2013).

The HTP introduced the so-called performance-for-pay (PFP) system and a number of benchmarking practices in hospitals alongside financial austerity measures for the public sector hospitals. As is the case for several national health systems in Europe, starting with France (Juven 2016), each medical act was made accountable and attributed performance points. While, before the HTP, doctors were paid salaries, with the PFP, their remuneration took into account the number of patients they see and the medical acts they realize (Gök and Altındağ 2015). In the public hospitals especially, the performance points collected by doctors at an individual level had an impact on the calculation of performance points for their department and even their hospital. In the private hospitals, these points were calculated on a more individual basis. The supplementary premiums or the profit shares for the OGs were negotiated with the hospital's management on an annual basis. They were based on various medical interventions and their 'values' in the performance system. According to doctors' unions in Turkey, this point-based system resulted in a deterioration in working conditions for health professionals, both in public and in private hospitals, due to increased workload and individual pressure (Turkish Medical Association 2018b). Since 2011, physical and verbal violence against health professionals also increased despite the augmentation of preventive measures (Hamzaoğlu and Türk 2019).

As a result, most of the OGs in my study were critical of the CS law and its associated regulations. They saw it as an authoritarian tool to further degrade their working conditions redefined by the HTP which was elaborated and implemented without the professional stakeholders' involvement (Wendt et al. 2013). They also believed that Turkey's conservative government aimed to use the law to gain greater control over both women and doctors. Considering the situation from a more macro perspective, some even claimed that the 'CS law' was part of the government's attacks on intellectuals in Turkey more generally. According to the OGs from the Turkish Society of Gynecology and Obstetrics that I interviewed, the 'CS law' had been passed without prior consultation with any professional organizations. This prompted them to file a legal challenge to the 'law' claiming it was a political intervention in their (scientific) practice. The OGs, like other specialist doctors, had already lost a number of privileges as a result of the HTP. For example, before the HTP was introduced, they could work part-time in a public hospital and part-time in their private practice. This structure was highly criticized by consumer groups because many doctors were suspected to recruit patients from the public hospitals in the mornings for a private, high-profit consultation in their practice in the afternoons. The HTP effectively forced doctors to choose between a job in the public sector and private practice. It became very difficult for them to combine the two because the AKP government overtaxed private practice as a dissuasive measure. Professional organizations, such as the Turkish Medical Association, criticized the new regulation for being a political strategy aimed at transferring doctors to the newly established private hospitals at a lower cost (Turkish Medical Association 2011). In other words, if their option to combine private practice and hospital work had not been constrained, it would have been difficult to convince them to work in private hospitals without offering very high salaries. The OGs who adhered to the government's political line more closely, however, such as the head of the maternity service at Public Hospital #2 in 2015–16, had a different appreciation of the HPT:

> There's also a false perception among doctors. They think that the (AKP) government's always working against us. This is a very common perception. Turkish doctors think 'I'm a specialist now so I should have my own office, and I should earn 50K, 100K per month'. Until the 2000s, they all thought like this, didn't they? Most of them still do. Does anybody earn that much in Europe? No. When I go to Spain, I meet fellow doctors who say 'We barely earn 5,000 euros a month. I go to Portugal to do some extra surgeries at the weekends'. When I go to Germany, my colleagues there say 'If you're a specialist doctor, you earn 4,000 euros here. If you're head of the clinic, you earn 6,000 or 7,000 euros, but then you mostly use the salary difference mainly for professional purposes' (…) What was the system like before in Turkey? I used to work as a state doctor in the eastern cities. Before, being a state doctor meant you went wherever the state wanted you to go. And then you worked for yourself (in your private practice) from morning to evening. It was enough just to do two surgeries a day in the public hospital, where you were employed, and then you would go back to your practice. I'm not going to lie, we used to earn 20 or even 30 thousand dollars a month doing this. As a specialist doctor. But the system couldn't go on like this. It was impossible.

Regardless of the OGs different reactions to the HTP, very few media commentators or public experts had linked up the boom in CS rates with the rapid rise in the number of private hospitals since the HTP was launched. The then prime minister Erdoğan's condemnation of CS delivery (describing it as murder) meant that the 'CS law' was seen more as an authoritarian, pronatalist, conservative tool than an intervention aimed at repairing the side effects of the government's neoliberal health project. As already mentioned, the expansion of private hospitals was one of the HTP's key objectives, but the 'abuse' of CSs engendered by the project now seemed to need to be brought under control. The AKP government officials in particular stressed the need to increase national fertility rates through the CS regulations in order to build a young, populated, 'big' Turkey that would be the strongest new force in the region. Another significant, albeit discreet, motivation for the 'CS law' was that it would lead to savings in public health expenditure (Ministry of Health of Turkey 2017), which had grown by 7.7 per cent over the last decade (compare to 1.9 per cent in Germany, for instance, in the same period) (Wendt et al. 2013: 93). The calculations were clear: birth costs almost doubled in case of a CS (Özer et al. 2016: 264). One of the OGs from TTB criticized this issue in the following way:

> They [the government officials] introduced the staff called the HTP, in order to seduce people and gain new votes. Then they realized that the national budget is not sufficient to implement it. They started to ask themselves 'How can I cut costs?' They realized that C-sections cost too much, that the cost of anaesthesia, operation room etc. are too much. They said to the PM: 'We should do economies on C-sections'. The PM replied: 'All right, I will deal with that'. And the next day he came in front of the cameras to say that C-section is a murder!

Public hospitals: Towards a new economy and politics of the maternal body

Supporting OGs, banning elective CSs

In Public Hospital #1, all the OGs I interviewed told me that they felt a high level of work pressure but that their salaries were satisfactory because of the performance points. Each had between fifty and seventy consultations in the polyclinic every afternoon, which meant that sessions lasted a maximum of approximately 2 minutes per expectant mother. In addition, once hospitalized for the birth, the women had no privacy because neither the labour wards nor the delivery rooms were closed off. There was also a high turnover of OGs in this public hospital. They frequently migrated to the private sector, particularly after the launch of the benchmarking system, which had added to their workload and stress, according to the interviewees. Moreover, hospitals now had to display the monthly CS rates for each OG by law, and these were presented on the wall behind the information desk at Public Hospital #1's maternity service entrance. Sanctions or compulsory training courses provided by the Ministry of Health had also been put in place to discipline any doctors 'abusing' CSs. During my first observation phase, one of the OGs had already been 'sent' to Ankara for having the highest CS rates a number of times. Although most of the OGs I met said they did not pay any attention to the law, the regulatory practices did seem to have an impact because the CS rate in Public Hospital #1 had fallen from 40 per cent to 31 per cent over three years. Moreover, in Public Hospital #2, the head of the maternity service explained in 2015 that the lowering of CS rates through better support for OGs was a major aim for his service:

C-sections became the modus operandi for OGs. And this still goes on. One of this year's quality goals in our hospital is to lower our C-section rates from 49% to 45%. To achieve this, we're focusing on the psychology and feelings of our doctors by reassuring them that they will not be left stranded in the event of an accident. The TCK 2004 law [the 2004 Turkish Criminal Code law n°5237] was a turning point for doctors in terms of medico-legal risks. It was adopted within the framework of a harmonization of our laws with those of the European Union. What I don't understand though is why these laws didn't cause any increase in CS rates in Europe, but at home they did. When I speak to doctors, they say 'The TCK law is destroying us, it (a vaginal birth) can cost us 1 billion, 3 billion.' Many legal actions were filed against the Ministry of Health. Some of them turned into lawsuits. But as far as public hospitals are concerned, very few accidents are judged to be a doctor's individual responsibility. Only around 3%. See? In 97% of cases, the state takes responsibility for them. What does the state look at? It looks at whether the OGs followed up their patient, whether their attitude resulted in an added complication or not. If the accident happens because of a medical complication, then the state takes responsibility for it. In this respect, there's a misunderstanding, an exaggeration of the medico-legal risks on the part of OGs.

In addition to Public Hospital #2's support for OGs and the dialogue it encouraged around the importance and safe nature of opting for vaginal birth, it also provided antenatal classes (six sessions) for pregnant women (and couples). The midwives who led these classes did not, however, supervise any deliveries, which were the responsibility of either the doctors or intern doctors. In Public Hospital #2, episiotomies in the case of a first birth were systematic, labour induction was frequent and birth on a gynaecological table was the rule. One of the midwives explained during our interview:

We don't deal with deliveries because intern doctors should learn how to supervise them. But to be honest, if you want to, nobody would stop you. I have for instance already attended deliveries, I also practised episiotomy. But you should show you are willing to. Last year, the hospital management ordered a survey. Among the 30 midwives working here, only three said they wanted to attend births. The rest of them think that birth assistance is a hard job. They don't want to be involved in it (…) Most women who come to the training sessions do not give birth here. They are followed by a natural birth doctor, etc. Doctors and interns here wouldn't want women to be too informed or too demanding either. They would be afraid to cope up with them, and not to be able to do their business-as-usual.

In Public Hospital #1, which was much smaller than Public Hospital #2, there was no antenatal classes provision at all during the research and writing-up period. Moreover, there were no major official incentives to make vaginal births more appealing to women. Some of the midwives took the initiative, purely on an individual basis, to attend alternative birth training courses, especially those provided by Dr Hakan Çoker, who founded the Birth-With-No-Regret Academy in Istanbul. This academy is quite a lucrative, upper-class antenatal education centre, located in a comfortable, central quarter of Istanbul, but Dr Çoker had also been giving conferences and training courses on a more affordable and sometimes voluntary basis all around the country since 2012. One midwife at Public Hospital #1 who had attended the courses in 2014 explained to me that she had been 'completely transformed' by this experience. However she was unable on her own to put her new knowledge (e.g. the fact that systematized episiotomy was not medically justified) into practice. The OGs and indeed most of the midwives at Public Hospital #1 believed, for instance, that attaching a pregnant women to monitoring devices for most of her labour process was a medical necessity, that delivery on a gynaecological table was the only legitimate birth position, that episiotomy was a must for safe first births (primipares) and that general anaesthesia was the best anaesthetic option in the case of a CS. It would take time and, more importantly, a change in mentality to replace these local 'truths' with others. It would also require a shift away from the quantitative regulation of the CS problem that the government proposed to a qualitative evaluation of the limitations of the dominant obstetric care system as a whole. Hence, the 8 per cent reduction in CS rates in the short term in Public Hospital #1 was related to factors other than a substantial change in birth practices. It seemed to be associated in particular with the fact that maternal demand for a CS delivery had been systematically refused since the 'law' had come into force. Before the 'law' was passed, it was easy for women who were anxious about a vaginal birth and who asked for a CS at their antenatal consultations to have their CS delivery scheduled.

Giving birth in a public hospital: Between obligation and choice

The women who gave birth in Public Hospital #1, where I conducted my ethnographic observations, had different motivations for choosing their place of delivery in the aftermath of the CS controversy. Most had chosen Public Hospital #1 either because they did not have sufficient financial means or health insurance to give birth in even a modest private hospital or because of personal reasons, such as the fact that a close family member worked there. If this had not been the case, they told me, they would have opted for a private hospital. A sizeable percentage of the women who had chosen the public hospital for financial reasons continued to be anxious about vaginal birth and thus still hoped to have an OG who would be understanding about their vaginal birth fears and not too intractable on the vaginal birth issue. For example, when Gülcan (twenty-three years old, 1st pregnancy) arrived at the hospital at 2:30 am with contractions, she was immediately taken to the labour ward because there was no medical reason for her to have a CS birth. In the morning, she would repeatedly cry in the labour ward, loudly enough so that the midwives could hear her. She told them a number of times that she could not bear the pain any longer and that she wanted a CS. At one point, she whispered to me, 'They're not taking me to the operating theatre because I'm Kurdish not Turkish'. She did not realize that the same procedure applied to everybody. She also cried when she told me that nobody was bothered about her labour pain in the hospital. All the pregnant women were attached to monitoring devices most of the time. They were not encouraged to walk about, and they had not been given any breathing training. The midwives mostly spoke to them in a gentle and patient way but either chose not to or could not spare the time to accompany them during labour. They often said that the most important thing was to 'have a healthy baby in one's hands'. Indeed, they themselves had not necessarily been trained in labour-related processes, such as breathing exercises. When Gülcan's daughter was born by vaginal delivery a few hours later, she made fun of her insistence on a CS during her labour. She told me, 'I'm happy now that they didn't do surgery on me. The labour pain was tough, but everything went well. I'm already up and feel good. The doctors didn't listen to me thankfully.'

By contrast, some women really did not want a CS birth and therefore came to the public hospital to increase their chances of having a vaginal birth, even though this meant a less comfortable stay compared with the private hospital. For example, Didem (thirty-six years old) felt lucky to have escaped a CS delivery when she gave birth to her first child in a university hospital in Ankara, although she would also have preferred not to have had an epidural anaesthesia:

> I had a negative experience with epidural anaesthesia. Your body loses all the strength it needs to push the baby out. I had this button in my hand that I had to press. The labour was just dragging on and on. In the end, the doctors came in and were annoyed with the interns and nurses because my baby had started to show signs of foetal distress apparently. They took the button out of my hand and speeded up the delivery. It was a big panic.

Didem was happy to be in a public hospital again for her second birth, especially because this was a more modest hospital where no epidural was offered at any point during my observations. She also chose Public Hospital #1 because she felt that one of the OGs who worked there had provided more satisfactory responses to her questions during her pregnancy compared with the doctors in the private hospitals: 'When I asked Dr B in the private hospital when I was eight months pregnant what the approximate weight of my baby was, he said "I'm not a fortune-teller Madam". A scientist would be able to tell you!' She also told me she was uncomfortable with the commercial dimension of the private hospitals: 'There's also another aspect. There's uncertainty around the prices in the private hospitals. A friend of mine who gave birth in the private sector (Private Hospital #1) couldn't get a bill when she left the hospital. Why not provide a bill? The prices apparently vary from one client to the next!'

Aysel (thirty-six years old, 1st pregnancy) also came to the public hospital with a clear preference for a vaginal birth. She explained to me in the early stages of her contractions:

> Normal birth is better for your health. Even if they offered me a billion lira, I wouldn't want to be cut for no reason. I think it's important as well to feel the birth pain. I feel that because of the pain I will love my baby even more. (…) I was told that birth pain was a bit like a tooth abscess pain or a kidney pain. I've had both of them so I'm not scared of it.

Aysel's labour lasted 8 hours. In the middle of her labour, she started to cry desperately and begged for a CS several times, saying that she could not bear the pain any longer. She hit the delivery room walls so hard that one of the student midwives felt the need to check with the chief midwife whether the wall might cave in because Aysel was quite strong. Aysel finally had a vaginal birth. She felt uncomfortable and insecure as the intern midwife was stitching her episiotomy. She cried frequently during the repair, complaining at the pain again. The midwife who had injected the anaesthetic 'in three places' in preparation reassured her that it was impossible for her to be able to feel the pain and that what she could feel was just a little scratch from the needle's point.

Finally, some women came to the public hospital with no clear preference for a CS or a vaginal birth. They were simply happy to follow what the doctor prescribed. However, some (like Didem) had also made contact with a private hospital so that they had an alternative option just in case they were 'forced' to have a vaginal birth or they were 'mistreated'. Indeed, during my two-month research stay at the public hospital, these kinds of situations occurred on a few occasions, prompting the women to go instead to a private hospital.

Azize (thirty-one years old, 1st birth) arrived at the hospital on the morning of her baby's due date, even though her contractions had not yet started. She registered and explained to the midwives at the information desk that her most recent ultrasound scan had shown her baby was breech and that the OG who had examined her had told her she would have to have a CS delivery if the baby had not changed its position by the due date. Azize was given another ultrasound scan, which confirmed that the baby was still breech. However, the OG on call that day was not the same OG who had examined her previously, and he was the only doctor in that maternity service who liked to 'try' vaginal births first in the case of breech babies. He thus told the midwives that Azize should be taken to the labour ward. Azize objected, explaining that she should have a CS. The on-call OG replied, 'I'm the doctor here, not you, so I decide which treatment to prescribe to my patients. If you don't want to try vaginal birth, you can leave.' Azize reflected for a few minutes and then retrieved her documents and left for one of the two private hospitals in the town. The midwives on duty strongly criticized the OG on this matter. They believed that he generally took unnecessary risks and that he expected women to do the same. They said Azize had the right to have a CS in this case.

The case of Nevra (thirty-three years old) was different because she had already had two CSs. Her third birth was therefore necessarily an elective CS delivery, and her doctor was insisting she had a tubal ligation. I was not allowed to attend these consultations personally, but the case was reported to me by the doctor in question. While I was interviewing him in his office, a midwife knocked on the door. She said, 'The patient with the planned C-section has accepted.' The doctor nodded his head, pleased at her response. He told me:

> Here's another sociological case for you. There's a pregnant woman who's going to have her third child. She had a C-section with the first two. Now she's going to have a C-section again. I'm the one who operated on her the first two times, and I'm due to operate on her again this afternoon. I told her, during the consultation today, that she'd also have to have a tubal ligation. She didn't want one. So I told her, if that was the case, I wouldn't be able to do her surgical delivery, that she'd have to find another doctor. Apparently she thought about it for a bit. She's accepted now, after some gentle persuasion (...) I can't bear any responsibility in such cases because, beyond the third, a caesarean operation is too risky.

Unlike Azize, Nevra did not have the means to go to a private hospital where, according to the private hospital OGs I interviewed, she would have been free to refuse tubal ligation. In other words, the more the public hospitals implemented authoritarian practices and restrictions (including restricted abortion service), the more the private hospitals were reframed as places where the woman's choice would be respected and abided by (provided she could afford it). In this respect, the 'CS ban' contributed to reinforce this positive image of the private sector. More importantly, it led to the privatization of a state service (i.e. elective CSs), just like abortion services were silently privatized (O'Neil 2017).

Private hospitals: Towards the privatization of women's 'choice'

From CS ban to commercial birth

In contrast to the public hospitals, there was no drop in the CS rates after 2012 for the two private hospitals studied. In Private Hospital #1 for instance, the rate increased from 79 per cent in 2012 to 83 per cent in 2013 and then to 85 per cent in 2014. Despite these very high CS rates (which the hospital justified by the prevalence of repetitive CSs), none of the OGs was sanctioned during the field research period, unlike in Public Hospital #1. The OGs and the hospital management at Private Hospital #1 both complained to me about the amount of government surveillance they were subject to. However, their complaints seemed more related to the new measures the government had put into place to prevent fraud associated with health insurance reimbursements. There had been many cases reported nationally over recent years of patients receiving treatment in private hospitals under other people's insurance policies because they themselves were not insured. To prevent this, the government had (at the time of the research) introduced a compulsory 'biometric finger and palm print' hospital registration system. This was a controversial measure denunciated by the TTB as a violation of privacy of personal information laws (Turkish Medical Association 2013). It was also considered by private health service providers, such as the Private Hospital #1's management, to be an insult to them. The CS 'ban' and its associated regulations seemed to concern them less. The chief executive of Private Hospital #1 recalled during our first interview that CS deliveries were 'banned' but then immediately added: 'As a result, women are knocking on the doors of private hospitals more.' Clearly, in his view, the 'ban' primarily concerned public hospitals. A similar perception also seemed to be prevalent in Private Hospital #2. One of the OGs there told me during our interview (in 2015):

> I don't know whether the sanctions for C-section abuse are still valid, or if they ever happened in this hospital. I was only appointed chief of the maternity service three months ago, so I don't know. I haven't seen a sanction case yet. But it can happen. The government wants to sanction OGs.

This same OG explained that the high CS rates in his hospital, which he confirmed were approximately '70 or 80 per cent, something like that',[7] were not likely to reduce because of women's preferences for CS:

ST: Why are the C-section rates much higher in the private sector than the public sector?

OG: Women's demand for C-sections is one major reason.

ST: Why do women in Turkey want to have a C-section in your opinion? Is it because of a lack of pain management, such as access to epidural anaesthesia?

OG: Yes, pain's an important factor. There is a lot of suffering in our society. People don't want to experience pain in childbirth or at any other time. Fear's also an important factor. There's a lack of education. Sex education for instance is very poor in our country. So women are afraid.

ST: Most women who come to your hospital have quite a specific socioeconomic status. Even they're lacking in knowledge? And I guess some of them would prefer a 'normal birth' to a caesarean birth?

OG: Yes, some of them come and say that they want a normal birth. But that's not really because they want it. It's because it's become fashionable to have a normal birth. Because the media promotes it. Water births have become quite trendy. Or some want to give birth crouching or standing. There are some alternative staff (« süslü püslü işler ») out there that became quite fashionable, a trend. Women don't ask for all these because they know what they want. The main problem is the preparation for the birth. There are no proper training courses for mums and dads beforehand. So when women who want to have a normal birth go into labour and start to feel the pains, they immediately ask for a C-section.

Although this OG cited the lack of antenatal classes for pregnant women as being one of the key determining factors, even his own prestigious and expensive hospital did not offer any training sessions to help women manage a vaginal birth. In 2017, it started to offer one-day birth seminars to women, but it does not include either physical exercises or group discussion sessions. It comprises only theoretical talks given by OGs, midwives and anaesthetists on, for instance, birth complications, breastfeeding and common infant illnesses.

It should be mentioned here that, over recent years, the private hospitals introduced 'birth packages' to make the prices more attractive. Surprisingly, antenatal classes are almost never mentioned in these packages, demonstrating they are not a priority either for the hospitals or for the women who choose to give birth in them. For instance, according to Private Hospital #2's call centre agents in early 2020, its 'birth package' included the following services as standard:

Call Centre (Private Hospital #2): I am just looking that up on the system for you. The system is just loading, thank you for your patience. So, the caesarean birth package includes: the rental of the operating theatre for the mother, the blood tests, 2 night's private room service for the mother and baby, 2 night's hosting of the birth partner with 3 meals a day, one breastfeeding training session provided by the nurse, nutritional diet advice for the mother, Turkish delights and sherbet offered to the visitors, a special celebration dinner for the new baby's parents, hairdressing service for the mother. For the baby, the package includes the routine blood tests, scans, a paediatric consultation after birth, an ophthalmologic examination, a hearing test, the first dose of the hepatitis B vaccination, all examinations and checks carried out during hospitalization, one follow-up visit at home by the medical team, a newborn baby pack containing baby plasters, shampoo, baby oil, lotion, photos of your baby and their publication on our 'e-bebek' website, a lifelong price promotion for the baby on his/her medical consultations at our hospital, with a 20% reduction on consultation prices during childhood, 10% reduction after the age of 18.

ST: Interesting. What is the content of the birth package in the case of a normal (vaginal) birth please?

CC: The same thing, if it is a single pregnancy. The only difference is that there is one night's hospitality for the patient and her birth partner instead of two.

ST: Are antenatal classes included in these birth packages?

CC: I'm just checking in the system, thank you for waiting... hmm, only the breastfeeding training and nutritional diet advice are included.

These birth packages, which did not include any birth preparation courses (unlike those offered by some European maternity hospitals, like breathing classes, group discussions, yoga, sophrology, acupuncture, haptonomy, etc.), cost 9,500 YTL (1,461 euros[8]) if the woman had public health insurance (SGK) and if she wanted her birth to be supervised by a top obstetrician (a professor or associate professor). The prices were the same for both a CS and a 'normal birth'. They were slightly lower if the mother settled for just a specialist OG (8,000 YTL) and slightly higher (10,000 YTL) if she had an epidural (vaginal) birth or a CS with an epidural or spinal anaesthesia instead of general anaesthesia. In cases where the woman had no health insurance cover, she had to pay an extra fee, which ranged between 5,800 and 7,400 YTL depending on the type of birth. These prices supposedly corresponded to the public insurance system's contributions to these packages. However, they were far beyond the contribution rates fixed for vaginal birth or CS alone (Özer et al. 2016). An OG from the TTB commented:

> Private hospitals offer hospitality services rather than health services, and they get good cover from the social health insurance system (SGK) for this. The more surgeries they perform, the more hospitalized patients they have. So they wouldn't want to reduce their C-section rates.

Indeed, according to official statistics, while in 2002, 76 per cent of hospitalizations took place in the public hospitals, 14 per cent in the university hospitals and 10 per cent in the private hospitals, in 2017, the rates were as follows: 55 per cent public hospitals, 14 per cent university hospitals, 30 per cent private hospitals (Ministry of Health of Turkey 2018: 166). The private hospitals thus clearly competed with public hospitals and took away from them a significant part of hospitalizations. Put differently, while between 2002 and 2017 the number of hospitalizations augmented by 81 per cent in the public hospitals, it rose by 627 per cent in the private hospitals. And among the latter, by 2017, the top 5 hospital chains made up for approximately 28 per cent of the total private hospital market in terms of beds (Union of Chambers and Commodity Exchanges of Turkey 2017). Furthermore, from 2002 to 2017, the annual volume of surgeries more than tripled countrywide. The ones realized in the public hospitals augmented by 160 per cent (from over 1 million to approximately 2.6 million), those in the university hospitals by 165 per cent (from nearly 307K to nearly 815K), while those taken in charge by private hospitals augmented by almost 584 per cent (from nearly 219K to over 1.5 million) (Ministry of Health of Turkey 2018: 166). The permanence of – and even increase in – private sector's CS rates should be evaluated by taking into account such structural changes and incitation mechanisms that transformed private hospitals into surgery 'paradises'.

Coming back to birth training for women, Private Hospital #1, where the prices were much lower (approximately a quarter of those in Private Hospital #2) and the birth packages more modest, had not put on any courses at all since the CS 'ban' had been introduced. The most significant change in this hospital in recent years had been the promotion of vaginal births under epidural anaesthesia. The hospital had been advertising them as a 'painless birth' and even as a 'princess birth' since 2017. However, this had not led to a rapid uptake in epidural births, which would have reduced the hospital's CS birth rate.

Choosing CS or dignity or both? Women's birth experiences in the private hospitals

The women who chose private (over public) hospitals for their childbirth reported different motivations, but an epidural birth (which most public hospitals did not offer) was not one of the main reasons cited. Their main motivations were rather privacy (each patient had a comfortable individual room with en suite shower and WC as well as a bed for their birth partner) and hygiene (some women reported rumours that 'rusty' episiotomy suturing needles were used in Public Hospital #1!). Most women who chose the private sector also wanted their birth supervised by a doctor rather than a midwife (as was the case in Public Hospital #1) and valued the personalized care on offer: they could choose their doctor from the outset and have both antenatal and delivery care provided by this doctor. Some women of low socioeconomic status had stretched their financial resources to have their birth in a private hospital for these reasons. As Selma (twenty-six years old, 1st pregnancy in 2014) explained: 'I started my antenatal care at the public hospital, but when I did my sums and took into account the minibus fares, etc., the private hospital is walking distance from my home but the public hospital isn't, it didn't really make a big difference. So why put up with the public hospital? (…) In the end, the bill was 1,500 YTL… or actually 2,000 YTL I think, if I count the trisomy 21 test when I was pregnant.' A homemaker with a high school diploma, Selma read a lot and was a passionate health and nutrition advocate. During her first pregnancy, she had told the OG in Private Hospital #1 that she really wanted to have a 'normal' birth:

During our monthly consultations, Dr F would listen to me carefully, but then she'd often say 'You can try a normal birth but we can't tell at this stage how things will turn out on D-day, so you shouldn't set your heart on it'. I read a lot of things on the internet. I watched videos on how to do the breathing exercises, and I started to practise them at home everyday. Sometimes I did the exercises with my husband. One afternoon, exactly 2 weeks before my son's due date, I felt my first contractions. I told my husband I didn't want to go to the hospital straight away though. I was thinking that if my labour was well advanced, they wouldn't just automatically take me to the operating theatre. But within an hour, my contractions had become so strong that I started to get a bit anxious, and we went to the hospital. My hospital bag was ready anyway. When I arrived, my doctor was there. She examined me straight away and told me that the birth had started, that my cervix was half dilated! I told her that I was ready. I then felt things all went a bit strange. Kind of … she was stressed. Yes, she seemed very stressed. And she made me feel stressed! She was looking straight into my eyes. I did the same back. I felt she was trying to decide whether to take me to the operating theatre or not. Finally, 20 minutes later, the midwife reexamined me, and they took me to the delivery room. The OG told me to follow all her instructions. Everything was fine afterwards. My son came quickly. Overall, it was only about an hour, two max, between being admitted to hospital and my son being born. I think I gave birth so quickly as a defense mechanism. I wanted to do it before they could take me to theatre.

A significant number of women I met in Private Hospital #1 either before or after their deliveries told me that they, like Selma, wanted to have a 'normal birth' rather than a CS. Not all got their wish, however. In 2014, Leyla (twenty-five years old), a high school teacher, felt strongly about having a vaginal birth and chose Private Hospital #1 because her husband's aunt was one of the OGs there. Leyla placed a lot of trust in her and thought that she was her only chance of having a vaginal birth. Her pregnancy had proceeded without any complications. On her son's due date, the aunt proposed not to hospitalize Leyla but to monitor the foetus daily until her contractions started. On the fourth day, however, Leyla said she became very stressed and was crying a lot. She was anxious about a vaginal birth. She had had no preparation for it. She was also impacted by her mother telling her that it was a pity she had decided to suffer instead of taking advantage of the CS opportunity. She suddenly felt powerless. She felt she would not be able to manage a vaginal birth. In the end, she and her husband's aunt made a joint decision to opt for a CS. Her aunt offered her an epidural, rather than a general, anaesthesia because she had initially wanted to actively participate in the birth of her child. However, after three attempts, the anaesthetist told the OG that they would need to use a general anaesthesia, adding, 'She's put on a bit of weight. I'm afraid I can't get the needle in the right place in her back.' Leyla was upset about having to have a general anaesthesia. Her trauma was redoubled when she was woken up after the birth of her healthy baby. As she held her son in her arms for the first time, she saw on her smart phone that photos of her newborn baby had already been 'liked' by more than 300 Facebook friends. Her husband had sent the first photos of their son to one of their best friends, who had then posted them on Facebook. Several hundred people had seen Leyla's baby before she had.

Zeynep (twenty-eight years old, 1st birth, 2nd day after birth) also really wanted to have a 'normal' birth. In preparation, she had read a lot during pregnancy, learnt the breathing exercises, walked a lot and had been careful not to put on more than 9 kilos. Her contractions had started at 6 a.m., and she arrived at the hospital at 9 a.m., just as her doctor was starting her shift. The OG examined her, told her she was '3.5-4 centimetres, which is good' and then asked the nurses to settle her into her own side room. At 2 p.m., the OG decided to accelerate the process by inducing Zeynep in order, they were all told, to 'give support to the birthing women'. Induction was a very frequent practice at this hospital. 'Apparently they did it because my baby was lazy,' Zeynep told me. She added, 'Everything was going all right until they induced me, contractions, everything. But afterwards, the pain became unbearable. So Dr N asked me if I wanted an epidural anaesthesia. I didn't. I'm scared of it. In the end, at 4 pm, because my labour wasn't advancing as much as it should, Dr N came and told me "We don't want to tire you or your baby out anymore. Let's go for a C-section". So that's how things finished up. It wasn't a very happy ending. Now I get a lot of bloating in my belly'.

Aysen (twenty-five years old, 1st birth) was luckier in a sense. She had also wanted a vaginal birth from the outset, but during her first vaginal examination in the third month of her pregnancy, her doctor had told her that she was not 'relaxed enough' so she would probably not manage to have a normal birth. He added that it could be risky for the baby because she was stressed. Aysen came to the hospital at midnight, after her contractions had started. She had been asked to come in two days before that because she had already gone past her due date, but she had not done so because she did not want to be induced. By 4 a.m., her pain had become too much for her, and she asked the midwife to call the OG to come to the hospital and operate on her immediately. The OG refused. He arrived instead at 9 a.m. for his shift, examined Aysen and told her that she was close to giving birth. The on-call midwife reminded him that the patient had asked for a CS several times during the night, but there seemed to be no need for one anymore. Aysen was taken to the delivery room in a wheelchair, and she gave birth to her daughter shortly after by vaginal delivery. She had changed her mind about having a CS several times during her labour, but in the end her labour had advanced so well that she had a vaginal birth.

Clearly, the OGs in Private Hospital #1 did not refuse the women's requests for a 'normal birth' during pregnancy, but neither did they really encourage vaginal births, as the above cases show. Generally speaking, in Private Hospital #1, all possible medical reasons for a CS, as defined by the government experts following the 'Robson classification' (Ministry of Health of Turkey 2010), were mobilized. A 'previous C-section' was the main reason recorded, because VBAC (vaginal birth after caesarean) was never practised in this hospital. The same was true of many private hospitals in Turkey, despite the fact VBAC is common practice in a large number of European countries since the early 2000s. IVF babies, twin babies, breech babies and 'big' babies (i.e. babies who, according to the ultrasound, weighed 4 kg or more) were also all automatic reasons for a CS. For the women who wanted to give birth 'normally', provided that none of the above medical reasons applied, a number of non-medical factors were also taken into account by the OGs when deciding whether or not they would 'give normal birth a chance', as one midwife put it. One was the woman's determination to have a vaginal birth, as Selma's case showed. The duration of labour (and birth) was another important factor, as we saw in Zeynep's case. Because of concerns relating to time management, many women in Private Hospital #1 ended up having CS deliveries after first 'trying' a vaginal birth. According to the hospital's birth register accounts, a prolonged labour was the main reason for emergency CS cases. However, what counted as 'prolonged' largely depended on the OGs' working hours (9:00–18:00). Finally, the 'chance to have a normal birth' inevitably depended, to some extent at least, on each OG's performance points agreements (some earned more if they did a CS, some less) (Topçu 2019: 156–7).

As a result, women only had a partial choice when it came to vaginal births. The situation for CS births was different. Women who had requested a CS from the start (i.e. not those who did not want a CS but who ended up having one during labour or because a complication had been identified[9]) had to pay the full cost of the operation. Indeed, an official new birth category (and billing structure) had been introduced within the private sector since the 'CS law' had come into force, called 'C-sections on maternal demand'. This category covered cases in which the pregnant women made an explicit demand for a CS from the outset (i.e. not during labour or when a complication, such as a breech position, was identified). In such cases, the women were asked to sign a document confirming they were aware they would not benefit from public health insurance cover. The women's choice to have a CS was thus transformed either into a commodity that could be sold or into an individual need or expenditure from which the state had withdrawn. It should, however, also be noted that, according to the interviews I conducted, when a pregnant woman could not fully afford the CS costs, it was possible to come to an 'arrangement' with the OG. The fact that vaginal birth anxiety was considered by law to be a medical reason for a CS facilitated such arrangements.

More research on the distribution of 'C-sections on maternal demand' vs. 'C-sections for medical reasons' in the private sector is necessary in order to fully understand whether Turkey has been facing a significant transfer of CS cost-bearing from the state to the individual (i.e. patients) or whether the change rather concerns a shift from state-funded CSs carried out in state hospitals to state-funded CSs carried out in private hospitals (with out-of-pocket fees for patients). I argue that in both cases, the private hospitals have emerged the winners from the 'caesarean law' because more and more women anxious about vaginal birth have come 'knocking on the doors of private hospitals', as one hospital manager put it. On the flip side of this, women, women's demands and women's needs for a safe, empowering birth experience seem to have been mostly pushed aside.

Conclusion

Whether by caesarean section or vaginally, giving birth in a hospital has become a traumatic experience for many women in the world (Diniz et al. 2018). Feminist mobilizations against obstetric violence have acquired a relevant international audience since early 2010s. The many issues denounced within the framework of these mobilizations include the verbal violence of health professionals, the lack of assistance to women, the denial of their suffering (as, for example, when local anaesthesia is not effective) and the unjustified interventions these women undergo such as 'abusive' C-sections, or episiotomy cuts, or the use of forceps. Too much medical intervention or too little individualized care can indeed have long-term, and even dramatic, consequences for women. Traumatic childbirth experiences can engender post-partum anxiety, depression and even suicide in the mother (see also Göbelez, in this volume). According to a survey conducted in 2011 of 1,010 Turkish women, approximately one-third of them was suffering or had suffered from post-partum depression, a rate much higher than that of countries like the UK (12.8 per cent), France (8.5 per cent) or Sweden (12.4 per cent) (Ünsal Altan et al. 2018).

The necessity of respecting the right of women to choose the way they want to live their birth experience is often put forward as a means of preventing such trauma. Despite its indisputably fair nature, such a proposition is, however, more theoretical than feasible in many contexts because giving birth in a hospital is more often than not governed by pre-established norms and protocols rather than by a large set of possibilities of choice that are offered to women. To take one example, even choosing one's childbirth position is impossible in many hospital environments around the world. Furthermore, as this chapter has demonstrated, when exigencies of security combine with other ideologies such as conservatism and neoliberalism, a 'woman's choice' serves above all as a strategic and discursive tool of governmentality, despite the fact that neither women nor their preferences or well-being are placed at the centre of political and medical concerns.

It can be safely argued that the brutish character of the governmental critique of an alleged nationwide CS epidemic ('caesarean delivery is a murder') in 2012 has contributed to the exclusion of women from what concerns them in the first place: the improvement of their childbirth conditions and the co-design of their (future) experience of childbirth. Indeed, the too openly conservative nature of the AKP's polemic about the legitimacy of CSs prevented, at least to a certain extent, the rise of social reflexivity on the inconvenience of CSs and of technocratic birth overall. Instead, it provoked a polarized controversy which did not involve a veritable critique of the techno-medical colonization of women's bodies and autonomy, via normalized CSs. The abuse of CSs as a health problem was rendered occult, whilst the debate was rather framed, by both regulatory bodies and medical actors, as 'for or against the governmental harassment of obgyns', or 'for or against a greater political control on women's bodies'. In short, criticizing CS was perceived, by many, as 'being against doctors', or instead, as 'being against women', 'being antifeminist', or 'supporting Erdoğan'. These were short-term developments.

The 'CS law' and the political-economic regulations that followed also came to play a paradoxical role, as far as the settings and the findings of this ethnographic study are concerned. It exerted pressure on public hospitals for the sake of greater efficiency, while the private ones, which theoretically were the major target of the government's CS regulations, seemed to maintain their autonomy, and even to boost their profits thanks to the 'law'. The category of 'CS on maternal demand' was formalized within this frame.

In short, the CS controversy was not followed by major institutional reforms capable of introducing deep changes in practices and mentalities towards a 're-humanization' of childbirth and a 're-empowerment' of women. As a result, a significant number of women continue to prefer and even *desire* a caesarean birth, as they want to avoid episiotomy cuts or the lack of care during painful labour. Those who prefer vaginal birth, on the contrary, either are not able to have it, especially if they choose a private hospital, or when they do undergo it, it is a painful process, for which sometimes they do not receive sufficient physical or psychological preparation before birth. In the middle of all these developments, to be sure, the critical evaluation of CS abuse as a health problem, but also as a feminist problem, as a cultural problem, and as a (bio) political problem, has to wait for a new tomorrow.

Acknowledgements

The author thanks the French National Research Agency (ANR 'Hypmedpro') who funded this research as well as the administrative team of the Centre for the Study of Social Movements (CEMS-Ehess) who provided technical support. She thanks the hospital administrations for having released the necessary authorizations and the medical teams and the anonymous interviewees for having made this research possible. She is also grateful to Hilal Alkan for her precious comments and inspiring insight on this chapter, and to Clare Ferguson and Ruth Mas for their help with the proofreading.

Notes

1   See, for example, 'Turkish Doctors Face Fines for Elective Caesareans', *The Guardian*, 13 July 2012, https://www.theguardian.com/world/2012/jul/13/turkish-doctors-fines-elective-caesareans

2   See, for example, 'Başbakan: Sezaryen cinayettir' (PM: Caesarean delivery is a murder), Kanal Türk, 27 May 2012, http://beyazgazete.com/video/anahaber/kanalturk-32/2012/05/27/basbakan-sezaryen-cinayettir-283466.html. Unless otherwise indicated, this and all subsequent quotations from Turkish sources have been translated into English.

3   'Çok sezaryen yapan hastaneler değerlendirmeye alınacak' (hospitals with high caesarean rates will be put under surveillance), CNN Türk, 10 February 2017, https://www.cnnturk.com/video/saglik/sezaryen-ile-dogumu-azaltmak-icin-yeni-yasa-geliyor

4   'Sezaryanla doğumu azaltmak için yeni yasa geliyor' (a new law is being introduced to decrease caesarean rates), CNN Türk, 15 December 2017, https://www.cnnturk.com/video/saglik/sezaryen-ile-dogumu-azaltmak-icin-yeni-yasa-geliyor

5   Fieldnotes, 16 February 2015, Public Hospital #2, Birth training room, Istanbul.

6   According to the 2004 Turkish Criminal Code law (n°5237) (26.09.2004), known as TCK 2004, provoking injury or pain in a person's body (including a pregnant woman) engenders a prison punishment of three to twelve months, or a financial fine (Article n°89).

7   It was not possible for me to access more accurate data on the CS rates for Private
    Hospital #2, where I did not conduct ethnographic observations, only interviews.
8   The minimum wage was 440 euros in the same period (January 2020).
9   According to a national survey, this was approximately 50 per cent of all women who
    had a CS delivery.

References

Acar, F. and G. Altunok (2013), 'The "politics of intimate" at the Intersection of Neo-
    Liberalism and Neo-Conservatism in Contemporary Turkey', *Women's Studies
    International Forum*, 41: 14–23.
Arman, A. (2015), 'Hastane ve doktor hatasına rekor tazminat: 2.5 milyon lira' [Record
    compensation for medical error: 2.5. million lira], *Hürriyet*, 4 January. Available
    online: https://www.hurriyet.com.tr/yazarlar/ayse-arman/hastane-ve-doktor-hatasina-
    rekor-tazminat-2-5-milyon-lira-27888991
Cindoğlu, D. and F. Sayan-Cengiz (2010), 'Türkiye'de Doğumların Medikalizasyonu:
    Feminist Bir Bakışla Sezaryen Problemini Düşünmek' [Medicalisation of childbirth in
    Turkey: Reflecting on the caesarean problem from a feminist viewpoint], in *2. Kadın
    Hekimlik ve Kadın Sağlığı Kongresi Kongre Kitabı* (*Congress Book of the 2nd Gynaecology-
    Obstetrics and Women's Health Congress*), 51–64, Ankara: University of Ankara Press.
Davis-Floyd, R. E. and C. F. Sargent, eds (1997), *Childbirth and Authoritative Knowledge.
    Crosscultural Perspectives*, Berkeley: University of California Press.
Diniz, S. G. and A. S. Chacham (2004), 'The "cut above" and "the cut below". The Abuse of
    Caesareans and Episiotomy in Sao Paolo, Brazil', *Reproductive Health Matters*, 12 (23):
    100–10.
Diniz, S. G., D. Rattner, A. F. Lucas d'Oliveira, J. M. de Aguiar and D. Y. Niy (2018),
    'Disrespect and Abuse in Childbirth in Brazil: Social Activism, Public Policies And
    Providers' Training', *Reproductive Health Matters*, 26 (53): 19–35.
Eren Vural, I. (2017), 'Financialisation in Health Care: An Analysis of Private Equity Fund
    Investments in Turkey', *Social Science and Medicine*, 187: 276–86.
Gaskin, I. M. (2008), *Ina May's Guide to Childbirth*, London: Vermilion.
Gök, M. S. and E. Altındağ (2015), 'Analysis of the Cost and Efficiency Relationships:
    Experience in the Turkish Pay for Performance System', *European Journal of Health
    Economy*, 16: 459–69.
Göbelez, S. (2021), 'Tactics of Women up against Obstetrical Violence and the
    Medicalization of Childbirth in Turkey', in H. Alkan, A. Dayi, S. Topçu, B. Yarar (eds),
    Politics of the Female Body in Turkey: Reproduction, Maternity, Sexuality, London: I.B.
    Tauris.
Hamzaoğlu, N. and B. Türk (2019), 'Prevalence of Physical and Verbal Violence against
    Health Care Workers in Turkey', *International Journal of Health Services*, 49 (4): 844–61.
Jordan, B. (1978), *Birth in Four Cultures: A Crosscultural Investigation of Childbirth in
    Yucatan, Holland, Sweden, and the United States*, California: Eden Press Women's
    Publications.
Juven, P. (2016), *Une santé qui compte? Les coûts et les tarifs controversés de l'hôpital public*,
    Paris: PUF.
Kitzinger, S. (2015), *A Passion for Birth: My Life: Anthropology, Family and Feminism*,
    London: Pinter & Martin.

Maffi, I. (2015), 'The Detour of an Obstetric Technology: Active Management of Labor Across Cultures', *Medical Anthropology*, 35 (1): 17–30.

Mc Callum, C. (2005), 'Explaining Caesarean Section in Salvador da Bahia, Brazil', *Sociology of Health & Illness*, 27 (2): 215–42.

Ministry of Health of Turkey (2010), *Management Guide for Vaginal and Caesarean Deliveries (Dogum ve Sezaryan Eylemi Yönetim Rehberi)*, Ankara: Republic of Turkey Ministry of Health.

Ministry of Health of Turkey (2017), *Women's Diseases and Birth Commission Report (Kadin Hastaliklari ve Dogum Komisyonu Raporu)*, Istanbul: Istanbul Directory of Health/Ministry of Health.

Ministry of Health of Turkey (2018), *Health Statistics Year Book 2017*, Ankara: Republic of Turkey Ministry of Health.

Morris, T. (2013), *Cut It Out. The C-section Epidemic in America*, New York: New York University Press.

Odent, M. (1992), *The Nature of birth and Breastfeeding*, New York: Praeger.

Omay, E.G.G. and E. Cengiz (2013), 'Health Tourism in Turkey: Opportunities and Threats', *Mediterranean Journal of Social Sciences*, 4 (10): 424–31.

O'Neil, M. L. (2017), 'Abortion Services at Hospitals in Istanbul', *The European Journal of Contraception and Reproductive Health Care*, 22 (2): 88–93.

Özer Ö., Ç. Gün and M. Saygılı (2016), 'Cost of Caesarean Section Rates in Turkey and Their Burden in the Turkish Health Economics', *Proceedings of the 24th International Academic Conference*, 28 June–1 July.

Roberts, E. F. S. (2012), 'Scars of the Nation: Surgical Penetration and the Ecuadorian State', *The Journal of Latin American and Caribbean Anthropology*, 17 (2): 215–37.

Sarda, G. (2011), 'Artificially Maintained Scientific Controversies, the Construction of Maternal Choice and Caesarean Section Rates', *Social Theory & Health*, 9 (2): 166–82.

Topçu S. (2019), 'Caesarean or Vaginarean Epidemics? Techno-Birth, Risk and Obstetric Practice in Turkey', *Health, Risk & Society*, 21 (3–4): 141–63.

Topçu S. and P. Brown (2019), 'The Impact of Technology on Pregnancy and Childbirth: Creating and Managing Obstetrical Risk in different Cultural and Socio-Economic Contexts', *Health, Risk & Society*, 21 (3–4): 89–99.

Turkish Medical Association (2011), 'Tam Gün mü? Ulus ötesi işbirliğine ucuz işgücü mü?' (Full time? Or cheap workforce for a supranational collaboration?), *Press Release*, 29 August.

Turkish Medical Association (2013), 'Özel hastanede avuç izi parmak izi verirken bir kez daha düşünün!' (Think twice before you give a finger and palm print in private hospitals !), *Press Release*, 3 December.

Turkish Medical Association (2018a), 'Sağlıkta Dönüşüm Programı Çöktü. Ne Dediler Ne Oldu ?' (The Health Transformation Programme collapsed. What did they promise and what happened ?), supplement to *Tıp Dünyası Gazetesi (Gazette of the Medical World)*, March.

Turkish Medical Association (2018b), *Özel Sağlık Sektöründe Çalışma ve Ücretlendirme Biçimleri (Forms of Work and Remuneration in the Private Health Sector)*, Istanbul: TTB Yayınları.

Union of Chambers and Commodity Exchanges of Turkey (Türkiye Odalar ve Borsalar Birliği) (2017), *Turkey Healthcare Landscape. A Report*. Available online: https://www.tobb.org.tr/saglik/20171229-tss-genel-bakis-en.pdf (accessed 10 November 2020).

Ünsal Altan, S., R. Öztürk, D. Güleç Satır, S. Ildan Çalım, B. Karaöz Weller, K. Amanak, A. Saruhan, A. Şirin and F. Akerca (2018), 'Relation between Mothers' Types of Labor,

Birth Interventions, Birth Experiences and Postpartum Depression: A Multi-centre Follow-up Study', *Sexual and Reproductive Healthcare*, 18: 13–18.

Visser, G. H. A., D. Ayres-de-Campos, E. R. Barnea, L. de Bernis, G. C. Di Renzo, M. F. Escobar Vidarte, I. Lloyd, A. H. Nassar, W. Nicholson, P. K. Shah, W. Stones, L. Sun, G. B. Theron and S. Walani (2018), 'FIGO Position Paper: How to Stop the Caesarean Section Epidemic', *The Lancet*, 392 (13.10.2018).

Wendt, C., T. I. Agartan and M. E. Kaminska (2013), 'Social Health Insurance without Corporate Actors: Changes in Self-regulation in Germany, Poland and Turkey', *Social Science & Medicine*, 86: 88–95.

World Bank (2018), *Turkish Health Transformation Program and Beyond*, Results Briefs, 2 April. Available online: https://www.worldbank.org/en/results/2018/04/02/turkish-healthtransformation-program-and-beyond

World Health Organization (2015), *WHO Statement on Caesarean Section Rates*. Available online: https://apps.who.int/iris/bitstream/handle/10665/161442/WHO_RHR_15.02_eng.pdf?sequence=1

Wolf, J. (2018), *Cesarean Section. An American History of Risk, Technology and Consequence*, Baltimore: Johns Hopkins University Press.

6

Monitoring pregnancies: The politics and ethics of reproductive health surveillance in Turkey

Seda Saluk

In November 2011, Kadıköy, one of the central and middle-class residential areas of Istanbul, made it to the newspapers with a unique story. According to the papers, family physicians working at the local and state-run family health centres had recently started to make unannounced home visits to residents. The aim was not only to introduce the newly established family medicine system at the primary level, but also to collect residents' health data for the centres' records. Many residents, however, were not happy with the unannounced home visits or the physicians' questions about – what they perceived as – intimate details of their personal lives. As a response, they started posting the following banners on their apartment blocks' entrance gates: 'Dilenci, satıcı, ve aile hekimi giremez' ('Beggars, salespeople and family physicians' 2011). The banners, which can be translated as 'Beggars, salespeople, and family physicians are not allowed', drew a fair amount of media attention, since they juxtaposed often belittled professions with a highly respected and historically well-regarded one in Turkey.

The same newspapers also published interviews with prominent public health bureaucrats who were puzzled by the neighbourhood residents' refusal to accept family physicians into their homes. Professor Dr Savaş Başar Kartal, then Deputy Manager of Istanbul Health Directory, stated his concerns in the following words:

> This is very sad. This situation happens in some regions of Izmir, too. You go to their doors... Doctors [from family health centers] come to their homes, but they say, 'I use somewhere else's service; their vaccines are of better quality.' It is us who provide almost all of the newborn vaccinations to private hospitals in Istanbul, which means the vaccines at the private hospitals and the family medicine units are the same. ('Beggars, salespeople and family physicians' 2011)

Professor Kartal later added that the home visits were part of the newly established family medicine system's comprehensive public health surveillance efforts. Not only adults in Istanbul but also all pregnant women and newborns were routinely monitored by family physicians. The achieved decrease in the country's infant mortality rates over the last couple of years, he claimed, was a result of those meticulous surveillance practices completed in the field. Professor Kartal also mentioned that the Turkish Ministry of

Health was trying to decrease the high rates of maternal mortality, similarly by closely monitoring pregnancies. According to him, the routine monitoring of pregnancies was crucial for detecting and preventing home births, especially in high-risk situations:

> Due to an expected storm on the Princes Islands, we brought to Istanbul all pregnant women who were at risk and whose delivery was fast approaching. Similarly, we brought all pregnant women in the high-risk category in Şile and Çatalca to our city hospitals so as not to endanger them due to adverse weather conditions. In the last year alone, more than 500 pregnant women took advantage of our services. ('Beggars, salespeople and family physicians' 2011)

What we see in Professor Kartal's remarks above is a combination of disappointment and anger at the residents of Kadıköy, but also high praise for the Justice and Development Party (JDP) government's newly established family medicine system and its controversial health monitoring practices. The JDP governments have routinely presented their decade-long healthcare reforms as a crystallization of their success in governing the country and bringing services to its citizens. According to Professor Kartal, the residents of Kadıköy not only refuse to receive these efficient healthcare services, but also misbehave towards physicians who represent the JDP-led Ministry of Health, hence the very representatives of the Turkish state itself.

The pairing of Kadıköy with the south-western city of Izmir in Professor Kartal's remarks is also interesting. JDP politicians and bureaucrats often perceive and present both places as strongholds of 'white Turks,' the Westernized secular elites living in the urban centres and voting for the Republican People's Party (CHP), the main opposition and the long-time rival of the JDP. By contrast, in this equation the JDP is presented, in President Recep Tayyip Erdogan's proud words, as 'black Turks,' the pious Muslim middle- and lower-middle classes of Anatolia, the underdogs who had long been neglected by the previous governments, until the JDP first came to power in 2003 (White 2014 'President Erdoğan: "I am proud of being a black Turk"' 2015; 'Erdoğan: "İnce, would I give you the time of my day?"' 2018).

In the second part of Professor Kartal's remarks, the high praise for the family medicine system and its controversial health monitoring practices becomes much clearer. Kartal alerts the audience about potential dangers that could emerge if the state institutions would not closely monitor pregnant women and their newborns. Without effective surveillance practices conducted by family health centres, he implies, the country would experience much higher rates of maternal and infant mortality. Through an invocation of compassion and care for the country's seemingly vulnerable women and children, the family physicians' unannounced and unwelcome home visits are normalized and even justified.

Using the case of family health centres and the public controversies around their health monitoring practices as a vantage point, this chapter provides a critical analysis of the recent changes in Turkey's reproductive healthcare system. These local centres, formerly known as *sağlık ocağı* (health home), were transferred to family health centres in 2010 and became the main provider of preventive and reproductive health services at the primary care level. This transition happened as part of the healthcare reforms led by the JDP government, which blended the international organizations' terminology of 'good governance' with the government's conservative pronatalist aspirations that situate the heterosexual nuclear family and its procreation at the centre of health services. Established in the aftermath of the Reproductive Health Program (2003–7) and the Health Transformation Program (2003–12), these reforms have resulted in a restructuring of state-run health centres, a renewed attention to maternal and infant well-being, and an increased reliance on standardized, data-driven reproductive health surveillance.

My argument in this chapter is twofold. First, I claim that the shift from the earlier *sağlık ocağı* (health home) system to a family health centre model constitutes an important case study for understanding the broader sociopolitical and economic changes happening in Turkey under the JDP governments over the past decade. These centres provide a compelling case study to unpack Turkish-style neoliberalism. The Turkish version is similar to Anglo-American accounts of neoliberalism and its counterparts in the Global South, in the sense that it produces changes in not only economic and material conditions (Harvey 2007), but also subjectivities and social relations between differently situated subjects (Rivkin-Fish 2005; Ong 2006; Li 2007). Yet, it also derives from the peculiarities of an increasingly neoconservative and authoritarian Turkey, where the state reorganizes itself and gains more power on issues of reproduction and family (Coşar and Yeğenoğlu 2012; Korkman 2015; Özbay et al. 2016). As a result, healthcare workers who mediate the new system and ordinary people who are subjected to it found themselves in new types of encounters, further complicating the implementation of these reform projects (Dayı 2019).

Second, I argue that the JDP's reproductive politics are central to these changes. Since the rise of demographic anxieties over declining birth rates in Turkey by the early 2000s, the figures of the pregnant woman and the newborn have increasingly played a critical role in debates about health policy and practice. These figures were both the driving force and a tool of legitimization behind many reform projects. The restructuring of family health centres, in particular, has played a central role in these reforms, due to these centres' historically significant role in monitoring population practices and reproductive behaviours. After the founding of the Turkish Republic, the state has increasingly been concerned with collecting the health data of both individuals and the population at large. The state-run health centres became the main institutions collecting these data, with a special emphasis on calculating birth and death rates, as well as fertility patterns (Gürsoy, Sümbüloğlu, and Eren 1982; Dole 2004, 2012). Although the methods of gathering and tracking of information have changed across time, monitoring of pregnancies has long been practised at these centres. While the centres used a paper-based, 'index card system' to 'individually chart medical case histories' in the 1930s (Dole 2012: 40), the 2000s witnessed the mushrooming of health information technologies (for example, big data platforms and centralized databases) to track patients' pregnancies (Saluk 2014).

Methodology and language

This chapter draws on my doctoral work on the politics and ethics of reproductive health surveillance in Turkey. For my dissertation research, I conducted eighteen months of fieldwork in Istanbul, Turkey, between 2014 and 2017. The analysis presented in this chapter is based on media and policy analysis, as well as ethnographic observations and interviews at family health centres. My research on media and policy analysis seeks to chronicle when, how and why reproductive surveillance mechanisms have emerged in Turkey. I collected and analysed news articles, TV shows and policy reports of the Turkish Ministry of Health, the European Commission, the World Health Organization and the World Bank. My research at the health centres attends to the implementation and impact of these mechanisms. I conducted participant-observation, especially at two family health centres. The first centre was in Kadıköy, a predominantly middle-class neighbourhood at the centre of the city, which is often marked as ethnically Turkish. The second centre was in Sultanbeyli, a predominantly low-income neighbourhood at the city's periphery, with residents hailing mostly from central Anatolia, Turkey's Kurdistan and, recently, Syria. I complemented my observations with in-depth, semi-structured interviews with twelve family physicians, twenty nurses, and twenty-five patients coming from different class and ethnic backgrounds.[1]

Like most of the state-run medical settings in Turkey, these family health centres are preconditioned to construct and serve normative subjects, bodies and desires. Queer, trans and refugee people and communities often find themselves excluded from these public spaces, with limited or no access to the state's health services (Shakhsari 2014; Yılmaz and Göçmen 2016; Mutlu et al. 2018). Therefore, the pregnancies I encountered during my fieldwork in health centres were exclusively of heterosexual, cis-gendered women with formal citizenship. Similarly, the nurses with whom I interacted were perceived or presented themselves as women, as nursing is a very (female) gendered profession in Turkey (Dal and Kitiş 2008). These conditions, as a result, have shaped the language and terminology in this chapter, as well as my decision to use words such as 'women' and 'mothers', instead of gender-neutral phrases such as 'pregnant people' and 'parents'.

Drawing on media and policy analysis, observations at the health centres and interviews with practitioners, I analyse the introduction, implementation and impact of reproductive surveillance mechanisms in health policy and practice in the rest of this chapter. I first situate these mechanisms at the nexus of national politics of reproduction and transnational governance, through a discussion of recent changes in Turkey's healthcare policy. I then turn to how healthcare bureaucrats imagine and talk about these mechanisms. Finally, I discuss the everyday implementation and impact of these mechanisms for nurses and their patients, who are subjected to these mechanisms on the frontline, but mostly absent in policy debates. I examine how the new forms of monitoring and documenting scripts generated by health surveillance reshape labour conditions, care practices and social interactions at the health centres, producing uneven outcomes for differently situated practitioners and patients.

A brief history of reproductive health surveillance in Turkey

The rise and circulation of reproductive health surveillance mechanisms in Turkey build on a long-time national tradition of maternal-infant health monitoring, as well as the JDP government's ongoing pronatalist agendas. It is also a result of transnational organizations' recent interventions in the Turkish healthcare system. State authorities have long cast procreation as a requirement for the Turkish nation's survival, military power and economic prosperity since the late Ottoman period and the early nation-building years of the Turkish Republic (Miller 2007; Balsoy 2015; Demirci-Yılmaz 2015). At the same time, the European Union (EU), as well as international agencies such as the World Health Organization (WHO) and the United Nations (UN), has approached the country's maternal and infant mortality statistics as a litmus test of its proximity to 'European standards' of civilization, democracy and modernity. Both local and transnational actors have often framed the high rate of maternal and infant deaths in Turkey as a social problem that needs to be addressed by means of techno-medical solutions (Ağartan 2012).

For the last two decades, in particular, Turkey has been subject to the revival of pronatalist state policies that aim at boosting population growth in the country. The ruling JDP identified Turkey's declining birth rates as a 'demographic crisis' in the early 2000s, even framing the use of birth control as national treason. The assumed urgency to solve this 'crisis' has eventually prompted various discursive, medical and legislative state interventions such as urging heterosexual Turkish women to have at least three children, as well as formal and informal restrictions on abortion, contraception and caesarean sections.

By the 2000s, the World Health Organization had also started to present the high rates of maternal and infant mortality in Turkey as a concern in its annual reports. These reports suggested that the state should allocate more financial and human resources to strengthening its maternal and infant care at the primary level (World Health Organization 2003, 2005; World Bank 2004; Akam 2010). Meanwhile, the European Commission identified Turkey's (reproductive) healthcare system as a site of needed intervention to modernize the country in line with 'European standards' (European Commission 2000, 2004). As a result, many healthcare reforms that took effect during the 2000s in Turkey targeted reproductive healthcare services, resulting in massive restructuring, standardization and computerization. As an outcome of this national-global interplay, over the last decade data-driven health surveillance mechanisms increasingly intent on monitoring reproduction rapidly went from novelty to routine.

In 2008, the Public Health Directorate of Istanbul launched a specific program: the Pregnancy, Newborn, and Postpartum Monitoring System, popularly known as *GEBLIZ* (*Gebe, Bebek, Lohusa İzlem Sistemi*). In the conventional sense, *GEBLIZ* is not a (new) reproductive technology actively used in human reproduction or monitoring the body, but a specific technology of knowledge that draws on information technology to keep regular health records on targeted populations. The project's primary goal is to collect, store and analyse numerical data on maternal and infant health in an electronic environment and to find ways to understand the mortality patterns. *GEBLIZ* collects this information through digital infrastructure composed of a software system and a centralized database that connects primary (e.g. family health centres), secondary (e.g. public and private hospitals) and tertiary (e.g. university hospitals) healthcare settings to each other. This integrated system compiles women's and newborns' health information in the form of digital data via electronic health records across and among these different medical institutions. The collected information includes, among others, eating habits, blood pressure, weight, first and last period dates, contraceptive usage, history of abortion, miscarriage and birthing.

Since the project's centralized database is linked to other electronic health databases, *GEBLIZ* tracks sexual and reproductive health information not only of pregnant women and new mothers, but of all women of childbearing age. In other words, *GEBLIZ* can detect and extract any recorded data related to reproduction in the national health information database. In a computerized aspirant to the *panopticon* in the digital age (Foucault 1995), the system sees all changes in one's reproductive life from a centralized viewpoint. It then combines routine and automatic data collection with medical examinations conducted by a team of family physicians and nurses in family health centres and during routine home visits by the same care team. Pregnant women registered in the system are monitored at least four times during their pregnancy. They receive a follow-up home visit when they give birth. During the postnatal period, their newborns are monitored for vaccinations, and routine medical examinations continue until the children reach four years of age.

The information collected and monitored under *GEBLIZ* is similar to the previous, paper-based version of reproductive health monitoring at health centres. What is different in the new version, however, is that monitoring practices are now digitized and tied to a performance management system. Under this new system, the Turkish Ministry of Health regularly audits family health centres' records and adjusts the healthcare practitioners' monthly salaries based on their work performance. The monthly salaries depend on the number and type of registered patients, the socio-economic development of the neighbourhood in which practitioners work, as well as preventive care practices that practitioners perform. Prenatal follow-ups for pregnant women, postnatal follow-ups for infants and children under five, and target vaccinations for children receive the highest performance points, hence the highest subsidiary salaries. If practitioners fail to conduct and report these prenatal and postnatal follow-ups, they receive salary deductions (World Bank 2013).

GEBLIZ: A controversial pregnancy monitoring program

In the summer of 2012, family health centres appeared in the news again, this time because of *GEBLIZ*. On the morning of 25 June, people woke up to the following newspaper headlines: 'Terrifying text message from the Ministry of Health to the father of the unmarried young woman: "Congratulations! Your daughter is pregnant"' ('Shocking message from the family physician' 2012; 'Congratulations' 2013). According to the sensationalist news stories, the Turkish Ministry of Health had recently adopted a controversial new policy across the country. It had started to collect the results of all pregnancy tests conducted in public and private medical institutions, to archive these in a nationwide, centralized database, and to send the test results to health centres. Thereafter, the health centres' responsibility was to inform women and their families if the results were positive and then to closely monitor pregnancies. In one such instance, a young, unmarried woman took a pregnancy test at a private medical centre. Her family physician at the health centre then accessed the information through the centralized database and sent a text message to the phone number registered in the system. The number, however, belonged to the woman's father, rather than the woman herself. When the father learned of his unwed daughter's pregnancy, he became furious and attempted to stab her. Although he was not able to harm the woman, he kicked her out of the house.

The incident coverage in the newspapers had as many internal contradictions as the reported new policy itself; yet, it paved the way for a highly polarized public debate in Turkey. *Habertürk*, a widely circulated Turkish newspaper, ran the story on the front page, alongside another, separate news item depicting the photo of a mufti, an Islamic scholar and official of the Religious Affairs Department, with his distinctive outfit composed of a white gown and turban. With this deliberately curated front-page placement and aesthetic, the pointed connection between the new policy of reproductive monitoring and pro-Islamic roots of the JDP government was salient, if not explicitly put into words. From a quick reading of the headline 'Congratulations! Your daughter is pregnant', one would think that the ministry had adopted the new policy not only to police, but also to punish unwed young women's sexuality, by informing their families of their pregnancies. Ali Tezel, a columnist and social security expert, who was the first to report the incident, described the policy as a human rights violation that could easily endanger women's security (Tezel 2012).

A closer reading of his column as it continued beyond the front page, however, revealed that notifying third parties without the knowledge or consent of women was not an intentional part of the policy, but the outcome of medical malpractice. The physician had texted the phone number registered in the system without knowing that the number belonged to the father instead of the woman herself. As Tezel argued, neighbourhood-based, state-run health centres had long been responsible for monitoring maternal and infant health, and now family physicians were doing the same. According to the healthcare legislation, he continued, family physicians were responsible for reproductive health monitoring to make sure that populations registered to themselves are healthy and receiving proper care. The aim was good, but the method was not, so he claimed (Tezel 2012). What he did not say was that the possible difference in the motivation to monitor pregnancies could be a fear of receiving salary deductions under the new performance management system imposed on Family Health Center staff, if they failed to report on pre- and postnatal follow ups.

Nevertheless, the media coverage and discussion of the new policy quickly escalated, and the issue of archiving women's information in a centralized state database and informing third parties without consent drew widespread public attention in the summer of 2012. This was how the highly controversial reproductive health surveillance program *GEBLIZ* entered the consciousness and agenda of many citizens. When *GEBLIZ* hit the national news, the government officials from the Turkish Ministry of Health denied that there existed a policy of notifying third parties without the women's consent. They defended the project for its success in decreasing Istanbul's high rates of maternal and infant mortality, in line with the United Nations (UN) Millennium Development Goals (MDGs). According to the officials, *GEBLIZ* was a successful materialization of the European Union membership requirements as well. It took Turkey's medical institutions above the level of modern European health services in terms of guaranteeing equal planning and distribution of healthcare services (Kartal et al. 2010).

Techno-medical fixes to social problems: The bureaucrats' perspective

The summer 2012 headlines were not the first time that *GEBLIZ* had appeared in the Turkish media, however. As attentive audiences would have noticed, *GEBLIZ* had already been in the news five months before the sensationalist media coverage about text messages being sent to fathers. In December 2011, viewers of the national public broadcaster *TRT* (Turkish Radio and Television Corporation) were presented with a mini-documentary about, in the channel's own words, 'a group of dedicated bureaucrats who decreased the high rates of infant mortality in the country with an innovative public health monitoring project' (Aksoy 2011). The documentary was broadcast as part of the program *Güzel Ülke* (Beautiful Country), whose slogan was: 'Beautiful things are happening in this country; you just need to turn and look in that direction.' The twenty-second episode of the program was dedicated to *GEBLIZ* and the persons behind its development and introduction to the healthcare system. Following the enacted journey of a team of five real-life, male bureaucrats, physicians and software engineers, the documentary revealed the behind-the-scenes of *GEBLIZ*, from the project's planning on paper to its implementation on the streets and in homes.

According to the documentary, the *GEBLIZ* team had initiated the project with the question of how to decrease the high rates of infant mortality in a crowded metropolis like Istanbul, where reaching out to pregnant women and new mothers has always been a problem, especially in working-class neighbourhoods with low formal education levels. Aziz Gürhan Birler, who at that time served as the Information Systems Branch Manager at the Istanbul Health Directorate, was the first to come up with the idea of a technological infrastructure composed of a software system and an electronic database to monitor the reproductive health of city residents. The documentary enacted the project development process with real-life actors in dark grey, ironed suits, all sitting around a round table with dozens of files and documents in front of them. The camera sometimes zoomed in on these actors, presenting short interviews with each. Birler, the leader of the group, talked straight into the camera:

> We can understand the development level of a country by looking at many different factors. If we would like to see its development level in the health area, one of the first things that we need to look at is maternal and infant mortality rates. We haven't reached our desired [development] level yet when we look at Turkey from this angle. We are the 77th country in the world in terms of the under-five mortality rate. These rates befit neither us nor our country. (Aksoy 2011)

Then came a male voice-over accompanied by scenes from crowded streets: 'This is Istanbul. In this megacity, there live millions of people. Every day, thousands of babies are born here. Thousands of babies mean thousands of happy families. However, in some homes, this happiness does not last long. Some lose this race from the beginning' (Aksoy 2011).

The voice-over argued that infant deaths were tragic, not only for families, but also for the nation as a whole. The camera once again turned to Birler, who argued that they knew the reasons behind these deaths, as well as what to do to prevent them from happening. The viewers were not presented with an explicit discussion of these reasons, however. What the healthcare bureaucrats could not do, Birler continued, was to reach out to women who did not use the state's medical institutions during their pregnancies and thus could not be detected by the national health system. The solution, then, would be to develop a technological infrastructure such as *GEBLIZ*, in order to electronically track and monitor each and every expecting woman in the city. This was not enough either, he continued, as these digital surveillance mechanisms should be combined with medical examinations and in-person home visits conducted by family physicians working in health centres that had direct access to city residents.

Only with such routine and integrated monitoring practices, so Birler argued, could they lower the maternal and infant mortality statistics according to the world standards. He mentioned that the infant mortality rate had totalled 28.5 per 1,000 live births in 2003, and that it had dropped to 10.9 in 2010 after the introduction of *GEBLIZ*. This rapid decrease, according to Birler, surprised even the officials from the World Health Organization. The WHO officials initially did not believe the statistics presented by the Istanbul Health Directory and ran their own statistical analysis. When they found the numbers accurate, they praised the project and the people behind it.[2] Then the bureaucrats presented the results to the Ministry of Health. The ministry was also pleased with the results and required from the team to expand the project to other parts of Turkey as well (Aksoy 2011; 'The project that impressed the health organization' 2011).

In these narrations, maternal and infant mortality are framed as social problems into which one needs to intervene with techno-medical solutions for the greater good and development of the nation. Pregnancy, in particular, becomes an object of constant monitoring, investigation and intervention. Both in the documentary and in their later writings, the bureaucrats described *GEBLIZ* as an innovative public health project that would help to better plan and distribute prenatal and postnatal care, to protect mothers and their newborns, and to improve the health and well-being of future generations. Yet, what we encounter in the documentary is a dramatization of the high rates of infant deaths in Turkey without any discussion about the reasons behind these high rates. The bureaucrats describe the primary target of the project as urban poor women, whom they see as illiterate and lacking proper knowledge about how to care for their bodies and their children. As such, they deflect the blame away from the deepening poverty in Turkey's urban centres, or the increasingly stratified healthcare services. *GEBLIZ*, then, is presented as a techno-medical intervention that would solve these issues through standardized, data-driven healthcare delivery. It would also fulfil the modernization requirements of transnational organizations and take Turkey above the European or world criteria in technological innovation in an increasingly globalizing healthcare market.

Changes in labour and care at the health centres:
The nurses' perspective

While the Turkish Ministry of Health defends *GEBLIZ* in neoliberal terms of efficiency and accountability, the everyday implications of the program are much more complicated. Similar to earlier periods in Turkey and the broader Middle East, the success of the newly adopted surveillance and data collection mechanisms often depends on reproductive healthcare workers, especially nurses, whose gendered labour and intimate relationships with their communities are essential for the operation of these mechanisms (Balsoy 2015; Shatz 2018).

While sipping from our glasses of black tea in the kitchen adjacent to the nurses' rooms during lunch break, the nurses in both the Kadıköy and Sultanbeyli health centres often complained about the dramatic changes in their work routines and in their interactions with the neighbourhood women due to the introduction of *GEBLIZ*. Zeliha, the eldest and most experienced nurse of the Kadıköy health centre, nostalgically remembering the old *sağlık ocağı* system, once explained that the assessment and monitoring of pregnancies had always been a common, central practice at the health centres:

> In the past, we would have closer relationships with neighborhood women, though. We would know all of them by their names and even the names of their children and the apartment numbers where they lived. Women would visit us regularly, and when they didn't show up for a long time, we would go and knock on their doors. We would assess and monitor their health through medical examinations, but also provide advice on diverse matters such as nutrition, breastfeeding, exercise, or sexual life, and contraceptive use after pregnancy.

What is different in the new system with *GEBLIZ*, however, is a proactive, standardized understanding of care, accomplished through collecting data points in computer-based information systems rather than detailed patient narratives. Healthcare providers now have to identify and register each and every pregnant woman in their neighbourhoods, regularly gather their health information and record the numerical data on paper as well as in the online database.

Due to hierarchies and the highly gendered division of labour among providers, it is the nurses, and not the physicians, who now performs all this labour undergirding the information technology. As part of the performance management system introduced with the new healthcare reforms, all healthcare providers receive subsidiary salaries for every pregnant woman whom they monitor at the health centres. It is also crucial to note that these subsidiary salaries are *only* for monitoring pregnancies, but not for other reproductive healthcare services, such as providing family planning or contraceptives. This practice in and of itself points to the pronatalist concerns behind such regulations. The Ministry of Health implements audit mechanisms to regularly inspect the centres' health records and compare them with those in hospitals' databases. During these inspections, as nurses explain, the ministry officials cut a certain amount from the salaries of both family physicians and nurses, if the centre misses registering a pregnant woman in the neighbourhood into *GEBLIZ* or does not collect and enter all the required information into the database. The nurses among themselves call this practice 'negative performance' system.

In our conversations, the nurses frequently mentioned that keeping up with all the required data collection of *GEBLIZ* is difficult and sometimes impossible, considering the large population of the urban city. Yet, these subsidiary salaries received for pregnancy monitoring cannot even cover the salary deductions resulting from 'failures' in collecting information, especially in low-income neighbourhoods such as Sultanbeyli, where birth rates are higher than in many other places. The nurses are affected by these salary deductions much more than family physicians, as their salaries are already lower when compared to physician salaries. Nurses said that, as a result of the performance management system, they became primarily concerned with detecting as many pregnant women as possible in their neighbourhoods and recording them into the system. Hence, they perceive the work required by *GEBLIZ* as an obligation and burden, rather than a crucial and vital part of their care practice. What the nurses termed 'negative performance' system is a clear example of what Chris Shore and Susan Wright call 'coercive accountability' measures in their work on the rise of 'audit cultures' (Shore and Wright 2015). As they argue, audit mechanisms produce a 'rapid and relentless spread of coercive technologies of accountability' (Shore and Wright 2000: 57). As a result, they reshape workers' conditions of labour, how they identify themselves and their work, and the accompanying subjectivities.

These new shifts in labour routines and interactions also create a certain amount of routinization and bureaucratization of care at the health centres. If a pregnant woman does not want to be registered and monitored through *GEBLIZ*, the nurses then have to fill in more paperwork and send a petition to the City Health Department to avoid salary deductions. As a result, the program creates burdensome paperwork routines for nurses, increases their workload and bureaucratizes the care practice cutting across both middle-class and low-income neighbourhoods. To keep up with all the required documentation, the nurses are now spending an enormous amount of time on collecting, transcribing and inputting information and filling in paperwork or petitions. Such a process of bureaucratization is another outcome that Shore and Wright describe as typical of many audit practices. As Vania Smith-Oka (2013) argues in her research on the public hospitals of Mexico, the bureaucratization of care does not solely or inherently come from the excessive amount of paperwork, nor the information technology *per se*. Rather, the bureaucratization happens since the nurses' everyday practices become increasingly routinized but also detached from pregnant women's needs, concerns and priorities (Smith-Oka 2013).

Due to this bureaucratization, as well as the obsession with collecting big data information, neighbourhood women's narratives and bodies in the end become numerical abstractions. One of the most consistent mental pictures from my fieldwork at the health centres features the nurses' spending hours and hours in front of computers or on phones. Subsequently, the nurses find themselves performing their assessment and monitoring tasks through computers or incessant calls to women's homes rather than through face-to-face communications or regular home visits, where conversations can be more wide-ranging and address issues that are not standardized data points. During these phone calls, the nurses ask short and direct questions to get instant information, rather than, for instance, inviting pregnant women and new mothers to the health centres. The priority is not given to having women-centred, in-person relationships, or to understanding home environments or family conditions. The priority is collecting and recording as much of the required 'health data' as possible before each inspection period. This is a striking contrast of *GEBLIZ* in action, when compared to the project description on paper, where the ministry officials argue that '"home visits" which had been neglected [before] were started actively by primary healthcare personnel, and preventive health service who stayed in the shadow of therapeutic health services came to life again' (Kartal et al. 2010: 289). The nurses, however, argue that over the past ten years there has been a steady decline in home visits by health centre staff. Standardized instruments such as *GEBLIZ* rely on what Sally Merry defines as 'simplified numerical representations of complex phenomena' (Merry 2011: 83). They reduce women's health experiences to a series of numerical abstractions and make nurses committed to digitalized forms of monitoring, even at the expense of providing the care that patients need or seek to receive.

All these changes in terms of a late capitalist logic of arranging labour (i.e. performance-management systems, audit mechanisms and bureaucratization) create very fragile, precarious[3] conditions for the nurses. By making healthcare workers implement information technologies through financial incentives and coercions, *GEBLIZ* has ended up producing systemic disempowerment and alienation in multiple and gendered ways. During a yet again busy day at the Sultanbeyli health centre, Nurse Hatice, one of the newest and most dedicated members of the centre, raised her head from the computer and approached the ringing phone on the table. Right before picking up the phone, she turned to me and said in an exhausted tone: 'See, we have turned into call-center workers here.' Working in a call-centre would require long hours of labour and repetitive searching, tracing, compiling or sitting and talking to people through technology without much job security. This analogy and many similar nurse narratives painfully capture the precarity of their labour at the health centres and the alienation they experience regarding their care practice.

To be monitored or not to be monitored: The patients' perspective

During my fieldwork, I observed that women's responses to being monitored differed vastly, based on their class and neighbourhoods. While women in the middle-class neighbourhood Kadıköy often perceived *GEBLIZ* as a suspicious surveillance mechanism and did not want to be monitored, women in the working-class district Sultanbeyli saw reproductive health surveillances as an act of care. Ayla, a woman in her late thirties, was an example of the former. She stormed into the Kadıköy health centre one day and headed to the nurses' room to talk to Nurse Nesrin, who had been calling her for a couple of weeks. 'How does my information enter your system, even though I did not provide it myself or never visited you?' Ayla asked. She added: 'You are calling my landline. I first thought it was a hoax.' Then she started to enquire about how her information could appear in the system, how practitioners could access that information, whether anyone else could access it and what other kinds of data were easily accessible and to whom without her knowledge. Nesrin explained that the information was not shared with any other non-medical constituencies, emphasizing that the reason behind the information collection was for statistical purposes.

Thanks to Nesrin's explanation, Ayla calmed down and said that she and her husband had been receiving in-vitro fertilization (IVF) treatments at a private hospital for more than a year, but that only the last one had resulted in conception. When the treatment was successful, the hospital entered the pregnancy information into the system, and thus it appeared in the *GEBLIZ* database. Since then, Nesrin had been trying to reach the woman to collect further information. Yet, what the database did not include was the fact that the successful IVF conception had later ended in a miscarriage, leaving the grieving Ayla profoundly angry at Nesrin's repeated phone calls. The last thing she wanted was to disclose her struggle to someone whom she had never met before, much less on the phone. For her, being called for pregnancy monitoring was a painful reminder of her miscarriage, which she wanted to leave behind as she was getting ready for the next treatment cycle.

Ayla's story reveals that the ability to keep their personal information confidential is indeed a significant concern for women using the health centres, especially when they are going through 'reproductive disruptions' (Inhorn 2008) such as infertility, miscarriage or abortion. At the same time, women's responses are not static but ever-changing, as their relationship with their environment, bodies and care providers evolves. Sometimes nurses joke about these changes, arguing that women become more mellow, especially after childbirth. 'When we tell them that we are doing this for the health of their babies,' say nurses, 'they stop complaining and start to call us or come to the health centre themselves. Motherhood softens them.'

Some women, however, never question reproductive health surveillance. Nurses in Kadıköy often compare their interactions with the neighbourhood's highly affluent women with their interactions in villages or urban poor neighbourhoods where they worked in the past, arguing that the latter never create problems over being monitored. Confirming the nurses' arguments, I rarely observed women getting into conflicts with their care providers in Sultanbeyli. In most of the cases, it was the woman herself who came to the centre to register her pregnancy. One day, as I was sitting next to Nurse Hatice in the Sultanbeyli health centre, Nazire, a woman in her mid-twenties, rushed into the room and started shaking her finger at the nurse. 'Why didn't you phone me last week?' she asked half-jokingly. 'I was expecting a call from you; you were supposed to invite me to the center for the monitoring. What if I were to forget my visit?' Hatice smiled: 'You are here, aren't you? I knew you would not forget.' She replied, 'How can I call each and every one of my patients? I do not even have time to catch my breath.' Nazire continued as if she had not heard the nurse: 'My upstairs neighbor says her nurse calls her all the time, and she is not even as pregnant as I am.'

That day, Nazire had come for her last pregnancy monitoring. She was a mother of two small children, aged 2 and 5, and she was expecting her third. After the nurse weighed her on the small scale in the corner of the room, Nazire said that she had gained some extra weight over the last couple of weeks and asked whether that was normal. The nurse said that everything was normal while noting the weight on a little yellow Post-it. Her computer had been broken for a couple of months, leaving her to write everything on little Post-its first. She was then entering the information into the *GEBLIZ* database from her family physician's computer, after the physician had left for home in the evening.

Glancing at all the Post-its randomly stuck on the nurse's desk, Nazire asked the nurse why her doctor had not yet fixed her computer. 'Do not lose mine,' she said, referring to the paper with her weight written on. 'I do not want to come again.' The nurse assured her that she would transfer all the information to a computer later. She then took out her Doppler ultrasound from the tiny drawer below her desk, headed to the door, locked it and asked Nazire to lay down on the dark grey exam table so that she could listen to the baby's heartbeat. Nazire asked if it was okay to record the heartbeat with her phone, since she wanted to make her husband listen to the sound as well. Hatice smiled and said that this would be okay. A tenuous pulsating sound filled the room as she moved the Doppler back and forth over Nazire's belly, while Nazire was now recording the sound with her phone.

Unlike the middle-class women in Kadıköy who prefer to go to private hospitals for pre- and postnatal care, women living at the margins of the city, such as in Sultanbeyli, come to these health centres every day with different stories, questions and demands to receive health services. Since their establishment in Turkey in the early 1960s, these state-run, publicly funded centres have been the main providers of primary care, where people can show up and receive free and accessible health services. Every day, many women arrive at the centres to get pregnancy tests or birth control pills, vaccinations or condoms, consultations or advice, and material and emotional support. In their struggle to care for their families, women also come to these centres to receive information on certain welfare services such as maternity or breastfeeding benefits, from their nurses or each other.

For pregnant women and new mothers in Sultanbeyli, *GEBLIZ* is a central part of their experience, even though they do not know or have never heard the name of the program. During our conversations, I always asked them how they felt about receiving phone calls from their nurses, coming to the health centre for routine monitoring, sharing their intimate details and having a record of their information in the centre's database. I sometimes recounted the earlier newspaper articles in 2012, where family health centres shared women's pregnancy information with third parties without consent. After my questions, they often stared at me and did not completely understand what I was trying to get at. I asked the same questions to women outside the centre, with whom I had no prior connections through the centre. Again, I received similar stares and responses. 'I am happy that my nurse calls me. It is like knowing somebody is taking care of you,' said some of them. 'I want them to know about my pregnancy. Here we get the service right next to our homes. I do not want to go to a hospital and spend my entire day going there and then coming back home,' said others.

These narratives reveal that, in contrast to affluent women, women in disenfranchised neighbourhoods do not perceive the state's reproductive health surveillance simply as a surveillance mechanism that functions to control and discipline. Instead, they recognize it as a form and space of care, where their stories of poverty, violence and affliction will be listened to, recorded and hopefully acted upon. What accounts for their willingness to be monitored by *GEBLIZ*, I argue, is *not* that they are grateful that the state is doing something it needs to be doing anyway, or that they trust the state more. (They would have little trust, mainly because some of these women carry transgenerational memories of state violence as they move to Istanbul after being forcibly displaced from Kurdish cities.) They are *not* looking to escape from the state's medical gaze, but they intentionally use it to generate new strategies to negotiate their everyday conditions. Their willingness does *not* come from a place of voluntary submission but constitutes a strategic agency that claims fair and just redistribution of public resources.

Conclusion

There is a widespread tendency to exceptionalize, focus on only national dynamics and discourses, or use 'religion' as the main analytical category to explain social and political changes in Muslim-majority countries such as Turkey. While local processes are one part of the picture, they might not be the only or the most crucial factor for understanding the dynamics of gender, reproduction and health. *GEBLIZ*, as a particular mechanism of 'reproductive governance' (Morgan and Roberts 2012), provides a compelling case study to debunk restrictive, yet dominant, narratives of non-Western contexts that mischaracterize the sexual and reproductive regimes that are currently at play.

In this chapter, I have situated the rise and circulation of reproductive health surveillance in a different temporal and relational order. First, I argued that this surveillance is not a new practice, but that it builds on a long history of monitoring of populations through neighbourhood-based, state-run health centres. Second, I argued that it also derives from the peculiarities of the 2000s, where we see a complex convergence between national politics of reproduction and transnational (health) governance. The JDP government's demographic concerns over declining birth rates and transnational organizations' requirements to standardize and modernize health services have intertwined and paved the way to controversial health surveillance mechanisms, where maternal and infant mortality rates are presented as social problems that require intervention with techno-medical solutions.

Rather than providing real-life solutions, the emergent surveillance mechanisms seem to further complicate the already existing concerns in the healthcare sector, by generating new types of labour conditions, care practices and social encounters between practitioners and their patients, sometimes putting them at odds with each other. They also produce particularly fraught discourses around women's bodies and reproduction, which often depoliticize engrained social problems – such as problems in access to health services or increasing poverty in urban centres. These discourses, in return, cast techno-medical interventions such as *GEBLIZ* as the ultimate solution to social problems and depict women, and particularly urban poor mothers, as needing routine and intensive state-imposed reproductive monitoring. These women, however, do not see reproductive health surveillance as a suspicious mechanism, as do their more affluent counterparts; rather, they use it strategically to access public resources.

Notes

1   In Kadıköy, there are thirty-six family health centres in total, all dispersed in different parts of the district. In Sultanbeyli, there are twenty-one centres in total. Apart from these centres, there exist also two migrant health clinics in Sultanbeyli, which employ Arabic-speaking staff and provide free public health services. Although Syrian refugees occasionally visit the Sultanbeyli health centre, there are always language barriers between the visitors and practitioners, which restrict their communication and access to health services.

2   It is interesting to note that the World Health Organization's official reports draw a picture different from Birler's statements in terms of infant mortality rates. According to the World Heath Statistics published by the WHO in 2015, the infant mortality rate was 33.7 per 1,000 live births in 2000 and dropped to 16.5 in 2013 (World Health Organization 2015). These numbers are much higher than the numbers presented by Birler in the documentary.

3   The term *precarity* refers to work or well-being conditions that lack security, predictability and welfare as a result of emerging neoliberal capitalist policies (Harvey 2007; Federici 2012).

Bibliography

Ağartan, T. (2012), 'Gender and Health Sector Reform: Policies, Actions and Effects', in S. Dedeoğlu and A. Y. Elveren (eds), *Gender and Society in Turkey: The Impact of Neo-Liberal Policies, Political Islam and EU Accession*, 155–72, New York: I.B. Tauris.

Akam, S. (2010), 'The Turkish Child Mortality Puzzle', *The Guardian*, 14 June. Available online: http://www.theguardian.com/journalismcompetition/the-turkish-child-mortality-puzzle (accessed 27 February 2018).

Aksoy, M. A. (2011), *Güzel Ülke: GEBLİZ (Beautiful Country: GEBLIZ)*, [TV Series Documentary] TRT. Available online: https://www.youtube.com/watch?v=ZDmIBRJbL90&t=1150s (accessed 21 March 2019).

Babül, E. M. (2017), *Bureaucratic Intimacies: Translating Human Rights in Turkey*, Stanford: Stanford University Press.

Balsoy, G. (2015), *The Politics of Reproduction in Ottoman Society, 1838–1900*, London: Routledge.

'Beggars, salespeople and family physicians are not allowed (Dilenci, Satıcı ve Aile Hekimi Giremez)' (2011), *Radikal*, 3 November. Available online: http://www.radikal.com.tr/turkiye/dilenci-satici-ve-aile-hekimi-giremez-1068434/ (accessed 1 October 2018).

'Congratulations, your daughter is pregnant (Tebrikler, kızınız hamile)' (2013), *Hürriyet Kelebek*, 20 June. Available online: http://www.hurriyet.com.tr/kelebek/saglik/tebrikler-kiziniz-hamile-23547603 (accessed 13 March 2018).

Coşar, S. and M. Yeğenoğlu (2012), 'The AKP and the Gender Issue: Shuttling Between Neoliberalism and Patriarchy', in S. Coşar and G. Yücesan-Özdemir (eds), *Silent*

Violence of Neoliberalism and Islamist Politics: The AKP Years in Turkey, 179–205, Ottawa: Red Quill Books.

Dal, Ü. and Y. Kitiş (2008), 'The Historical Development and Current Status of Nursing in Turkey', *OJIN: The Online Journal of Issues in Nursing*, 13 (2).

Dayı, A. (2019), 'Neoliberal Health Restructuring, Neoconservatism and the Limits of Law', *Health and Human Rights*, 21 (2): 57–68.

Demirci-Yılmaz, T. (2015), 'Osmanlı ve Erken Cumhuriyet Dönemi Türkiye Modernleşmesinde Annelik Kurguları (1840-1950) (Motherhood Constructions in Ottoman and Early Republican Turkish Modernization [1840-1950])', *Cogito*, 81: 66–90.

Dole, C. (2004), 'In the Shadows of Medicine and Modernity: Medical Integration and Secular Histories of Religious Healing in Turkey', *Culture, Medicine and Psychiatry*, 28 (3): 255–80.

Dole, C. (2012), *Healing Secular Life: Loss and Devotion in Modern Turkey*, Philadelphia: University of Pennsylvania Press.

'Erdoğan: "İnce, would I give you the time of my day?" (Erdoğan: "İnce, ben seni muhattap alır mıyım?")' (2018), *İznews*, 17 June. Available online: https://www.iznewsagency.com/erdogan-ince-ben-seni-muhattap-alirmiyim/ (accessed 1 October 2018).

European Commission (2000), *Turkey 2010 Progress Report*, Brussels: European Union.

European Commission (2004), *Issues Arising from Turkey's Membership Perspective*, Brussels: European Union.

Federici, S. (2012), *Revolution at Point Zero: Housework, Reproduction, and Feminist Struggle*, Oakland: PM Press.

Foucault, M. (1995), *Discipline and Punish: The Birth of the Prison*, trans. A. Sheridan, New York: Vintage Books.

Gürsoy, Y., K Sümbüloğlu and N. Eren (1982), 'Ocak Kayıtları (Clinic Records)', in N. Eren and Z. Öztek (eds), *Sağlık Ocağı Yönetimi (Health Clinic Governance)*, 167–207, Ankara: Hacettepe Üniversitesi Toplum Hekimliği Enstitüsü.

Harvey, D. (2007), *A Brief History of Neoliberalism*, New York: Oxford University Press.

Inhorn, M. C., ed. (2008), *Reproductive Disruptions: Gender, Technology, and Biopolitics in the New Millennium*, New York: Berghahn Books.

Kartal, S. B., A. G. Birler, D. Özkul, S. Ünlüer, S. Gürleyük, A. Yamak, Y. Öztürk and A. B. Topuzoğlu (2010), 'The Improvement of Prenatal, Postnatal, Newborn and Preschool Child's Health Care Services in Istanbul: GEBLIZ', *TAF Preventive Medicine Bulletin*, 9 (4): 289–96.

Korkman, Z. K. (2015), 'Blessing Neoliberalism: Economy, Family, and the Occult in Millennial Turkey' *Journal of the Ottoman and Turkish Studies Association*, 2 (2): 335–57.

Lampland, M. and S. L. Star (2009), *Standards and Their Stories: How Quantifying, Classifying, and Formalizing Practices Shape Everyday Life*, Ithaca: Cornell University Press.

Li, T. (2007), *The Will to Improve: Governmentality, Development, and the Practice of Politics*, Durham: Duke University Press.

Merry, S. E. (2011), 'Measuring the World: Indicators, Human Rights, and Global Governance', *Current Anthropology*, 52 (S3): 83–95.

Miller, R. A. (2007), 'Rights, Reproduction, Sexuality, and Citizenship in the Ottoman Empire and Turkey', *Signs: Journal of Women in Culture and Society*, 32 (2): 347–73.

Morgan, L. M. and E. F. S. Roberts (2012), 'Reproductive Governance in Latin America', *Anthropology & Medicine*, 19 (2): 241–54.

Mutlu, B., N. Şen, N. Erten, N. Polat, S. Saluk and Ş. Kılıçtepe (2018), 'Cinsellik, Üreme/Doğurganlık, ve Sağlık Politikaları Üzerine Sohbet (Conversations on the Politics of Sexuality, Reproduction, and Health)', *Kültür ve Siyasette Feminist Yaklaşımlar*, 33–4: 123–54.

Ong, A. (2006), *Neoliberalism as Exception: Mutations in Citizenship and Sovereignty*, Durham: Duke University Press.

Özbay, C., M. Erol, Z. Umut and A. Terzioğlu, eds (2016), *The Making of Neoliberal Turkey*, London and New York: Routledge.

'President Erdoğan: "I am proud of being a black Turk" (Cumhurbaşkanı Erdoğan: "Zenci bir Türk olmaktan şeref duyuyorum")' (2015), *Sabah*, 25 June. Available online: https://www.sabah.com.tr/webtv/turkiye/cumhurbaskani-erdogan-zenci-bir-turk-olmaktan-seref-duyuyorum (accessed 1 October 2018).

Rivkin-Fish, M. (2005), *Women's Health in Post-Soviet Russia: The Politics of Intervention*, Bloomington: Indiana University Press.

Saluk, S. (2014), 'Üreme Politikaları Üzerine Bazı Notlar: Sağlıkta Dönüşüm Programı, Aile Hekimliği ve Gebliz Sistemi (Reflections on Turkey's Reproductive Politics: Health Transformation Program, Family Medicine, and the GEBLIZ System)', *Kültür ve Siyasette Feminist Yaklaşımlar*, 24: 23–38.

Shakhsari, S. (2014), 'The Queer Time of Death: Temporality, Geopolitics, and Refugee Rights', *Sexualities*, 17 (8): 998–1015.

Shatz, J. R. (2018), 'A Politics of Care: Local Nurses in Mandate Palestine', *International Journal of Middle East Studies*, 50: 669–89.

'Shocking message from the family physician to the single woman's father: Congratulations, your daughter is pregnant (Aile hekiminden bekar genç kız babasına şok cep mesajı: Tebrikler kızınız hamile)' (2012), *Hürriyet*, 25 June. Available online: http://www.hurriyet.com.tr/gundem/aile-hekiminden-bekar-genc-kiz-babasina-sok-cep-mesaji-tebrikler-kiziniz-hamile-20837705 (accessed 13 March 2018).

Shore, C. and S. Wright (2000), 'Coercive Accountability: The Rise of Audit Culture in Higher Education', in M. Strathern (ed.), *Audit Cultures: Anthropological Studies in Accountability, Ethics, and the Academy*, 57–89, London: Routledge.

Shore, C. and S. Wright (2015), 'Governing by Numbers: Audit Culture, Rankings and the New World Order', *Social Anthropology*, 23 (1): 22–8.

Smith-Oka, V. (2013), 'Managing Labor and Delivery among Impoverished Populations in Mexico: Cervical Examinations as Bureaucratic Practice', *American Anthropologist*, 115 (4): 595–607.

Tezel, A. (2012), 'Gebelik testi sonucu eş ve babaya mesajlanıyor (Pregnancy test results are reported to husbands and fathers)', *Habertürk*, 25 June. Available online: https://www.haberturk.com/yazarlar/ali-tezel-1016/753574-gebelik-testi-sonucu-es-ve-babaya-mesajlaniyor (accessed 16 July 2018).

'The project that impressed the health organization (Sağlık örgütünü hayran bırakan proje)' (2011), *Zaman*, 11 July. Available online: http://m2.samanyoluhaber.com/saglik-orgutunu-hayran-birakan-proje-haberi-714128.html (accessed 13 March 2018).

White, J. (2014), *Muslim Nationalism and the New Turks*, Princeton: Princeton University Press.

World Bank (2004), '*Millennium Development Goals for Health in Europe and Central Asia: Relevance and Policy Implications*', 33, Washington, DC: World Bank.

World Bank (2013), *Turkey Performance-Based Contracting Scheme in Family Medicine: Design and Achievements*, Washington, DC: World Bank.

World Health Organization (2003), *Maternal Mortality in 2000: Estimates Developed by WHO, UNICEF and UNFPA*, Geneva: World Health Organization.

World Health Organization (2005), *Highlights on Health in Turkey*, Geneva: World Health Organization.

World Health Organization (2015), '*World Health Statistics 2015*', Geneva: World Health Organization.

Yılmaz, V. and İ. Göçmen (2016), 'Denied Citizens of Turkey: Experiences of Discrimination Among LGBT Individuals in Employment, Housing and Health Care', *Gender, Work & Organization*, 23 (5): 470–88.

7

Egg-freezing narratives of women: Between medicalization and marketization

Azer Kılıç

Introduction

New reproductive technologies have the potential to bring about radical changes regarding women's bodies and reproductive behaviours, as well as family and population structures. Once seeming like a natural phenomenon, reproduction is now a medical issue, subject to scientific scrutiny and intervention, while medical markets provide goods and services to satisfy emerging needs and desires. Egg-freezing technology – one of the latest reproductive technologies – medicalizes the postponement of motherhood and the age-related decline in fertility and enables the market to expand into the new domains of life.

This chapter examines the narratives of twenty-one women in Istanbul who either recently froze their eggs or were undergoing this process due to declining ovarian reserves and age-related fertility decline. I start by reviewing the literature on egg freezing vis-à-vis broader issues of medicalization and marketization. I then explain the study's methodological approach and describe the context in terms of local regulations and relevant social indicators. Subsequently, I focus on three major aspects of women's narratives of egg freezing from a socio-economic perspective. First, egg-freezing technology is represented in the mainstream Western media as an instrument enabling women to focus on their career endeavours by preserving fertility and postponing motherhood. However, our interviewees' narratives suggest that it is not future career goals but rather past experiences of work and education that influence women's decisions to freeze their eggs. Second, egg-freezing technology primarily attracts single women, and this target population underlines the moralized issue of virginity in Turkey, as egg-freezing methods are usually transvaginal. However, we

İstanbul Bilgi University. The author conducted the interviews underlying this chapter in collaboration with İpek Göçmen, whom she thanks. She also thanks Bülent Urman, Ayşen Boza, Zehra Özdinç, Büşra Kartal and Melek Güre Turan for their help with accessing egg-freezing women, as well as Simla Serim and İzem Aral for their help with interview transcription. The author also thanks Istanbul Bilgi University for its support.

see that virgin women who opt for egg freezing begin medicalizing and redefining virginity, as medical markets offer various remedies to alleviate women's concerns. Third, egg-freezing women employ ideas such as risk management and self-investment to explain their behaviours. With the individualization of risk and responsibility and the idea of human capital becoming particularly popular in the neoliberal era, egg freezing has plausibly become a site of neoliberal femininity. The chapter ends with a brief summary.

Egg freezing at the intersection of medicalization and marketization

One of the major manifestations of modernization has been the influence of medical sciences over society. Several factors, including scientific advances, secularization, rights struggles and governmental initiatives, have contributed to the rise of medicalization, leading to everyday life and human behaviour becoming increasingly subject to medical scrutiny. For instance, some behaviours that used to be considered sinful or criminal have begun to be defined as health matters. Once social problems become defined in terms of health, medical intervention begins to seem legitimate and necessary (Conrad 1992). As such, individuals are no longer responsible for the existence of a given problem but rather for taking the necessary action to solve it. For instance, rather than castigating individuals who become sick, we judge them irresponsible if they are sick but do not visit a doctor or do not comply with a prescribed treatment. Hence, medical science assumed the dual roles of imposing social control and protecting individuals against the other institutions of social control, such as religion and law, by medicalizing deviance (Zola 1972; Conrad 1992, 2008).

In this vein, human reproduction has also become a matter of medicalization: a physical condition subject to medical scrutiny, intervention and manipulation. Even before medicalization, reproduction was not completely seen as a 'natural' phenomenon. For people holding superstitious beliefs, successful experiences of reproduction are seen as a blessing, with those able to bear children interpreting this as a 'gift from God'; meanwhile, those unable to reproduce attribute this to 'fate', seeing it as a punishment by God, accepting personal responsibility or even blaming others for this unfortunate situation (Spar 2006). Religious beliefs may still influence individual efforts to understand and orient reproductive behaviour in contemporary societies (Conrad 1992; Czarnecki 2015; Göknar 2015; Inhorn et al. 2020); yet the influence of medical advances on reproductive behaviour seems all the more radical.

Medical advances regarding reproduction first manifested in improved understanding of the biology of reproduction and the discovery of hormones (Spar 2006). Next came the invention of *in vitro* fertilization (IVF) and assisted reproductive technologies (ARTs). Egg-freezing technology – or oocyte cryopreservation in medical terms – is one of the latest ARTs. This technology is based on procedures similar to IVF: ovaries are stimulated to produce eggs via hormone medication, and the produced eggs are retrieved in a clinical setting to be frozen unfertilized and stored for future use (Cil et al. 2015).

Egg-freezing technology has been developed as an alternative to embryo freezing and egg donation, both of which face resistance in countries such as Italy (Martin 2010). Yet other potential benefits came to be recognized: egg freezing seems a helpful measure for fertility preservation in situations where reproductive functions might be threatened by illness and medical treatment. Hence, cancer patients can be among those who freeze their eggs for medical reasons (Inhorn et al. 2017). Egg freezing also seems helpful for non-medical reasons, particularly age-related fertility decline. We see various terms in the literature for such uses: social egg freezing, egg freezing for lifestyle reasons and elective egg freezing (Savulescu and Goold 2008; Linkeviciute et al. 2015; Martinelli et al. 2015; Lewis et al. 2016; Baldwin 2018; Inhorn et al. 2018). Of importance here is that a woman does not need to be in a relationship to have her eggs frozen.

This second type of egg freezing – i.e. to resist age-related fertility decline – has been depicted in the mainstream Western media as a technological advance that empowers women. Egg freezing is particularly seen as a rational strategy for reconciling career and family goals (Myers 2014; van de Wiel 2014). Academic studies also highlight the benefits that egg freezing may offer women. These benefits usually centre around gaining time: instead of rushing into having a partner (whether straight or gay), getting married and bearing children, they can focus on educational and career goals, benefitting from some psychological relief vis-à-vis their biological clock (Harwood 2009; Stoop et al. 2011; Robertson 2014). Women who have decided to freeze their eggs confirm such expectations in interviews (Waldby 2015a; Myers 2017; Baldwin 2018; Brown and Patrick 2018; Göçmen and Kılıç 2018; Inhorn et al. 2018).

Some studies have been critical of egg freezing, citing the risks of medical procedures, such as hyperstimulation of the ovaries, psychological risks, such as false hopes, and other risks, such as the possibility of misinformation and exploitation by actors in medical markets (Mertes and Pennings 2012; Stoop et al. 2014; Lewis et al. 2016).

Criticisms have also been voiced from a feminist perspective. Some argue that egg freezing cannot be seen as simply a matter of choice based on free will, since women may need to postpone motherhood and freeze their eggs due to economic and institutional constraints. Meanwhile, ARTs such as egg freezing are financially beyond the means of many women in the absence of social insurance coverage (Cattapan et al. 2014). Other studies on fertility behaviour in general take a similar line: while women increasingly participate in the labour force in contemporary societies, they have also witnessed flexibilization in labour markets and retrenchment in some welfare state services. Such factors negatively influence women's reproductive behaviours (Streeck 2009; Esping-Andersen 2015). Against this background, we need to remember how egg freezing came to the public agenda in the United States: a few years ago, the mainstream media reported that companies such as Facebook and Apple were covering egg-freezing costs within the insurance package for female employees (Miller 2014). Hence, another concern is that women might feel pressure to freeze their eggs due to employer expectations and competition in working life (Robertson 2014).

Furthermore, the medicalization of age-related fertility decline via egg freezing establishes a new responsibility for women – the responsibility to preserve fertility – while not interfering with the underlying structures that negatively influence women's reproductive decisions (Cattapan et al. 2014). There is also the view that egg freezing reflects and reinforces some of the traditional social norms about family, motherhood and childbearing (Waldby 2015b). Research on egg freezing in countries such as Turkey and Israel supports this view (Kılıç and Göçmen 2018; Rimon-Zarfaty 2019). On this note, it is also worthy to underline that empirical articles published on egg freezing in the last decade focus on 'predominantly white, heterosexual, and middle class' women mostly from Europe, the United Kingdom and the United States (De Proost and Coene 2019: 359).

In addition to these concerns, two further aspects of egg freezing warrant consideration from a socio-economic perspective: the interaction between markets and morals, and the role of neoliberal femininity. The medicalization literature notes the importance of marketization in the healthcare sector (Conrad 2008). Medical markets play an important role in the provision of ARTs services, and the history of capitalist development shows that market expansion may lead to changes in social norms, as shown by Viviana Zelizer's seminal works in economic sociology.

Zelizer (1978), for instance, tells the story of how the market for life insurance developed in the United States in the nineteenth century. Potential customers initially objected to the idea of buying insurance for their loved ones due to moral concerns (e.g. profiting from the death of a loved one) and superstitious beliefs (e.g. accelerating the death of a loved one). However, the economic actors in this newly emerging market were eventually able to reframe the issue and overcome social resistance by redefining life insurance as a matter of familial responsibility. Moral norms were, thus, redefined in the face of newly defined needs and the market remedies to satisfy them. In our analysis below, we will consider the virginity issue and the definition of egg freezing as a woman's responsibility in this light.

Finally, we also need to consider how the ideas of the neoliberal period relate to egg freezing. As noted above, egg freezing is depicted in the mainstream Western media as a rational choice and an empowering strategy for women who aim to pursue both career and family goals (Myers 2014; van de Wiel 2014). The egg-freezing women in our sample also appear comfortable with the ideational approaches common to the neoliberal era, such as the individualization of risk and responsibility (Rose 2004) and the human capital theory (Repo 2016; Rottenberg 2017). Egg-freezing women appear to embrace a calculative rationality of investment, cost and benefit. Many frame egg freezing as an insurance mechanism, a savings account, a responsible act or a self-investment (cf. Myers 2014). These examples raise the question of whether egg freezing emerges as a showcase for neoliberal femininity. Here I am influenced by Ozyegin's (2015) discussion of 'neoliberal masculinity' among university students in contemporary Turkey, and suggest that the egg-freezing narratives of women in this study also indicate a mode of femininity shaped by neoliberal conditions and ideas; hence, women are supposed to act like entrepreneurs investing in their human capital while managing risk.

Methods

The chapter draws on interviews that I and İpek Göçmen conducted with twenty-one women in the second half of 2016. All interviewees were women who had either had their eggs frozen in the preceding twelve months or were undergoing the egg-freezing process. I approached three private fertility clinics in Istanbul, and only one of them agreed to help access egg-freezing women. We accessed eighteen of the women through this clinic; the other three were accessed through either the women we interviewed or our personal contacts. Both researchers were present in half of the interviews, while only one researcher was present in the other half. In addition to the interviews with egg-freezing women, I also had informal conversations with the staff of the mentioned clinic and made phone calls to several other private fertility clinics in the city to get information about medical procedures and patient profile.

The median age of the sample was forty years old. All but one of the women were employed or self-employed; their occupations included engineer, lawyer, medical doctor, nurse, clinical psychologist, academic and manager (mid- and high-level). One woman had a high school degree, whereas all the others had a university degree and one-third had a graduate-level degree. All the women were unmarried at the time of the interviews: three were divorced, five were currently in a relationship, two had never had any experience of romantic relationships and six had not experienced sexual intercourse.

For data collection, we chose to conduct semi-structured interviews. This method enabled us to explore women's experiences of egg freezing, bearing in mind both the debates in the literature and the peculiarities of women's stories. We asked the women how they came to know about egg-freezing technology, how they decided to freeze their eggs and what kind of expectations they had. We also posed questions about their life stories regarding family, romantic relationships, education and working lives.

Interviews were transcribed verbatim by two research assistants, and interviewees were assigned pseudonyms by the researchers. Interview data were later coded manually by the researchers, bearing in mind both the major concepts seen in the literature and the peculiarities of stories in our sample. This chapter prioritizes the socio-economic perspective on aspects of egg-freezing experiences.

This study's main limitation is its biased sample. As we reached egg-freezing women via a private fertility clinic, the sample comprises women with high levels of education and income potential. Further research should examine women with different levels of education and income, especially those who have their eggs frozen at public hospitals or who cannot afford the procedure. Considering the dominant trends in Turkey regarding marriage and first childbearing, which women commonly experience in their early twenties (as elaborated below), egg freezing might be more common among the group of women represented in our sample.

Setting the scene: Local regulations and social indicators

Since 2014, it has been legal to freeze eggs in Turkey in situations such as a decline in ovarian reserves, a family history of premature menopause or aging, in addition to disease-related reasons. Such criteria imply a limited approach to elective egg freezing: young healthy women with high ovarian reserves are not eligible for egg freezing – hence the high median age in our sample. This depicts egg freezing as primarily a last resort against anticipated infertility. Elective egg freezing has also received little coverage in the Turkish media, unlike in the West, and has not been a subject of political discussions. This lack of attention might be attributable to the prevalent gender norms and practices mentioned below. Although egg freezing is particularly aimed at single women, the use of frozen eggs for IVF is allowed only for married heterosexual couples, thus endorsing the heteronormative family model.

Such limitations on age and marital status may appear confusing considering the recent policy approach of pronatalism in Turkey and compared to regional countries such as Israel, where the government has similarly been pronatalist and allowing both egg freezing for non-medical reasons for younger women from the age of 30 on (see Israel Ministry of Health 2020) and the use of frozen eggs by single women for IVF (Rimon-Zarfaty 2019). It is also important to note that Cyprus has been an important travel destination for the Turkish citizens who want to pursue ART services not accessible in Turkey – a phenomenon which has led to Turkish legislative steps to ban travel for third-party reproductive assistance (Gürtin 2011; Mutlu 2019). As a result of local prohibition on the use of IVF by single women, one of our interviewees, for instance, initially went to Cyprus with her boyfriend to freeze embryos and later decided instead to freeze eggs in Turkey due to relationship reasons. In a similar vein, as discussed below, two interviewees were also trying to get some eggs frozen and banked in the United States due to local prohibition on sperm banks.

Prices vary between fertility clinics, and we await reliable data on the number of fertility clinics offering egg-freezing services and on segmentation in the emerging egg-freezing market. There is also partial public insurance coverage for the limited number of public hospitals where the procedure is available. At the private fertility clinic in Istanbul where we conducted most of the interviews, the procedure has been provided since the 2014 changes in regulations and costs about USD 2,000 per cycle (including clinic visits and egg retrieval, as well as optional psychological counselling). Meanwhile, the market price for hormone medications is about USD 500 per cycle, and storage fees cost about USD 200 per annum. Hence, egg freezing is likely beyond the financial means of single women outside the middle- to high-income groups.

As the regulations imply, prevalent social norms underline marriage as a requirement for childbearing, as children born out of wedlock are regarded as illegitimate (Çarkoğlu and Kalaycıoğlu 2012). Marriage and motherhood are strong gender norms in Turkish society, where childlessness can be a source of stigmatization (Göknar 2015). The male-breadwinner family model prevails as the ideal form, as backed by the welfare system (Kılıç 2008).

Statistics also suggest delayed marriage and motherhood to be uncommon phenomena: in 2013 the median age at first marriage was 21 for women, and for those aged between 25 and 49, the median age at the first child's birth was 22.9 (HÜNEE 2014). Conversely, the same study reported that 6.8 per cent of women aged between 35 and 49 were childless (HÜNEE 2014). A recent comparative study shows that the propensity to lifelong singlehood, especially among highly educated women, is greater in societies where traditional norms prevail concerning gender roles, demonstrating limited adaptation to the changing roles of women (Bellani et al. 2017). The uncommon characteristics of the women in our sample concerning age, marital status and childbearing can also be seen in this light.

While marriage during the early 20s is a prevalent norm, premarital sexuality is still taboo. According to the findings of a World Values Survey (2014), sex before marriage was never justifiable for 76.7 per cent of respondents in Turkey. This is an extremely high figure compared to Western countries (e.g. 8 per cent in Germany and 13.5 per cent in the United States, while the question was not asked in surveys conducted in other regional countries such as Iraq, Lebanon and Egypt). Virginity before marriage also remains an important norm for many upwardly mobile women (Scalco 2016), as seen in our sample, while the local medical market offers hymen reconstruction services (Güzel 2018), as well as transabdominal procedures for egg retrieval as discussed below. Resistance to transvaginal procedure for egg retrieval (in case of egg freezing for both elective and medical reasons) is mentioned for countries across the Middle East and North Africa (MENA) including Israel, Lebanon, Egypt and Tunisia, due to concerns about intact hymen; an issue causing clinicians to suggest transabdominal and transrectal procedures (Abdelwehab and Samy 2017; Khalife et al. 2019; Rimon-Zarfaty 2019; Ghazeeri and Khalife 2020).

Education statistics also demonstrate the unusual social placement of our sample. Tertiary education attainment has been increasing in the last decade, but is still low: in 2014, it was 13.2 per cent for women aged 25 and above. Graduate-level education is even rarer among women: in 2015 just 1.4 per cent had attained master's level and 0.2 per cent doctoral level (World Bank 2017). By contrast, as mentioned above, all but one of the women in our sample were university graduates, and one-third had postgraduate degrees.

Linked to education, female labour force participation is also low in Turkey. The nationwide rate was 35 per cent in 2015, with participation concentrated in the services sector, characterized by low-paying and low-skilled jobs. The rates of employed women with managerial and professional occupations were, respectively, 2.2 and 14.3 per cent in 2015 (TURKSTAT 2016). These are important indicators to understand the privileged status of the women interviewed for this study, as they occupy either managerial or, more commonly, professional positions. The resulting picture is also consistent with the stereotypical profile of egg-freezing women depicted in the mainstream Western media (Myers 2014; van de Wiel 2014).

Egg freezing in Turkey has not previously been studied from a social-science perspective, except for the research on which this chapter relies (see also, Kılıç, and Göçmen 2018; Göçmen and Kılıç 2018). Meanwhile, the studies conducted by medical professionals are very limited in number and focus on issues such as demographic profiles, fertility awareness, reproductive outcomes and decision regret (Akın et al. 2019; Cil et al. 2019; Boza et al. 2020).

Women's narratives of egg freezing

Freezing eggs for careerism, or a problem of decreased capabilities?

In the mainstream Western media, egg freezing is depicted as an instrument that may enable women to focus on their careers while preserving their fertility (see van de Wiel 2014). However, none of the women in our sample stated career goals among their reasons for egg freezing. The main reason stated by almost all of them was the lack of a suitable partner for a long-term relationship in which they could consider having children. Other reasons they gave include the desire not to rush into finding a partner, getting married and pregnancy. The desire not to rush has previously been reported by egg-freezing women in other case studies in the United Kingdom, the United States and Israel (see Waldby 2015a; Inhorn et al. 2018; Baldwin et al. 2019).

Notwithstanding their stated reasons, the life stories of egg-freezing women suggest that their experiences of extended education and training, as well as flexible working lives, might have paved the way to egg freezing. In other words, rather than being an intentional decision with the aim of achieving career goals, egg freezing may be a consequence of women's capabilities being limited by a number of historical conditions, including career paths. We know that educational and working conditions (e.g. long-working hours, spatial mobility, uncertainty) may limit opportunities for romantic relationships, marriage and childbearing, thus contributing to the decision to postpone motherhood (Esping-Andersen 2015). Turkey, in particular, has among the longest working hours of any OECD country: female employees' total declared employment is 41 hours per week, compared to the OECD average of 33 hours (sector-specific data not available; see OECD 2019). Hence, it seems reasonable to consider egg-freezing behaviour in this light as well.

For instance, Esin (age 40) discussed how challenging it was for her to become a medical doctor in terms of family and maternal goals:

> If you choose to study at medical school, you are already at a disadvantage. Although I have friends who did it, it is terribly difficult to bear and raise children before you reach a certain point [in your career]. Frankly, I didn't want to take that responsibility. I was quite a nerd… It was difficult to even think about marriage before I finished school, did my internship, and completed specialty training.

It is important to note that medical training can take many years to complete in Turkey, with an average of six years' study at medical school and four years' specialization.

We see the existence of similar constraints in the stories of academics. Çağla (41) studied at university in Istanbul then moved to the United States to pursue a PhD degree. After earning her PhD, she moved from one state to another across the United States as a postdoctoral fellow until she finally found a tenure-track position. Although her uncertainty and mobility then decreased, she still had to work long hours and did not have enough time for socializing:

> Çağla: In the first year I came to [my current state], I was working for 15 hours a day. Hence, I had no time to go anywhere. I could hardly cook for myself… Loneliness was a problem mainly after graduating from school… once I started working. For instance, I spent one year in [another US state]. In that year I had no time to make friends [both friends in general and boyfriend candidates in particular]. In the second year, I moved to [another state]… I had no time to make friends there either. After that, I moved to [my current state]. Again, I had no time to make friends for another year. Once [my job] became permanent, [I had time] in the second year.

Author: When you say you had no time, do you mean that you were working long hours?

Çağla: Yes, and I was also looking for a job. Because the positions were only for one year.

Yasemin (40) studied engineering and currently works as a manager at a big company in Istanbul. She argued that her experiences of romantic relationships were not influenced by her working conditions, but her story reveals similar patterns of high mobility and hectic work schedules:

Author: You said you love working and wandering. Do you think this might have influenced your past relationships not evolving in the direction [of marriage and motherhood]?

Yasemin: No, no way... I am abroad for 80 to 90 days a year. This is very challenging. [However], let me say this, you can plan things. So there was not anything exaggerated, like I could not have time for my boyfriend, I could not care for him, or like my priority was something else.

Another engineer, Ece (38), works at the Istanbul branch of an international company. She described how her previous working conditions damaged her private life, leading to her decision to change job:

I was very busy in my previous work. I had a very good position but with lots of traveling. Then I suffered from a health problem because of working too hard. Since I realized it was damaging my health, I quit my job. My current job is calmer and my goal is to have a family. Because my clock is ticking... I want to have a family and a calm job – a regular job. I want to have regular working hours and no irregular traveling. That's why I found this job. It's very interesting: it was one year after I started my current job that I met my boyfriend. Marriage did not happen, but if it did, we could have had children.

In addition to the issues of education and working life, familial responsibilities such as elderly care can further complicate the work–life balance for women. Ayşe, a 41-year-old project manager, said that she would not be able to have a child now even if she had a suitable partner: 'I have too many other responsibilities... My mother is sick, and because I'm her only child, I undertake the medical and financial responsibilities... these might change with the support of a partner, but still...'

One can, of course, think of many factors that might influence the individual experiences of romantic relationships, marriage and childbearing. The stories of egg-freezing women in our sample highlight some of the socio-economic factors. Experiences of extended professional training appear to be one important factor. Although women in our sample have prestigious professions, we also see that their working lives are not without problems. Women's capabilities in private life might have been limited by work-related factors such as hectic schedules, job insecurity and uncertainty about the future, as well as high mobility due to travelling or relocating for work. It therefore seems more plausible to regard egg-freezing behaviour as a consequence of how professional training, working life and the lack of institutional supports limit women's capabilities, rather than as a voluntary choice to focus on career goals.

The question of virginity and egg retrieval

As noted above, medicalization leads to changes in the definition of personal responsibility, as ever more problems are defined in terms of health and disease. This leads to either individual exemption from moral responsibility or a new notion of individual responsibility to conform to socio-medical expectations (Zola 1972; Conrad 1992). On the medicalization of age-related fertility decline via egg freezing in Turkey, we see similar change in some women's views of virginity and responsibility. Six of the twenty-one women we interviewed stated that they had not had sexual intercourse. Five of these six women defined virginity as a matter of moral responsibility and values. However, the same women began negotiating virginity once they decided to have their eggs frozen. The need for this arises because egg retrieval methods are usually transvaginal, causing the hymen to be 'broken'. While the very concepts of virginity and the hymen can be problematized from the perspective of medicalization, we point here to the narratives of egg-freezing women on how they dissociate the notion of the hymen (*kızlık zarı*) from their (re-)definition of virginity. We also see that the medical markets offer some measures against this dilemma, as elaborated below, and thereby support women in their decision to opt for fertility preservation services over virginity preservation (cf. Zelizer 1978).

Sezen is a 41-year-old academic. At the time of our interview she was undergoing hormonal treatment, prior to having her eggs retrieved. Sezen stated that she opposes premarital sex because of the moral values she holds and her family upbringing. However, she recalled having no hesitation with respect to virginity once she had decided to have her eggs frozen. We see that Sezen started to redefine virginity in the process of egg freezing; she now approaches virginity in terms of health, rather than as a moral matter. Through the medicalizing approach, Sezen became exempt from responsibility for preserving her hymen as an indicator of her chastity:

> Virginity was important for me. I was a virgin; however, to be frank, when I had to make that choice [losing my hymen to allow retrieval of my eggs], I did not care about it at all. I concluded that the person I marry will understand that this may be my only opportunity [for pregnancy]… Look at this like an illness. You do whatever is necessary for illness; for health.

Similarly, Çağla also started to redefine virginity during the process of egg freezing. She now defines it in behavioural terms, rather than with reference to the hymen:

> But what is virginity anyway?… It is the existence of a membrane… If what is called virginity, a membrane, gets broken because of an illness, one will still be a virgin. The same applies for an operation… So we also need to think about the

definition of virginity... I do not care about it at all, because the definition of virginity is clear. What I have done is to get a membrane broken for an operation, for an ultrasound, that is it. [Am I] still a virgin? But of course.

While Sezen and Çağla are Muslims, Damla (43, accountant) is a Christian and she noted that her upbringing in the Church is the major reason why she is virgin. She elaborated thus:

I don't care if other people engage in [premarital sex] or not. For me what matters is the brains. It is up to individuals. If they engage in [premarital sex], that's very normal. But I always told myself that I wanted to wait until marriage.

Damla has been in a relationship with her boyfriend for three years and they plan to marry. She reported talking to her boyfriend about egg freezing and its impact on the hymen: 'To make things easier', she linked her decision to freeze her eggs to the existence of some cysts in her ovaries; in truth, she was actually worried about reproductive aging, and her decision to freeze eggs was not linked to the presence of cysts. Consequently, her boyfriend also evaluated the issue in terms of health and supported Damla:

I told him that I have cysts, that's why we will store some eggs. I really had some cysts too. I told him that the doctor treats me by [egg freezing]. I also told him how the doctor said that 'once the [egg retrieval] procedure is done, it will be like you had intercourse', and how I felt sad about it. And [my boyfriend] said, 'no problem, what matters most is health.'

Ela (43, engineer) offered a different perspective on virginity, arguing that she is virgin due to relationship dynamics, rather than her moral values: 'I've never attached importance to virginity; however, over the course of my relationships, I got the feeling from the other party that this [virginity] is something that needs to be preserved until marriage.' As virginity is widely seen as a prerequisite for marriage in Turkey, it leads to different definitions of responsibility for women and men. While the traditional norms make women responsible for protecting their virginity, men are expected to either wait until marriage or take responsibility – eventually getting married – in the case of having premarital sex. Ela pointed to the difficulties such social expectations cause for relationships:

[Virginity] turned into something like a barrier in my life; hence, it does not matter anymore. If I had a boyfriend at the moment, it could have been different. When I had long-term relationships in the past, it was like 'wait a second' for the guys, because I think they hesitate about being the first.

Çağla, Sezen and Damla noted that they would still not engage in premarital sex. When re-approaching virginity in health and moral-behavioural terms, they problematize the significance of intact hymen, but they do not reject the idealization of female chastity. Hence, this is different from the moralizing approach to virginity that is seen among the educated, upwardly mobile young women studied by Ozyegin, an approach which is expressed as 'virginity is not between the legs, it resides in the brain' (Ozyegin 2009: 109).

On the other hand, Ela was open to the idea of premarital sex. She believes that her changing situation regarding virginity will not be a problem in her future relationships. However, she also referred to the hymen reconstruction option offered by medical markets for those worried about virginity (see also Güzel 2018): 'If you want to cheat about it, you are able to. Hence, this is not a concern in my opinion. How many people are out there who value virginity nowadays? Well, [not many] in my social circles.'

Damla also judgingly mentioned how some women undergo hymen reconstruction to ensure their future husbands regard them as virgins – a procedure she would not personally choose to do (neither Sezen nor Çağla mentioned this option, and we did not question them about it). Yet Damla is more optimistic about another option offered by the medical markets: the provision of a medical document certifying that the hymen was 'broken' by the egg retrieval procedure. Medical doctors explained to us that in cases of transvaginal medical intervention, it was common in Turkey to provide patients with a medical report explaining the intervention and its impact on the hymen. However, we need to consider such reports not simply as medical epicrises but also as measures devised due to social norms and the risks they may pose for 'deviant' patients: hence, they serve to protect individuals from other institutions of social control (cf. Conrad 1992; Zola 1972) or, alternatively, to reconcile medical services with prevalent social norms. Asked what she thought about the offer of medical documents, Damla replied, 'Yes, they said that they can give me a report. And I said, ok, fine. My sister told me that I should have it... not for showing to any men though.'

Another option offered by the medical markets in Turkey targets women who want to both preserve their hymen and freeze their eggs. This is the method of laparoscopy, which entails retrieving eggs transabdominally; it is less internationally common than the transvaginal retrieval method (see, for instance, Mayo Clinic 2019). We do not know how many clinics in Turkey offer the laparoscopy method. The fertility clinic through which we recruited interviewees does not offer laparoscopy; one of the coordinating staff described it as a medically inefficient egg retrieval method. However, the same personnel told us that they sometimes receive phone enquiries about the method's availability, and they think that patients concerned about the hymen might be going to the clinics that offer laparoscopy. We also contacted some of the major fertility clinics in Istanbul about the method: at least one major clinic confirmed that it offers laparoscopy for those reluctant to undergo transvaginal retrieval.

Overall, we see that virgin women facing the risk of declining fertility might give up on preserving the hymen as an indicator of chastity. Virgin women in our sample started to medicalize the issue, framing it in terms of health needs or behaviour, thereby overcoming the pressure of moral responsibility (cf. Conrad 1992; Zola 1972). Here it seems helpful that ARTs separate sex and reproduction (cf. Spar 2006). Through egg freezing, virgin women can take reproductive measures without engaging in sex. However, the decision to give up the hymen – having preserved it for many years due to moral concerns – is not an easy one to make. For those women who may feel conflicted in making this decision, medical markets offer important remedies to help reconcile the egg-freezing service with moral norms, and even contribute to redefining those norms (cf. Zelizer 1978). Similar concerns on hymen are seen among religious Jewish women considering elective egg freezing in Israel (Rimon-Zarfaty 2019) and among religious Muslim and Druze parents of female adolescent cancer patients in Lebanon (Khalife et al. 2019); in the former case, medical professionals are also endeavouring to overcome these concerns by using alternative procedures such as laparoscopy. Medical researchers from Egypt also argue that the social norm of having an intact hymen until marriage poses an obstacle to egg freezing; hence, requiring procedures other than transvaginal ones (Abdelwehab and Samy 2017). Still, we need more studies on the topic for a systematic comparison. In sum, it is not merely virginity that is being medicalized and redefined here: the preservation of fertility against the risk of reproductive aging, in the form of egg freezing, is also being defined as a new responsibility of women. On that note, we also need to consider reflections of the neoliberal period in the narratives of egg-freezing women.

The rhetoric of risk management and self-investment

Women in our sample cited a number of reasons to explain their decision to freeze their eggs, such as the absence of a suitable partner with whom to have a child. We also analysed how women's educational and working life trajectories seem to have contributed to the postponement of marriage and motherhood. Beyond these considerations, a third line of thought appeared often in women's narratives about the reasons for egg freezing, with echoes of the neoliberal period. This type of reasoning offers an individualistic take on egg freezing. Women depict egg freezing as a rational choice to take precautions against the risk of reproductive aging. Accordingly, they seem to accept the 'individualization of risk and responsibility' (Rose 2004) concerning fertility preservation (cf. Myers 2014). Some women's narratives also show that they subscribe to the human-capital approaches (Repo 2016; Rottenberg 2017), with the idea of maintaining or increasing their value in the dating market by freezing eggs. Overall, this decision-making approach and some expectations of women depict egg freezing as a potential showcase for neoliberal femininity (cf. Ozyegin 2015).

Discussing her decision-making process, Deniz (42, clinical psychologist) reported considering her goals and available options before reaching what she considers to be a rational choice:

> I thought about what I wanted now. I said: 'I want to have a child.' But I don't have a serious relationship right now and I don't want to miss the train. Yet, at the same time, I don't want to rush into finding someone, getting married, and having a child either… I didn't want to make a wrong decision.

Ela, a 43-year-old manager with degrees in engineering, gave an account explicitly underlining a calculative rationality:

I am trying to increase the probability [of childbearing]. I am a rational person, an engineer, therefore I can deal with probabilities… When deciding, you should consider both cause and effect when projecting for the future. Engineering is about finding an optimum solution under given constraints.

Ela decided to undergo three cycles to freeze an 'optimum' number of eggs. Her gynaecologist suggested collecting twenty eggs in total, but Ela aims to freeze thirty to ensure 'a higher probability of eventually having at least three healthy eggs fertilized'. When asked about the high financial cost of undergoing multiple cycles (recall the prices in the previous section), she said that she did not mind and regarded it as not particularly high considering the probability of having a child in the future and the potential future costs of raising a child. Of course, we see here the effect of high-income potential on the calculation of costs and benefits.

Most of the women we interviewed talked about egg freezing in terms of risks and responsibility. References to 'risk management' were abundant, with perceived risks including age-related fertility decline, possible inability to achieve pregnancy in the future, and consequential potential difficulties with a future partner. By contrast, the medical risks associated with the egg-freezing procedure were not seriously considered. For instance, Ekin (37, attorney) explained her decision to freeze her eggs as follows: 'There is a risk here; there might be a negative situation in the future, and I now have the chance to prevent that situation. So, I've made use of that chance.'

Sezen, a 41-year-old academic working in the United States, gave a more detailed account of risk calculation. She has decided to freeze her eggs in both Turkey and the United States. Although egg freezing is cheaper in Turkey, where the costs may vary between USD 4,000 and USD 7,000 (La Ferla 2018), Turkish law prohibits the use of frozen eggs for IVF through sperm donation. Like the other interviewees, Sezen's priority is to have a child within marriage, yet she is also open to becoming a single parent in the United States via sperm donation. Hence, considering such legal and societal constraints, she decided to undergo the egg-freezing procedure in the United States too: 'if I get married, I can use [the eggs] in Turkey. But there is a chance that I won't, so I think that I'd better have a few eggs in the US as well. So, I feel like I have to distribute the risk.'

Some women used the prudential metaphors of 'insurance plan' and 'savings account' for egg freezing (cf. Myers 2014). Defne (29, a doctoral researcher) commented, 'I feel like I have deposited money in the bank. When the day comes and everything [fertility] is over, I will have at least a chance to try [pregnancy].' Similarly, Ayşe (41, project manager) said, 'I am making a deposit in the bank. It's not certain if I'll use it or not, but I feel at ease.' By minimizing risks and gaining time, women expect relief and empowerment.

We mentioned above the emerging definition of egg freezing as a new responsibility due to the medicalization of reproductive aging. The approach of individualized risk management also depicts egg freezing as a matter of individual responsibility. Therefore, the definition of egg freezing as a woman's responsibility seems to be located at the intersection of medicalization and marketization. Here, responsibility for fertility preservation not only addresses the risks of future infertility but also reflects, for some women, a duty to future partners, whose approval they anticipate.

When asked how they expected having frozen eggs to impact on their future relationships, many women predicted a positive effect. Merve (38, clinical psychologist) considered some future scenarios:

> I think I will be appreciated. I think I will hear something like: 'I am glad that you thought about this and have done this'... This is actually one of the reasons behind my decision. If we really want to have a child at some point, I do not want to say, 'I heard about it, there was an opportunity, but I did not do it.'

Sezen also anticipated an affirmative reaction from a future partner. She elaborated by particularizing what other couples experience during IVF treatment and undertaking individualized responsibility for preparing her eggs in advance:

> I think the man I marry will thank me for doing this... The man who takes me will be lucky because I have prepared everything for him. Sometimes men have to go through this in a marriage, and they financially and emotionally share [the burden]. I will prepare everything and then present it to him.

The ideas of fertility preservation as a woman's responsibility and anticipation of a future partner's approval relate to some women's efforts to maintain or increase their perceived value in the dating market – that is, to preserve their marriageability. For instance, by keeping open her option to have a child, Deniz believes she has increased her chances of having a future long-term relationship:

> Let's imagine that someone wants to have a child. He might wonder how this woman, at the age of 42, could have a child, and think it better to end the relationship before it's too late, otherwise it would be harder, and better to leave her before becoming too attached. But now, on the contrary, if we want to have a child, we will still have the option.

The issue of women's perceived value further links to one interviewee's allusion to self-investment. Merve, the clinical psychologist mentioned above regarding anticipated approval, also framed her decision to have eggs frozen as follows:

> Primarily, so to speak, I've made an investment in myself. Thank God, I have no illness; I have no [boyfriend] in my life either. It's not something urgent for me. I primarily see this as an investment.

The narrative of self-investment, coupled with individualized risk management, connects to the notion of human capital, which has become popular in the neoliberal era and has already been applied to gender policies (see Repo 2016; Rottenberg 2017). By freezing their eggs, women appear to be maximizing their human capital – their reproductive attributes, in this case – and, hence, increasing their value. Coupled with approaches in the mainstream media, women's embrace of the economic calculus of investment, cost and profit, as well as the individualization of risk and responsibility, depicts egg freezing as a showcase for a neoliberal mode of femininity. On the one hand, women's lived experiences of relief at gaining time and their expectations of future benefits concerning pregnancy and relationships may be seen as empowering aspects of egg freezing, as we have elaborated elsewhere (see Göçmen and Kılıç 2018). On the other hand, we see the further extension of market rationality into life domains, such as women's future reproductive capacity, with women encouraged to act and think like entrepreneurs and invest in their own human capital (cf. Ozyegin 2015; Repo 2016; Rottenberg 2017).

Conclusion

This chapter presented the findings of a study on women's narratives of egg freezing in Istanbul. Considering the intersecting issues of medicalization and marketization, we discussed three major aspects of women's narratives from a socio-economic perspective, after overviewing debates in the literature on egg freezing.

First, in postponing motherhood and deciding to freeze their eggs, the women in our sample were not focusing on their future career goals. However, their past experiences of extended education and flexible working life, as well as the lack of institutional supports, might have formed the constraints that influenced their decision on egg freezing. We need more empirical studies to explore the link between women's capabilities and working conditions and the decision to freeze eggs.

Second, egg freezing initially appears to conflict with some moral norms in Turkey, such as the preservation of the hymen as an indicator of virginity. However, virgin women in our sample prioritized preserving their fertility over preserving their hymen. This moral decision seems to have been made smoothly thanks to the medicalization of reproductive aging and the remedy measures provided by medical markets for those concerned about virginity; hence, egg freezing is reconciled with moral norms in the case at hand and may even imply the redefinition of norms and responsibilities. The issue of virginity and transvaginal egg retrieval appears to be a concern across MENA; this topic definitely needs further investigation both within Turkey and from a comparative perspective, and should be considered alongside other services offered by medical markets, such as hymen reconstruction.

Finally, the ways that egg-freezing women explain their decisions show parallels to ideas such as individualized risk management and human capital, suggesting that women are supposed to act like entrepreneurs. This picture reflects the neoliberal period and points to the question of neoliberal femininity. This issue is also linked to how the socio-economic environment influences women's behaviour (in freezing their eggs) and their subjectivities. Overall, there remains much to learn from a systematic exploration of the socio-economic aspects of egg freezing in capitalist societies.

References

Abdelwehab, S. and M. Samy (2017), 'Obstacles Facing Oocyte Cryopreservation in the Middle East', *Obstetrics & Gynecology International Journal*, 7 (2): 00238.

Akın, O. D., A. Boza, K. Yakin and B. Urman (2019), 'Awareness of Fertility and Reproductive Aging in Women Seeking Oocyte Cryopreservation, Reproductive Aged Controls, and Female Health Care Professionals: A Comparative Study', *European Journal of Obstetrics & Gynecology and Reproductive Biology*, 233: 146–50.

Baldwin, K. (2018), 'Conceptualising Women's Motivations for Social Egg Freezing and Experience of Reproductive Delay', *Sociology of Health & Illness*, 40 (5): 859–73.

Baldwin, K., L. Culley, N. Hudson and H. Mitchell (2019), 'Running Out of Time: Exploring Women's Motivations for Social Egg Freezing', *Journal of Psychosomatic Obstetrics & Gynecology*, 40 (2): 166–73.

Bellani, D., G. Esping-Andersen and L. Nedoluzhko (2017), 'Never Partnered: A Multilevel Analysis of Lifelong Singlehood', *Demographic Research*, 37 (4): 53–100.

Boza, A. et al. (2020), 'Factors Associated with Decision Regret Following Oocyte Cryopreservation in Patients with Diminished Ovarian Reserve and/or Age-Related Fertility Decline', unpublished manuscript.

Brown, E. and M. Patrick (2018), 'Time, Anticipation, and the Life Course: Egg Freezing as Temporarily Disentangling Romance and Reproduction', *American Sociological Review*, 83 (5): 959–82.

Çarkoğlu, A. and E. Kalaycıoğlu (2012), *Türkiye'de Aile, İş ve Toplumsal Cinsiyet*, Istanbul: Istanbul Policy Center.

Cattapan, A., K. Hammond, J. Haw and L. A. Tarasoff (2014), 'Breaking the Ice: Young Feminist Scholars of Reproductive Politics Reflect on Egg Freezing', *International Journal of Feminist Approaches to Bioethics*, 7: 236–47.

Cil A. P. et al. (2015), 'Oocyte Cryopreservation as a Preventive Measure for Age-Related Fertility Loss', *Seminars in Reproductive Medicine*, 33: 429–35.

Cil A. P. et al. (2019), 'A 5-year Analysis of Demographics, Cycle Characteristics and Reproductive Outcomes of 907 Egg Freezing Cycles in Patients with Diminished Ovarian Reserve and Age-Related Fertility Decline', *Fertility and Sterility*, 112 (3): e108.

Conrad, P. (1992), 'Medicalization and Social Control', *Annual Review of Sociology*, 18: 209–32.

Conrad, P. (2008), *The Medicalization of Society: On the Transformation of Human Conditions into Treatable Disorders*, Baltimore: Johns Hopkins University Press.

Czarnecki, D. (2015), 'Moral Women, Immoral Technologies: How Devout Women Negotiate Gender, Religion, and Assisted Reproductive Technologies', *Gender & Society*, 29: 716–42.

De Proost, M. and G. Coene (2019), 'Emancipation on Thin Ice: Women's Autonomy, Reproductive Justice, and Social Egg Freezing', *Tijdschrift voor Genderstudies*, 22 (4): 357–71.

Esping-Andersen, G. (2015), *The Incomplete Revolution: Adapting to Women's New Roles*, Cambridge: Polity Press.

Ghazeeri, G. and D. Khalife (2020), 'Challenges in Fertility Counseling of Cancer Patients: A Developing Nation Perspective', in H. A. Azim et al. (eds), *Fertility Challenges and Solutions in Women with Cancer*, 93–101, Cham: Springer.

Göçmen, İ. and A. Kılıç (2018), 'Egg Freezing Experiences of Women in Turkey: From the Social Context to the Narratives of Reproductive Ageing and Empowerment', *European Journal of Women's Studies*, 25 (2): 168–82.

Göknar, M. D. (2015), *Achieving Procreation: Childlessness and IVF in Turkey*, New York and Oxford: Berghahn Books.

Gürtin, Z. B. (2011), 'Banning Reproductive Travel: Turkey's ART Legislation and Third-Party Assisted Reproduction', *Reproductive BioMedicine Online*, 23 (5): 555–64.

Güzel, H. (2018), 'Pain as Performance. Re-Virginisation in Turkey', *Medical Humanities*, 44 (2): 89–95.

Harwood, K. (2009), 'Egg Freezing: A Breakthrough for Reproductive Autonomy?' *Bioethics*, 23 (1): 39–46.

HÜNEE (2014), *2013 Türkiye Nüfus ve Sağlık Araştırması*, Ankara: Hacettepe University Population Studies Institute.

Inhorn, M. C. et al. (2018), 'Ten Pathways to Elective Egg Freezing: A Binational Analysis', *Journal of Assisted Reproduction and Genetics*, 35 (11): 2003–11.

Inhorn, M. C., D. Birenbaum-Carmeli and P. Patrizio (2017), 'Medical Egg Freezing and Cancer Patients' Hopes: Fertility Preservation at the Intersection of Life and Death', *Social Science & Medicine*, 195: 25–33.

Inhorn, M. C., D. Birenbaum-Carmeli, M. D. Vale and P. Patrizio (2020), 'Abrahamic Traditions and Egg Freezing: Religious Women's Experiences in Local Moral Worlds', *Social Science & Medicine*, 253: 112976.

Israel Ministry of Health (2020). 'Egg Freezing'. Available online: https://www.health.gov.il/English/Topics/fertility/ovum_preserving/Pages/ovum_preserv.aspx (accessed 9 September 2020).

Khalife, D. R., W. Kutteh, H. Tarhini, A. Khalil, C. Beyrouthy and G. Ghazeeri (2019), 'Parental Attitudes toward Fertility Preservation in Female Adolescent Cancer Patients in Lebanon', *Journal of Pediatric and Adolescent Gynecology*, 32 (5): 522–9.

Kılıç, A. (2008), 'The Gender Dimension of Social Policy Reform in Turkey: Towards Equal Citizenship?' *Social Policy and Administration*, 42 (5): 487–503.

Kılıç, A. and İ. Göçmen (2018), 'Fate, Morals and Rational Calculations: Freezing Eggs for Non-Medical Reasons in Turkey', *Social Science & Medicine*, 203: 19–27.

La Ferla, R. (2018), 'These Companies Really, Really, Really Want to Freeze Your Eggs', *New York Times*, 29 August.

Lewis, E. I., S. A. Missmer, L. V. Farland and E. S. Ginsburg (2016), 'Public Support in the United States for Elective Oocyte Cryopreservation', *Fertility and Sterility*, 106 (5): 1183–9.

Linkeviciute, A., F. A. Peccatori, V. Sanchini and G. Boniolo (2015), 'Oocyte Cryopreservation beyond Cancer: Tools for Ethical Reflection', *Journal of Assisted Reproduction and Genetics*, 32: 1211–20.

Martin, L. J. (2010), 'Egg Freezing, Genetic Preservation and Risk', *Gender & Society*, 24: 526–45.

Martinelli, L., L. Busatta, L. Galvagni and C. Piciocchi (2015), 'Social Egg Freezing: A Reproductive Chance or Smoke and Mirrors?', *Croatian Medical Journal*, 56: 387–91.

Mayo Clinic (2019), 'Egg Freezing'. Available online: https://www.mayoclinic.org/tests-procedures/egg-freezing/about/pac-20384556 (accessed 3 September 2019).

Mertes, H. and G. Pennings (2012), 'Elective Oocyte Cryopreservation: Who Should Pay?' *Human Reproduction*, 27: 9–13.

Miller, C. C. (2014), 'Freezing Eggs as Part of Employee Benefits: Some Women See Darker Message', *New York Times*, 14 October.

Mutlu, B. (2019), 'Transnational Biopolitics and Family-Making in Secrecy: An Ethnography of Reproductive Travel from Turkey to Northern Cyprus', PhD diss., Massachusetts Institute of Technology, Massachusetts.

Myers, C. E. C. (2014), 'Colonizing the (Reproductive) Future: The Discursive Construction of ARTS as Technologies of Self', *Frontiers*, 35 (1): 73–106.

Myers, K. (2017), 'If I'm Going to Do It, I'm Going to Do It Right': Intensive Mothering Ideologies among Childless Women Who Elect Egg Freezing', *Gender & Society*, 31 (6): 777–803.

OECD (2019), *OECD Employment and Labour Market Statistics*. Available online: https://www.oecd-ilibrary.org/ (accessed 3 September 2019).

Ozyegin, G. (2009), 'Virginal Facades: Sexual Freedom and Guilt among Young Turkish Women', *European Journal of Women's Studies*, 16 (2): 103–23.

Ozyegin, G. (2015), *New Desires, New Selves: Sex, Love, and Piety among Turkish Youth*, New York: New York University Press.

Repo, J. (2016), 'Gender Equality as Biopolitical Governmentality in a Neoliberal European Union', *Social Politics*, 23 (2): 307–28.

Rimon-Zarfaty, N. (2019), 'Freezing for the Fourth and Fifth Child" The Usage of Social Egg Freezing among Israeli Religious Women: An Intracultural Perspective', *International Expert Symposium: Comparative and Transnational Perspectives on Technologies of Fertility Preservation and Extension*, 13 June, De Montfort University Leicester, UK.

Robertson, J. A. (2014), 'Egg Freezing and Egg Banking: Empowerment and Alienation in Assisted Reproduction', *Journal of Law and the Biosciences*, 1 (2): 1–24.

Rose, N. (2004), *Powers of Freedom: Reframing Political Thought*, Cambridge: Cambridge University Press.

Rottenberg, C. (2017), 'Neoliberal Feminism and the Future of Human Capital', *Signs*, 42 (4): 329–48.

Savulescu, J. and I. Goold (2008), 'Freezing Eggs for Lifestyle Reasons', *American Journal of Bioethics*, 6: 32–5.

Scalco, P. D. (2016), 'The Politics of Chastity: Marriageability and Reproductive Rights in Turkey', *Social Anthropology*, 24 (3): 324–37.

Spar, D. (2006), *The Baby Business: How Money, Science, and Politics Drive the Commerce of Conception*, Boston, MA: Harvard Business School Press.

Stoop, D., J. Nekkebroeck and P. Devroey (2011), 'A Survey on the Intentions and Attitudes towards Oocyte Cryopreservation for Non-Medical Reasons among Women of Reproductive Age', *Human Reproduction*, 26 (3): 655–61.

Stoop, D. et al. (2014), 'Fertility Preservation for Age-Related Fertility Decline', *Lancet*, 384: 1311–19.

Streeck, W. (2009), 'Flexible Employment, Flexible Families, and the Socialization of Reproduction', Max Planck Institute for the Study of Societies Working Paper Series, Köln.

TURKSTAT (2016), *Labor Force Statistics*. Available online: http://www.turkstat.gov.tr/ (accessed 15 December 2016).

van de Wiel, L. (2014), 'For Whom the Clock Ticks: Reproductive Ageing and Egg Freezing in Dutch and British News Media', *Studies in the Maternal*, 6: 1–28.

Waldby, C. (2015a), '"Banking Time": Egg Freezing and the Negotiation of Future Fertility', *Culture, Health & Sexuality*, 17 (4): 470–82.

Waldby, C. (2015b), 'The Oocyte Market and Social Egg Freezing: From Scarcity to Singularity', *Journal of Cultural Economy*, 8 (3): 275–91.

World Bank (2017), *Education Statistics*. Available online: http://databank.worldbank.org (accessed 2 May 2017).

World Values Survey (2014), Wave 6, 2010–14. Official aggregate v.20150418. Available online: http://www.worldvaluessurvey.org/ (accessed 20 December 2016).

Zelizer, V. A. (1978), 'Human Values and the Market: The Case of Life Insurance and Death in 19th-Century America', *American Journal of Sociology*, 84: 591–610.

Zola, I. K. (1972), 'Medicine as an Institution of Social Control', *The Sociological Review*, 20 (4): 487–504.

8

Tactics of women up against obstetrical violence and the medicalization of childbirth in Turkey

Selen Göbelez

The dynamics of the over-medicalization of childbirth for Turkish women

'Medicalization' refers to the process whereby medicine as an institution of social control increases its influence on the everyday life of individuals by becoming the new repository of truth, based on the judgements of allegedly neutral experts in the name of health (Zola 1972: 487). With the rising involvement of men in childbirth around the turn of the century, traditional woman-centred home-birthing practices have been replaced by technologically guided hospital births, dominated by male doctors and reinforced by the expectation that increased medicalization would make birth safer and more comfortable. This change, portrayed by the historical account of Leavitt as a 'negotiated process' between the women from middle and well-to-do classes and healthcare professionals, did not lead to an immediate decline in infant and maternal mortality. Deprived from the network of supportive female friends and relatives, women increasingly underwent alienating birth experiences outside of their homes and 'alone among strangers' (Walzer Leavitt 1986: 171). The fundamental paradigm of modern obstetrical practice – otherwise defined as the 'medical model' by Rothman (1982) or the 'technocratic birth model' by Davis-Floyd (1992) – originates from the idea that if the deficient female body is connected to perfectly functioning diagnostic equipment, a 'better outcome' will result.

The pioneering critiques of the medicalization of childbirth, notably Oakley (1980) and Katz Rothman (1982), have unfolded the larger cultural and social structures to show the trends that turn babies into commodities and erode the autonomy of pregnant women (Fox and Worts 1999: 328–9). It is within the purposes of this chapter to situate childbirth practices in contemporary Turkey as practices of capitalist techno-medicalization that are influenced by a conservative undercurrent.

In Turkey, the medicalization of pregnancy and childbirth started in the late nineteenth century and continues on in Republican norms and practices, which are inseparable from modernization and pronatalist policies. Among the limited studies on the medicalization of childbirth in Turkey, the rigorous works of Balsoy (2013),

Beyinli (2014) as well as Cindoğlu and Sayan-Cengiz (2010) unanimously portray how the quality and quantity of the population have been a primal concern for the young Turkish Republic to the same extent as they were in the late Ottoman Empire, whereby women were perceived either as the producers of the population or as agents that would nurture and reproduce the seeds of the nation (Beyinli 2014: 43).

Partly due to the segregation of the feminine and masculine spheres in Ottoman society, replacement of midwives by male physicians has taken longer than it took to eventuate in Europe. When population became a concern for Ottoman elites, their policies focused on reducing infant and maternal mortality, prohibition of abortion and introducing a modern regulation of traditional midwifery. Instead of disqualifying midwives completely, they implemented a policy of 'qualifying' and registering midwives so that their roles were then subordinate to doctors. The first steps to remove birth from the home to a hospital setting were taken with the opening of Haseki Women's Hospital in 1847 (Balsoy 2013).

The governing of female bodies through medicalizing maternity continues in the new Turkish Republic as the experience and knowledge of midwives become progressively subordinate to scientific male-dominated knowledge that is legitimized by male authority. Despite the reforms for women's participation in the public space, 'a new form of patriarchy that defines itself as modern, progressive, Western and enlightened was born' and has pervasively propagated into the spheres of life that were 'traditionally women's domains, most notably the healing arts and especially childbirth'. (Cindoğlu and Sayan-Cengiz 2010: 223).

Pregnancy and childbirth practices since the year 2000 can be defined as almost entirely medicalized, technology-dependent and situated in hospital settings.[1] Some of the components of medicalization include systematic procedural interventions such as intravenous infusions and oxytocin in labour, continuous electronic foetal monitoring, epidural analgesia, routine vaginal examinations, forced dorsal position and delivery in lithotomy as well as caesarean sections. Although some non-evidence-based interventions (such as enemas, pubic shaving and episiotomy) are not informed by the World Health Organization (WHO) guidelines, they have become routine in Turkey. Another dimension of over-medicalization is the treatment of pregnant and birthing women as 'sick' and consequently categorizing them as 'patients'. Thus, often women are not only perceived as physically deficient so as to be obliged to use wheelchairs, for instance, but also as incapable of participating in decision-making processes about their maternity care. They are forced into relying on the experts' knowledge as their embodiment and experience-based knowledge of pregnancy, birth and reproduction are undermined.

Within the varied corpus of research on childbirth in Western contexts, empirical evidence shows that while some women were alienated by the experience of medicalized birth, some women, across social classes, accepted medical interventions at hospital settings and reported their satisfaction (Sargent and Stark 1989; Davis-Floyd 1992; Lazarus 1994). The findings of the study at hand indicate a similar diversity in reactions from women. The satisfaction levels from birth outcome depend on multiple factors that range from expected delivery method to the existence of support. Yet, the need of treatment with dignity and respect for privacy as well as physical and emotional support before, during and after birth appear as the prominent issues that are important for women. In this research, I adopt a double-layered approach in order to analyse the experiences and the agencies of women alongside the consideration of the macro social structures. The real-life experiences of women involved in this qualitative study portray hybrid interpretations, which sometimes surpass the dichotomies of caesarean vs. vaginal, natural vs. medical, home vs. hospital, or male doctor vs. female midwife.

In understanding the unspoken, unusual and unexplored experiences that challenge the dualities of the binary systems, belonging to the fluid and complex, almost 'abject', sentiments around pregnancy, childbirth and motherhood, methodological and theoretical toolkit of the approaches in queer studies may offer opportunities to expose the multifaceted singularities of the mothers' subjectivities and gender performances during childbirth. Whilst queer scholarship is more often concerned with examining the experiences of sexual/gender minorities, a 'queering' of heterosexual relations has previously been argued for (Browne and Nash 2010: 5). Thus, in situating my heterosexual cisgender female informants' narratives in a broader and more critical discussion, it is seminal to question the possibilities of 'queering of childbirth' in line with Mikdashi's appeal to queer Middle East studies, suggesting a methodology of queering as 'a way of interrogating normative practices of and assumptions about race, class, the state, and the body' (Mikdashi 2013: 350). Allouche's recent account of cis heterosexual couples, which engages queer theory beyond sexuality through the specific context of Lebanon, is not only a successful response to Mikdashi's call but also an effective methodological 'queering' of heterosexual relations to subvert hegemonic interpretations of 'man and wife' by identifying the political potential of romantic love. (Allouche 2019). Visions of the anti-normative queer scholarship in destabilizing, challenging and critiquing accepted 'stabilities' (Browne and Nash 2010) might assist us in interpreting how normative social categories can be disrupted through everyday performances of resistance.

In the dim light of such theoretical and methodological concerns, this chapter elaborates how, in their heterogeneous, multilayered and amorphous childbirth experiences, women in Turkey develop flexible tactics that go beyond spatial and institutional borders. By tactics, I mean the individual decisions, actions and/or silence women adopt during childbirth to overcome, bypass or cope with the various biomedical exertions within the overarching framework of the dominant institutions. (De Certeau 1984). Meanwhile, it is vital to recall Abu-Lughod's eminent reminder about the 'romance of resistance' in interpreting 'all forms of resistance as ineffectiveness of systems of power and of the resilience and creativity of the human spirit in its refusal to be dominated' (Abu-Lughod 1990: 42).

Neoliberal strategies in health services

The modern childbirth practices in Turkey, as the champion of caesarean operations (Topçu 2019), are highly marked by the credo of neoliberalism along with the increasing religious and authoritarian discourses that govern predominantly through the control of women's bodies. In 2003, the 'Health Transformation Program' introduced the paradigmatic shift, which imposed the performance criteria that would lead to further deregulation, precarization, individualization, stratification and an increase in health inequalities. Reducing personnel expenses for 'maximum efficiency' and then introducing 'performance payments' instigated competition among health workers, leading to quantity being the priority rather than the quality of care, in turn influenced the relations between the healthcare personnel and the patients (Dayı and Karakaya 2018). The performance-based system increased the workload of health workers which resulted in intolerance and lack of communication within such intensive and exhaustive tempo (Öcal 2017: 85). Such neoliberal incentives had a considerable impact on the childbirth sector, as admitted by one of the OG (obstetric-gynaecologist) interviewees of Bülbül: 'Working in private institutions means not taking risks or making errors... All in all it becomes a job, there are no more patients. There are customers and also bosses to please' (Bülbül 2012: 42–3). It also had a negative effect on the caesarean decisions of obstetricians in the public sector, after the enactment of the so-called caesarean law in 2012. As analysed in Topçu's chapter in this volume, despite the recent regulatory measures targeting caesarean 'abuse' in public and private sectors, high C-section rates in Turkey have not been reduced by a considerable level. Indeed, the decrease in caesareans in public hospitals due to punitive measures was neutralized by the increase in C-section operations in private hospitals.

With this 'Healthcare Reform', which led to an explosive increase in the number of private hospitals, the number of caesarean operations has almost doubled, confirming the positive correlation between the rise in C-section operations and commercialization of childbirth. Similar to the Turkish case, in Brazil, for instance, caesarean rates in private hospitals (80–90 per cent) are considerably higher than in the public sector (35–45 per cent) (Nakamura-Pereira et al. 2016: 246).

A new legal term: Obstetric violence

Although it has been almost half a century that second-wave feminism and Women's Health Movement in the United States have challenged medicalization of childbirth and gynaecological violence, the recent appearance of the concept of 'obstetrical violence' has brought in a new legal term. Officially formulated in 2007 in Venezuela,[2] obstetric violence refers in general to disrespectful, non-consented care and abusive treatment of women by healthcare providers as well as a failure to adhere to evidence-based care, along with professional authoritarianism and sexist attitudes towards women.

Starting from 2014, five Obstetric Violence Observatories, founded in Chile, Spain, Argentina, Colombia and France, released a common statement declaring obstetric violence as one of the most invisible and naturalized forms of violence against women and a serious violation of human rights (Sadler et al. 2016: 50). In October 2019, Parliamentary Assembly of the Council of Europe adopted a resolution on 'Obstetrical and gynecological violence', which, though not binding, nevertheless constitutes a major step for the political recognition of obstetrical violence.[3] It is also significant to frame the discussion of abuse and disrespect within the broader field of structural inequalities and violence against women. It is in the aims of this chapter to situate the various mistreatments women experienced during their childbirth as fragments of obstetrical violence whether or not women themselves define their experiences as such. I adopt such an approach mainly because lack of consent is an important component of obstetrical violence and that even in the case of consent, sometimes women either interiorize or, through softer tactics, they develop a self-perception as non-victims, as shall be elaborated in the following pages.

Within the agenda of the feminist movement in Turkey highly charged with abortion rights and femicide, there has not been a lively reflection of the international obstetrical violence debate, with the exception of a few health professionals, mainly midwives and doulas, sensitive to the topic. Thus, in the lack of a structured movement against obstetrical violence, this empirical research aims to contribute to the feminist criticism.

Methodological framework

Two years after my own caesarean experience in a luxuriously medicalized private hospital in Istanbul, I conducted preliminary fieldwork in 2013 interviewing one midwife, two OGs and one doula, to understand the various aspects of high caesarean rates. This preliminary fieldwork indicated to adopt a broader conceptual tool than caesarean sections, towards medicalization of birth and the importance of the experiences and voices of women themselves. Thus, mothers were recruited through mainly a mixed method of convenience sampling and snowball sampling. The women interviewed through convenience sampling were predominantly educated women from middle and higher classes living in the central neighbourhoods of Istanbul, who have given birth in their late 30s. With the need to include the voices of women with differing social and educational levels, through snowball sampling, I interviewed women from lower-income and -education groups who have given birth before the age of 25. Meanwhile, with the interest as to the possibilities of more respectful childbirth practices, I followed a doula-training program, which also helped me to conduct participant observation of childbirth practices and the milieu of doulas, some of whom I also interviewed for this research.

I conducted semi-structured face-to-face, in-depth interviews between 2016 and 2017 with a sample of thirty-seven women who gave birth in Turkey within the last twenty-five years. In order to provide a plurality of experiences, the field consists of mothers from various districts of Istanbul, who gave birth at private institutions, public hospitals or at home, by vaginal or caesarean delivery. These women whose age at first birth varied between 14 and 40 belong to differing social classes, with educational levels varying from illiterate to PhD graduate. Twenty of the participants were younger than 25 years old when they gave birth to their first child. The main differences between the younger mothers and the older mothers in this research correlate with the results of the Turkish Population Survey in the sense that the younger the age of birth, the lower the education and income level of the women (Hacettepe Institute of Population Studies 2019: 55). Moreover, the majority of the younger mothers have given vaginal births at public hospitals. The interviews also portray how in the urban and cosmopolitan setting of Istanbul with its high levels of rural immigration from all corners of the country, the local and the global, the traditional and the modern and the 'natural' and the medical intermingle together to create hybrid practices around childbirth.

In the next section, some of the common constituents of over-medicalization such as routine episiotomy, vaginal examination, verbal and/or physical violence, and disrespect for intimacy are discussed. This discussion is based on the analysis of the transcripts of the recorded interviews that lasted between 60 and 90 minutes. In the final section, some examples of the ways in which women resist, negotiate or bypass and manoeuvre mistreatments are elaborated.

Researching the voices of women in the face of obstetrical violence

Cutting below

In the highly medicalized maternity services in Turkey, among the foremost-routinized interventions of enema administration[4], amniotomy[5] and fundal pressure, women found the episiotomy[6] as the most disturbing procedure. One recent Cochrane review that could not identify any benefits of routine episiotomy for the baby or the mother concludes that the rationale for conducting routine episiotomies to prevent severe perineal trauma is not justified by current evidence (Jiang et al. 2017).

There is no official national data or any nationwide research in Turkey on episiotomy. According to one study, in 2007, episiotomy was conducted in more than 65 per cent of hospital births and 90 per cent of the primiparous (Hotun Şahin, Yıldırım, and Aslan 2007). The same year, the average national rate of episiotomy was reported to be 70.33 per cent in another study, which concluded that 96.72 per cent of primiparous and 51.85 per cent of multiparous women experienced episiotomy (Sayıner and Demirci 2007). Consent is a substantial criterion in defining a medical intervention as obstetrical violence. In my research, none of my interviewees was asked for consent before episiotomy. Women who gave birth twenty years ago as much as women who recently gave birth remember episiotomy as one of the most terrible and painful moments of birth.

Ayfer,[7] who gave birth 23 years ago, admits she didn't know anything about episiotomy before: 'They did seven, eight, nine stitches... all the way behind... up to my butt... It is terrible. They suture you alive, without asking. I suffered a lot in the beginning' (Ayfer, age 46, 1 child).

Münevver also remembers vividly her experience of episiotomy in the most popular state hospital for childbirth in Istanbul.

> It hurt a lot, I still remember very well the moment of cutting, although it was 20 years ago... The child gets out, you forget everything, and you feel relieved. But I still can't forget the cut and the stitches...I don't know if it is easier for the doctor or what. (Münevver, age 41, 1 child)

Actually the application of certain medical procedures is based on unquestioned habits of medical staff that they have acquired throughout their medical training, more than the consideration of the actual needs and respect for the bodily integrity of the women.

For instance, Burcu who, for her first birth in 2015, didn't want to have an episiotomy tried to talk to the hospital staff into not applying it. However the response was: 'we learned that way during our education, we can't do otherwise' (Burcu, age 24, 1 child).

'Fingering' – repetitive vaginal examinations

Another disconcerting routine for women is the frequent pelvic examinations (especially if conducted by several male interns) to determine the opening of the cervix during the labour stage. Most of the mothers stated that they found pelvic examinations not only painful but also uncomfortable and sometimes embarrassing. One of the interviewees, who gave birth to her second child in a private hospital in 2005, narrates her experiences as following:

> Various interns came and examined me. It is as if they made experiments on us. Both men and women came. I contracted myself when it was a man 'fingering'. I was closing my legs when it was the male interns and they were getting mad at me. (Fadime, age 38, 3 children)

However, despite WHO's (2018) recommendation, vaginal examination of the same woman by multiple caregivers around the same time or at different times is a common practice, especially at education and research hospitals. Ayfer, who had her first vaginal examination in 1995 when she was pregnant, describes her experience as dishonouring:

> I had found it very humiliating. The nurse lined us all and told all the women to take off their skirts and panties. Half of our bodies naked, we opened our legs and started waiting. I felt terrible, it was very mean and I felt humiliated. Doctors don't even look at your faces. He put the device (*speculum*) in and all the interns looked inside. I was traumatized. (Ayfer, age 46, 1 child)

Kapsalis, who elaborates on the public exposure of female 'privates' in the performance of the pelvic exams, argues that gynaecology is not simply the study of women's bodies, but that it also defines and constitutes them. In that sense, 'if the pelvic examination is not performed properly, […] if the patient is not sufficiently transformed into an object […], the examination of non-compliance threatens the stability of the medicalization of this object' (Kapsalis 1997:14). In her analysis of the politics of tactility formed at the intersection of violence, intimacy and sex/gender transgressive lives, Zengin examines the sensory apparatus, precisely diverse forms of violent touch by institutional actors. Her enquiry in two fields, namely trans women in public hospitals and gay men in military hospitals, reveals the institutional preoccupation with (penile) penetration whereby penetration becomes 'a medico-legal abstraction for gender identity and sexual orientation' (Zengin 2016). In a parallel vein, I suggest that systematic exercise of tactile penetration (palpation, bimanual, speculum, etc.), particularly without informed consent and respect for the intimacy of the women, may serve as an intimidating act in the process of constructing potentially docile bodies.

Class and violence

Although not exclusively, narratives of mistreatment during birth are more recurrent in the case of less educated women with lower incomes who gave birth in public hospitals, at younger ages as exemplified in the following cases. Similarly, the findings of a recent cross-sectional study in four countries (Ghana, Guinea, Myanmar and Nigeria) show that young age and lack of education are the primary determinants of mistreatment during birth (Bohren et al. 2019).

In the highly stratified and medicalized birthing culture in Turkey, women from lower socio-economic classes are subject to double-folded symbolic violence. Some women who gave birth at public hospitals and were not content with the approach of health professionals claimed that they would prefer a private hospital if they could afford it because of the possibility of having a private room, intimacy and more personalized care. In their passage into motherhood some of these women have experienced verbal insults at different levels by doctors, midwives or nurses. Some of the phrases reported by different women include: 'Even those elephants give birth to those huge babies, why can't you do it?'; 'The baby would have been born by now but the patient is incompatible'; 'Look, I put an extra stitch for you' (*looking at the husband*).

Among the narratives of violence, the example of Merve who abstained from conceiving a second baby after her first birth experience, in 1997 in one of the most known public hospital in Istanbul, is worth mentioning. 'Nobody helped me. The nurses were shouting at me... They even used bad words: "you knew how to do that thing and now why are you screaming?"' (Merve, age 43, 1 child).

Merve, who continues her story with tears in her eyes, also admits, during our interview, that it is the first time she explains her childbirth experience to someone:

> I get goose bumps when I hear the name of that hospital. I want to forget these. After birth, they were putting stitches. As I was moving up the bed with pain, the midwife was saying: 'If your husband will accept you this way, go. Instead of soothing me and taking care of me,' she said 'I will see you here next year'. I replied, 'Yes, You will!!' I never wanted to have a second child... That's why I hate midwives... Not everyone is rich enough to afford a private hospital. (Merve, age 43, 1 child)

Neslihan, who gave birth in 2016 at the age of 22 in a university hospital, had a similar souvenir of disrespect: 'After the birth I was waiting at the birthing bed and I was so cold I was begging them to let my husband and mother bring socks. The rooms were clean but I did not like their attitude, they shouted a lot, you couldn't ask any questions, you couldn't say anything to them' (Neslihan, age 22, 1 child).

Such silencing by healthcare personnel faced with women screaming during labour is repeatedly recounted by participants. In order to understand this phenomenon, Shabot argues, 'laboring bodies are at least potentially perceived as antithetical to the myth of femininity, undermining the feminine mode of bodily comportment under patriarchy and thereby seriously threatening the hegemonic powers... Violence, then, appears to be necessary in order to domesticate these bodies, to make them "feminine" again' (Shabot 2015).

Some critics point out the links between oppressive social structures and the appropriation and medicalization of childbirth, as being rooted in a patriarchal approach that 'perceives women as essentially abnormal, as victims of their reproductive systems and hormones', which needs to be controlled (Cahill 2001: 334). The narrative of Sibel is an accurate example of violence exerted on the pretext of the endeavour of controlling the uncontained and unruly birthing body. 'My doctor was late, the emergency gynecologist was very rude. After birth he came and said the reason he was so rough was "to keep the birth and the mother under control" and then he apologized' (Sibel, age 30, 1 child).

In parallel with my results about the class-based variation in the healthcare professionals' attitude towards birthing women, Cindoğlu and Sayan-Cengiz point out the significance of the education and the background of the patient. 'While physicians and midwives defend their attitudes, they usually make loaded references to the concepts of "modern" and "traditional". Being uneducated and coming from a village seems to correspond to being "traditional" or "backward," not knowing how to behave in a modern building and how to talk to physicians, displaying uncontrolled and undisciplined behavior, such as screaming unnecessarily during birth. These are presented as justifications to harsh or neglectful attitudes' (Cindoğlu and Sayan-Cengiz 2010: 240).

On the other hand, the older interviewees who mostly were from more urban and educated layers repetitively defined their experience of first passage into motherhood as that of an 'ignorant' moment. In explaining their birthing experience, many women defined themselves as 'young', 'inexperienced', 'not knowing', 'novice', 'shy', 'ashamed', 'humiliated', 'disrespected', 'passive', etc. Often they felt vulnerable in the face of medical practices and the authority of medical professionals. It is the stigma, humiliation and lack of respect for intimacy, which seem to have left a mark in their memory more than the birth pain itself.

Losing control of their own bodily powers and their ability to decide is an experience described by some women, sometimes irrelevant of their educational, social and economical statuses. This has been the most astonishing aspect for Ezra, who has been teased due to her weight by her gynaecologist. As a human and women's rights advocate, she finds it difficult to understand how she could surrender to such disrespectful attitude: 'In front of my husband and my mother who weighs 40 kilos, he said: "I hope the baby looks like your mother instead of you". At each consultation, I was under pressure about my weight' (Ezra, age 33, 1 child).

Moreover, Ezra was very much disturbed because her arms were tied up during the C-section operation, despite her will. Attaching the arms and establishing vascular catheter to both arms impede mothers from touching their babies after the caesarean birth, which might lead to the delay of mother–baby attachment. She explained: 'I told them not to tie me but they didn't listen to me. Those leather belts reminded me all the torture court files I was involved as a lawyer' (Ezra, age 33, 1 child).

Multiple tactics of women during birth

Self-silencing

As 'maternal bodies are socially, sexually, ethnically, class specific bodies that are mutable in terms of their cultural production' (Longhurst 2008: 3), the reactions and the responses of women up against mistreatment are varied ranging from acceptance to developing mechanisms of resistance. Some women act in accordance and use a tactic of self-silencing, in some cases to behave like a 'good girl', due to potential fears of leaving a bad impression. Internalized technologies of gender serve to make birth more difficult for women and often cause them not to ask for what they need while giving birth and not to put themselves at the centre of the birth experience (Martin 2003: 59).

Self-silencing, deeply related with social structures, rooted in the gender norms designated by the culture, emerges from an attempt to 'fill a gender role marked by passivity, body shame, fear and vulnerability, and niceness' (Jack and Ali 2010: 141). Gender norms about docile and silent behaviour for women foster an over-eye, which can be comprehended 'as the cultural, moralistic voice that condemns the self for departing from culturally prescribed shoulds' (Maji and Dixit 2019: 4). Such social norms of domination can be reproduced by the dominated as explained by Bourdieu with the concept of symbolic violence, 'exercised only through an active knowledge and practical recognition which takes place below the level of the consciousness and will and which gives all its manifestations – injunctions, suggestions, seduction, threats, reproaches, orders or calls to order –their "hypnotic power"' (Bourdieu 2001: 42). 'The dominated applies categories, which are constructed from the point of view of the dominant to the relations of domination, making them appear natural... This can lead to a kind of systematic self-depreciation, even self-denigration' (Bourdieu 2001: 35). In cases of incorporation of gender-based hierarchy, the acceptance of mistreatment is accompanied by almost a normalization of violence. Jale, for instance, who had her first child in 1995, says, 'The doctors were good to me. Anyway I am a shy person. That male doctor was shouting not at us but others. Those who were having their second or third children were screaming too much. The doctors were right.' When she had to go to the toilet, she wasn't allowed by the nurses who shouted at her claiming that the baby might fall. 'That's normal. What else shall she do? Of course she will shout. I am not the only one at the hospital. That was normal, there were many other women; I mean that is normal, really normal' (Jale, age 39, 2 children). Jale who is a housewife, from a lower class, has become mother at the age of 17. Albeit not necessarily, the findings of my research emphasize that class and education levels play some roles in the normalizing interpretation and description of violence.

In a similar vein, another participant, Hanife, who gave birth at the age of 17, says:

> I had a relative who was telling me scary things about childbirth saying that they hit and shout at the hospital... Sometimes I give them right. I didn't see it because there was a curtain but the doctor shouted and spanked the woman next to me. If you do what the doctor says, believe me there is no problem. We don't know but

the doctor is telling you. If you aren't stupid you understand. He says to push and she screams. The doctor is a human being too. You should do what he says for your and his comfort. (Hanife, age 44, 2 children)

During the interviews, rarely women themselves defined the treatment they received as a form of violence. Often it turned out at the end of the interview that a little less than half of the women weren't fully satisfied with their childbearing experiences. Some of the criteria of satisfaction were hygiene, respect for intimacy, physical and emotional support, and positive communication with the health professionals. Those who felt understood, respected and valued reported to have better remembrances of their birth experiences.

Women with memories of violence refer to feelings of infantilization and the diminishment of self. The unequal power relation between the doctors with authoritative knowledge and the women in the position of patient is amplified with the responsibility and moral obligation of carrying the foetus which almost paralyses women in their transition to motherhood.

As Ezra recounts:

I don't understand how I could put myself in that situation of patient whereas I am a defender of rights. My mission is to empower people against the malpractice. I was in such a psychology of a sick patient that I couldn't protect my own rights. If I couldn't do that, how can a simple woman on the street defend her rights in that system? I am an educated woman with a master's degree on human rights, who struggle with police at the police station. And I couldn't do a single thing when a nurse told me to shut up. I don't know why I acted like a sheep ready to be sacrificed. I guess I thought I must be like that, passive. (Ezra, age 33, 1 child)

The responsibility she felt for the foetus combined with the fact that she is in an unfamiliar environment contributed to her temporarily acceptance of the role of less knowledgeable patient vis-à-vis the 'expert' doctor.

Some of those women admit that, if they were to give birth again, they would do things differently: insist more on their own needs, not allow the healthcare personnel yell at them and ask for more information before complying with the orders of the health personnel. Sometimes women develop negotiation strategies, acts of rebellion or resistance. However, none of these have turned into legal actions, nor into some forms of organized or collective resistance as far as the women included in this study are concerned. Although complaint lines about violation of patient rights have been established with the Health Reform, none of the women interviewed have complained verbally or in writing to the hospital authorities.

This research is also an attempt to make visible women's action (and refusal of action) and make audible their voices (and their silences) in their struggle for comfort, dignity and autonomy in the face of physical or psychological violence, in a context of absence of organized and overt resistance. Instead of portraying women as passive objects of medical surveillance, it is important to take into account the fact that women are active participants with some level of power whether they respond to reproductive technologies via assimilation, compliance or resistance. Thus, such self-silencing is to be related with an almost willing submission to reproductive technologies and medical intervention, mainly in the lack of other possible alternatives. Women, who are better off in terms of socio-economical status with an access to alternative information and opportunities, on the other hand, may opt for other solutions such as doula support or care provided by private OGs specialized in natural birth.

Lines of flight

When the power is too compact to confront directly, some women develop certain tactics that I call the 'lines of flight'.[8] Rather than predetermined resolutions, such spontaneous tactics of escape are less about anticipating a future outcome than it is about the process of becoming. Such lines of flight can take the form of bending of authority often in a silenced manner. For instance, Fadime heard that they shouted to the woman next to her saying, 'it was good when you were taking it in, is it bad now to take it out?' She laughs and explains almost 'impishly': 'You try to develop a psychology so that they don't shout at you. It was forbidden to have water at the "pain room".[9] They told me not to drink but I couldn't stand it. I wrapped a bottle of water inside my clothes. Then I had to go to the toilet but they wouldn't allow me go to the bathroom either. I drew the curtains, secretly pulled the garbage bin under my body and started peeing' (Fadime, age 36, 2 children, pregnant for the third one during our interview).

Concentrating on their embodied needs and desires by turning a deaf ear and ignoring the authority become ways of creating lines of flight for some women. Such a response is often likely in subsequent pregnancies. One strategy is to delay going to the hospital as much as possible. In very few (and marginal) cases opting for a home birth is another alternative. Actually we can claim that those women respond to the interpellations of medicalization by 'ignoring the call', as Jale explains:

> For the second birth I said I would not go to the hospital even if I were dead... You become more experienced after the first one. I had some pain, but I said to myself I will not go. I said to my mother that I would not go so early. They were forcing me to go to the hospital. However, I knew it, I tried to spend as much time as possible at home. (Jale, age 39, 2 children)

Ignoring, oblivion and silence may become forms of coping with the authoritarian modes of governing women's bodies. Silence acts as a means of coping with traumatic birth memoires. Some women talked about the details of their birth stories first time with me. 'I didn't tell these to anybody before, not even my husband, and nobody asked me anyway,' says Ayşe (age 39, 4 children).

Humour becomes another way of dealing with the violence and the memory of that violence. Those who have witnessed some sort of mistreatment related with their birth would either cry or laugh narrating that experience. Humour is the way Nuriye, for example, handled the violence she had observed at the medical structure. She said: 'The doctor was shouting at the woman who was giving birth next to me. I was the only one who didn't scream. If I listened to the other women around, psychologically

I would be scared and scream myself. I continuously made fun of the situation and joked with the doctors' (Nuriye, age 32, 1 child, pregnant for the second one during our interview).

Cutting above

Finally, the two outstanding birth stories of Fazilet are worth mentioning in detail, because it portrays how the birth experiences can be empowering or devastating depending on the attitude and the support. Although Fazilet, a 32-year-old university-graduate, wanted to have a vaginal birth, her gynaecologist (in a private hospital) pushed her to have a caesarean. He tried to convince her in the following way: 'I will cut you either from down if you have normal birth or from up if you have C-section.' He also threatened her by saying: 'You will not be able to give birth, you will die at the birthing table and the child will die in your womb.'

> He threw to me the Electronic Fetal Monitoring results and said 'I told you 2 weeks ago to have a caesarean. Now go away and give birth at another hospital. You waited 40 weeks, now you will return home with empty arms'.... My husband wasn't there and my parents-in-law begged the doctor to accept me. I was sitting there in one corner silently, in shock. Then he said 'I accept this stubborn goat only for your sake. Otherwise I wouldn't bother.' (Fazilet, age 32, 2 children)

Later on she found out that the vaginal deliveries were almost non-existent in that private hospital. 'Due to commercial reasons all the doctors opt for surgical births,' she says. Although she wanted to, she didn't sue the doctor for the fear of seeing his face again. She felt very desperate and helpless, like she was 'punished for something she wished for'. During her difficult postnatal period that lacked support, she tried to drown herself. She was saved by her husband who broke the door to find her fainted in the bathtub. Subsequently she went through a long therapy, followed private birth classes, read every possible material about birth and became a VBAC (vaginal birth after caesarean) advocate. Five years later she gave birth to her son, assisted by a gynaecologist experienced in VBAC, an experienced midwife in natural birth and a doula. After her totally natural vaginal birth, she felt she was reborn herself giving birth:

> It was as if my femininity was born as I was pushing the baby out of my vagina... As the child was coming out, it came with a strange sound that I never thought I could make normally. As I pushed, I felt the baby coming out, it slipped away and they put it on my belly directly. It was a grandiose relief, a vey beautiful feeling... close to a feeling of orgasm... As if I had butterflies fluttering around. I couldn't concentrate on anything else. I wanted to live that feeling until the end without focusing on other things. I didn't even think about taking photos, I didn't want to ruin that moment. It was something like orgasm. (Fazilet, age 32, 2 children)

After her second birth, she reports feeling special and beautiful: 'I have not felt myself beautiful for a long time. I have not felt like a woman. Actually I have been feeling like a piece of furniture satisfying the needs of my husband... With my second birth I felt strong enough to stand on my feet and found the power to tell my husband that I did not want him in my life anymore... I said to myself I want to live my sexuality fully.'

The narrative of Fazilet exhibits vividly how the process of childbirth has a life-changing effect on women physically and emotionally, affecting the relation between all family members. The trajectory of Fazilet can also be interpreted as a distortion of the patriarchal consensus to define women's sexual intimacy as it relates to procreation and social reproduction rather than pleasure as well as the collapse of the 'honour codes' of Turkish hegemonic masculinity which recognize women's sexuality as the property of men, family or society rather than women themselves (Koğacıoğlu 2004; also referred by Zengin 2016: 229).

The importance of respect for privacy and intimacy, personalized care, encouragement and communication is a common value emphasized by many women. Similarly, Duru, a doula, who felt that her birth choices were not respected, underlines the importance of kindness, compassion and understanding necessary for women to feel empowered by their birth experience:

> I felt ignored. I was just any woman who had a caesarean. I wasn't there like an individual, more like a part of mass production. You try to say something but nobody wants you to say that and they suppress you with the defensive structure of the system. It is as if once that box is open, something will come out, like the fear of the patriarchal society from the women. Like they know a force will come out of it, no one dares to open that box. Unless women are aware of their own strengths, nobody in the society says, 'come on, you can do it!' (Duru, age 35, 1 child, pregnant for her second child during our interview)

Re-appropriation of their birth within a respectful framework is crucial for women to feel satisfied about their childbirth experience. Rusen, who had felt not only humiliation but also too much pain during vaginal examination, mentions lack of privacy due to the existence of too much staff in the room as one crucial problem. Although she was disturbed about the existence of too many people around her, she couldn't say it. She draws a direct connection between the mistreatment and the problems of bonding with her baby and even the effects of her psychological postnatal condition on the stress level of her son: 'Actually at that moment nothing is about you. You live something that you want to be special. At the same time you are in pain. It is my day today and I am suffering, and nobody really cares' (Rusen, age 28, 1 child).

Conclusion

'Freedom of a country can be measured by the freedom of birth' – Agnes Gereb

In the neoliberal governmentality of contemporary Turkey, authoritarian and pronatalist strategies based on neoconservative family values cooperate with the dominating medicalization and violence against women during childbirth practices. As some of the narratives illustrate, considering perinatal experiences of women requires an interpretation that reconstructs the subjectivities of women as active agents, rather than victims. Thus it is important to make visible the struggle of women, for their comfort, dignity and autonomy in the face of obstetrical violence by underlying the tactics and the capacities to act and resist. The intention of such an interpretative opportunity is to disclose the power of the birthing feminine body defined as a 'biopolitical womb' (Miller 2007) in the discourses of political elites and rendered vulnerable within the boundaries of medicalized and commercialized maternity settings. However in such a pursuit, the trap of dichotomies such as natural vs. medical requires attention. As pointed out by Wackerhausen, countering such medicalizing strategies with a strong emphasis on 'natural' or 'normal' may be more of a burden than a blessing, more a source of confusion than a source of clarification (Wackerhausen 1999: 1110). The Australian organization Birthtalk describes traumatic birth as a birth that 'stays with you… It might not look "that bad" to an outsider… It could have been a caesarean or a natural birth. It might have taken 30 hours or 3 hours. A bad birth is defined by the way you feel, not just the events that occurred' ('What Is a Bad Birth?' 2013).

Yet, the hierarchical relations between women and health personnel within the existing system create a gap, which may lead to rather unsatisfied birth expectancies. The uniqueness of each woman's experience is devoured in the factory-like functioning of the hospital setting, with a central accent on efficacy, whereby women can feel ignored and unvalued which impact negatively their postnatal period, sometimes leading to depression and even to suicide attempts, as in the case of Fazilet. Nearly half of the interviewees didn't have satisfying birth experiences, five of whom reported symptoms of possible postnatal depression, which were left undiagnosed. Eight of the interviewees reported to have experienced some form of violence, whereas three interviewees reported to have witnessed violence done to other women during their birth.

The present research correspondingly reveals that the comfort and satisfaction of women about their childbirth is related more to the manner they are treated than the method of birth. Brubaker and Dillaway (2009) discuss that the natural childbirth approach, with class and race bias, may deny women choice and agency, by 'essentializing' women's childbirth experiences. Thus, in the struggle against disrespectful mistreatments against women during birth, rather than attributing mystifying ahistorical and absolute traits such as 'natural' or 'normal', I suggest elucidating the dignity and power in the tactics of survival.

Furthermore, the results of the interviews highlight that the lack of empathy, understanding, intimacy, respect, personalized care and information are the main factors of dissatisfaction during the childbearing process. Women who have physical and emotional support before, during and after birth, for instance, by a doula, however, tend to have better comfort outcomes.

The reinforcement of the feminist criticism of medicalization and violence during childbirth, as have done the Women's Health Movement in the United States, in the context of recent legal changes instigates debates around obstetrical and gynaecological violence around the globe. It is imperative that, along with further academic research into the possibilities of respectful childbirth practices in Turkey, such legal attempts are employed for the protection of women's rights and dignity during pregnancy and childbirth.

Acknowledgments

I would like to thank The Raoul Wallenberg Institute of Human Rights and Humanitarian Law (RWI) for the short-term scholarship to fund this research partially, the editors for the meticulous work, Emma Dubois for her precious comments on proofreading my work and all the participants for their sincere contribution.

Notes

1   By 2018, the rate of births at health facilities is around 98 per cent, whereas it was around 60 per cent in 1993 (Hacettepe Institute of Population Studies 2019).
2   This was followed by Argentina in 2009 and the Mexican states of Durango, Veracruz, Guanajuato and Chiapas, in 2007, 2008, 2010 and 2012.
3   Resolution 2306 (2019) Parliamentary Assembly, Origin – Assembly debate on 3 October 2019 (34th Sitting).
4   Enemas, injection of liquid or gas into the rectum, to expel its contents during labour, have been routine practice in many countries and settings.
5   Artificial rupture of membranes (AROM), 'breaking the water', is the intentional rupture of the amniotic sac by an obstetrical provider. WHO (2014) notes, 'in spite of the common use of amniotomy for prevention of labor delay in clinical practice there is no clear evidence that the potential benefits outweigh harms.'
6   Episiotomy is a surgical incision of the perineum and the posterior vaginal wall during second stage of labour to quickly enlarge the opening for the baby.
7   All names used are pseudonyms.
8   'Line of flight' is a concept developed by Gilles Deleuze and Félix Guattari. Translated as line of flight, *ligne de fuits* in French implies the act of fleeing or escaping as well as flowing and leaking rather than flying (Deleuze and Guattari 1987).
9   In Turkey, the labour room is called 'pain room'.

References

Abu-Lughod, L. (1990), 'The Romance of Resistance: Tracing Transformations of Power Through Bedouin Women', *American Ethnologist*, 17 (1): 41–55.
Allouche, S. (2019), 'Queering Heterosexual (Intersectarian) Love in Lebanon', *International Journal of Middle East Studies*, 51 (4): 547–65.
Balsoy, G. (2013), *The Politics of Reproduction in Ottoman Society, 1838–1900*, London: Pickering & Chatto.
Beyinli G. (2014), *Elleri Tılsımlı: Modern Türkiye'de Ebelik*, Ankara: Ayizi Yayınları.
Bohren, M. A., H. Mehrtash, B. Fawole, T. Maung Maung, M. D. Balde, E. Maya, S. S. Thwin, A. K. Aderoba, J. P. Vogel, T. A. Irinyenikan, A. O. Adeyanju, N. O. Mon, K. Adu-Bonsaffoh, S. Landoulsi, C. Guure, R. Adanu, B. A. Diallo, A. M. Gülmezoğlu, A. Soumah, A. O. Sall and Ö. Tunçalp (2019), 'How Women Are Treated during Facility-based Childbirth in Four Countries: A Cross-sectional Study with Labour Observations and Community-based Surveys', *The Lancet*, 394 (10210): 1750–63.
Bourdieu, P. (2001), *Masculine Domination*, trans. R. Nice, Stanford: Stanford University Press.

Browne, K. and C. J. Nash, eds (2010), *Queer Methods and Methodologies: Intersecting Queer Theories and Social Science Research*, London: Ashgate.

Brubaker, S. and H. Dillaway (2009), 'Medicalization, Natural Childbirth and Birthing Experiences', *Sociology Compass*, 3 (1): 31–48.

Bülbül, G. (2012), 'İstanbul'da Çalışan Kadın Hastalıkları ve Doğum Uzmanlarının Doğum Şekli ile İlgili Görüş ve Önerileri', MA diss., Marmara University, Istanbul.

Cahill, H. A. (2001), 'Male Appropriation and Medicalization of Childbirth: an Historical Analysis', *Journal of Advanced Nursing*, 33 (3): 334–42.

Cindoğlu, D. and F. Sayan-Cengiz (2010), 'Medicalization Discourse and Modernity: Contested Meanings over Childbirth in Contemporary Turkey', *Health Care for Women International*, 31 (3): 221–43.

Davis-Floyd, R. E. (1992), *Birth as an American Rite of Passage*, Berkeley: University of California Press.

Dayı, A. and E. Karakaya (2018), 'Transforming the Gendered Regime Through Reproductive Politics: Neoliberal Health Restructuring, The Debt Economy and Reproductive Rights in Turkey', *Les cahiers du CEDREF*, 22: 158–92.

De Certeau, M. (1984), *The Practice of Everyday Life*, trans. S. F. Rendail, Berkeley: University of California Press.

Deleuze, G. and F. Guattari (1987 [1980]), *A Thousand Plateaus*, trans. B. Massumi, Minneapolis: University of Minnesota Press.

Fox, B. and D. Worts (1999), 'Revisiting the Critique of Medicalized Childbirth: A Contribution to the Sociology of Birth', *Gender & Society*, 13 (3): 326–46.

Hacettepe University Institute of Population Studies (2019), *2018 Turkey Demographic and Health Survey*, Hacettepe University Institute of Population Studies, T.R. Presidency of Turkey Directorate of Strategy and Budget and TÜBİTAK, Ankara, Turkey.

Hotun Şahin, N., G. Yıldırım and E. Aslan (2007), 'Evaluating the Second Stages of Deliveries in a Maternity Hospital', *Journal of Clinical Obstetrics and Gynecology*, 17 (1): 37–43.

Jack, D. C. and A. Ali, eds (2010), *Silencing the Self across Cultures: Depression and Gender in the Social World*, Oxford: Oxford University Press.

Jiang, H., X. Qian, G. Carroli and P. Garner (2017), 'Selective versus Routine Use of Episiotomy for Vaginal Birth', *Cochrane Database of Systematic Reviews*, 2.

Kapsalis, T. (1997), *Public Privates: Performing Gynecology from Both Ends of the Speculum*, Durham: Duke University Press.

Koğacıoğlu, D. (2004), 'The Tradition Effect: Framing Honor Crimes in Turkey', *Differences: A Journal of Feminist Cultural Studies*, 15 (2): 119–51.

Lazarus, E. S. (1994), 'What Do Women Want?: Issues of Choice, Control, and Class in Pregnancy and Childbirth', *Medical Anthropology Quarterly*, 8 (1): 25–46.

Longhurst, R. (2008), *Maternities: Gender, Bodies and Space*, New York: Routledge.

Maji, S. and S. Dixit (2019), 'Self-silencing and Women's Health', *International Journal of Social Psychiatry*, 65 (1): 3–13.

Martin, K. A. (2003), 'Giving Birth Like a Girl', *Gender and Society*, 17 (1): 54–72.

Mikdashi, M. (2013), 'Queering Citizenship, Queering Middle East Studies', *International Journal of Middle East Studies*, 45 (2): 350–2.

Miller, R. A (2007), *The Limits of Bodily Integrity: Abortion, Adultery, and Rape Legislation in Comparative Perspective*, Aldershot: Ashgate.

Nakamura-Pereira, M., M. do Carmo Leal, A. P. Esteves-Pereira, R. M. Soares Madeira Domingues, J. Alves Torres, M. A. Bastos Dias and M. E. Moreira (2016), 'Use of Robson Classification to Assess Cesarean Section Rate in Brazil: The Role of Source of Payment for Childbirth', *Reproductive Health*, 13 (128): 245–65.

Oakley, A. (1980), *Women Confined: Towards a Sociology of Childbirth*, Oxford: Martin Robertson.

Öcal, F. (2017), 'Neoliberal Sağlık Politikalarının Etkinlik Analizi', *Fiscaoeconomia*, 1 (1): 77–98.

Rothman, B. K. (1982), *In Labor: Women and Power in the Birthplace*, New York: W. W. Norton and Co.

Sadler, M., M. JDS Santos, D. Ruiz-Berdún, G. L. Rojas, E. Skoko, P. Gillen and J. A. Clausen (2016), 'Moving beyond Disrespect and Abuse: Addressing the Structural Dimensions of Obstetric Violence', *Reproductive Health Matters*, 24 (47): 47–55.

Sargent, C. and N. Stark (1989), 'Childbirth Education and Childbirth Models: Parental Perspectives on Control, Anesthesia, and Technological Intervention in the Birth Process', *Medical Anthropology Quarterly*, 3 (1): 36–51.

Sayıner, F. D. and N. Demirci (2007), 'Prenatal perineal masajın vaginal doğumlarda etkinliği'. *Florence Nightingale Hemsirelik Dergisi*, 15: 146–54.

Shabot, S. C. (2015), 'Making Loud Bodies "Feminine": A Feminist-Phenomenological Analysis of Obstetrical Violence', *Human Studies*, 39 (2): 231–47.

Topçu, S. (2019), 'Caesarean or Vaginarean Epidemics? Techno-birth, Risk and Obstetric Practice in Turkey', *Health, Risk & Society*, 21 (3–4): 141–63.

Topçu, S. (2021), 'Banning Caesareans or Selling "Choice"? The Paradoxical Regulation of Caesarean Section Epidemics and the Maternal Body in Turkey', in H. Alkan, A. Dayı, S. Topçu, B. Yarar (eds), *Politics of the Female Body in Turkey: Reproduction, Maternity, Sexuality*, London: I.B. Tauris.

Wackerhausen, S. (1999), 'What Is Natural? Deciding What to Do and Not to Do in Medicine and Health Care', *BJOG: An International Journal of Obstetrics and Gynaecology*, 106 (11): 1109–12.

Walzer Leavitt, J. (1986), *Brought to Bed: Childbearing in America 1750 to 1950*, New York: Oxford University Press.

'What Is a Bad Birth?' (2013), *birthtalk.org*™. Available online: http://birthtalk.org/had-a-bad-birth/what-is-a-bad-birth/ (accessed 12 November 2020).

World Health Organization (2014), *Recommendation on the Use of Amniotomy Alone for Prevention of Delay in Labour*, Geneva: World Health Organization.

WHO Reproductive Health Library (2018), *WHO Recommendation on Digital Vaginal Examination*, The WHO Reproductive Health Library, Geneva: World Health Organization.

Zengin, A. (2016), 'Violent Intimacies: Tactile State Power, Sex/Gender Transgression, and the Politics of Touch in Contemporary Turkey', *Journal of Middle East Women's Studies*, 12 (2): 225–45.

Zola, I. K. (1972), 'Medicine as an Institution of Social Control', *Sociological Review*, 20 (4): 487–504.

Part Three

Governing the sexualized body: Neoconservatism, authoritarianism and counter strategies

9

Misogynist Body Politics under the AKP Rule in Contemporary Turkey

Esra Sarıoğlu

In July 2018, a young Istanbul woman appeared on SHOWTV news, a nationwide television channel, in a pink sleeveless cotton shirt, jean shorts, and sneakers, wearing her hair in a low ponytail that kept it off her face. She paced herself as if she were just a local resident casually traipsing through the neighbourhood until the camera zoomed in on her face to reveal two black eyes she had suffered after neighbourhood bullies punched her in the face. A closer look also revealed the white bandages wrapped around both of her knees as well as the fact that she was visibly shaken. She had been attacked at night by a group of men, she explained, after giving a hug to her boyfriend, who walked her home where she lives with her parents. Upon seeing the couple on the street, a neighbourhood woman insulted the young woman and told her not to engage in public displays of affection in the presence of children, insinuating that what she had done was obscene. A group of local men, including the neighbourhood woman's husband, arrived at the scene, became violent and attacked the young woman, punching her in the face several times, pulling her hair, pushing her to the ground and dragging her body along the street. The young woman reported the incident to the police and initiated legal action against her attackers. One of the perpetrators spoke to the cameras and explained why he assaulted the young woman: 'My wife saw them while they were doing something inappropriate. I have been living here for thirty-five years and have never let anything obscene like this happen in my neighborhood. If someone came to my street and behaved in a way I did not want them to, not just me but the whole neighborhood would do the same thing again' (*Show Ana Haber* 2018).

One cannot help feeling appalled while watching the male perpetrator maliciously speak to the cameras. Instead of feeling guilty or expressing regret, he vindictively justified his anger and aggression, his body posture domineering, his voice loud and hand gestures imposing, calling the victim to account for her allegedly immoral act. When asked about the other perpetrators' identities, he turned to his fellow residents, a group of men strolling far behind him in front of a house on the street. 'Tell me guys! Is it just me who beat her up, or?' he yelled at them. Then facing the cameras again with a grin on his face, he answered, 'Yes, the whole neighborhood!' looking satisfied with the clever answer he had come up with and appearing totally unconcerned about the legal repercussions of his actions, as if he had legal immunity or some sort of moral entitlement.

He is not the only man who has recently inflicted harm on women who allegedly transgressed gendered moral codes in Turkey. In fact, over the last few years, vigilante violence against women – a paradigmatic act of misogyny – has been on the rise again in the country. Between September 2016 and July 2018, nineteen cases of vigilante violence against women were documented in Turkey, where male vigilantes meted out violent punishments to women who did not conform and failed to adhere to so-called moral norms in public places.[1] In other words, male vigilantes, rather than attacking women across the board, target women selectively and punish them by creating a public spectacle. Women whose *habitus*, including their demeanour, posture, confidence, elocution, dress and bodily comportment, does not evince a strong commitment to a particular understanding of feminine propriety – a gendered construct deriving largely from localized gender hierarchies infused with Islamic norms – are the ones who are most likely to be subjected to vigilante violence as they navigate public spaces in densely populated cities such as Izmir, Antalya, Istanbul, Bursa and Adana. Indeed, women have been violently assaulted over the last few years for no other reason than wearing shorts, walking in the supermarket, smoking cigarettes, sitting cross-legged in public, engaging in public displays of affection and exercising in parks. The recent recurrence of vigilante violence against women is limited to large cities; in small towns and rural areas, norms about feminine propriety and modesty have always been strict. In densely populated cities, on the other hand, the embodied public presence of the women who do not conform to norms of propriety and chastity is fairly strong. Nevertheless, women who feel less encumbered by the weight of gendered norms are at an increasing risk of becoming the victim of vigilantism in today's Turkey.

Violence against women is widespread and well documented in Turkey. A study on domestic violence found that 34 per cent of women reported to have experienced physical violence from their partners (Altinay and Arat 2007). Domestic violence, as a certain type of male violence, however, manifests different patterns than that of vigilante violence. While domestic violence affects women across the board, vigilante violence in contemporary Turkey targets particular groups of women, those who ostensibly do not conform to localized norms about feminine propriety. And unlike domestic violence against women, which is often committed in the confines of the home and even disguised as a private matter, vigilante violence is deliberately public, not hidden from sight and committed with the aim of creating a public spectacle by male attackers who the victims do not know personally.

This chapter sets out to explore gendered power dynamics of contemporary vigilantism in Turkey. It specifically investigates moral notions that figure prominently in the justifications vigilante men utilize. Vigilantism, its resurgence in public places and deliberate performativity, I argue, can be understood as a *new* mode of coercive power operating on women's bodies in Turkey, a form of power that has become staggeringly visible in the post-2008 period. This mode of power is directed at particular embodiments of femininity, not with the aim of regulating and disciplining bodies, but with the aim of attacking, injuring and punishing feminine selves, humiliating them by taking advantage of their embodied vulnerability. Far from being anchored in legal-juridical concepts, this modality of power exclusively relies on, and operates through, the moralization of embodied selves. A particular understanding of moral transgression enables this rather masculinist power to function in a period in Turkey when legal and social changes have considerably unburdened women's bodies from the weight of feminine modesty. In this moralistic framework, vigilante men present themselves as moral actors who are concerned about women's moral transgressions and actively invoke notions of feminine modesty to justify the violence they inflicted on women in public places.

The chapter focuses on the recent male involvement in feminine bodily comportment, as opposed to women's own understandings or practices of bodily comportment, to examine gendered dynamics of vigilante violence and its larger implications for the AKP's (Justice and Development Party) gender politics. First, I illustrate how vigilante men, in an effort to reassert the male entitlement to bodily control, draw on the notion of moral transgression. By claiming an active relationship with women's modesty, perpetrators provide justifications for their public enactments of violence. Men recast vigilantism in terms other than those defined in legal debates by framing their violent acts as legitimate punishments through which women receive what they deserve because of their moral infractions.

An analysis of vigilante violence also offers insights into the changing body politics in Turkey in the post-2008 period, a phase when misogyny has become more pronounced with the resurgence of punitive practices such as vigilantism. The practice of utilizing the notion of feminine modesty in the service of asserting male entitlement to bodily control is not confined to vigilante men. The concept of moral transgression seems to occupy a recognizable place in the AKP's recent gender politics too with the government condoning punitive practices against the women who allegedly commit moral infractions. This chapter shines a spotlight on the notion of 'gender justice', a new gender paradigm that the AKP-led government has introduced over the last few years, to investigate into possible connections between punitive practices, moral transgression and the AKP's authoritarian rule. Of particular importance here is the idiosyncratic notion of 'fair treatment' the AKP's concept of (gender) justice entails. By teasing out the gendered logic embedded in the notion of fair treatment, I show how the AKP's concept of (gender) justice might facilitate an understanding of masculinist fair treatment that juxtaposes moral transgression and punishment, hostility against certain groups of women and moral norms, male entitlement and violence together.

Part of my thinking on the misogynistic direction that body politics have taken in the post-2008 era in Turkey is shaped by the discussions of backlash and backlash politics. It is possible to situate both vigilantism and the AKP's gender justice paradigm as part and consequence of the backlash politics. A focus on backlash allows us to consider the AKP's conservative turn as a reactionary political response to women's increasing empowerment in Turkey. The AKP's recent gender politics, in this light, is not simply a conservative turn but also one that exemplifies the backlash politics fomented by the AKP to counter the gender equality as well as the improvements in women's status gained in the early 2000s.

The chapter presents qualitative data from an ongoing project on the transformation of body politics in contemporary Turkey, which draws on a diverse set of sources, including data on vigilantism provided by women's organizations, media reports, court cases and the interviews I carried out in June 2017 and March 2018 with three feminist activists, three lawyers and ten women whose embodied comportment does not conform to localized norms about feminine propriety. While interviews with feminist activists and lawyers offered insights into the legal and political dynamics of vigilantism, by listening to the narratives of insubordinate women, I was able to understand how women navigate a social environment in which they are likely to encounter misogyny. The chapter begins with an account of the sharp turn that gender politics has taken in Turkey in the post-2008 period. It then proceeds to a discussion of vigilantism in Turkey and offers an examination of some cases of vigilante violence in order to shed light on the connections between misogyny, morality and women's embodied comportment. The penultimate section attends to the AKP's version of justice as well as the discourse on gender justice formulated and promoted by women's associations that back the government, elucidating how fair treatment and punitive practices are coupled together within this framework. The conclusion draws some broader implications from my argument about the relationship between misogyny, body politics and the ascendance of anti-equality politics.

The AKP's gender politics after 2008: A backlash against gender equality?

The conservative turn in gender politics during the second term of the AKP government has inspired a flood of research and speculation about the larger dynamics underlying this shift. Studies have highlighted the government's efforts to blend neoliberalism with neoconservatism (Bugra 2014). According to these studies, the AKP government implemented between 2002 and 2007 a neoliberal economic program as Turkey integrated itself into the European and global markets. During the same period, the government also carried out gender equality measures following Turkey's candidacy for EU membership. After 2008, however, the government began to pursue staunchly a politics of strengthening the patriarchal family (Kandiyoti 2010; Acar and Altunok 2013; Korkman 2016; Cindoğlu and Ünal 2017). For many scholars, the main tenet of the change in the government's gender agenda in the post-2008 period was the rising power of the neoconservative ideology in the AKP's politics. Studies showed how this conservative gender ideology, often framed by moderate Islamism, lent the welfare regime an increasingly masculine and paternalistic character (Acar and Altunok 2013; Koyuncu and Özman 2018). Others illustrated the morality discourse the AKP embraced in order to advocate for a conventional gendered division of labour and modest feminine subjectivity (Cindoğlu and Ünal 2017).

While existing studies underscore the importance of the neoliberalism/ neoconservatism nexus to explain how the AKP came to foreground moralism in gender politics, scant attention has been paid to the link between the AKP's increasing moralism and its anti-equality politics in the post-2008 era. By conceptualizing the AKP's emphasis on conservative morality as a form of reactionary politics that emerged just as Turkey was witnessing increasing gender equality, I claim that the AKP's gender politics in the post-2008 era represent a backlash[2] against gender equality. Here, I adopt Mansbridge and Shames's (2008) concept of backlash, which they define as 'the use of coercive power to regain lost power as capacity' (Mansbridge and Shames 2008: 625). From this perspective, the AKP's conservative turn in the post-2008 era has not just been a regular political transition in which the party's inherently conservative agenda has found its full expression as the party has consolidated its power after 2007 elections. Rather, it could also be seen as a reactionary politics that operates under the mantle of moralism against women's increasing autonomy in Turkey.

The current backlash, I argue, seeks to eliminate the empowerment of women that followed out of the gender equality reforms that the AKP carried out in the early 2000s, which disentangled women's bodies from an order based on public morality, honour and chastity, thereby enhancing women's bodily autonomy. The concepts of virginity, chastity and honour historically underpinned men's entitlement to women's bodies (Parla 2001; Ozyegin 2009). The removal of these concepts from the penal code in the early 2000s decisively circumscribed male capacity to control women's bodies. Initially, the reforms were carried out as part of Turkey's efforts to become a member of the European Union; the government was not substantially invested in the project of deepening gender equality in the country. However, the feminist movement in Turkey, which is quite strong and militant, seized the moment and exerted pressure on the government through lobbying and activism. Thanks to feminists, what started as a minimal legal change that took no account of women's needs grew into a full-blown legislative project that more integrally codified gender equality in the country. The new Turkish Civil Code, according to Deniz Kandiyoti, was 'arguably the most progressive legislation for women since the Kemalist reforms of the 1920s and the 1930s' (Kandiyoti 2010: 174). Further, the new penal code, which went into effect in 2004, eliminated the distinctions between married and unmarried women, and virgins and non-virgins, in punishing sexual crimes, and acknowledged, for the first time, honour killings as aggravated homicides.

These legal reforms were accompanied by structural changes that improved women's lives. For instance, by the early 2000s, the total fertility rate had fallen from five births to two and an unprecedented rise was recorded in the educational attainment of women in Turkey. Certainly, the restructuring of the global economy extended the effects of gender equality reforms, prompting a change in employment opportunities from manufacturing to services, from muscle power to cultural capital, and from male to female (Keyder 2005), all of which drew more women into the labour market in urban areas and transformed the decades-long downward trend in women's labour force participation rates (Sarioğlu 2013).

One distinctive aspect of the backlash politics the AKP pursued in the post-2008 era was the government's reactionary response to gender equality. Take, for example, President Erdoğan's statements against gender equality. As early as 2008, he became quite outspoken against the principle of gender equality and claimed that it was alien to Turkish culture. Later, Erdoğan repeatedly declared his belief in the Islamic *fitrat*, which denotes the idea that there are inherent, God-given differences between men and women. A few years later, the AKP introduced a new paradigm: gender justice. As opposed to the contemporary notion of gender justice, which seeks to eradicate all forms of gender inequality, the notion of gender justice that the AKP promotes is informed by Quranic notions of fair treatment of different genders (Yılmaz 2015; Diner 2018). Moreover, the concept echoes strongly the premodern Ottoman imperial notion of justice, an ideology that serves to justify and reinforce the fundamental hierarchies and differences between Muslim/non-Muslim, ruling elite/common people, as well as men/women. Viewed as aspects of the backlash politics, these manoeuvres illustrate how the AKP's enthusiasm for moral conservatism has become the government's major line of attack against gender equality.

Unlike regular political opposition, the backlash exclusively relies on the use of coercion to restore power. This understanding of backlash helps to account for why misogyny is ascendant in contemporary Turkey, with men physically attacking women in public spaces in the name of a moral order. Seen in this light, male resort to vigilante violence is closely tied to the men's struggle around controlling women's bodies, a struggle aggravated by the limits placed on male entitlements following the entrenchment of gender equality in the country in the early 2000s. It is against this background that men invoke moral transgression to assert male power over women's bodies and that women are subjected to hostility and violence due to the alleged moral transgressions they committed.

Here, I draw on the concept of misogyny that Kate Manne put forth in her book *Down Girl* (2017). Manne defines misogyny as a hostile form of gendered oppression 'in which women are liable to encounter hostility due to the enforcement and policing of patriarchal norms and expectations – often, though not exclusively, insofar as they violate patriarchal law and order' (Manne 2017: 19). Morality and hostility are central to Manne's account, which explains how misogyny threatens to harm and penalize a woman if she transgresses the moral norms that keep the patriarchal order intact.

This chapter also shows how hostile emotional energies, such as the resentment encapsulated in misogynistic acts such as vigilante violence, are enabled by and exacerbate a larger backlash politics. This brand of anti-equality politics thrives on the notion of Ottoman justice and separates those groups who are seen as deserving of paternalist protection from those who are not. In this framework, matters pertaining to gender are regarded not as political disputes to be settled through political discussion among social actors, but as moral issues that can be understood and resolved through the binary of moral transgression versus conformity, a criterion that serves as a pretext for punitive practices.

Vigilantism against women in Turkey

Women's so-called punishment by men for their alleged offences against morality used to be a widespread misogynistic practice in Turkey and has been historically enabled by particular discourses such as those of shame and honour, in which men maintain their honour through controlling women's sexuality and body. However, vigilantism has not always operated under the mantle of morality. In the 1990s, for instance, when the headscarf ban was in effect, vigilantism, especially in large cities in the western part of Turkey, took the form of secularist vigilance against women wearing headscarves in public places.

Throughout the early 2000s, vigilantism, in both its moralist and secularist streaks, was far less common, and it seemed like the practice had been consigned to the dustbin of history until the news about a vigilante incident forcefully made the headlines in June 2013 during the Gezi resistance. The news revealed to a shocked public the gruesome details about a young woman wearing a headscarf who was viciously assaulted by male protestors. Known as the *Kabataş* incident, the only eyewitness to the alleged crime was the victim herself, a young woman who claimed to have been attacked by a gang of seventy male protestors in the centrally located neighbourhood of Kabataş in Istanbul. The half-naked men wearing black leather pants and leather gloves, the woman explained, first verbally harassed her, then beat her, crushed the stroller carrying her baby and finally urinated on her and her six-month-old child, leaving the woman lying on the street unconscious. When a small number of journalists from the mainstream media testified that they watched the video footage showing the incident, AKP officials lashed out against the Gezi Park protestors. Recep Tayyip Erdoğan, then prime minister, seized the moment and accused the Gezi protesters of moral turpitude, galvanizing his political base by bemoaning on media channels: 'They harassed and beat my fellow head scarf-wearing sisters' (Erdoğan 2013).

The period of the Gezi protests was one of the turning points in the AKP's strategy to tighten their hold on power, in which political opposition to the government was depoliticized and framed as a moral insult to the larger Sunni majority in the country. The government, in the meantime, worked diligently to push particular practices such as the consumption of alcoholic beverages, abortion, women's sexuality and coed living out of the sphere of political negotiation by framing them as moral transgressions. It was not until two years after the Kabataş event that the video footage was finally leaked to the press and it was proven that the allegations were grossly distorted, with some parts entirely fabricated. The footage showed a group of six young men who seemed to be walking past the young woman and verbally harassing her.

It is in this context that moral vigilantism resurfaced in Istanbul in 2015, where cafés and art galleries involved in so-called immoral activities, such as serving alcohol during an art exhibition, were threatened by resentful groups of religious, nationalist youths.[3] Sometimes, mixed-gender groups consuming alcoholic drinks in public spaces were intimidated by local small business owners. Vigilante incidents that exclusively target women, on the other hand, erupted after the democracy vigils in 2016. Instigated by President Erdoğan, the vigils started on the night of 15 July 2016, when a faction of the Turkish military initiated a coup against the AKP government. That night, Erdoğan appeared on a live CNNTürk broadcast via the anchorwoman's smartphone on FaceTime and called on the people to go out, violate the curfew and stop the attempted coup. Held nightly for weeks in urban streets and squares, the vigils often drew thousands of participants. Islamic calls, *Sala*, were recited from mosques, not to call to prayer, but to spark off civilian resistance against the attempted coup and urge believers to pledge allegiance to the AKP regime. Never before had a political government in the history of the Turkish Republic called the masses to the streets to display resistance against a military intervention. Tayyip Erdoğan's call on that night was met with enthusiasm by AKP supporters, and large masses of men and a small number of women took to the streets to join the vigils. During this period, men easily assumed the role of vigilantes protecting the regime.

The first vigilante attack on a woman for her alleged moral infraction was reported just a few weeks after the vigils ended. On 12 September 2016, Ayşegül Terzi, a 23-year-old nurse, was violently attacked on a public bus for wearing shorts. The male perpetrator later defended himself in court by claiming that at the time of the incident, his moral and national feelings were particularly intense (Terzi v. Çakıroğlu 2016). On 20 September 2016, a woman in Bursa stepped in to intervene in a bullying incident on the subway where an older man verbally harassed a younger man for playing music at a high volume through his headphones. When the woman told him to stop swearing, the older man threatened her by reminding her vulnerability to violence with an allusion to Ayşegül Terzi: 'You know what happened to that woman wearing shorts on the bus. And you are still talking!' he retorted. Two months later, İpek Atcan, a 22-year-old music writer based in Istanbul, was at the subway station, waiting for the train when a man kicked her in the legs, furiously shouting, 'You can't sit here with your legs crossed like this' (İpek Atcan'a 2016). By the end of July 2018, nineteen cases of vigilante violence against women, in which women were attacked by men for their alleged moral infractions, had already been documented.

Vigilantism: Misogyny under the cloak of morality

Vigilante men seem to harbour resentment and hostile feelings towards certain groups of women, and when they encounter them in public places, such as on the bus, in the subway, on the street, at parks or at a supermarket, they assault them. Recently, performativity of violence is not confined to vigilantism and an increasing number of domestic violence incidents repeat the pattern. For instance, the percentage of women murdered in public places in the presence of witnesses is reported to be on the rise (bianet Şiddet 2020). Feminist activists and lawyers I interviewed also drew attention to the performativity of male violence across cases. One feminist activist pointed out that acts of femicide committed by men have become more gruesome and extreme. 'Now', she said, 'men are killing women by using torture methods, with intense hatred, and by using lethal electroshock weapons, for instance. Or else, they kill women by placing explosive devices in women's cars.'

In the cases of vigilante violence, moral infractions allegedly committed by women often instigate these attacks. Vigilantism refers to the use or threat of extralegal violence in response to an alleged criminal act, violation or transgression. In contemporary Turkey, male vigilantism exhibits an unequivocal desire to reinstate a gendered moral order. A 53-year-old woman in Istanbul, for instance, was attacked by a man in a supermarket on the grounds that her style of walking was inappropriate (İstanbu'da 2016). As the woman was walking down the aisle in the grocery store, a man shouted at her and ordered her to 'walk properly'. He then attacked her, breaking the woman's nose and bruising her arms. Indeed, all of the nineteen cases of vigilante violence documented between September 2016 and July 2018 in Turkey attest to the pervasiveness of moral vigilantism, a type of vigilantism where violence or the threat of violence is cloaked in an appeal to higher moral orders and sovereignties. Vigilante men, in a sense, call upon moral norms to justify their attacks and actions to the public, including witnesses, the media and state officials.[4]

Moralism – the framing of political disputes as moral issues – serves as a pretext for punitive and violent hostility against women. Vigilante men are fixated on providing moralistic justifications for their crimes. The accounts given by male vigilantes of their actions suggest that men present themselves as actors exacting penalties on women for their moral transgressions. Some vigilantes, for instance, explicitly invoke religious morality; that is, Islamic norms, according to which feminine modesty is both a virtue and a Quranic mandate. In these cases, the use or threat of violence is directed against women primarily for their ostensible transgressions of Islamic codes of feminine propriety. For instance, Abdullah Çakıroğlu, an Istanbul man who brutally kicked Ayşegül Terzi in the face on a public bus, defended himself in court by citing Ayşegül Terzi's alleged moral transgression. His statement was as follows:

> It was the Feast of Sacrifice [*Eid al Adha*]. My national and moral feelings were heightened and intense. Every single day, some moral values in our country are made to erode further. It was one of those days. I don't think my action was right. I don't think it was constructive. The woman's way of dressing was not normal. It offended my moral feelings. A woman should appear chaste and in order to do that, she should dress according to the norms and position herself accordingly. If she had been dressed decently, we would not have been morally offended and would not have acted this way. We would have been less offended if she had at least put on trousers or a tracksuit. They are ruining our mental and spiritual chemical balance. I have been fasting for the last four years. However, because of these people, I cannot turn towards the eternal life and cannot have a peaceful religious life. (Terzi v. Çakıroğlu 2016)

Abdullah Çakıroğlu lapses into the first-person plural when offering a justification of his own action, a crime he committed by himself without the involvement of any other persons. The use of the first-person plural in his statement seems to have multiple meanings. Primarily, his use of the first-person plural, 'we' (*biz*), denotes a strategy of humble self-referencing, a culturally specific use of 'we' in colloquial Turkish that communicates the speaker's observance of particular norms about cultural conformity and the avoidance of putting himself before others. In this system of self-reference, one's individual identity, instead of accentuating a free-floating ego, signals a humble self that is subordinated to a larger community. It also enables the person to tacitly claim certain entitlements on the basis of being a member of the community, such as the entitlement to surveil others in order to uphold the community's moral order. This sense of entitlement informed Abdullah Çakıroğlu's belief that he should be subjected to fewer legal and moral penalties for his action. Çakıroğlu, in his defence, also evoked an understanding of 'we' as a bounded collectivity. Through the statement, 'They are ruining our mental and spiritual chemical balance', he sets up an obvious antagonism between 'us' and 'them', with those who do not belong being malicious, corrupt and self-indulgent, as opposed to members of the group, who are presented as being religious, morally decent, plain-spoken people. One can readily identify parallels between the moralizing discourse that the AKP mobilizes and the 'us versus them' rhetoric that Çakıroğlu resorts to. It is partly through this antagonism, which draws the boundaries between insiders and outsiders and which stigmatizes certain women as outsiders to be weeded out, that vigilante men draw on the notion of moral transgression to mark particular women as outsiders and use violence against women.

The pernicious moralism that male vigilantes evoke does not always explicitly draw on Islamic codes, but sometimes operates through localized understandings of gendered propriety; which are only loosely associated with Islamic norms. For instance, Dilay Özel, a twenty-year-old young woman, her aunt, and her mother were attacked on the street in Antalya for their so-called audacious behaviour – that is, smoking cigarettes. Upon seeing Dilay walk home in the company of her mother and aunt, who was smoking a cigarette at the moment, the two male attackers grew furious and began loudly heckling the women: 'Look just how reckless they are. How dare women smoke on the street!' (Laf attı 2017). When Dilay's aunt confronted them and told them to mind their own business, one man, in just a blink of an eye, punched the aunt in the chest and attacked the mother, while the other man took the lit cigarette and extinguished it on Dilay's neck. Here, women were reproved and attacked not for failing to comply with norms of religiosity but for being audacious and smoking, an act which, according to the men, constituted the crossing of boundaries of feminine modesty.

Despite male perpetrators' claims about women's moral transgressions, vigilante men do not actually know whether their female victims are religious or not, whether they are Sunni or Alevi, whether they believe in God, whether they observe and celebrate religious holidays, or whether they fast during the month of Ramadan. Targeted women, however, appear immodest and lacking in piety, because they are ostensibly not engaged in the project of self-constitution in accordance with the local norms of Islamic modesty and do not wear a headscarf. It appears that it is women's embodied comportment in public places that incites vigilante attacks. The embodied ways women inhabit the city – women's demeanour, posture, confidence, elocution, clothes and bodily comportment – seem to offend men. To be more specific, vigilante men regard women's embodied capacities as signs of moral transgression and punish women for their alleged offensive behaviour. Take, for instance, the case of Canan Kaymakçı, an Istanbul woman harassed by a man on the street for wearing 'provocative clothing' and 'turning people on' (Eminönü'de 2017) or that of Çağla Köse, a young woman in Istanbul was asked by a security guard to leave a public park where she was hanging out with her friend on the grounds that her outfit was inappropriate. When the woman told him to mind his own business, the security guard told her: 'There are families here and you are disturbing people by dressing up like that' (Woman harassed 2017).

In some of the cases of vigilante violence, it becomes evident that the ways in which women inhabit spaces in urban zones and the ways they use their bodies do not just offend, but also intimidate men. For instance, Ercan Kızılateş, an Istanbul man who attacked Asena Melisa Sağlam, a university student, for wearing shorts on a minibus during the month of Ramadan in 2017, was utterly appalled when the young woman fought back. 'She came to her feet and started yelling at me "Who are you to push me?" she shouted. At that moment, I thought she was an athlete because she attacked me with great courage and force' (Asena Melisa 2018). Partly on the basis of this incident, I believe that there are serious grounds to think that men's moral vigilantism is intimately linked to women's refusal to adhere to certain norms. These norms encompass an amalgam of local norms about feminine bodily comportment. Male vigilantes punish those women whose embodiment conveys a sense of insubordination, the most explicit form of insubordination being the rejection of the moral obligation to obey the male authority. In fact, a closer look reveals that male vigilantes are more likely to resort to physical violence when women confront them by talking back or fighting back – acts which convey women's autonomy, an unwillingness to obey male authority. Consider Abdullah Çakıroğlu again, who attacked Ayşegül Terzi on a public bus. His description of the attack tells us that what threw him into a rage was not her alleged violation of moral norms, but the moment when she confronted him: 'The way she sat was obscene. When I told her to sit properly, she made a facial gesture which meant none of your business. I wasn't able to stomach that. It was an involuntary reflex what I did… I warned the plaintiff but she didn't care and didn't change the way she sat. Then this event occurred' (Terzi v. Çakıroğlu 2016).

In a similar vein, two young women in Izmir were heavily battered by male police officers on the street when the women, instead of remaining silent, requested to file a report of sexual harassment against men who harassed them. The two women asked two nearby police officers for help, but the police officers, instead of helping, chastised them for their outfits and said: 'You actually deserve more with this outfit. Look at yourselves.' One of the police officers assaulted the two women when they protested against what he had said (İzmir'de tacize 2017). Such incidents suggest that at those times when women question, explicitly reject the masculine authority or take action against male violence and harassment, men are more likely to resort to violence.

Why do vigilante men seize on morality to justify their violent actions? What is it about moral transgression that enables men to advance their claims over women's bodies? It seems that alleged moral infractions function as an occasion for hostility and violence against women in two explicit ways. First, by drawing on the notion of religious morality, men attempt at framing women's embodied actions in terms of moral transgression and conformity. A particular understanding of morality enables male actors to advance their claims of unchecked authority on women's bodies and to enforce a moral order, all without being held accountable, at least fully, by the police. Second, the masculine authority that male perpetrators wanted to exercise is rooted in a particular interpretation of moral transgression. According to this understanding, woman's body is the repository of man; men can watch women's conduct and even resort to violence when women commit moral infractions. It is this understanding of morality that male perpetrators utilize to circumvent many of the barriers that gender equality poses to male resort to violence. Men, by hewing closely to the notion of moral infraction that makes women's bodies vulnerable to attacks, often give themselves licence to commit violence against women.

Such a moral authority is indeed very difficult to obtain, because the legal and social orders, both of which are based on the principle of equality, place severe constraints on attempts to subjugate women. Under Turkish law, the practice of vigilantism is punishable as a criminal act. And despite the fact Turkish courts have often handed down reduced sentences in cases of violence against women, vigilante men have been convicted of assault and punished, not least because feminists' sustained efforts to raise public awareness about vigilante cases have often proven to be quite successful. Confronted with severe legal limitations put in place to reduce male entitlements, men turn to an understanding of morality, which strongly resonates with an inverted notion of justice, a notion that grants men the capacity to take justice into their own hands. Such a notion of justice that opens the door for punitive practices has been brought back to politics by the AKP's justice discourse.

The curious link between justice and misogyny

In *Down Girl*, Kate Manne primarily provides an analytical account of misogyny, but, at times, her account also offers glimpses into misogyny from the first-person point of view by imagining how misogyny might feel to a male misogynist:

> If it feels like anything at all it will tend to be *righteous*: like standing up for oneself or for morality, or – often combining the two – for the 'little guy.' It often feels to those in its grip like a moral crusade, not a witch hunt. And it may pursue its targets not in the spirit of hating women but, rather, of loving justice. (Manne 2017: 20)

Perhaps the most curious connection between justice and misogyny in contemporary Turkey is the particular version of justice touted by the AKP, which envisions a restoration of justice in the country. The influence of justice in Turkish politics, however, stretches far beyond AKP politics. The concept continually appears throughout the history of the modern Turkish Republic, with the majority of right-wing political parties drawing on the discourse of justice to articulate their political vision, whereas left-wing politics and social-democratic parties historically have embraced primarily the principles of equality and freedom (Bora 2019). For instance, the centrist right-wing party founded in 1961 and a prominent political party throughout the 1960s and 1970s was called the Justice Party. Moreover, Necmettin Erbakan's Welfare Party, founded in 1983, appealed to Sunni populations through the populist 'Just Order' program, a form of popular rule that sought to fuse economic redistribution with Islamic morality.

Justice in these usages is not necessarily connected with the modern understanding of justice, which entails the rule of law. Rather, justice as it has been appropriated by right-wing political parties in Turkey often tends to hark back to the imperial Ottoman notion of justice, a government philosophy that denotes a particular relationship between the ruler and the ruled. Drawn out of the Quran, the Ottoman notion of justice, set behavioural norms for all spheres of life, including economics and politics, represents an alternative to secular law (Mardin 1991). What is salient in this notion of justice is that it hinges on, and naturalizes, a society rooted in inequalities. Justice here refers to the way in which the ruler treats the empire's subjects. The Ottoman notion of justice thus accommodates entrenched social hierarchies while at the same time promising those at the bottom of the hierarchy a paternalistic type of protection or fair treatment. For instance, it stipulates that non-Muslims, common people and women, those at the very bottom, should be shielded from brutal treatment as long as they know their place in the hierarchy and do not challenge the status quo (Eldem 2017). When they do, justice requires punishment, because the very notion of fair treatment is based on the idea that, if an offender breaks the law, she in return suffers. This notion of justice, in which the distinction between fair treatment and brutal forms of mistreatment is blurred, allowed Ottoman Muslims, as opposed to non-Muslims, to advance their claims as belonging to the community of the just, a moral community that contrasted with outside, non-moral communities (Mardin 1991). This version of justice, however, historically began to lose its command over politics in the late nineteenth century. In 1856, *Islahat Fermanı* (The Royal Edict of Reform) marked a momentous shift, replacing Ottoman justice with the principle of equality, which, in particular, meant acknowledging the legal equality between Muslims and non-Muslims (İrem 2008).

In contemporary Turkey, the Ottoman notion of imperial justice has recently undergone a renaissance. This has been fostered most prominently by the shift in the AKP's politics towards anti-equality in the post-2008 period. In the early 2000s, when the AKP first came to power, the AKP's concept of justice promised to correct the injustices of past militarist rule and Kemalist authoritarianism and emphasized fair treatment of popular classes through an array of paternalist welfare policies. However, beginning in 2008, the party's concept of justice began to take on hostile and revengeful undertones, with the government singling out and chastising those groups who deserve punishment in accordance with the imperial, Ottoman principle of fair treatment. How has this specific understanding of justice recently gained currency in the field of gender politics? A look at the AKP government's recent discursive practices makes it possible to grasp the sense in which a punitive understanding of justice and gender is connected. Of particular importance here is the notion of gender justice that the government introduced and promoted through the establishment of civil society organizations focused on women's rights (Diner 2018).

Gender justice, to begin with, just like the Ottoman notion of justice, is neither complementary to, nor associated with, the principle of equality. Instead, gender justice has been introduced with the aim of supplanting gender equality (Akyüz and Sayan-Cengiz 2016). In an article on gender justice, then associate professor Sare Aydın Yılmaz, the founding president of the Women and Democracy Association (KADEM), a civil society organization established to disseminate and popularize the AKP's gender politics and gender justice discourse in Turkey, outlined the notion in the following way: 'This framework centers on justice, in opposition to the approach that seeks to establish "equality" enshrining the same rights and responsibilities for men and women in social life' (Yılmaz 2015: 107). Second, gender justice, in the same way as the Ottoman notion of justice, is predicated upon the concept of fair treatment. For the author, Sare Aydın Yılmaz, who criticizes the notion of gender equality for failing to recognize the differences between men and women, the concept of gender justice accommodates so-called cultural specificity of Turkey by introducing the notion of fair treatment. As such, fair treatment prescribes genders to receive differential treatment on the basis of their *fitrat*, those essential and God-given differences between genders.

This alternative to gender equality grants a man a higher rank in the gender hierarchy. It is worth pausing over man's purported superiority for a moment, since Sare Yılmaz, who became an AKP member of parliament in 2018, in the same article claims that men's superior position in the hierarchy follows from the natural differences between a man and a woman. 'Some differences inherent in men and women may require that men could be regarded as *primus inter pares* (first among equals) in some cases,' she writes (Yılmaz 2015: 114). At least in some cases, the understanding of gender justice that takes supposed innate gender differences as sufficient evidence for men's superiority resonates well with the Islamic approach to gender, in which men and women are not taken on their own as individuals, but as parts of a whole that complement each other in the family. Yılmaz positively affirms the overlap between gender justice[5] and the Islamic order:

> The view of Islam toward women and men also supports this argument. Islam regards women and men as human beings and identifies differences in what they can do. It considers women and men as parts of a whole that complement each other, stating that 'women constitute the other half as men, complementing a whole' by accepting that 'the two spouses cannot be reduced to each other, cannot be blended with each other but cannot be separated either'. (Yılmaz 2015:112)

And finally, the AKP's gender justice discourse, like the notion of Ottoman justice, might readily lead to mistreatment, punishment or other forms of punitive practices in the guise of fair treatment. Since the notion emphasizes not only the inherent differences but also hierarchies between genders and bases its conception of fair treatment on this ontology of gender, it promotes a heavily gendered and all too often a sexist logic of fair treatment. It creates vicious hierarchies among women themselves by splitting women into two categories: those who deserve punishment and those who deserve fair treatment (benign paternal protection). Because fairness is a virtue possessed by those sitting in the higher ranks of the hierarchy, such as God and the ruler, fair treatment, by the same logic, becomes the bastion of men. Women are expected to be protected by men as long as they squarely comply with the gender norms, which mandate that women live according to their *fitrat*. There is already an abundance of empirical evidence that the politics of the AKP – and not just the behavioural propensities of individual men – promotes paternalistic, masculinist behaviours, in which morally conforming women are treated benevolently (Toksöz 2016). This ethos of gender justice finds strong expression in the implementation of paternalistic social policies and welfare assistance for some underprivileged women, and particularly mothers, widows and caretakers.

However, the ethos of gender justice easily backslides and fosters hostility against women who are seen as deserving punishment. Insubordinate women, offbeat women, women who aspire to equality, those who want to believe in themselves and also have confidence in their bodily capacities, those who are unwilling to obey male authority or those who just exercise in public parks whilst pregnant might face vilification, punishment, stigmatization and humiliation. What lurks right beneath the ethos of gender justice is the basic assumption of misogynistic thinking: punishment is actually a form of fair treatment reserved for those women who transgress moral norms. This is the exact point where the AKP's concept of gender justice intersects with the logic of vigilantism against women.

Seen in this light, violence against women for alleged moral transgressions raise unsettling questions about the connections between male vigilantes, the AKP's notion of gender justice and misogyny. Moral transgression, pivotal both to vigilantism and to the AKP's moralizing political strategy, is one key aspect of anti-equality politics in Turkey. Vigilantism against women, we can argue, is ascending in urban Turkey despite its illegality largely because corporal punishment of women from below aligns with the misogynistic anti-equality politics that the AKP advances. In other words, male vigilantes' masculinist street justice overlaps with the AKP's version of justice in Turkey.

Discussion and conclusion

Vigilantism, in which men deliberately inflict harm on women's bodies in the name of moral norms, forces us to examine a new form of coercive power operating on women's bodies in contemporary Turkey. In this chapter, I argued that this new modality of coercive power, which targets embodied selves, does not aim at disciplining and regulating women, but aims at punishing, injuring and assaulting them. A localized understanding of moral transgression enables the operations of this new form of coercive power in a period when legal and social changes have, in many respects, freed women's bodies from the burden of feminine modesty. I also argued that moral vigilantism is, in fact, a component of the contemporary political backlash against women, which counteracts the remarkable gains for women's autonomy made in the early 2000s. Finally, by highlighting the overlap between street justice, male vigilantes' performance and the Ottoman imperial notion of justice that the AKP is bringing back into politics, I drew attention to the unique collusion between civilian men from popular classes and AKP rule in Turkey. My analysis suggests that grasping misogyny as an autonomous sociopolitical force is vital for understanding the different directions that body politics have taken in the post-2008 era in Turkey.

Backlash politics, as cases of moral vigilantism demonstrate, derives its emotional energy from hostile feelings and a moral entitlement to assert and regain power. These actions deepen social hierarchies in a particular way: those who arrogate for themselves the position of superiority establish their superiority through acts of degradation, that is, by brutally forcing other groups into an inferior or subordinate status in public. It is in this context that misogyny animates and drives the current backlash in Turkey. However, very few studies have been conducted on misogyny in contemporary Turkey and the broader implications it has in Turkish society and politics. To gain more insight into the operations and various strands of misogyny in institutions such as the family, the market and the state, we need to carry out more studies that treat misogyny as an autonomous force, a force that awakens and mobilizes hostile feelings against women in a given society.

Here, it is important to underline that women are not the only target of the backlash politics that have taken hold in Turkey; so too are groups who aspire to, or benefit from, the improvement of political equality, including Kurdish people and the queer movement. Driven by a pressing sense of urgency to reinstate inequality by violently degrading the status of certain groups in society, the backlash politics, as a politics of anti-equality, is not limited to vigilantism, but encompasses a variety of different strategies and practices targeting different groups. It is thus also important for future studies to empirically examine the direction, trajectory and varied manifestations of backlash politics in different fields of social and political life.

Notes

1   The data on vigilantism is provided by the We Will Stop Femicide Platform (Kadın Cinayetlerini Durduracağız Platformu), a women's organization that strives for ending femicide in Turkey and ensuring women's protection from violence.
2   For a deeper discussion of backlash in gender politics in Turkey, see Sarıoğlu (2018).
3   Please see Basaran (2015) for a detailed account of those vigilante incidents.
4   In this section, while discussing the vigilante violence cases in Turkey, I draw on my earlier work (Sarıoğlu 2018).
5   Although Sare Yılmaz does not specifically address how gender justice manifests itself in different parts of life, it is not difficult to imagine a myriad of ways in which gender justice paradigms can go awry and undercut gender equality in social life. To begin with, the emphasis on embodied gender differences serves to reinforce an ideology of familialism, which regards the family unit as the primary ordering element of society and predicates the social relationship between men and women on familial relations exclusively. After all, the view that a woman and a man complement each other follows directly from the spousal model. This familialism also entails a heterosexual, gendered division of labour, in which women are heavily burdened with a host of reproductive tasks, whereas men, freed from those tasks, are granted certain privileges, such as the privilege to act as primus inter pares.

References

Acar, F. and G. Altunok (2013), 'The "Politics of Intimate" at the Intersection of Neo-Liberalism and Neo-Conservatism in Contemporary Turkey', *Women's Studies International Forum*, 41 (1): 14–23.

Akyüz, S. and F. Sayan-Cengiz (2016), '"Overcome Your Anger if You Are a Man": Silencing Women's Agency to Voice Violence against Women', *Women's Studies International Forum*, 57 (July): 1–10.

Altınay, A. G. and Y. Arat (2007), *Türkiye'de Kadına Yönelik Şiddet*, Istanbul: Punto.

'Asena Melisa Sağlam yalnız değildir' (2018), *Haber Türk Hayat*, 11 March. Available online: https://hthayat.haberturk.com/yasam/guncel/haber/1051443-asena-melisa-saglam-yalniz-degildir (accessed 19 May 2019).

Basaran, P. (2015), 'Türkiye'de "Toplumsal Hassasiyetler" ve Tophane Vakası', *T24*, 27 May. Available online: https://t24.com.tr/haber/tophaneli-kendi-adaletini-kendi-uyguluyor,298293 (accessed 17 August 2019).

'bianet Şiddet, Taciz, Tecavüz Çetelesi Tutuyor' (2020), *Bianet*, 20 September. Available online: http://m.bianet.org/kadin/bianet/133354-bianet-siddet-taciz-tecavuz-cetelesi-tutuyor (accessed 20 September 2020).

Bora, T. (2019), 'Adalet Dairesi', *Birikim Dergi*, 13 March. Available online: https://www.birikimdergisi.com/haftalik/9401/adalet-dairesi#.XOFqBFIzZdg (accessed 19 May 2019).

Bugra, A. (2014), 'Revisiting the Wollstonecraft Dilemma in the Context of Conservative Liberalism: The Case of Female Employment in Turkey', *Social Politics: International Studies in Gender, State & Society*, 21 (1): 148–66.

Cindoğlu, D. and D. Ünal (2017), 'Gender and Sexuality in the Authoritarian Discursive Strategies of "New Turkey"', *European Journal of Women's Studies*, 24 (1): 39–54.

Diner, C. (2018), 'Gender Politics and GONGOS in Turkey', *Turkish Policy Quarterly*, 16 (4): 101–8.

Eldem, E. (2017), 'Osmanlı İmparatorluğu'ndan Günümüze Adalet, Hukuk, Eşitlik ve Siyaset', *Tarih ve Toplum*, 288 (December): 24–37.

'Eminönü'de bir kadına kıyafeti bahanesiyle sözlü saldırı: Milleti azdırıyorsun' (2017), *Yarın Haber*, 29 June. Available online: http://yarinhaber.net/kadin/55507/eminonude-bir-kadina-kiyafeti-bahanesiyle-sozlu-saldiri-milleti-azdiriyorsun (accessed 19 May 2019).

'Erdoğan: Başörtülülere saldırdılar' (2013), *Ntv.com.tr*, 9 June. Available online: https://www.ntv.com.tr/turkiye/erdogan-basortululere-saldirdilar,MY8fETQDTESWrDoEc5_tbQ (accessed 19 May 2019).

'İpek Atcan'a metroda tekmeli saldırı' (2016), *Hürriyet Gazetesi*, 29 November. Available online: http://www.hurriyet.com.tr/gundem/ipek-atcana-metroda-tekmeli-saldiri-40292008 (accessed 19 May 2019).

İrem, N. (2008), 'Klasik Osmanlı Rejimi ve 1939 Gülhane Kırılması', *Muhafazakâr Düşünce Dergisi*, 15 (Winter): 147–72.

'İstanbu'da bir markette "Düzgün yürü" diyen erkek, 53 yaşındaki kadına saldırdı' (2016), *Siyasi Haber*, 7 October. Available online: http://siyasihaber4.org/istanbuda-bir-markette-duzgun-yuru-diyen-erkek-53-yasindaki-kadina-saldirdi (accessed 19 May 2019).

'İzmir'de tacize uğrayan kadını döven polis hakkında soruşturma başlatıldı' (2017), *T24 Gazetesi*, 13 August. Available online: https://t24.com.tr/haber/izmirde-tacize-ugrayan-kadini-doven-polis-hakkinda-sorusturma-baslatildi,419571 (accessed 19 May 2019).

Kandiyoti D. (2010), 'Gender and Women's Studies in Turkey: A Moment for Reflection', *New Perspectives on Turkey*, 43 (Fall): 165–76.

Keyder, Ç. (2005), 'Globalization and Social Exclusion in Istanbul', *International Journal of Urban and Regional Research*, 29 (1): 124–34.

Korkman Z. (2016), 'Politics of Intimacy in Turkey: A Distraction from "Real" Politics?' *Journal of Middle East Women's Studies*, 12 (1): 112–21.

Koyuncu, B. and A. Özman (2018), 'Women's Rights Organizations and Turkish State in the Post-2011 Era: Ideological Disengagement versus Conservative Alignment', *Turkish Studies*, 20 (5): 728–53

'Laf attı, boğazında sigara söndürdü, serbest kaldı' (2017), *Cumhuriyet Gazetesi*, 16 May. Available online: http://www.cumhuriyet.com.tr/haber/turkiye/742031/Laf_atti_bogazinda_sigara_sondurdu_serbest_kaldi.html (accessed 19 May 2019).

Manne, K. (2017), *Down Girl: The Logic of Misogyny*, Oxford: Oxford University Press.

Mansbridge J. and S. L. Shames (2008), 'Toward a Theory of Backlash: Dynamic Resistance and the Central Role of Power', *Politics & Gender*, 4 (4): 623–34.

Mardin, Ş. (1991), 'The Just and the Unjust', *Daedalus*, 120 (3): 113–29.

Ozyegin, G. (2009), 'Virginal Facades: Sexual Freedom and Guilt among Young Turkish Women', *European Journal of Women's Studies*, 16 (2): 103–23.

Parla, A. (2001), 'The "Honor" of the State: Virginity Examinations in Turkey', *Feminist Studies*, 27 (1): 65–88.

Sarioğlu, E. (2013), 'Global Economy and New Gender Identities: A Study of Saleswomen in Turkey', PhD diss., Department of Sociology, Binghamton University, NY.

Sarıoğlu, E. (2018), 'Vigilante Violence against Women in Turkey: A Sociological Analysis', *Kadın/Woman 2000*, 19 (2): 51–68.

Show Ana Haber (2018), 'Sevgilime sarıldım, mahalleli beni dövdü', [TV programme] SHOWTV, 18 July. Available online: https://www.facebook.com/ShowAnaHaber/videos/1306068892862088/UzpfSTczMDA3MDIyODoxMDE1Njc0MDk1OTEwMDIyOQ/ (accessed 19 May 2019).

Toksöz, G. (2016), 'Transition from "Woman" to "Family": An Analysis of AKP Era Employment Policies from a Gender Perspective', *Journal für Entwicklungspolitik*, 32 (1/2): 64–83.

'Woman Harassed by Security Staff Faces Prosecution for 'insulting public officer'' (2017), *Bianet*, 7 October. Available online: http://bianet.org/english/print/190400-woman-harassed-by-security-staff-faces-prosecution-for-insulting-public-officer (accessed 28 April 2019).

Yılmaz, S. (2015), 'A New Momentum: Gender Justice in the Women's Movement', *Turkish Policy Quarterly*, 13 (4): 107–15.

10

Disciplining pious female bodies/sexualities in the authoritarian times of Turkey: An analysis of public moral discourses on the 'Süslümans'

Betül Yarar

Introduction

The public debates on and criticisms of *tesettür* (known as "hijab" in some places, a practice whereby some Muslim women cover their hair/faces, wear long, all-enveloping garments and avoid contact with men) and the *başörtüsü* (headscarf) are not new. Turkey has been confronted with such issues ever since the late Ottoman period and modernization process that accompanied it. This process created an opposition between the religious-conservatives and secularist-modernists who held contrasting views about what an authentic culture should consist of with respect to gender roles and femininity. While acknowledging this long history, this chapter aims to study instead the more recent political discourses on the issue of the proper form of dressing for Muslim veiled women by focusing particularly on current debates on the *Süslüman*, a derisive and belittling concept that proposes a critique of younger 'pious' veiled women for their indulgence with consumer culture and social media and for exposing their bodies in the social media in a manner that many secular and religious authorities do not approve.

The term *Süslüman* originally derives from the new conservative youth culture as a way to mock newly expanding Islamic bourgeoisie women in respect to their unusual and non-conventional attitudes and tastes dispositioning not only their class but also their Muslim identity and Islamic habitus. The term eventually turns into a concept that is used by radical and authoritarian conservatives to express their reactions against religious youth culture which is framed not only by consumerism and Islamic fashion industry, but also by new communication technologies such as social media. By pointing at these newly expanding sociopolitical and economic cleavages that are deepening among religious conservatives along lines of social class, gender and age, this chapter analyses this ongoing discursive struggle over the concept of *Süslüman* and in turn over the proper female subjectivity and public sexuality, as *Süslümans* are criticized for transgressing existing borders drawn by norms of *mahremiyet* in Islamicate culture of Turkey. According to Sehlikoglu

(2016: 143), '*mahremiyet* operates as an institution of intimacy that provides a metacultural intelligibility for heteronormativity based on sexual scripts, normative spaces, and gendered acts'. It functions as a boundary-making mechanism in the Islamicate context which includes various versions of the religion Islam and the diverse Muslimhoods. Within the heterosexual *mahremiyet* culture of Turkey, the term public sexuality is used in reference to 'the making and remaking of (hetero) sexed bodies of women and men in public (and inevitably in private)' (Sehlikoglu 2016: 144).

Within this context, the chapter aims to address the tensions among different views of various authorities (politicians, journalists and intellectuals) on how women should practise and perform their religious identities. Here it is their dressing codes and other related public performances of religious women in such heterosexual social spaces as the social media is under scrutiny. Along this line, the chapter goes beyond the analysis of the old tension between the secularists-modernists and religious-conservatives and focuses more on recently increasing tensions among people within each category. The discourses of public authorities that signify these differences and conflicts are investigated within the unique historical context of the rise of authoritarianism that emerged under the leadership of the ruling Justice and Development Party (AKP) in Turkey in the late 2000s. Throughout this period of authoritarianism in Turkey, despite the common sense perception, not only non-veiled but also veiled women have turned into a subject of close surveillance and symbolic/physical violence along the line of tension that was emerging between more liberal and authoritarian-conservative conceptions of feminine subjectivity and public sexuality. Here the term *Süslüman*, which represents the opposition not between secular and religious femininities, but between 'imitation/artificial' and 'authentic' Muslim femininities, is used as a starting point to expand an analysis of new disciplinary and authoritarian practices targeting some veiled (inevitably also unveiled) women. It looks at the discursive strategies and mechanisms which are used to build and maintain some limits and boundaries between gendered bodies through regulating the public performances of veiled women. As Sehlikoglu (2016: 145) states, 'This is related not only to normality and (hetero)sexuality in Turkey as an Islamicate context but also to the ways women need to deal with the fragility of their privacy in public in an era when the institution of intimacy (…) is undergoing change.'

To conclude, this study assumes that the analysis of political and journalistic discourses on the *Süslüman* might delineate new discursive strategies, positions and conflicts that are emerging and widening beyond the old-fashioned opposition between 'Islamists' and 'Laïcists', but along the lines of class, ethnicity and generational difference within conservative as well as secular sections over the issues concerning the public sexuality and fragile privacy of veiled women in Turkey. It argues that these new conflicts have emerged under the impact of neoliberalism and gained a new momentum in the recent times of authoritarianism. In this sense this analysis requires us to address and be aware of the diversity of the forms of self-making and performing religious piety and as well as of the views about the rules for regulating public sexuality. The chapter achieves this aim through a discursive analysis of statements of politicians and journalists on the concept of *Süslüman* and by shedding light on the authoritarian, critical and mockery tunes of their comments which generally condemn their public performances and form of visibility in the social media in moral terms. In addition, the chapter points at not only the kind of heteronormative Muslim femininity and female sexuality that have been promoted, but also sociopolitical uses and effects of these critical comments on *Süslümans* which are addressing popular fears and anxieties, on which the AKP has widened social legitimacy for its authoritarian regime and the new power block in the last decade. Such an analysis delineates also how combined effects of gender and class conflicts and political and economic crisis can be transformed into a moral language that translates them into a moral crisis concerned with the women's sexuality and sexual purity. It is this gendered emotional language of *mahremiyet* through which politicians and public figures managed a lot more easily to build some connections with the popular masses and create legitimacy for widening their authoritarian views and practices. As Sehlikoglu (2015: 77) states, 'The use of the language of *mahremiyet* in contemporary politics not only enables what can seem to be a meta-cultural intelligibility that guarantees popular support, but also distances any critique as strange or foreign.'

In line with the aims explained above, the chapter studies, in the first part, the historical background of the issue surrounding mainly the headscarf. This analysis starts from the period when it was banned by the military regime in response to the rising power of the Islamist movement that continues until now. It underlines not only the official politics, but also the impacts, of the counter protests of Islamist and religious women's groups, which became prominent throughout that period, and which transformed the headscarf into the most representative political symbol of the Islamist movement in Turkey in the 1990s. The chapter then moves on to the earlier period of the Justice and Development Party (AKP), which came to power in 2002 with a proposal on gender reforms. Claiming to represent a modern view of Islam, the AKP's earlier gender politics, which were framed by its so-called 'Conservative Democracy' project, is here analysed within the context of the expansion of the Islamist movement under the conditions of global neoliberalism. However, in the late 2000s, the AKP's earlier model of neoliberalism that is in tune with conservative values and tradition comes to the end of its production of further solutions to the emerging social problems of Turkey and results in what has recently become the strengthening of its authoritarian conditions and neoconservative stand which is in resonance with radical conservatism. This historical review herein ascertains the socio-economic and political parameters that made the emergence of the concept of the *Süslüman* possible and defines the limits of the discursive field on this issue. Later, the chapter returns to the discursive analysis of the concept of the *Süslüman* with the aim of scrutinizing the new parameters of power relations that have evolved and crystalized in this authoritarian period around conservative moral values and issues concerning the body and sexuality of religious women. Therefore, it not only addresses new discursive positions that emerge in response to such issue as the *Süslüman* which reflects new lines of social conflicts and breaks that cut across conservative sectors along the lines of gender, class and age difference. It also argues that these are the social conflicts to which authoritarian forces have managed to appeal in order to constitute their own social basis and legitimacy.

This anonymous concept, which is a play on two words, the Müslüman (Muslim) and Süslü (dressy), was first used by young social media users in 2009 as a critique and outright mockery of the young veiled women who had also acquired visibility in social media and whose relationship with modern or/and luxury consumption was conspicuous. Therefore, in general, the concept defines a specific group of veiled women who adopt a luxury and/or modern Islamic lifestyle and who wish to construct a new generational and class habitus that is in line with their Islamic identities. In this sense the concept signifies a crack within the Muslim identity which has been assumed as homogenous not only by modernist secularist but also by Islamist conservative sectors while the latter has attributed increasingly stronger and radical conservative definition to it. The concept of *Süslüman* was brought into mainstream media in 2013. Ever since then, the concept has been widely used in virtual space across various genres, such as a subject or title in online dictionaries, and in videos, poems, columns, short stories and news reports in both the social and mainstream media. In this study, only articles, commentaries, columns and press interviews that have been published since 2013 in diverse newspapers on the concepts of the 'Süslüman', the 'headscarf' and of 'tesettür' have been collected in a Google search. The data is thus analysed in detail with the use of critical discourse analysis to understand the diverse positions that are taken in respect to this new phenomenon called the *Süslüman*. Documents from social media are included in this analysis only as complementary material. Hence, the data does not include actual statements of pious women who are named *Süslüman*. Excluding views of these women's responses to such critical discourses, rather the chapter studies discourses of those who develop the concept as a mockery or a critique that targets these women and their ways of practising Muslim identity. Since these discourses on the concept of *Süslüman* define and regulate the codes of female intimacy and privacy, an analysis of these discourses unveils not only various discursive positions that are held in respect to this specific issue among various intellectuals with different political stands, but also their potential effects in stabilizing and normalizing particular forms of knowledge in creating compliant subjectivities.

A brief historical review of the headscarf controversy

As Partha Chatterjee (1993) states in the context of Indian anti-colonial nationalism, the desire to construct an aesthetic form, which is modern and national (yet recognizably different from the West), constitutes an important aspect of nationalisms. Chatterjee states that this comes into being along with important changes to patriarchy and to the position of women, and results in the transformation of the domain of the family and the emergence of the new women. The same process requires also the transformation of more subtle mechanisms of constituting subjectivities and technologies of the self-embedded in what Sehlikoglu calls the culture of *mahremiyet*. Sehlikoglu defines this 'not only as an institution of intimacy regulating everyday sexual relationships between individuals in public, but also as a system enabling the operation of social normalcies through the creation of boundaries and privileges' (Sehlikoglu 2015: 77). As Sehlikoglu states *mahremiyet* as a boundary-making mechanism creates boundaries not only between spaces and individuals but also within the body of the individual. They mark *mahrems* ('forbidden', such as same-sex individuals and opposite sex relatives) as insiders and non-*mahrems* as outsiders, segregate spaces and differentiate parts of the body. In the culture of *mahremiyet*, the gaze and seeing are the most important phenomenon defining who can see whom and how. An intersectional analysis (emphasizing both gender, religious, class and ethnic aspects of the issue in relational terms), based on the Bourdieu's concept of habitus (Bourdieu 1984), might help us to place the changes in the micro fabric of everyday culture and culture of *mahremiyet* into the historical context of power struggles and lead us to ask how new classes have built their own habitus by challenging and changing earlier gendered moral norms of intimacy and privacy. Moreover, Foucault's theory of power would also lead us to relate these dynamics to the changing modes of governance (which brings us, at the last instance, to the question of subjectivity at the interplay of various technologies, i.e. technologies of power/domination and technologies of the self) (Foucault 1988).

In the context of Turkey, the long history of the discussion on the headscarf issue very much accompanies the process of Westernization/modernization that started in the late period of the Ottoman Empire (Göle 2000a; 2000b; Yeğenoğlu 2011; Turan 2013; Alimen 2018). This process implies the emergence of a new nation-state and nationalism, and the transformation of rules of the public sexuality in *mahremiyet* culture (or rules of privacy/secrecy, decency and modesty in Foucauldian terms) which is beyond the control of secular laws and Islamic rules, as its historical, temporal, spatial and sociable dimensions complicate women's relationships with it (Sehlikoglu 2016: 148). When the public sphere of the newly founded Turkish Republic was established, it was identified with the state's constitutive principle of laicism (Suman 2000). Ever since, the founding state ideology has supported and made use of the image of a 'modern woman with an uncovered head', in opposition to the 'traditional veiled woman' who were seen to be backward (Elif, Kara, and Kavuncu 2008). In this process of modernization, which includes a movement from a homosocial female-bounded world into a heterosocial public space, the idealized form of a female body has transformed and included women's voluntary adaptation of what Najmabadi calls an 'invisible metaphoric veil' [veil of chastity] (Najmabadi 1993: 489 in Sehlikoglu 2016: 149). In line with this, in the early republican period, women were also expected to be 'modern' and unveiled in appearance, yet were still required to preserve the 'traditional' virtue of chastity and sexual purity (Durakbaşa 1988).

Despite this relatively radical process of transformation which aimed to bring a new woman into being, Atatürk (the founder of the Turkish Republic) only promoted unveiling, but did not pass laws to restrict the headscarf, or enforce veiling bans. The first regulation called 'the Dress of Personnel Employed in Public Institutions' came into force in 1982 after the coup d'état of 12 September 1980 (Buğdaycı 2008). This initial attempt by military power has been the sole basis for the subsequent bans that were issued throughout the following years (Report 2010). The Islamist movement was on the rise, and expressed the responses of religious groups against the crisis of old modernist nation states. In the age of the neoliberal globalism that expanded worldwide under the hegemony of the countries of the North, the aim was to prevent the emergence of the radical tendencies of this global movement, and to control these tendencies by force (Buğdaycı 2008; Tuğal 2009).

Hence the historical opposition between secular modernists and religious conservatives buttresses Chatterjee's argument about anti-colonial nationalisms. For instance, in the 1980s, Kemalist laicist sections of society supported the idea of banning the headscarf, since for them it signified not the women's moral and sexual purity but their underdevelopment, backwardness and oppression by men. The headscarf was associated also with Islamic radicalism and signified as the symbol of the newly enlarging Islamist ideology of establishing an Islamist state. They preferred to use the word 'türban' by asserting its difference from the 'headscarf' (*basörtüsü*) in order to shape its negative connotation and to stigmatize those who used the headscarf as representative of a newly widening Islamist resistance throughout the 1980s and 1990s (İlyasoglu 1994; Report 2010).

In the 1990s, the reactions against the criminalizing of the practice of veiling were immediately felt in Islamic circles and transformed the headscarf into a real battlefield between laicist and Islamist groups. During the same period, the Islamic women's movement has also gained serious momentum and its growth has accelerated under the impact of the headscarf debates (Çakır 1990; Ilyasoğlu 1994; Yılmaz 2015). Throughout these years, Islamist female activists expanded their new struggle in the 1980s mostly in conjunction with the rise of the Islamic movement, but have also taken inspiration from the perceived sisterhood of feminism. They have tightened and expanded their woman-to-woman organizations independently of male-dominated conservative parties and religious communities.

In the 1990s the first generation has given way to a new generation of Islamist female activists and intellectuals who started to produce arguments that were not only opposed to modernist laicism but also to traditional conservatism. They have also critically reviewed feminism, and offered a feminist critique of Islamist male counterparts. In their search for the reform of Islam, this second generation also criticized, from a woman's perspective, the religious interpretations and Islamic viewpoints of the conservative men that belonged to their circles (Yılmaz 2015). For instance, by taking up more effective roles in the public sphere as writers, journalists, activists and politicians, many Islamist women were able to critically review feminist theory from Islamic and post-colonial perspectives. They categorized feminism as a White Western imperialist or Orientalist project that was exclusionary to women from other regions and origins, and aimed to construct a new more authentic women-centred view of Islam. On the one hand, these religious female intellectuals retained some interest in certain feminist issues and supported policies concerning women's equal participation at work and in education, in political representation and with respect to the law of inheritance. On the other hand, in the context of the body politics and sexuality, they differentiated themselves from secular feminists by shifting to faith (*iman*) and biological sexual difference-based discourse (Yılmaz 2015: 160). In short, despite being caught between Islamist, feminist and Kemalist discourses, these conservative women played a great role in constituting their own subjectivities by reconciling and articulating these diverse discourses.

As opposed to the colonial image of a silent Muslim woman under the shroud of the hijab, which is a powerful symbol associated with the 'backwardness' of Muslim culture, the second generation of religious women reinvent the tradition by modifying not only its form but also its meaning as the symbol of their resistance against what they call the colonial approach of modernists and part of their search for a new Islam and Islamic identity. For them, neither the term *türban*, nor the form of veiling of rural women is acceptable, since the latter follows the tradition without question. Excluding the term 'burqa' (*çarşaf*) from their discussions, however, for them donning the *tesettür* in its new modern form was represented a conscious choice and turned into part of their political battle.

Figure 10.1 'Veiled Women's Struggle in the 1990s' (Başörtülü Kadınların Mücadeleleri) Source: https://bianet.org/bianet/kadin/161062-basortusune-ozgurluk-icin-elele-zincirlerinden-bugune

Figure 10.2 'Never Without Headscarf' (Başörtüsüz Asla) Source: https://islamipaylasimlar.tumblr.com/post/63391081347/ba%C5%9F%C3%B6rt%C3%BCs%C3%BCz-asla

Since they embody the intimate/Islamic everywhere, they transform the public space, participating into which is typically rendered as non-*mahrem* to them. In other words, in a Butlerian sense, their performative acts of wearing the headscarf do not simply reproduce male discourses; they also articulate them through new means and strategies, which nevertheless sustain classical distinctions like external/internal, intimate/non-intimate, *mahrem*/*non-mahrem*, but at the same time lead them to transgress the social boundaries associated with them. Hence they involve into the process of producing a 'truth' about what is the public and the private, and secular and religious. Hence, by using the headscarf, these women remove spatial borders by converting them into corporeal boundaries signified by their veils. In other words, they marked the borders onto their own bodies through the headscarf (Yılmaz 2015: 191). The increasing number of women with the *tesettür* in the 1990s was a challenge against laicist Kemalism and its control over personal preferences and public spaces (Göle 2012; Yılmaz 2015).

In the late 1990s when the Islamist conservative Welfare Party (RP) was active, the demand that the headscarf be permitted in the public sphere (in businesses and in educational institutions) became the basic heading of the growing Islamic women's movement public action. Within a short period, conservative men attempted to take control of both the Islamic women's organizations and their headscarf movement, and the incentive of RP excessively politicized and transformed the debate into a harshly contested arena (Çakır 2000; 2013). Later, this radicalization resulted in the 1997 'postmodern military coup' after which Turkey's long-standing prohibitions on the headscarf gradually intensified.

Under these circumstances, the neoliberal and neoconservative AKP came to power in 2002 with an alternative political project titled 'Conservative Democracy' promoting a new model of modernization in harmony with traditional Islamic values as well as neoliberal austerity rules (İnsel 2003; Keyman 2007; Hale and Özbudun 2009). Hence, in the first period of its rule that is from 2002 until 2007, the AKP has followed the path of liberal Islam and aligned Turkey's trajectory with neoliberal processes of globalization (Tuğal 2009). Within this context, the AKP applied a new strategy based on a politics of non-defiance (Turam 2008), which means that in the name of building a new consensus around its neoliberal and neoconservative project, it has avoided getting involved with issues of conflict, like that of the headscarf. This enabled AKP politicians to associate the defiance and street protest of earlier Islamic activists with extremism. Despite its historically religiously conservative roots, the AKP adopted many liberal views. Following some liberal Islamist female activists, the AKP has also promoted women's rights such as equal participation in education and economy and formulated policies against domestic violence. To draw a modern profile that was opposed to the old traditional conservative parties, the AKP also put some gender-sensitive legal and institutional reforms into practice.[1] Displaying a women-friendly face has also found a support of the EU members and also functioned positively in Turkey's continuing negotiation with the EU for membership therein.

The interaction of Islam with the neoliberal market economy has been in effect ever since the 1980s when the Mother Land Party (ANAP, the first neoconservative party) was in power, but the relationship has become much more prominent and has accelerated in the period of AKP rule. The conservative bourgeoisie grew tremendously under the impact of the increasing flow of hot money capital because of the standby agreements with the IMF, and in their existent cronyism with, and patronage of, the AKP (Tanyılmaz 2015). In line with this, the AKP has not only depoliticized but also economized old political issues like that of the headscarf by inserting them into a growing Islamic market economy. Within this process of the integration of Islam with capitalism, the number of Islamic magazines, television channels, publishers, Islamic music and fashion firms, and conservative touristic hotels has grown huge. This has made a real impact on the experiences of veiled women by increasing their public existence and visibility. Under the impact of all these changes, the political meaning of the headscarf has changed throughout the 2000s due to the evolution of a new *tesettür* fashion that has turned the headscarf into a consumer good (Yılmaz 2015: 186). Hence, the headscarf became a symbol that signifies not only religious, but also class, differences among conservatives. In its earlier period, the AKP's rule relatively balanced social conflicts previously proliferated between secular and Islamic sections of society by presenting the attributes of liberal-reformism with the defence of modern Islam and some women's rights policies. Hence the issue of the headscarf has lost its earlier public weight not only with respect to the new political approach of the government but also parallel to its increasing economic value in widening *tesettür* fashion.

With their highly political and challenging subjectivities, the female piety and public sexuality of the 1990s have gone through important changes particularly under the impact of the integration of Islam with neoliberal market economies and the growth of a conservative bourgeoisie in the 2000s. Here, the impacts of neoliberalism and neoconservatism are intermingled rationalities (Brown 2005, 2006, 2018) that are perceived not simply as suppressive/oppressive but also as enabling and positive and which lead to the constitution of various subjective practices, spheres and habits. In this process of the articulation of Islam with capitalism, the religious communities functioned well in the decreasing significance of old nation-state institutions and led the development of the Islamic market economy including various sectors ranging from Islamic magazines, television channels, publishers, music producers, to fashion firms. All these not only resulted in the reformation of Islam but also in its adaptation to the needs of capitalism. Consequently, not only religious-oriented universities, hotels, cafés and restaurants where women and men can go together have emerged, but even the mosques have been transformed on the grounds of new understandings of female and male equality. Social media has also engendered new religious websites and blogs where pious women and men are active.

In this context, where not only neoliberal conservatism has spread but also a neoconservative bourgeoisie has emerged, the wearing of *tesettür* clothing, as the assumed symbol of Islamic belief and tradition, evolved into a new sector (Çakır 1990; Meşe 2015; Durur and Şimşek 2017). Beyond being transformed into a sector, towards the 2010s, the wearing of *tesettür* clothing also became highly globalized. Moreover, in a newspaper column, Alphan (2017) generally predicted that the global Islamic market would surpass US$ 5 trillion in 2019 and stressed the potential that it bore for the global economy. In the conservative fashion sector, what was mainly desired was, on the one hand, to include the Islamic tradition in the public sphere, on the other hand, to reinvent the tradition by adapting *tesettür* clothing to modern norms. While the Islamic moral codes (linked to such values as modesty and piety) to which veiling is related require you to deemphasize class differences and revalue your community membership, fashion redefines you in the very layered terms of the economy of taste and of cultural distinctions in Bourdieu's (1984) terms. Meşe, who analyses the conservative fashion magazine called *Aysha*, summarizes this seemingly contradictory transformation as follows: 'The magazine brings together veiling industry and consumers, and even shape them in accordance with class and aesthetic pleasures. In this sense, while the magazine integrates Muslims with modern life through fashion, at the same time it decomposes them by offering an exclusive identity' (Meşe 2015: 146). This new ambivalence of a cultural context, that is surrounded by the fashion industry and market relations as much as it is by Islamic culture, articulated the class, gender and generational differences as well as created some tensions, which have become more apparent and deeper within conservative sectors in the last decade. Sim (2017: 45) states under these circumstances, by veiling, the woman turns her body into not only a site of religious classification, but also one of class. Although the relations of these women with fashion have many sites of negotiation between Islam and aesthetics, politics and the desires of their socio-spatial environments (Gökarıksel and Secor 2012), in the final analysis, their subjectivity as fashion objects creates new ambivalences and leads to, as Meşe states, a new representational crisis.

Furthermore, not only have class differences and social gaps been deepened by the market economy, new social spaces of individualism and self-reflexivity have also expanded. As Alimen states, in this global era, 'the diversification and horizontalization

Figure 10.3 'Süslüman Turkey Is the First in The World of Fashion' (Süslüman Türkiye Moda Dünyasında Birinci). Source: https://odatv.com/susluman-turkiye-3007151200.html

of religious authorities and sources, and the rapidly changing circumstances of many areas of everyday life (such as consumption spaces and the internet) result in reflexivity and reflexive responses that leads to instauration of religious habitus' (Alimen 2018: 10). Social media 'reveals the intrinsic hybridity of multiple modernities and traditions in which individuals (mainly conservative youngsters) selectively utilize and creatively reinterpret religious and other cultural resources as they negotiate their way through the heterogeneity of the present' (Alimen 2018: 11). As they allow individual creativity and multiple Islamic interpretations beyond the control of religious elites and authorities, these new cultural, political and economic dynamics have increased ambiguities and ambivalence, as well as fears and anxieties among conservatives.

Threatening cultural unity that was dreamed by Islamist, as of the mid-2000s, while conservative circles, nurtured by economic interests, have become the main actors in state politics, tensions deriving from new class habituses and class conflicts in economic and political terms between them deepened. In the same period, the liberal alliance on which the AKP was based has gradually been disintegrated and the project of 'Conservative Democracy' has lost its hegemony. The sudden step back in the peace process with the Kurdish movement, the disintegration of the Erdoğanists' political alliance with the Gülen community, the Gezi revolts and the dissolution of the process of Turkey's membership into the EU can be read as the main denominators of this growing crisis. Added to this is the dissatisfaction – due to widening economic depression – with existing socio-economic policies that have expanded in the reactions of the lower classes against the earlier reformist policies of the AKP. An earlier period of the AKP rule, which was marked by the acceleration of the demands of the Kurdish movement towards democratic solutions to the Kurdish question, the expansion of women's rights along with the widening of socio-economic gaps between classes, and the marketization of religious values and ties, was on the way to end as the critique against these politics have aroused among popular masses. The AKP responded to this growing crisis by strengthening the authoritarian elements of its regime and by building new political and class alliances between radical nationalist and conservative power groups (Bruff 2014, 2016; Bruff and Tansel 2018; Kaygusuz 2018; Tansel 2018). Particularly after 2010, the foundation of the earlier liberal coalition in Turkey has weakened and has been replaced with a radical nationalist-conservative power bloc that aims to close ranks, especially against the secular Kurdish and feminist movements, and to re-establish state authority. Hence, in order to be able to appeal to popular classes, the AKP has shifted to a 'single nation – single flag – single land – single state' discourse, which emanates from the new synthesis of 'native and national' ideology of its power bloc, and has also adopted an anti-gender equality stance (Yarar 2020).

In this new context, women are exposed to ubiquitous disciplinary body politics at multiple levels where technologies of subjection, knowledge and power operate together in a complex manner. For instance, in authoritarian contexts, where nationalism, Islamism and neoliberalism are smoothly blended into each other, it appears that political rule is reinforced by a patriarchal framework that is based on the promotion of family values, and on discourses that are against gender equality and are backed up by patriarchal, family-based and pronatalistic policies (Acar and Altunok 2013; Cindoğlu and Ünal 2017). Hence, women's bodies became subjects of ubiquitous local surveillance and deeply enmeshed within increasing conflicts and struggles. Definitions of what is considered a threat to the national unity have been filtered through gendered and sexualized anxieties about national virility, sovereignty and integrity (Bedford 2008). As opposed to this increasing political and popular concerns about the national and moral integrity, the image of veiled women along with other gendered and sexualized fantasies appeared as an important symbol in bringing together often-contradictory ideological elements under a single rubric in order to achieve a coherent narrative against the imagined Others. The subjects of these critical nationalist discourses are not only secular female figures, but also conservative religious women of the 2000s.

As opposed to these increasingly moralized and religiously informed nationalist discourses and images, not only secular feminists, but also some young Muslim veiled women, who have grown up under the impact of an Islamic market-economy and consumer culture, have appeared as dangerous others. Ironically, this new period begins with the break in the AKP's silence over the issue of the headscarf when it abolished the bans on the use of the headscarf on university campuses (2008). However, the new attempt of the AKP to lift the ban on the headscarf has not only provoked the debate and the old opposition between laicists and religious conservatives, it has also resulted in a new type of representational crisis in religious circles. This representational crisis is what this chapter aims to analyse in the enlarging discussions on the proper public appearance of conservative religious women, and on the concept of the *Süslüman*. These discussions resonate with the popular feelings of social groups who are uncomfortable with the impact of the earlier mode of the AKP's neoliberal governmentality. This new conjuncture is what has forced the AKP to build new political alliances with radical conservative and nationalist groups and with the authoritarian regime that became particularly visible after 2010 and 2015.

Süslüman as the subject of political discourses in authoritarian times

The emergence of the Süslüman as a popular issue in the social media and its transformation into a political issue

Neoliberalism, while depoliticizing cultural forms through their integration with the market economy, has also constituted a basis for new social conflicts, tensions, ambiguities and crisis. The same process brings also the attempts to establish norms of *mahremiyet* (privacy and modesty) and to control public sexualities of new generations into being. These contradictory dynamics can partly be seen as the natural outcomes of social-historical process of change and transformation, but the same contradictions and tensions are also related to the combined effects of neoliberalism and neoconservatism. As has been already mentioned above, these two forms of rationalities have historically been a basis for the expansion of the individual reflexivity and cultural diversity that has emerged through the prism of consumer culture as much as of conservative-authoritarian moral reactions. As Brown argues, neoliberalism as a form of governmental rationality is a fruitful basis not only for the evolution of liberal aspects like individualism, self-reflexivity and anti-statism but also for strengthening the state, nationalism and religious conservatism. She constitutes continuous but non-functional or non-causal symbiotic relationship between neoliberal, neoconservative and authoritarian rationalities and forms (Brown 2005, 2006, 2018). Here, in the context of the discursive field on the female sexuality, the headscarf and the *Süslümans*, we can trace all these contradictory trends as well as the emergence of new technologies of power and the self. In the late 2000s, the concept of the *Süslüman* emerged within this context of deepening socio-economic tensions resulting from the effects of neoliberalism and neoconservatism and reflects the great ambiguity and crisis constructed around Islamic-pious femininity that has been once constructed by Islamist political activism.

As it was mentioned earlier, the concept of *Süslüman*, which is a play on two words, the *Müslüman* (Muslim) and *Süslü* (dressy), was first used by young social media users in 2009 as a critique and outright mockery of the young conservative women who had also acquired visibility in social media and whose relationship with modern or/ and luxury consumption was conspicuous. Throughout the research I have conducted on social media about the concept of *the Süslüman*, I have collected materials ranging from videos, pictures and poems under the heading of the *Süslüman*. While they reflect various feelings ranging from satire, mocking, anger, disgust, criticism, shame and so on, these materials make it possible for us to realize not only the way how these feelings emerge but also the ways in which above-mentioned social and cultural crisis has been gendered and moralized through these feelings directed against the *Süslüman*.

Süslüman

Tight pants on them
Now these are the
süslüman
They have become
painted with
Make-up on their
faces
These are the
süslüman
They smoke hookah
at cafes

They dance the *halay*
at folk song bars
I swear to God, it's
true
These have become
very sweet
These are the
süslüman
They put on nail
polish,
Their lips are painted

When they walk, they
have a lot of style
You remember,
worldly goods were
Forbidden by religion
Didn't you know,
süslüman?
Muhlis Şutanrıkulu
Recording Date: 10
March 2015, 16:45:00

Reflecting and expressing diverse feelings, this and many other similar poems circulating in the social media are generally written as definitions of what the Süslüman is in a critical or mocking manner in conservative circles. Condemning the new *tesettür* fashion, new clothing styles with makeup and clothing exposing the bodies of women to the gaze of non-*mahrem* others, these texts criticize many young middle- and upper-class veiled women, who appear shamelessly beyond the rule of religious modesty and privacy. In this sense, the unintentional desire behind these poems, like many other statements along the same lines, seems to build the radical conservative as opposed to liberal Islamic rules and norms of *mahremiyet*. In these texts, these young veiled women (*Süslümans*) are clearly denied, *for* transgressing social boundaries that differentiate not only modern-secular from traditional-religious but also *mahrem* from non-*mahrem*. Their performances are perceived as synthetic subjectivities who act under dangerous impacts of secularism, modernism and consumerism.

Few years after its first emergence in the social media in this line, the concept of *Süslüman* turns into a subject of political debates in the mainstream media. Through the analysis of these discourses on the *Süslüman*, one can trace the sings of rising new radical conservative and the authoritarian views and practices that express themselves in the subtle forms in the field of *mahremiyet*. These political discourses tend to moralize existing social problems through the language of *mahremiyet*. For instance, we see how the *Süslüman* turns into a common subject of the critiques of those intellectuals and politicians with different political positions against the AKP's earlier politics. As it is shown below, on this common ground, their voices began to resonate with each other and they both condemned the AKP's earlier liberal but still religiously informed policies for degenerating the youth. You can also see how the AKP appropriated these reactions against its earlier liberal policies and made a new manoeuvre towards authoritarian and conservative politics. As it is also shown below, in the same context, there had been some liberal ideas which are critical about authoritarian and conservative discourses mentioned above but challenge neither neoliberal capitalism nor patriarchal norms of sexuality.

New conservative political standpoints as opposed to the AKP's earlier neoliberalism and the Süslümans

In 2013, the radical conservative newspaper *Vahdet* published a commentary on a young conservative woman sitting on the shoulders of her male friend in a crowd at a concert on a university campus in the provincial city of *Düzce* in the north-western part of Turkey. Pointing at her appearance in a crowd without a necessary physical distance from presumably a non-*mahrem* male body despite her headscarf, the author expresses his frustration in the news title: *Is this what we have struggled so long for? Such a disgrace is not acceptable.* The image of this girl later circulates in both social and mainstream media, and turns into a visual signifier for the concept of the *Süslüman*. As soon as it is published in *Vahdet*, the news also attracts other newspapers like the radical nationalist and Kemalist known *Sözcü* (See Figure 10.4).

This strategy of re-presenting the already presented news in a new setting or framework repeats itself through other very similar news on expanding moral issues/ problems among conservatives in gendered moral terms and leads to a shallow critique of the AKP government. In these articles, popular concepts such as *Süslüman* become a way of deciphering the failure of the AKP's project in raising a new devout generation that had been declared by Erdoğan himself a few times in his public statements. For instance, in an article, Hande Zeyrek ('*Süslü Müslümanlar*' – Dressy Muslims – 22 October 2013, the Sözcü newspaper) defines these women as 'the *nouveaux riche* created by the AKP' and states: 'They also have names: *Süslüman* ... It is one

Figure 10.4 'We Have Raised Not Muslims but Süslümans' (Müslüman Değil Süslüman Yetiştirdik). Source : https://odatv.com/musluman-degil-susluman-olduk-0103151200.html

of the most talked about concepts in recent periods. This name has been given to conservatives who lived a disproportionate life of luxury, even if the luxury-lifestyle of the "*Süslümans*" is criticized with the words, "Religion has become the entertainment of the rich"; everyone is watching them.' Here, the author adds a class dimension to this political discussion of the concept by defining these newly rich religious groups as a newly emerging class who are engaged with disproportionate wealth and live in real luxury. The phrase like 'religion is the entertainment of the wealthy' signifies the suspicions of the author about the sincerity of the religious faith of these people.

In the same year, Nilay Örnek, in her highly influential popular magazine article (the impact of the article can be seen only by looking at how often it is cited in other commentaries and columns written by secular and conservative authors as well as by some social media users), writes on the concept of the 'Süslüman' and defines the term with reference to 'a group of well-educated young beautiful women with headscarves' who are given this name in social media. Accordingly, the concept signifies their age as well as their socio-economic class. She states, 'They are continuously sharing on Instagram their exaggerated lifestyles, their "brand-name" items, gold USB sticks or eyeglasses with rose reliefs, and stylish designer "outfits"' (Örnek 2013a). She argues that what these young veiled women constitute are imitations of 'secular' forms, 'It is as though I am following a different version by Tuba Ünsal [a famous secular Turkish model]... If Ünsal was putting a towel and vodka on the beach, this girl was also

putting a luxurious brand of soda next to her towel as well as a "Ted Baker" iPad bag'
(Örnek 2013a). As in this phrase, synchronic correspondences are made between
high-brand 'Islamic' and 'secular' consumer goods to reproduce and maintain
differences between these categories. For instance, in the social media photos of these
pious women, a 'luxury brand of soda' or a cup of 'salep' (a hot traditional drink), the
non-alcoholic Hookah that had been consumed at the modern Huqqa (an alcohol-free
restaurant) replaces the 'cocktail' or the 'vodka' served at Lucca. The replacement of
symbols (i.e. brands or products) which signify the Islamic life style with those which
are associated with the secularism by pious women is what Örnek calls 'bad imitations'
or 'bad copies' of what already exists in (mainstream pop-culture) in Turkey. What
makes these social media photos 'unbearable' in Örnek's term is 'the nonexistence of
creativity' or 'their pure imitation'. She also reaches the conclusion that what defines the
performances of these women on social media is 'the condition of transforming their
religious obligations into entertainment on a live stream'. Here the headscarf is seen not
as the symbol of devotion but as 'a means of socialization or social communication', as
Örnek calls. As it is easy to notice, the classical binary oppositional thinking between
the secular and the Islamic remains here in a manner, which leads the author to
conclude, 'these women are not anymore sincere in their religiosity'. But this time,
the reason is not over politicization of this symbol, which was a common view of the
Kemalists or modernists laicists in the 1990s, but its integration into consumer culture.
Here what seems (irritating) is the disappearance of the assumed connection between
modesty and religiosity represented through the bodies of veiled women. Since the
notion of modesty here is defined in association with not only the gender but also
class, the critique of these veiled women's public performances is criticized as being
over-expressive of not only their femininity but also their wealth.

It is true that in the name of performing their class and religious identities, these
women make use of the cultural sources provided by the Islamic fashion industry,
which makes room for them to create 'difference' through 'repetition'. It functions
as a space for the hybridization of a previously distinguished binary (secular versus
religious; modern versus traditional) so that the new generation can reinvent their
religious habitus through religiously informed class codes. Following Judith Butler
(1988), this can also be conceived as performance that produces associative semantic
meanings that signify their class origin along with their religious affiliation and gender
identities and sexualities. For Butler no performance can be seen as a simple repetition,
replication or imitation of existing orders or sources (i.e. language, gestures, all manner
of symbolic signs) by already constituted social agents. Performance is an act, which
is constitutive of the subject, not constituted by the subject, and identity (gender,
religious and so on) is not a stable entity or locus of agency, but tenuously instituted
in time through the stylized repetition of acts, which are internally discontinuous. In
this sense, public performances of these veiled women destabilize the existing order of
certain binary categories and transgress borders defined by *mahremiyet* culture, such
that they might appear to many as awkward or funny, along with some other negative
feelings (Butler 1988).

However, as in the case of this example, the earlier politically embedded and
destructive or aggressive approach of the laicists against certain forms of head covering

seems to have been replaced with more ironic and caricaturizing approaches; one can also catch a glimpse of class envy and resentment. Here, the subject of these critiques is not always the expansion of capitalism even among religious sections of society, or a shared patriarchal system, but the ways in which new religious bourgeois women perform their own class habitus in some 'banal' and 'bizarre' ways and, in doing so, stand in opposition to both certain Islamic and secular cultural patterns and moral norms. All these discourses might seem to reflect sociocultural anxieties about destabilization of moral orders and national fears of losing authentic identities. These fears are concerned with expanding liberal forms of Islam alongside market relations, which is the common ground that both laicists and conservatives seem to share.

One might argue here that all these popular feelings and fears constitute the social basis of rising populist authoritarianism and banal nationalism in the 2010s. Both groups perceive the images of these female conservatives as being destructive to their understanding of 'national' culture, which, in their mind, is divided into material and spiritual domains (Chatterjee 1993). The spiritual, which is represented by religion, women, the family and so on, has real purchase for their diverse nationalisms in marking their difference from the modular forms of other nationalisms. Despite the claimed difference, and just as it is for Kemalist elitists, the spiritual sphere is desired also by those conservatives who want it to be constituted with moral codes. For religious nationalists, the national spirit should be defined by women with *tesettürs*, as opposed to figures like not only the *Süslümans*, but also feminists, secularists, Western Christians and so on.

In his article on 'Süslümans', the conservative author Akif Emre explains his negative feelings about Süslümans who for him represents moral degeneration of religious youngsters of contemporary times. He states that under the impact of market forces, neoliberalism managed what 'Jacobin secularism' could not do: the secularization of religious people, and the transformation of the meanings of religious obligations and feelings. This article, which associates the criticism of neoliberalism with the criticism of laicist modernism, brings us to an interesting point concerning the definition of conservatism:

> In the neoliberal period during Turkey's adventure with westernization and the process of modernization were virtually completed, the relations established with the world system were not through politics but only through the market, (…) we are talking about a secularized environment. (…) Now we have reached a point where conservatism has gradually become secularized, and there cannot be a response to the debate made in the environment that a synthesis started to reconcile differences in the formulation of 'Praise be to God! We are laic.' (Emre 2016)

For Emre, in the present situation, which makes society more materialist, Islam, by being wedged into the private sphere, is reduced to an individual matter and choice, and this is what laicist or modernist conservatism has created. Hence, Islam has also been removed by conservative modernism from the position of being a determining factor in life or the sole principle of ruling society (Emre 2016). Since they both aim for the withdrawal of religion from the public sphere, conservative modernism, which as terms resonate

1990   2000   2012   2020   2030

BU İŞİN SONU NEREYE VARIR

Figure 10.5 'Moral Pessimistic View on History: Quo Vadimus?' Source not identified, widely circulated on social media.

with the concept of the 'Conservative Democracy' of the AKP, is not very different from 'secular modernism'. It seems that this essentialist and anti-liberal stance acquired more clarity around the mid-2000s and gradually increased its weight and place in the public statements of conservative politicians and intellectuals, as well as of other public figures. It is interesting to see how this historical narrative and the critique of the AKP reflect themselves on the discourse surrounding the headscarf and the 'Süslümans'.

Figure 10.5 is an image that has been widely shared in social media. It illustrates how the above-explained historical narrative is symbolized by the changing Islamic dress codes of veiled women. The picture not only reflects different discourses, but also represents the existing anxieties of conservatives about the present and the future, while it glorifies the past.

The AKP's neoconservative and authoritarian manoeuvre

But this periodical rapprochement of Kemalists and radical conservatives against the claimed degenerating impacts of the AKP's earlier relatively liberal and reformist politics has not remained too long as the AKP's politics began to resonate with these popular feelings going parallel with radical nationalism and conservatism. A year after these first commentaries on the concept of the *Süslüman* appeared in the mainstream media, conservative and authoritarian commentators, as opposed to the critiques they had made in the past of the AKP regime, entered into explicit or implicit dialogue with the interpretations of AKP politicians while the politicians of the AKP increased their conservative tone in respect to not only national identity but also gendered morality concerning female sexuality as its strong signifier. In 2014, a pro-AKP radical conservative newspaper named *Akit* presented the same news about the young girl sitting on the shoulders of her male friend in a crowd at a concert in Düzce exactly with the same title and same picture (this time the face of the girl was even openly exposed without hesitation) (see Figure 10.4), as if this event had just happened on the date when the news was republished, and this time with the addition of some statements made by an AKP deputy on the disgraceful behaviour of the girl. As soon as it was published, this fake news spread all over the local/national media and social media with a quotation from *Akit*. In addition, the *Akit* tweeted the same fake news and received a high rate of response from the readers who kept humiliating and insulting the girl in the photo.

In some columns *Süslümans are referered to* not as a subject but as 'abject' beings, to use Julia Kristeva's definition, who evoke feelings of fear, disgust, anger and repulsion among radical conservatives (Kristeva 1982). For instance, in an article by Mehmet Şevket Eygi (2015a), *Süslümans* are called 'pests' (*haşarat*) and the language of anger is elevated in the differentiation of Muslims from *Süslümans* who are perceived as not only being totally immersed within a lifestyle of luxury but who have also, immorally, become addicted to it. In his another article, he differentiates a Muslim (*Müslüman*) from a *Süslüman* (Eygi 2015b) and states that 'A Müslüman woman wraps herself in *tesettür* attire appropriate to the Holy Koran, to the Sunna and Islamic law that does not draw the attentions and carnal evil eyes of non-mahrem men; a *Süslüman* woman with multi-coloured, vermillion, reddish and purplish attire with bells, wearing a headscarf the color of a rainbow, and by her flirtatious walking, draws the attentions of men more than women who are uncovered'. Associating these women with the traditional understanding of women as the source of sin and evil aiming to attract men, he continues with critical comments on what kind of terrible acts a *Süslüman* indulges in. So far, apart from the strong language critical of these women, his statements seem in line with many other news and commentary on the same issue. Yet, upon closer examination, this also brings to light the intertextual character of his text, with its many references to earlier moral public statements of some well-known AKP politicians and leading Islamist figures on the proper public manners of women in the Islamic tradition. For instance, while explaining how badly a *Süslüman* behaves in public, he refers to Bülent Arınç's[2] statement about chastity as a moral norm which expects men not to be womanizers and women to be careful about their attitudes, such as not laughing in public (Dearden 2014). In another column, Eygi (2015c) responds to the increasing tension between the so-called Erdoğanist group and the Gülen community in the AKP, and strongly criticizes the latter on moral terms and calls their members *Süslümans*. Hence, a *Süslüman* turns into a derivative concept which can be used to signify various other subjects who seem to constitute a threat to the present regime.

Through this and many other similar texts, an Exclusive definition of proper Islamic femininity is attempted to be defined and fixed as opposed to the concept of the *Süslüman*. The latter is defined as being expressive, far from modest, inordinately proud and arrogant, ostentatious, extravagant, addicted to status, and neglectful of religious obligations and of the responsibilities of motherhood and religious education, and who, like feminists, keeps trying to be equal with men. Here, along with the use of gendered moral language, the terminology of class resentment finds its expression through such words like 'immodest' and 'arrogant'. For conservatives too, the sincerity of the religious identity of these women is in question. In sum, we see in these texts how social tensions related to socio-economic and political issues have been discursively transformed into moral anxieties about the social order and disorder, which is defined in religious and gendered terms that connote the authentic culture of a supposedly non-colonialist nation. By continuously evoking the fear that women may have flagrantly violated Islamic norms in the name of their material-worldly desires which are normally not promoted and pursued by religious rules, the statements of these conservative authors may reflect and constitute moral panic, which can be considered as a popular aspect of recently expanding authoritarianism.

Is there any line of flight[3]?: On the limits of liberalism

In the columns, commentaries and news published by both secular and conservative authors, *Süslümans* are seen as representative of a new religious bourgeoisie and are condemned this time not for political reasons, as was the case in the 1990s, but for class-contained economic instrumentalism and moral decadence. This 'non-qualified', 'non-holy', 'deviant' and 'imitative' approach has awakened the feelings of 'insincerity', 'estrangement', 'outrage', 'mockery', 'resentment' and 'anger' amongst not only secularists but also conservatives. These feelings are expressed with the use of derivative language, which does not include a critique of capitalist mass-culture or class conflicts but of class resentment and moral language that is concerned with boundaries of *mahremiyet* and sexuality, which is tacitly expressed through negative feelings about the public performances of newly wealthy veiled women. The most obvious expression of this shift in the discursive position of secularists as well as conservatives is the replacement of the opposition of *türban* versus *headscarf* with *Süslüman* versus *Müslüman*. By being put in a position of neither traditional nor modern, and as such, as unidentifiable hybrid compositions and performances, the new dress and headscarf styles of women called *Süslümans* create an ambivalence in which they end up as the subjects of the moralizing discourses from both secular and religious viewpoints. Despite being seemingly critical of the expansion of Islamic culture, these discourses are shared by both secularists and traditional conservatives who use moral gendered terms in their critiques.

At this point one can ask if there is any alternative position and any hope of flying out of this discursive paradigm, which seems to be providing a large social basis for the present authoritarian populist regime. Ruşen Çakır, who is known as a specialist on Islam and conservative politics, designates the gendered aspect of public criticism against pious women labelled with the fictitious concept of the *Süslüman*. Çakır argues that although it is the men who actually articulate the religious sectors of consumer society by way of creating financial resources that substitute it, the critical gaze is focused not on men but on conservative veiled women. For Çakır, to pay insufficient attention to the male dimension of this issue and to only see the role of women, and to criticize and, moreover, to accuse them is simply not just (Çakır 2013). He also does not find it right to associate this trend only with the AKP, since the transformation of the *tesettür* clothing into a successful sector extends back to the 1980s, much earlier than the AKP: 'it is useless to caricaturize only some religious women and to try to produce from this point anti-Islamist (and anti-AKP) criticism.' Yet he neither brings a deeper analysis of neoliberal capitalism's impact on our identities and worldviews, nor points to the importance of these and other seemingly 'trivial' gendered debates on the constitution of social legitimacy to the rising authoritarianism. Differently from Çakır, Eren Erdem (2013) takes a leftist stance and points at the relationship between the Islamic lifestyle and capitalism. However, this does not prevent it from being short on analysis, as it has no recourse to an intersectional perspective that could help him grasp the widening social basis of the rising authoritarian regime.

There are also various veiled female authors who are in line with Çakır's position and put forward women-friendly views on the issue of the *Süslüman*. While second-generation authors have sadly underlined the fact that the political meaning of the headscarf is on its way to disappear (Aktaş 2000, 2017), some others point at the male-centred criticisms that are on the rise. For example, Hilal Kaplan (2015) says:

> In the past, when wearing headscarf patterns were turned into a topic of debate, (…) there were young girls who would rightly cry out 'do we have to be veiled like our grandmothers?' Now there are young girls who live in a country where the headscarf ban is largely abolished and wear daily clothes worth thousands of dollars and cry out to those who criticize them: 'Do we have to be covered like our grandmothers?' Who would say that one day the same sentence uttered by the veiled women against a ban which excluded them from all areas of life would be repeated by women who reduce their subjectivity to the status of being a fanatic fashion consumer?

Although some conservative female authors (mainly from second- and third-generations) find it natural for devout women to follow fashion and develop new consumer habits, and to desire being fashionable as much as their counterparts, secular women, they do not seem to completely approve of the extravagant ways in which these women appear on social media.[4] Yet, like other conservatives, for them the matter is one of morality concerning the public sexuality of these women. For instance, describing this issue in sociological terms, Özlem Albayrak argues that the increase in the number of young women who do not wear the headscarf or who wear it in ways which have led them to being called *Süslümans* is neither political (secularists) nor moral-individual (radical conservatives) but a sociological phenomenon, which can be understood and solved not by blaming the new generation of pious women or the AKP's policies but by looking at the long-term sociological process that she calls 'rapid modernization and secularization'. Albayrak argues, bringing Turkey closer to the standards of 'material civilization', this process breaks us from 'our spiritual side' and the traditional values that are expected to guide us (Albayrak 2019a). Like other conservatives, she also conceptualizes the present crisis in moral terms, yet differently from radical conservatives like Akif Emre, she does not reject the notion of modernization, but rather favours a form of modernity that is in harmony with tradition. In this sense, Albayrak represents a liberal position, which sounds similar to the 'Conservative Democracy' of the earlier AKP. In line with this, and despite their common moralistic approach, she critiques conservative male authorities who also desire to regulate the conservative women's public sexuality and privacy as much as Kemalists. With reference to 28 February's military intervention, which created a basis for Kemalists to use insulting concepts like *türban*, *sıkma baş* (woman wearing headscarf), and 'Ninja' to criticize forms of head cover makes that the conservative men who call pious women *Süslümans* fall into line with Kemalists (Albayrak 2013; see also Albayrak 2019b).

Albayrak does not see any class conflict (i.e. differences in wealth and expressing them publicly), but points more at the generational tensions in her comments.

She says, 'According to them, if you are a young woman who does not contradict the *tesettür* verse of the Holy Koran, but who is in search of elegance for instance, and place importance on the harmony of colours in your clothes, from now on, you are off the cuff called a Süslüman. (…) if you are covered, you should not tie it like this or that; above all, you should never think of abandoning the cover or else, they will make you suffer so much for your decision that you will regret it' (Albayrak 2013). In short, Albayrak criticizes the tendency of conservative men to generalize their views to all the *young* religious women who simply follow fashion, while ignoring the conservative men who control the wealth. In line with Albayrak, some authors argue further and underline that the *tessettür* clothing concerns not only women, but also men.[5] In this sense men can also be called a *Süslüman* and can be subject of criticism for their style of dress. But there aren't enough statements such as this to change the fact that *Süslüman* is a feminized concept.[6] Despite her critique of conservative male authorities, she cannot avoid but problematizing the behaviour of young religious women and to blame the high-speed process of modernization. Hence, the class content of the issue disappears and instead of capitalist modernization, the high speed of modernization is defined as the main source of emerging moral problems.

Due to the lack of an intersectional analysis in all these perspectives, the connection between authoritarian-conservative discourse and the present authoritarian populist regime is missing. However, as is identified and pointed out in this chapter, during the period when authoritarian populism evolves and the legal ban on the headscarf no longer remains, the worries of secular and Islamic conservative sectors begin to ascribe a new gendered moral tone that mainly targets women from the growing Islamic bourgeoisie. These shifts in the parameters of the epistemic field on the issue of the headscarf find their symbolic expression in the replacement of the opposition between '*türban* and *headscarf*' with the binary opposition of '*Süslüman* versus *Müslüman*'. Here, the latter turns into a new label that is stamped on veiled or hijabi women this time not only by the secular establishment, but also by the conservative one. Although their criticism seems to be aimed at the *nouveaux riche*-conservatives called *Süslümans*, the term seems to be used loosely by conservatives to refer to every pious woman from all classes in order to specifically disciplining the new generations who have the capacity to challenge traditional religious and patriarchal authorities.

As a last word

The analysis of discourses on *Süslümans* in their interactions demonstrates the concept's relation to the deeper social fears and anxieties of various sectors. It also shows how these fears are transformed into a political truth claims through the language of *mahrem* about the social order and disorder that exist in direct correlation with the transformation undergone by Islam under the impact of modernization for many years. On the one hand, recent changes in Islamicate culture have widened social gaps; on the other hand this led to an increase in initiatives by religious veiled women to reinterpret and practise Islamic requirements in hybrid modes that interact with feminist and other modernist discourses. Also, consumer culture and communication technologies have led these veiled women to perform their subjectivities in the hybridized spheres, where they managed to distance themselves from the control of traditional conservative and patriarchal authorities. Under these circumstances, these discourses not only deepen existing popular fears, but also transform these popular fears into a crisis defined in moral, rather than political, terms. In other words, it seems possible to conclude that in Turkey's post-Kemalist and authoritarian period, widening fears and anxieties deriving from various impacts of neoliberalism find their reflections as well as expressions in the gendered moral terms that aim to discipline such deviant subjects like the *Süslümans*. In creating moral panic, these discourses provide wider social legitimacy for authoritarian views and practices. In an earlier period, all these dimensions led the success of the AKP, which claimed to be raising a new religious generation, to be opened to debate as is indicated by the case of the young women who are called *Süslümans*. Against this potentially powerful critique of the regime, the AKP made a new political manoeuvre and strengthened authoritarian and conservative aspects of its project while regretting the earlier liberal framework of its politics in order to appeal to the moralizing approach of many conservatives targeting the new liberal and consumerist pious generation. In line with these pro-AKP journals and authors began to collect such critiques of *Süslümans* and appropriated these issues into the AKP's discourse. Hence, it ironically re-presented itself as the solution for what it once was the only one to enable, or at least, to support.

Therefore, despite the abolishment of the headscarf bans at the legal level and the regression of Kemalist forces in politics and economy, it cannot be said that the waters are now clear in these sectors. In the veins of widening problems created by neoliberalism, authoritarian and conservative forces are actively dragging emerging reactions against social problems into gendered moral panic and strengthening not only existing authoritarian power relations, but also patriarchal ones. By transforming social reactions against these problems into a social desire for a higher moral order that is maintained through patriarchal and authoritarian means, these conservative discourses on *Süslümans* have wider implications than simply the disciplining of veiled as well as unveiled women and their bodies. A critical analysis of the discourses on the concept of the *Süslümans* once again shows us the importance of an intersectional analysis that is sensitive to class, gender and religious axes of power relations. This might help us to go beyond existing conservative and secular paradigms that fail to tackle such issues like *Süslümans* beyond existing discourses. In this context, the current debates that have gone on around the headscarf for so long deserve an analysis that goes beyond the opposition of the laicist and Islamic sectors, and lets us highlight new cracks within the social basis of the power-block that might emerge along class, gender and generational lines.

Notes

1   See Güneş-Ayata and Doğangün (2017).
2   He served as the 22nd Speaker of the Parliament of Turkey from 2002 to 2007 and as a Deputy Prime Minister of Turkey between 2009 and 2015.

3   The line of flight is a Deleuzian concept that covers not only the act of fleeing or
     eluding but also of flowing, leaking and disappearing into the distance. It has no
     relation to flying, but relates instead to the concept of multiplicity.
4   For Aktaş it is still a type of resistance against the secular establishment (see Aktaş 2013).
5   Aktaş (2015).
6   In a later article of hers, Örnek (2013b) mentions the concept of 'Cülusman' as
     the male version of the same concept. But from my analysis, I can state that this
     alternative concept has not been used by many.

References

Acar, F. A. and G. Altunok (2013), 'The "Politics of Intimate" at the Intersection of
    Neo-Liberalism and Neo-Conservatism in Contemporary Turkey', *Women's Studies
    International Forum*, 41: 14–23.
Aktaş, C. (2000), 'Kamusal Alanda İslâmcı Kadın ve Erkeklerin İlişkilerindeki Değişim
    Üzerine: Bacıdan Bayana' (On the changes in relations between Islamist women and
    men in Public Sphere: From the sister to miss), *Birikim Dergisi*, 137: 36–47.
Aktaş, C. (2013), 'Güzelliğimizi nasıl tanımlayabiliriz … ' (How can we define our beauty),
    Dünya Bülteni, 24 April. Available online: http://www.dunyabulteni.net/?aType=yazar
    Haber&ArticleID=19021 (accessed 14 January 2019).
Aktaş, C. (2015), 'Tesettür Beraberliği' (Tessettür collectivity), *Nihayet*, 10 November.
    Available online: http://www.nihayet.com/genel/tesettur-beraberligi-cihan-aktas/
    (accessed 15 June 2019).
Aktaş, C. (2017), 'Başörtüsü aynı açıklama değil artık' (The headscarf is not the same
    decleration), *Gerçekhayat*, 21 August. Available online: http://www.gercekhayat.com.tr/
    yazarlar/basortusu-ayni-aciklama-degil-artik/ (accessed 15 June 2019).
Albayrak, Ö. (2013), 'Süslüman!' *Yeni Şafak*, 1 June.
Albayrak, Ö. (2019a), 'Anomie, Murder', *Yeni Şafak*, 11 January.
Albayrak, Ö. (2019b), 'Açılan başörtülüler' (Women with headscarves who took off), *Yeni
    Şafak*, 23 January.
Alimen, N. (2018), *Faith and Fashion in Turkey: Consumption, Politics and Islamic
    Identities*, London: I.B. Tauris.
Alphan, M. (2017), 'Podyumlar tesettüre neden kucak açtı?' (Why have podiums
    opened their arms to the tesettür?), *Hürriyet*, 19 November. Available online: https://
    www.hurriyet.com.tr/yazarlar/melis-alphan/podyumlar-tesetture-neden-kucak-
    acti-40614790 (accessed 20 November 2019).
Ayata, A. G. and G. Doğangün (2017), 'Gender Politics of the AKP: Restoration of a
    Religio-conservative Gender Climate', *Journal of Balkan and Near Eastern Studies*, 19
    (6): 610–27.
Bedford, K. (2008), 'Holding It Together in a Crisis: Family Strengthening and Embedding
    Neoliberalism', *IDS Bulletin*, 39 (6): 60–6.
Bourdieu, P. (1984), *Distinction: A Social Critique of the Judgment of Taste*, Cambridge:
    Harvard University Press.
Brown, W. (2005), 'Neo-Liberalism and the End of Liberal Democracy', in W. Brown
    (ed.), *Edgework: Critical Essays on Knowledge and Politics*, 37–60, Princeton: Princeton
    University Press.
Brown, W. (2006), 'American Nightmare: Neoliberalism, Neoconservatism and De-
    democratization', *Political Theory*, 34 (6): 690–714.

Brown, W. (2018), 'Neoliberalism's Frankenstein: Authoritarian Freedom in Twenty-First Century 'Democracies'', *Critical Times*, 1 (1): 60–79.

Bruff, I. (2014), 'The Rise of Authoritarian Neoliberalism', *Rethinking Marxism*, 26 (1): 113–29.

Bruff, I. (2016), 'Neoliberalism and Authoritarianism', in S. Springer, K. Birch and J. MacLeavy (eds), *The Handbook of Neoliberalism*, 107–17, New York: Routledge.

Bruff, I. and C. B. Tansel (2018), 'Authoritarian Neoliberalism: Trajectories of Knowledge Production and Praxis', *Globalizations*, 16 (3): 233–44.

Buğdaycı, Ç. (2008), 'The Absence & Presence of the "Veil" and National Ideologies of Turkey', *The International Journal of the Humanities: Annual Review*, 6 (6): 159–64.

Butler, Judith (1988), 'Performative Acts and Gender Constitution: An Essay in Phenomenology and Feminist Theory', *Theatre Journal*, 40 (4): 519–31.

Çakır, R. (1990), *Ayet ve Slogan: Türkiye'de İslami Oluşumlar* (Ayet and slogan: Islamic compositions in Turkey), İstanbul: Metis Press.

Çakır, R. (2000), 'Dindar Kadının Serüveni' (Adventure of a religious woman), *Birikim*, 1 September.

Çakır, R. (2013), '"Süslüman" taşlamak' (Pelting "Süslüman")', *Gazete Vatan*, 22 May.

Chatterjee, P. (1993), *The Nation and Its Fragments: Colonial and Postcolonial Histories*, Princeton: Princeton University Press.

Cindoğlu, D. and D. Ünal (2017), 'Gender and Sexuality in the Authoritarian Discursive Strategies of "New Turkey"', *European Journal of Women's Studies*, 24 (1): 39–54.

Dearden, L. (2014), '"Women Should Not Laugh in Public," Says Turkey's Deputy Prime Minister in Morality Speech: Bülent Arınç Condemned "Moral Regression" and Consumerism', *Independent*, 29 July.

Durakbaşa, A. (1988), 'Cumhuriyet Döneminde Kadın Kimliğinin Oluşumu' (Construction of women's identity during republican time), *Tarih ve Toplum* (History and society), 51: 37–48.

Durur, E. K. and D. C. Şimşek (2017), 'Modern Tesettürlü Kadının Dönüşümü: Âla Dergisi Örneği', *Tarih Okulu Dergisi* (TOD) (*Journal of History School*, JOHS), 10 (31): 377–97.

Elif, S., S. Kara and S. Kavuncu (2008), 'Tanzimat'tan 2000'lere Başörtüsü Sorununun Tarihçesi' (History of the headscarf issue from the Tanzimat until the 2000s), *Artizan*, 27 November. Available online: http://feminisite.net/index.php/2008/09/tanzimattan-2000lere-basortusu-sorununun-tarihcesi/ (accessed 12 November 2020).

Emre, A. (2016), 'We are Secular. Praise Be to God!' *Yeni Şafak*, 28 April. Available online: http://www.yenisafak.com/yazarlar/akifemre/sekuleriz-elhamdulillah-2028616 (accessed 12 November 2020).

Erdem, E. (2013), 'Süslüman taşlamak ve Ruşen Çakır', *Aydınlık*, 23 May. Available online: https://www.aydinlik.com.tr/arsiv/susluman-taslamak-ve-rusen-cakir (accessed 11 March 2019).

Eygi, M. Ş. (2015a), 'Nereden Zuhur Etti Bunca Süslüman Haşarat?' (From where all these Süslüman pests have emerged), *İstiklal*, 28 March.

Eygi, M. Ş. (2015b), 'Müslüman ve Süslüman' (Muslim and Süslüman), *Milli Gazete*, 30 September. Available online: https://www.milligazete.com.tr/makale/850776/mehmed-sevket-eygi/musluman-ve-susluman (accessed 11 March 2019).

Eygi, M. S. (2015c), 'Süslümanlara beddua etti … (He blasts Süslümans). Available online: https://www.saskarahaber.com/suslumanlara-beddua-etti/ (accessed 13 November 2020).

Foucault, M. (1988), 'Technologies of the Self', in L. Martin, H. Gutman and P. Hutton (eds), *Technologies of the Self: A Seminar with Michel Foucault*, 16–49, Amherst: The University of Massachusetts Press.

Göle, N. (2000a), 'Giriş' (Introduction), in N. Göle (ed.), *İslamın Yeni Kamusal Yüzleri İslam ve Kamusal Alan Üzerine Bir Atölye Çalışması*, Istanbul: Metis Yayınları.

Göle, N. (2000b), 'Modernist Kamusal Alan ve İslamcı Ahlak' (Modernist publish sphere and Islamist morality), in N. Göle (ed.), *İslamın Yeni Kamusal Yüzleri İslam ve Kamusal Alan Üzerine Bir Atölye Çalışması*, Istanbul: Metis Yayınları.

Göle, N. (2012), *Seküler ve Dinsel: Aşınan Sınırlar*, İstanbul: Metis Yayınları.

Gökarıksel, B. and A. Secor (2012), '"Even I Was Tempted": The Moral Ambivalence and Ethical Practice of Veiling-Fashion in Turkey', *Annals of the Association of American Geographers*, 102 (4): 847–62.

Hale, W. and E. Özbudun (2009), *Islamism, Democracy and Liberalism in Turkey: The Case of the AKP*, London and New York: Routledge.

İlyasoğlu, A. (1994), *Örtülü Kimlik* (Veiled identity), İstanbul: Metis Press.

İnsel, A. (2003), 'The AKP and Normalizing Democracy in Turkey', *The South Atlantic Quarterly*, 102 (2/3): 293–308.

Kaplan, H. (2015), 'Babaannem Gibi Örtünemem (I cannot cover my hair like my grandma)', *Sabah Gazetesi*, 11 May.

Kaygusuz, Ö. (2018), 'Authoritarian Neoliberalism and Regime Security in Turkey: Moving to an "Exceptional State" under AKP', *South European Society and Politics*, 23 (2): 281–302.

Keyman, F., ed. (2007), *Remaking Turkey: Globalization, Alternative Modernities and Democracy*, Oxford: Lexington Books.

Kristeva, J. (1982), *Powers of Horror: An Essay on Abjection*, trans. Leon S. Roudiez. New York: Columbia University Press.

Meşe, İ. (2015), 'İslami bir moda dergisi örneğinde moda ve tesettür: Ne türden bir birliktelik?' (Fashion and tesettür in the case of an Islamic fashion magazine: What kind of a togetherness), *Fe Dergi*, 7 (1): 146–58.

Najmabadi, A. (1993), 'Veiled Discourse – Unveiled Bodies', *Feminist Studies*, 19 (3): 487–518.

Örnek, N. (2013a), 'Kim bu Süslümanlar? sorusuyla başladı her şey', *Akşam Gazetesi*, 19 May.

Örnek, N. (2013b), Alkolsüz mojito o kadar da masum değildir!" (Mojito without alcohol is not innocent)', *Akşam Gazetesi*, 26 May.

Report (2010), 'Convention on the Elimination of All Forms of Discrimination Against Women 46th CEDAW Session *Turkey's Sixth Report on Its Compliance with the Convention on the Elimination of All Forms of Discrimination against Women* ', June, The Coalition for the Partial Preliminary Evaluation Report by 71 Non-Governmental Organizations of Turkey.

Sim, M. A. (2017), 'Unveiling The Secret Stories: Conservative Female Blogosphere in Turkey'. *Galatasaray University Journal of Communication*, 26: 39–63.

Suman, D. (2000), 'Feminizm, İslam ve Kamusal Alan' (Feminism, Islam and the Public Sphere), in N. Göle (ed.), *İslamın Yeni Kamusal Yüzleri İslam ve Kamusal Alan Üzerine Bir Atölye Çalışması*, Istanbul: Metis Yayınları.

Sehlikoglu, S. (2015), 'Intimate Publics, Public Intimacies: Natural Limits, Creation and the Culture of Mahremiyet in Turkey', *Cambridge Journal of Anthropology*, 33 (2): 77–89.

Sehlikoglu, S. (2016), 'Exercising in Comfort: Islamicate Culture of Mahremiyet in Everyday Istanbul', *Journal of Middle East Women's Studies*, 12 (2): 143–65.

Tansel, C. B. (2018), 'Authoritarian Neoliberalism and Democratic Backsliding in Turkey: Beyond the Narratives of Progress', *South European Society and Politics*, 23 (2): 197–217.

Tanyılmaz, K. (2015), 'The Deep Fracture in the Big Bourgeosie of Turkey', in N. Balkan, E. Balkan and A. Öncü (eds), *The Neoliberal Landscape and the Rise of Islamist Capital in Turkey*, 89–117, New York and Oxford: Berghahn Books.

Tuğal, C. (2009), *Passive Revolution: Absorbing the Islamic Challenge to Capitalism*, Stanford: Stanford University Press.

Turam, B. (2008), 'Turkish Women Divided by Politics', *International Feminist Journal of Politics*, 10 (4): 475–94.

Turan, N. S. (2013), 'Modernleşmeyi Semboller Üzerinden Okumak: Son Dönem Osmanlı Kadın Kıyafetlerinde Değişim ve Toplumsal Tartışmalar' (Reading modernisation through symbols: Changes in dresses of the last Ottoman period and social discussion), *Kadın Araştırmaları Dergisi*, 1 (12): 103–38.

Yarar, B. (2020), 'Neoliberal and Neoconservative Feminism(s) in Turkey: Politics of Female Bodies/Subjectivities as the Constitutive Part of the AKP"s Drift to Authoritarianism"', *New Perspectives on Turkey*, 63: 113–37.

Yegenoğlu, M. (2011), 'Clash of Secularity and Religiosity: The Staging of Secularism and Islam through the Icons of Atatürk and the Veil in Turkey', in J. Barbalet, A. Possamai and B. S. Turner (eds), *Religion and the State: A Comperative Sociology*, 225–45, New York: Anthem Press.

Yılmaz, Z. (2015), *Dişil Dindarlık: İslâmcı Kadın Hareketinin Dönüşümü* (Feminine religiosity: Transformation of Islamist women's movement), İstanbul: İletişim Press.

11

Guiding the female body through the *Alo Fetva* hotline: The female preachers' fatwas on religious marriage, religious divorce and sexual life

Burcu Kalpaklıoğlu

Over the last years, we have witnessed the deepening of the role of the Directorate of the Religious Affairs (*Diyanet*) in governing religious, social and familial affairs in Turkey in line with the neoliberal and conservative policies of the Justice and Development Party (AKP), which promotes a discourse of 'family values' and 'saving families' claimed to be 'in crisis'. When the *Diyanet* was established in 1924, its regulatory role was centred on controlling religion by restricting it to the domain of belief and private activity. This role has now changed through its operation as a social service institution, which has been expanding in the public sphere in collaboration with other state institutions. The task of the female preachers, whose numbers have also increased in the last two decades, is vital in this role. The spaces and spheres in and through which, the *Diyanet* directly interact with women have expanded considerably as the female preachers act as mediators between the *Diyanet* and families. The *Alo Fetva* (fatwa) telephone hotline is one of the spaces where the female preachers, along with the male preachers, respond to fatwa questions concerning worship, daily life matters or any other issue, and give advice to the fatwa seekers.

The male officials of the Muftiates[1] have been responding to the questions about religious matters by using the private telephones of the Muftiates long before the *Alo Fetva* hotline was institutionalized. In 1999, Nevin Meriç (Nevin *Hoca*),[2] one of the protagonists of this chapter, was appointed as an employee responsible for delivering fatwas by telephone in the Muftiate of Istanbul. In the first three years, she was the only woman delivering fatwas, but then the *Diyanet* authorized female preachers, the employees whose primary task is giving sermons in the mosques, to deliver fatwas with her. In 2012, the name of this service, *Alo Fetva*, was changed to *Alo 190 Dini Soruları Cevaplandırma Hattı*[3] (Hello 190 The Hotline for Responding to Questions Concerning Religious Matters), and became free of charge. Through this hotline, calls coming from each city are transferred to the Muftiate of that city. When I conducted my fieldwork in the women's fatwa room *(bayan fetva odası)*, located in the service building of the Muftiate of Istanbul (which is a part of the social complex of Nuruosmaniye Mosque), two preachers as well as Nevin *Hoca* were answering phone calls. There were more than eighty female preachers working in Istanbul Province at that time.[4] They were responsible for giving fatwas in the women's fatwa room based on a rotation system called a 'fatwa shift', through which each preacher would work twice a year for one week.

These female preachers must be graduated from Theology Faculties, and are selected on the basis of competitive examinations that test their knowledge of hadith, Islamic jurisprudence, exegesis, Arabic language and so on. After being elected to the institution, the tenured preachers attend education seminars in which the most experienced preachers deliver knowledge about more practical issues. Nevertheless, most of my interlocutors, who were covenanted employees, told me that they had not attended the training, but instead had learned the practical issues and gained experience on the job. The women's fatwa room is the space where the female preachers learn to give advice to individuals about their ethical problems, and to transmit their knowledge of Islamic jurisprudence in relation to the stories the questioners tell them.

Here is how the *Alo Fetva* hotline works: When one dials 190 on the phone, s/he hears three options: (1) women's fatwa; (2) men's fatwa and (3) family counselling. The callers who choose 'men's fatwa' are transferred to the men's fatwa room, which is also located in the same building. Those who choose 'family counselling' are transferred to the next room, the Family Guidance and Counselling Bureau (*Aile İrşat*[5] *ve Dini Rehberlik Bürosu*, AIRB) of the Muftiate of Istanbul, where the coordinator of AIRB responds to questions related to family matters. Although the specific option of 'family matters', it should be noted that a considerable number of questions posed to the women's fatwa room are also about familial and marital issues. It is very well possible that the authority of the term 'fatwa' might lead the individuals who have questions about family matters to prefer 'women's fatwa', rather than 'family counselling'. The preachers generally transmit the *Diyanet*'s fatwas issued by the High Council of Religious Affairs (*Din İşleri Yüksek Kurulu*)[6] to the questioners. When a preacher does not know the specific answer to a question or is not sure about it, she can keep the caller waiting on the phone and search for it in the *Diyanet*'s *ilmihal* (manual of Islamic, faith, ethics and worship), or apply to online database that includes the *Diyanet*'s fatwas. In the case of complex ethical questions, they consult Nevin *Hoca* because she is the most experienced woman employee in the Muftiate. And, also, if a fatwa seeker submits a difficult question, which has to do with family matters, they sometimes transfer it to the next room, to the AIRB. Sometimes, they also transfer the questions concerning financial issues to the men's fatwa room. Also, when the question is considerably complicated, especially with regard to religious divorce, they advise the questioners to call the telephone line of the High Council of Religious Affairs through which authoritative experts on Islamic jurisprudence in the institution respond to questions.

This chapter draws on in-depth ethnographic research conducted in the women's fatwa room throughout five months in 2014–15, as well as semi-structured interviews conducted with ten female preachers and religious experts. I aim to analyse how the female preachers, as mediators between the *Diyanet* and individuals, reinterpret the *Diyanet*'s fatwas on religious marriage and divorce, as well as on marital and extramarital sexual relationships, depending on the lived experiences they listen to. First of all, I will begin with conceptualizing the practice of delivering fatwas in the context of neoliberal and conservative politics promoted in Turkey, and discuss the ways fatwa operates as a technique that governs the women's bodies, and marital and sexual lives. Then, I will discuss the various ways in which marriage and sexuality are articulated, negotiated and governed through the preachers' responses. Here, the preachers have a large room for interpretation that ensues from the gap between the existing fatwas and social realities, as well as the gap between religious law and civil law. Inspired by Saba Mahmood's use of the term 'agency' in which norms are not conceptualized as either consolidation or subversion but, instead, as 'performed, inhabited, and experienced in a variety of ways' (Mahmood 2005: 22), I suggest that, in female preachers' interpretative space, multiple norms, discourses and authoritative knowledges overlap, are transmitted, communicated and negotiated in myriad ways. The female preachers attempt, on the one hand, to stay within the boundaries of the government's discourse on family as well as the gender hierarchy constructed in Sunni Muslim legal tradition, and, on the other hand, to protect the female fatwa seekers' religious and legal rights and challenge the patriarchal interpretations of the Sharia. At the same time, they draw a line between their reasoning and that of feminists whom they consider as informed by Western secular ideas. In this way, I examine the female preachers' modes of reasoning, references, arguments, pedagogies and the ways in which they draw on multiple discourses in their responses.

The practice of giving fatwas as conduct of conduct

In the Islamic jurisprudential traditions, fatwas are non-binding learned opinions that may concern any issue, from practices of worship to ethical problems pertaining to the details of one's daily life. Hussein Ali Agrama draws attention to this ethical capacity of the fatwas and suggests that fatwas could be understood as a mode of 'the care of the self', 'as a practice by which selves, in the multiplicity of their affairs, are maintained and advanced as part of Islamic tradition' (Agrama 2010: 13). Through 'the care of the self', the term which means attending to oneself, being concerned with oneself, Michel Foucault describes a particular relationship with oneself within a particular period of history, namely, the ancient Greek and Roman and early Christian periods (Foucault 1998, 2005). In this regard, a fatwa is, first, an ethical practice that reproduces Muslim selves in showing the right path to the fatwa seekers. Taking into account its guiding, moving, changing and affecting efficacies, it is an act of ethical cultivation rather than of transmitting information. Nevertheless, discussing the *Alo Fetva* only in terms of its ethical dimension would not be enough to elaborate the way it works in contemporary Turkey. Ethical cultivation in the *Alo Fetva* often goes hand in hand with governmental practices. In this sense, Foucault's notion of 'governmentality', where the notions of the care of the self are openly linked to issues of power, is also useful in the analysis of the *Alo Fetva* as a service, works at the intersection of the moral, the social and the political.

Foucault employs the term 'governmentality' in order to depict the political rationalities and technologies, which emerged in Europe in the eighteenth and nineteenth centuries. The term 'government' does not refer to the political structures or the management of the state; 'rather it designates the way in which the conduct of individuals or of groups might be directed: the government of children, of souls, of communities, of families, of sick... To govern, in this sense, is to structure the possible field of action of others' (Foucault 1982: 790). Thus, governmentality is 'the conduct of conduct', and 'to conduct' refers both to activity of conducting (others), and the way in which one conducts oneself and is conducted by others (Foucault 2007: 258). Governmentality and the allocation of power, in this sense, is not a one-way or top-down mechanism; rather, government constitutes the 'contact point' where how 'the individuals are driven by others is tied to the way they conduct themselves' (Foucault 1993: 203). Hence, the female preachers' moral guidance, their activity of leading, affecting and shaping the practices of fatwa seekers could be understood as an effectuation of 'the conduct of conduct'.

According to Jacques Donzelot (1979), the 'social' is the new formula through which the act of governing is affected. That is to say, as if it were a naively apolitical act, political power acts upon people's action in relation to a given social norm and constitutes their experiences within a social form. This formula of government constitutes a form of knowledge in relation to the professionals who have the authority to act as experts in constituting and spreading truth claims through strategies of social rule (Miller and Rose 2008). Donzelot (1979) argues that the family becomes the target that conveys the norms of the state to the private sphere through certain methods and technologies. It is a target of political rationality that enables the control of sexuality and the reproduction of the population, as well as an instrument for moralising the nation since it is the locus of daily life, the sacred and the emotions.

Although, in Turkey, secular reforms have regulated the institution of marriage and the family since the end of the nineteenth century, during the AKP era, the role of the family in the political and economic transformation of the country has deepened and new means and techniques are being used for interventions into the family. Families are governed through social experts and multifarious political discourses that permeate the social lives of individuals, in alliance with the laws that have been implemented. In this regard, women are recognized in the public primarily in the context of their rights and roles in the family[7] and there has been huge public debate around abortion, the desirable number of children in families, contraception, women's sexuality and gender roles, their right to alimony and minimum marriage age, and their employment (Akınerdem 2019). In this regard, the Directorate of Religious Affairs, as a state institution that aims to define a particular religion mostly as an amalgam of government's norms and discourses and the patriarchal interpretations transmitted in Sunni jurisprudential tradition, has turned out to be one of the principal actors supporting the strategies of the government.

One of the most crucial novelties in the AKP period is the government's authorization of the *Diyanet* to largely carry out social services. While the number of other social service institutions aiming to empower women is quite low, and even decreasing in the AKP period, the role of the *Diyanet* as a new social service mechanism that seeks to preserve the families through various discourses and techniques has been gradually increasing (Eralp 2018). The female preachers are dominant actors in the fulfilment of this social service organized by the *Diyanet*, in conducting the lives, bodies and sexualities of women they consider as central to the institution of family. Along with their task in the *Alo Fetva* Hotline, within the scope of the project of Religious Services with Social Initiative, the female preachers also give personal advice in the Family Guidance and Counselling Bureaus. They visit orphanages, women's shelters, hospitals, alms-houses and prisons in order to give moral support and/or to give lessons to those who live there. By performing service (*hizmet*), it seems that the *Diyanet* is not involved in 'politics' but just operates in the sphere of the social and the moral. However, it could be said that the state-sponsored preachers disseminate the *Diyanet*'s, and, by extension, the government's and the Sunni legal tradition's discourses and truths through these services. Put differently, in a sense, the state enters the houses, listens to the most private secrets of its citizens and authorizes professionals to solve their problems. And, the solutions are in accord with the neoliberal and patriarchal policies through which the AKP intended to promote gender inequality, to preserve the family and to strengthen the morality of the population and the nation.

Yet the ambivalences, the multiple actors and discourses, and the complex negotiations should be taken into account in analysing the female preachers' fatwas in the *Alo Fetva*. While responding to questions, the female preachers always oscillate between two sides. On the one hand, as state employees who undertook formal education in theology faculties, female preachers transmit fatwas issued by a state institution. At times, they speak on behalf of the *Diyanet* or state their position as representing the institution. In particular cases, the *Diyanet* issues inflexible fatwas hardly opened to the interpretation of the preachers, such as its fatwas on abortion and contraceptive methods, and the preachers here engage in and promote these fatwas through their uncompromising styles of responding. On the other hand, the female preachers have different subjectivities and life experiences, which, in turn, implies that they do not represent the *Diyanet*. Accordingly, it would be unfair to claim that they are simply actors who only transmit the *Diyanet*'s fatwas as predicated on the discourse on gender and family promoted by the government as well as by the Sunni Muslim legal tradition. Instead, they employ various discourses as well as strategies and pedagogies in their interpretive room between canonical knowledge and the social facts provided by fatwa seekers.

The female preachers' interpretive space between the Islamic jurisprudence and women's lived experiences

The female preachers' interpretive possibilities first draw on the epistemic gap within the *Diyanet*'s discourse. Like all other legal systems or authorities, the Islamic jurisprudence promoted by the *Diyanet* has no capacity to define and regulate all the detailed practices of its adherents. Accordingly, daily life and marital issues are the very realms that can be permeated by the state discourse only to a limited extent forasmuch as everyday practices include various detailed complexities that divert the state's authority and grant strategies (De Certeau 1984). By this, I mean that when the female preachers deal with the women who have daily life problems, and despite the fact that the *Diyanet* is always within the conversation, it is not only the *Diyanet*'s voice that is heard on the phone. In this woman-to-woman conversation, the female preachers and fatwa seekers talk about daily complexities, sexual life, marriages, husbands, children, their rights or responsibilities, that is, the detailed issues which the *Diyanet* cannot strictly regulate. Although the government, along with the Islamic jurisprudential tradition, produces certain discourses that influence the preachers' responses, the preachers still have a space of their own that ensues from the gap between the law and the social reality (Messick 1993). It could also be argued that, although the family and intimate sphere become the site of proliferating forms of political intervention today, and as the very part of the neoliberal governmental activity again, family matters are at the same time considered to be intimate and secret (Sirman 2005; Agrama 2012) and hence are interfered with only to a certain extent. This ambivalent nature of conservative and neoliberal family politics thereby leaves some space for interpretation to the female preachers as women who are attentive to the other women's experiences.

In addition to that, and differently to other modern legal systems, Islamic jurisprudence (*fıkıh*) has a particular flexibility and fluidity, deepening the gap between the law and lived realities (Messick 1986, 1993; Mir-Hosseini 2000). While the Sharia, which literally means 'path' or 'way' in the Arabic language, refers to the ethical path revealed by God that constitutes what is the good life for Muslims, *fıkıh* is a humanly constituted interpretation of that divine truth (Messick 1993; Mir Hosseini 2000; Hallaq 2003–2004). Therefore, *fıkıh* itself is a human product and includes multifarious interpretations, and therefore has a capacity to accommodate social change and individual needs. In the context of marital issues and gender rights, *fıkıh* has been constructed in a patriarchal way such as to assume the inequality between men and women, thereby giving men particular privileges over women. However, it is usually understood to be divine, inflexible and unquestionable, and almost equated with Islam itself today. The challenge of Islamic feminists to the jurisprudential tradition has come into play in this framework in which gender hierarchy is considered inherent to Islam. Islamic feminists are seeking to deconstruct certain assumptions and redefine certain legal concepts in line with Islamic ethical values (Wadud 1999; Mir-Hosseini 2015; Tuksal 2018). At times, the female preachers' act of listening to the women's stories as well as their personal experiences as women compels them to produce new rationales and solutions in accordance to women's needs, in line with the discourses of the Islamic feminists. Nevertheless, in doing so, they clearly stress the difference between their approach and feminist perspectives. Here, it is also worthy of note that the preachers did not refer to anything concerning Islamic feminism in our conversations. According to them, feminism is a priori a 'secular' Western ideology, which tends to corrupt the institution of family and is not capable of understanding and responding to women's demands and troubles completely.

Lastly, the discrepancy between Islamic jurisprudential interpretations and civil law regarding marital issues in Turkey also expand the female preachers' room for interpretation. As we will see below, the *Diyanet*'s fatwas on religious marriage and divorce based on classical legal tradition are irrelevant to the Turkish Civil Code. They give men some privileges over women and cause injustice for women not only because of the underlying gender hierarchy of the Islamic jurisprudential tradition but also because women's having no chance to seek their religious rights in a court or any other institution in the context of Turkey. At that point, it should be noted that some of the preachers told me that the *Diyanet* is incapable of producing new fatwas in conformity with social realities in a modern world and that religious marriage and divorce are the very issues that need clear solutions. Because of this reason, within the knowledge of the authorities in the institution of the *Diyanet*, the female preachers certainly seek to find strategies of responding to these questions drawing on civil law as well as the jurisprudential traditions and enable a constant negotiation to take place between these two different realms of law.

Governing the sexual life, governing women

Sexual ethics and sexual practices constitute a significant part of the questions that arise in the women's fatwa room, primarily because of both the anonymity of the fatwa seekers and the gender of the fatwa deliverers. Talking woman-to-woman without knowing each other paves the way for the fatwa seekers to tell their most private stories and to ask questions in all their details. Once, a female fatwa seeker was shy about posing her question concerning a sexual matter. Then the preacher relaxed her by saying: 'We are here for your questions. In order to get your answer, you should first ask your question. There is no shame in religion.' 'There is no shame in religion' implies that one should not be ashamed to pose a question or to learn about an issue in relation to religion. The preacher here, on the one hand, speaks on behalf of both the institution and the Islamic tradition by using the term 'we' and referring to an idiom, which is well known in Islamic societies, 'there is no shame in religion'. On the other hand, it is the tacit authority of speaking as a woman that persuades the fatwa seeker to pose her question and feel better.

While responding to the questions about sexual life, the preachers mostly benefit from their 'epistemic authority' (Hallaq 2003–2004) that ensues from their personal experiences as women and the practical knowledge they obtained in the fatwa room, along with their theoretical knowledge gained in theology faculties. In our interview, one of the preachers told me the way in which her personal experience of marriage improved her responses:

> Firstly, you respond to the extent you know and transfer what you don't know to the other preachers. But, it changes over time. Experiences in human life also affect it. For example, at first, I was not married and I couldn't answer the questions regarding marriage since I didn't have enough knowledge. Child, sexuality, not being able to have sexual intercourse, and so on… As I gained experience, I began to respond to these questions.
>
> Personal Interview, 18 March 2015

In our conversations, many preachers mentioned the inadequateness of the theoretical knowledge they gained in the theology faculties. The training seminars they attended also helped them to overcome this difficulty, particularly in advising on sexual life. One of the preachers told me that,

For example, previously I didn't know incest cases were so common, and women's suicides as well. We had courses on sexual pathologies and sexuality in the family. The professors who issue fatwas on marital issues gave courses as well. We took theoretical knowledge about divorce in the university, but of course it is very different in practice. In the earlier stages, I was going into panic and praying so that these kinds of questions were not posed to me.

Personal Interview, 25 February 2015

The female preachers are attentive to the women's questions and sometimes they share similar experiences with the fatwa seekers. Comparing their ways of responding with that of male preachers and claiming that they understand and protect women more than male preachers do, they describe how they pose various questions to the fatwa seekers in order to understand the story or 'real intent' behind their questions and to give them detailed responses. A female preacher discussed this comparison in the following:

The question a woman posed to me: 'Is anal intercourse permissible?' If a woman asks this question, it means that she is compelled to do it. We should understand this, understand the amount of violence she is exposed to, and tell her Islam's approach. A male preacher might say 'It is *haram* (forbidden)' and then put down the phone. Yet, we say that God gave you these rights and nobody has a right to compel you. This is the way in which women's fatwas are different from men's fatwas.

Personal Interview, 11 May 2015

It is worth mentioning that encouraging fatwa seekers to not be ashamed in posing a fatwa question about sexual life and the preacher's certain pedagogies of responding are undergirded by the common view that interpretations in the Muslim legal tradition have a positive view of sexuality that recognizes women's and men's sexual desires and pleasures, albeit in a hierarchical way in which men's desire is seen as more active. However, as Kecia Ali stresses, such a recognition of sexuality also coexists with another view that treats 'female sexuality as dangerous, with potentially disruptive and chaotic effects on society' (Ali 2006: 8), which is familiar to us from the arguments that oppose women's participation to public space or conceive sexual ethics in the public space primarily in terms of women's bodily acts. In the Islamic jurisprudential traditions, both male and female sexuality are, first of all, regulated through the institution of marriage in which one is able to have lawful sexual relationship with a lawful partner. Extramarital sexual relationships therefore are considered to be *haram* (forbidden) and have the capacity to lead to social disharmony. The Islamic jurisprudence also regulates marital sexual relationships in deciding lawful sexual activity in the marriage as well as interpreting the issue of the sexual availability of the partners. In addition to the above narrative concerning lawful sexual positions, the female questioners also pose a considerable number of questions to the *Alo Fetva* about their experience of extramarital sexual relationships as a single or married person or their husbands' experience along with the problems of sexual life in their marriages. Based on the content of the questions, the advice given is therapeutic/confessional in form or aiming to solve the ethical problems faced. Now I will turn to female preachers' advice about these questions and examine their different pedagogies and their interpretations of the interpretations transmitted in the Sunni Muslim legal tradition.

During my fieldwork in the women's fatwa room, I have listened to a vast number of responses given to the questions posed by women who had had a previous extramarital sexual relationship and then regretted this experience. In such cases, the callers tell their most private secrets, so the practice of fatwa sometimes takes the form of a confession. The preachers most of the time advise the callers to repent (*tövbe etmek*) and pray. For instance, once I listened to a response given to a caller who cheated on her husband twenty-seven years before, then broke up with him. She was still regretting it. The preacher advised her to repent and be attentive to her prayers. She explicitly told the caller what she did was to commit adultery (*zina*) and disobey the commandments of God, but she also relaxed her by saying that God would forgive her. She also advised her not to tell anyone her experience.

In such occasions, as in the case above, the fatwa seeker sometimes seeks a kind of therapeutic authority (Miller and Rose 2008) in which the preachers' speech soothes the fatwa seeker. One of the extreme examples of this therapeutic role of 'women's fatwa' was the case of a woman who became obsessive because of the adultery (*zina*) she had committed in the past. She had been calling women's fatwa hotline because of this reason since 1999. The female expert who had responded to this woman for years, Nevin *Hoca*, told me,

> We transfer twenty per cent of the questions in the fatwa room to the doctors [advise the questioner to go to doctor]. If doctors know that we do this, they [the doctors] will communicate with us. For example, *vesvese* (delusion-obsession) cases... I have a patient from the first years. She has been calling me for 15 years and sees my voice as a solution now. We took seminars from doctors as well. I asked doctors about this case. I am not responding to her specific question anymore but respond to her other questions. This is what a doctor advised me to do.
> Personal Interview with Nevin Meriç, 13 February 2015

This case is striking in for how it epitomizes the ways in which different authoritative knowledges overlap or communicate in female preachers' advice. As a religious authority, she uses the discourse of medicine in referring to the fatwa seeker as her 'patient', and by responding in a way that a doctor advises her to do. Almost all of the preachers employ medical discourses in *vesvese* cases and advise the fatwa seekers to go to a doctor. Nevertheless, concerning the other cases in which the fatwa seekers are in trouble, they sometimes compare their ways of responding with that of psychologists and explain how the latter is inadequate to respond to women's troubles and demands. Many preachers with whom I interviewed explained that psychologists easily lead women to divorce and do not take women's conditions into account, and employ a discourse which is incongruous with that of pious women. One of the preachers asserted that, in contrast to psychologists, their language involves certain concepts that belong to Islamic vocabulary, such as *haram* (forbidden), *helal* (not forbidden), *hak* (right), *sabır* (patience), *ahiret* (afterlife), *fıtrat* (inborn nature), *emanet* (entrusted) and so on. Transmitting and redefining these concepts embedded in the social imagination of all Muslims (Mardin 1989) makes the fatwa seekers feel better and the female preachers more authoritative and trustable. According to the preacher, these concepts help the callers to make a proper decision that is attentive to both their and their families' conditions.

The female preachers' conduct with fatwa seekers who ask advice about their experience of *zina* is not always in therapeutic and confessional form. Sometimes, especially for married individuals, it might bring forth serious ethical problems to which the preachers have great difficulty in responding. In such complex situations, the preachers usually attempt to find their best solutions for the sake of all the parties involved in each situation. If the case is very difficult to advise, the preachers suggest callers to contact the High Council of Religious Affairs, where experts in Islamic jurisprudence respond to their questions. In one occasion, a man called and recounted his troublesome situation. He was married but had a long-term relationship with another married woman. The married woman had given birth to two children since they had started the affair. However, the woman's husband thought that these children were his own. The man asked if he should tell the children the truth and take care of them. After transferring the question to the High Council, the preacher said:

> This case has certainly a provision in Islamic jurisprudence. I know that, according to the Shafi school, although a child is the outcome of an adulterous relationship, the husband is considered to be the father. Instead of a situation in which the man and the husband kill each other, I think that it's better if the husband and children do not know the truth. But, in this case the children are considered to be descended from the husband and accordingly would be entitled to the husband's inheritance. It is a very difficult case to comment on.
>
> Personal Interview, 27 January 2015

Another preacher explains how she had difficulties responding to a question:

> She cheated on her husband and asked what she should do now. You are stuck in a burdensome situation. The questioner's sincerity, the emotion she makes you feel... Is she praising herself [because of the sin she committed]? You feel it during the conversation. You never say 'do this this way' or 'do that that way'. You just make this person think and open up her horizons. But she herself should come to a decision. We shouldn't say 'get married' or 'divorced'. Rather than despising her sin, we should see her as a respectable woman regretting her sin. One who has committed sin doesn't lose her need for respect
>
> Personal Interview, 3 November 2014

Almost all of the preachers with whom I conducted interviews underlined that they do not give fatwas prescriptively but show the fatwa seekers the possible results of their prospective decisions. This is the very point that illustrates very well how the preachers' practices can be conceptualized under the terms 'governmentality' and 'conduct of conduct', the terms that denote structuring possible field of action of others while at the same time letting others conduct themselves. Albeit not prescriptively, most of the time they steer women in the direction of 'saving' their families. Besides, although the preachers challenge the patriarchal jurisprudential interpretations concerning marital issues, in some cases, this occurs only to a certain extent. The following case will help me to elaborate my point.

Once, after putting down the phone, a preacher recounted the story she has just listened to: A woman's husband cheated on her and then she swore by saying that if he cheated once again, she would not get into the same bed with him anymore. But, to her regret, her husband did it again. Therefore, they have been sleeping in different rooms for five years. Her husband went to Umrah[8] and then changed. He didn't cheat on his wife again. The woman did not know that she could break her oath. The preacher advised the woman to atone for (*kefaretini ödemek*) her oath and said: 'Do this immediately and return to your family life. You have behaved unjustly (*zulmetmişsiniz*) both towards yourself and your husband until today. Human beings might make mistakes.' The woman here was willing to return to her husband, so advising her to return to her family after atoning for her oath is an advice that helps to solve her problem. However, there are two crucial insights to be highlighted here. First, the preacher 'conceptualizes' the act of separating of beds (and consequently, the rooms) as *zulüm* (unjust act, cruelty). And, second, she formulates the action of the husband as a 'pardonable' mistake. There is a discrepancy between what the preacher expects of the husband and the wife in these two accounts, which, in turn, leads to the undermining the woman's oath which indeed empowers her. What I have seen implicitly in this case, along with some other cases, is that preachers maintain the classical conception of marriage promoted by the Sunni jurisprudential traditions, though not in a strict form. Let me briefly describe the way sexuality is deployed in the patriarchal interpretations of the classical jurisprudential tradition and then discuss it in the context of the response of another preacher.

In Muslim legal traditions, the jurists define marriage as a contract of exchange that establishes a set of rights and obligations for each party, which, in turn, revolves around two themes, namely, sexual access and compensation. Mir-Hosseini describes it as the following: '*Tamkin*, obedience or submission, specifically sexual access, becomes the husband's right and thus the wife's duty; whereas *nafaqah*, maintenance, specifically shelter, food and clothing, becomes the wife's right and the husband's duty' (Mir-Hosseini 2015: 15). It would not be right to claim that the preachers promote the submission of wives to their husbands in their advice; nevertheless, it seems that they consider sexual access as the substantial responsibility of the wife. Although they recognize it as the husband's responsibility as well, their emphasis on sexual access as the wife's duty and sexual desire as a primarily male desire is apparent in their responses, albeit at times implicitly.

Another example helps me to clarify the point. Once, a female fatwa seeker called and explained that she didn't want to have a sexual intercourse with her husband since he always criticized and humiliated her. She wasn't sure about getting divorced, and her husband didn't want it either. The following are some notes I took while they were conversing:

Because of this reason [not having sexual intercourse], your marriage does not end, but if it leads your husband to *haram*, getting divorced would be better, also for your children… This is unfavourable in terms of religion. Staying married but not having sexual intercourse… Nobody should pay such a *vebal*.[9] Lady, you bear the *vebal* for this action… Religious divorce is not necessary to end a marriage; a civil divorce also ends it. If you want to maintain your marriage, you should make an effort. It would be better if you could take pleasure from having good time together. If your husband asks you to be patient, then be patient and try to have intercourse, even if just a bit. You can also go to therapy. There is nothing to do if you undertake this *vebal*. Is it difficult to spend time with such a person? Do not think only in terms of the bedroom. Handle it as a whole.

Personal Interview, 27 January 2015

In this case, the preacher explicitly advised the woman to divorce if she didn't want to maintain the marriage and didn't encourage her to save her marriage necessarily. However, she also insisted that it was *her vebal* not to have sex while staying married, because, in this way, she might cause her husband to commit sin. Accordingly, we see a discrepancy similar to the one mentioned above. On the one hand, there is the husband who humiliates his wife but who also doesn't want to get divorced; on the other hand, the wife doesn't want to have sex because of the chill she is feeling ensued from the husband's behaviours. In this articulation, *vebal* is credited to the wife. The reasoning, which takes the husband's prospective illicit relationship into account, draws on the unequal construction of male and female power of desire in Muslim legal traditions in which male sexuality is naturally considered as more powerful and active than that of females (Tucker 1998: 152). I also suggest that the argumentation of the wife's *vebal* in this relationship is highly undergirded by Islamic jurisprudential understandings of marriage in which women's sexual obedience, along with men's compensation, is a constituent element. In the preachers' responses, albeit not formulated in terms of 'obedience', sexual access is considered one of the major duties of the woman without which a marriage could not be maintained. In this context, the female preacher's discourse on sexuality clearly diverges from the feminist or Muslim feminist discourse in which women's supposed inborn nature (or *fitrat*, Abou-Bakr 2015: 54) and gender inequality stemming from this natural difference are challenged.

Within this framework, the pedagogy of responding to the family problems upheld by the Coordinator of AIRB is worth mentioning. In the interview I conducted with her, she told me how she promotes a way of thinking that focuses on the concept of 'duty' (*vazife*) instead of the concept of 'right' (*hak*):

I told the mufti I worked with together formerly the following: Please inform men about their duties towards their wives, and let us inform the women about their duties towards their husbands. If we inform women about their rights and you inform men about their rights and women's duties, marriages become hell. One always focuses on rights; let us do the contrary.

Personal Interview with the Coordinator of AIRB, 26 May 2015

Although informing both men and women about their duties in marriage seems to serve 'equality', in a society in which women are deprived of their rights, informing women about their duties rather than rights invokes the discourse of the state and patriarchy. The *Alo Fetva* articulates the goal of promoting the concept of duty and the preservation of the family by employing religious discourse. However, this religious discourse most of the time communicates with neoliberal policies through which the family becomes an instrument for the governance of the population and a patriarchal discourse in which women are recognized only through their roles and responsibilities in their families. It could be argued that a particular understanding of religion is integrated into the governmental rationality in and through which the *fetva* operates as 'effective advice' (Donzelot 1979) that moralizes and regulates the women who carry the family and, by extension, the nation.

The statements of the Coordinator of AIRB are important since they, in a sense, reflect the official discourse of the AIRB. These statements are, however, not the sole discourse in the women's fatwa room. On the contrary, the preachers make a great effort to inform women about their rights and challenge the patriarchal understanding of the Quran and other Islamic sources. In problems in daily life, men might manipulate religious law in conformity with their interests and women thus might be unaware of their rights. Especially, when they are in disagreement with their husbands, they doubt the rights that Islam accords to them and call women's fatwa hotline in order to ask what falls within the range of their rights according to Islam. In attempting to preserve women's rights in various cases, the preachers are indeed in internal dialogue with feminists. Nevertheless, according to my interlocutors, as I said above, feminism is a position that a Muslim woman should avoid. Once a preacher said to me that they work on slippery ground and should be careful not to slip into feminism. In this sense, in our conversations, many preachers compare their own positions and ideas on marriage with 'feminists'. Focusing on the concept of 'duty' instead of 'right' also includes a latent critique of feminism. When telling women of their rights in their marriages, in another preacher's words, the preachers are careful not to incite them against their husbands. This is a preclusive step that preachers take in order not to harm their marriages. Through their responses, the female preachers tread a precarious path between the religious and the secular, opening themselves up to the secular critique of feminists. In wanting to protect women, they sometimes get too close to feminism, which for them is a rejection of the religious, and at other times, they find themselves supporting a patriarchy they do not necessarily agree with.

Religious marriage and religious divorce

The interpretations of classical Sunni jurisprudence have seen marriage as a way to channel sexual desire, which is considered as powerful and male-centred. Sexuality has been regulated by the institution of marriage so that it cannot lead to 'illicit unions, unclaimed children, and, at worst, a social anarchy bred by unregulated sexual contracts' (Tucker 1998: 149). In that sense, through their advice on religious marriage and divorce, the female preachers also govern women's sexual lives by deciding whether their existing religious marriage is valid, which also means whether they are committing adultery, whether they can prefer religious marriage as a way of legitimizing their sexual relationships or whether they divorced from their husbands according to religious law and so on. In these responses, different discourses, secular and religious, state-approved ('saving families') or patriarchal jurisprudential and 'feminist' (protecting women's rights) discourses sometimes overlap, and at other times they are conflicting or negotiating. In this way, the female preachers give religious advice that involves their points of view drawing on their experiences as women, but they hardly exceed the boundaries of the Islamic jurisprudential traditions and the discourses of the *Diyanet*.

During my fieldwork in the women's fatwa room, I listened to a considerable number of advice about religious marriage (*dini nikah*, more commonly *imam nikahı*). In Turkey, along with civil marriages, most couples get married with ceremonies performed by *imams*[10] or family elders. Most of the time couples have a religious marriage ceremony after or before formal marriage as supplementary to the latter,[11] but some couples only have a religious ceremony, even if it is not legally recognized. The permissibility of religious marriage ceremony without the civil one is a very controversial issue among the religious authorities in Turkey. Some argue that two witnesses and dower (*mehir*) are sufficient for a marriage and religious marriage fulfils these requirements. Yet, since the civil law does not recognize religious marriage, women cannot acquire formal rights in it. And, their religious rights defined by the Islamic jurisprudence most of the time are violated by their partners/husbands. Besides, sometimes relatives, friends or neighbours are not informed about the marriage because couples want to keep it secret, which, in turn, as some religious authorities argue, contravenes the requirement of the publicity of religious marriage. Most of the time, men do not consider the religious marriage as an institution in which couples have some responsibilities and rights, but solely use it as a means by which they legitimize their sexual relationship and persuade their partners to its legitimacy. In some cases, men are already married to a woman and want to marry another by way of religious marriage. For these reasons, female preachers argue that religious marriage (without civil marriage) causes injustice for women and therefore do not approve it.

In one occasion, a woman explained that her husband died two years ago and asked whether she could get married (by way of religious marriage) to her aunt's son. Yet, the preacher understood the 'real' question and asked whether he was already married. The answer was 'yes'. Then the preacher asked if they would declare the marriage and the woman answered 'no' and stated that her aunt's son was planning to visit her only on weekends. After she hung up, the preacher interpreted the case to me as the following: 'The man was bored and wanted to enjoy himself on weekends. I told her that the basic principle of a marriage is its declaration to other people and that this form of marriage will cause her injustice.'

Considering that religious marriage mostly harms women, the preachers don't approve it and seek to protect women questioners' rights in the face of what they consider to be injustice. Yet it could also be said that another reason for their negative stance on religious marriage is their reasoning that getting married without any responsibility and declaration is not different from the act of *zina* and hence it would morally corrupt the institution of the family and the society. According to them, marriage is a contract that serves the needs of the community, rather than two individuals, and thusly leads to the achievement of social harmony and stability (Tucker 1998: 46). Accordingly, examining the issue only in terms of protecting women's rights does not explain the cases in which women themselves insistently desire the religious marriage for certain reasons without caring their rights. For example, in one case, a divorced woman with two children stated that she did not trust anyone because of her prior marriage experience, so she didn't want to get married anymore. Yet she wanted to contract a religious marriage with her partner because she felt lonely. The preacher said, 'You want to legitimise your relationship with imam marriage. If he convinces you, marry formally… Allah creates woman and man on the ground of responsibility… If you marry, your daughter and your husband would be *mahrem* (within a relationship that is forbidden for marriage) to each other, so they will have a father-daughter relationship.' The woman here does not want to make a contract in which she has certain rights and responsibilities, but she wants to have an emotional and sexual relationship with a man. From the preacher's perspective, however, it is not permissible because it would not be declared openly in society and would thereby contribute to social disorganization. This view regulates women's sexuality in the context of the well-being of the family and society, and in that sense, constitutes one of the preachers' main differences from 'secular' feminists.

On the other hand, when a woman who is already married to someone within the framework of a religious marriage (or as a second wife) asks about the permissibility of it, and about male polygamy, the female preachers are not able to say that they are not permissible. One of the preachers says,

> The male preachers say that a man can take a second wife. If a male fatwa seeker is planning to do this, we say to him that it is not permissible so that he will not be able to do this. Because a marriage should be declared, formally recognised, and woman should have certain rights in it. On the other hand, however, claiming its impermissibility is not religious, because according to Islamic jurisprudence, two witnesses are sufficient for contracting a marriage.
>
> Personal Interview, 10 March 2015

During a phone call, a woman said that her husband had got married to a woman without asking her for permission. She asks if his marriage is religiously valid without her permission. The preacher told the woman that she cannot say that it is not valid. After she put down the phone, she explained,

> Of course, he should have got her permission but we cannot say that their marriage is not valid because of this reason. That would mean that they are committing adultery. We should here also consider the other woman. That would also mean that the second wife's children are illegitimate (*veled-i zina*). However, the point in question here is about what constitutes 'rightful share' (*kul hakkı*). He didn't get his wife's permission, so he violated her right (*hakkına giriyor*).[12]
>
> Personal Interview, 11 February 2015

According to classical Islamic jurisprudential interpretations, the requirement of the legality of a marriage before the state is not necessary. Since the *Diyanet* has not produced any official fatwa concerning religious marriage, the female preachers claim the impermissibility of religious marriage only to a certain extent because in some cases the rights of another woman or the *neseb* (lineage/genealogy) of a child are at stake. Particularly, the issue of *neseb* limits their interpretative space, as the paternity and legitimacy of the offspring are the key factors in examining sexual and reproductive processes in the classical Islamic jurisprudence (Tucker 1998: 150).

In the women's fatwa room, what was the most surprising for me is that a considerable number of questions centred on religious divorce (which is not recognized by civil law). This made visible the substantial authority of Islamic jurisprudence in individuals' marital lives. Although there are different forms of divorce in Islamic jurisprudence,[13] because of the absence of legal institutions that are mostly necessary for other types of divorces, I have seen that only questions about *talaq* (repudiation of the wife by the husband) are posed to *Alo Fetva*. For this reason, I will refer to *talaq* when I use the term 'religious divorce' in what follows. *Talaq*[14] gives absolute power to man in terminating his marriage: he can divorce his wife at any time, in any place, without requiring his wife's consent or her presence (Tucker 1998; Mir-Hosseini 2000). Differently from the husband, however, the wife can apply either for *khul* divorce, which they can obtain only with the consent of the husband and in return for compensation like the dower, or for *tatliq* in which she applies in court but which has much more restricted rationales.

According to the *Diyanet*'s fatwa, the pronunciation of a proper divorce formula (most commonly *boş ol*) by the husband to his wife results in revocable divorce. If he decides to return to his wife, he can return within the waiting period (equivalent to the wife's three menstruation periods) without the requirement of a new marriage contract, but if the waiting period is over, the couple should make a new marriage contract. If the husband repeats the divorce formula in three different occasions, it results in irrevocable divorce in which they can come together only after the wife marries another man and then separates from him (Diyanet 2017). The women whose husbands pronounce the divorce formula get worried about the legitimacy of their sexual relationships and the fate of their marriage and call the *Alo Fetva* hotline. If the question is simple, such as if the husband pronounces the formula once, the female preachers respond to it; but if it includes complexities or the questioner needs a more authoritative response, the preachers transfer it to the High Council of Religious Affairs. It is presumed that questioners take the Council's responses more seriously than that of the preachers. For example, in one case, a woman's husband pronounced 'I divorce you' in two different occasions. She wondered whether they were divorced or not. In a serious tone of voice, the preacher said that if he pronounces it one more time, they would be irrevocably divorced. Here, her answer is explicit but she nevertheless advised her to call the High Council and strongly emphasized that her husband should certainly stand beside her while calling. In such situations, the preachers want to be sure that the husband is informed. The preacher in the case above stated the following after she hung up: 'The women suppose that their marriage ended. So they don't have sexual intercourse with their husbands for religious reasons. The men thus become further estranged. The women then get worried. For this reason, I tell women that their husbands should also call the hotline.'

In the fatwa room, I also listened to numerous stories in which husbands refused to accept formal divorce with the excuse that they had not pronounced the religious divorce formula. In our interview, one of the preachers told me the story of a woman who came to the AIRB in order to pose her question:

A woman got married to her uncle's son. She did not love him and did not see him as a husband. The man was an *imam*. They got divorced and then the woman got married to someone else. Her uncle's son claimed that he never divorced her and claimed that her second marriage was invalid. He did not give her his blessing (*hakkını helal etmiyormuş*). Her new husband was an irresponsible man. She thought she was in this situation [referring to the new husband's irresponsibility] because he [the first husband] had damned her. In order to ask about this, she went to a mufti in Tokat. The mufti told her that she was still his [the first husband's] wife. I said that if the judge divorced you, then, it is a divorce. But you asked a man [the mufti]. On the one side, you have mufti/imam; on the other, a female preacher: you are confused, so, it would be better if we call the High Council. And the High Council's fatwa was the following: 'You did not love him; it is a reason for divorce. You didn't commit adultery, did nothing; there is no reason for *vebal*. You stated that you didn't want him before you married. Is Allah so cruel, does He oblige you to remain with him while you don't want him? It is your [second] husband's irresponsibility.

Personal Interview, 3 November 2014

This story carries compelling points since it reveals the ways in which these female preachers protect female fatwa seekers' rights as well as the ways in which men violate women's rights by manipulating the duality of secular and religious law. In contrast to the female preacher, the mufti who works in a province supported the ex-husband who claimed that they were still married, although this claim went against the *Diyanet*'s approach on this issue. More importantly, the preacher emphasized that her advice was considered to be less authoritative than that of the mufti. The woman could not trust her absolutely, solely because she was a woman, which, in turn, displays the female preachers' inferior position with respect to male officials' in the eyes of the individuals. Certainly, it is not always the case, but still it points to a reality to which the female preachers are often exposed. Lastly, the High Council's response, which suggests that not being in love with a spouse is a reason for divorce, is also surprising to me due to the fact that the *Diyanet* mainly invokes a conception of marriage grounded on the classical jurisprudential conception of marriage defined in terms of duties and rights rather than emotions – here, it definitely diverges from that conception.

Conclusion

In their responses to fatwa questions, the female preachers employ various discourses and pedagogies, through the knowledge they obtained from different authorities as well as their own personal experiences. Although they draw on the interpretations in classical Islamic jurisprudential tradition and the conservative family policies of government, the flexibility of the Islamic jurisprudence as well as the discrepancy between religious law and social and legal reality gives them interpretive room. In this interpretive room, their conversations on extramarital sexual life are either therapeutic or confessional in form in which the callers feel regret and the preachers advise from the discursive position of psychologists, or they tend to solve the ethical problems experienced after an illicit relationship. Fatwas on marital sexual life are mostly about lawful sexual activity or the sexual apathy experienced by women. Besides, a great number of women whose husbands have extramarital sexual relationships submit questions in order to seek a proper way to continue or end their marriages. The preachers' responses generally hold the assumption that men and women have different inborn nature (*fıtrat*) and recognize their sexual desires in a hierarchical way. For the preachers (and for Islamic jurisprudential tradition) marriage is the only way of legitimizing sexual activity. Hence, in their advice about religious marriage and religious divorce, they govern women's sexualities and preserve the well-being of the family and the society, but they also are attentive to women's religious and legal rights. In this structure, they try to strike a delicate balance between religious obligations and women's rights, i.e. between state policy and their point of view as women who have similar experiences with the female questioners.

Analysing how these female preachers deliver fatwas on sexual life, religious marriage and religious divorce, this chapter sheds light on the question of how *Diyanet* governs women's bodies and their marital lives. Considering preachers as mediators between the institution and individuals, who have differences, inconsistencies and hesitations, I conceive of the *Diyanet* not as a static institution but as a flexible entity, which is formed by 'small figures' (Miller and Rose 2008) and practices. I argue that what is at stake here is not solely the government's or the *Diyanet*'s intervention into the private sphere but an interpretative practice that is open to negotiation, performed by a multilayered structure composed of the government, Muslim legal traditions, the *Diyanet* and numerous female preachers.

Notes

1   Muftiates are offices of Muftis in cities and districts, in which religious affairs are administered.
2   *Hoca* is a word which is used for schoolmaster as well as one who has knowledge and wisdom. Since all the preachers call her Nevin *Hoca*, I prefer using this term here.
3   Although its official name has changed, the preachers as well as questioners still use the term *Alo Fetva*.

4   For the increasing numbers of female preachers employed in the *Diyanet* in the last two decades, see Hassan (2011).

5   *Irşad* literally means 'to show the right path to someone'. For an analysis of the *Diyanet's irşad* strategy, see Maritato (2015).

6   The High Council of Religious Affairs consists of religious experts on Islamic jurisprudence, who are authorized to product the *Diyanet's* fatwas.

7   In this context, in 2011, the name of the Ministry Responsible for Women and Family was changed into the Ministry of Family and Social Policies and the name of the 'women' was erased.

8   Umrah is a pilgrimage to Mecca, performed by Muslims that can be undertaken at any time of the year. In contrast to the obligatory Islamic pilgrimage (Hajj), Umrah is optional.

9   In Arabic, *vebal* literally means that a pasture has abundant grass. In this regard, it is metaphorically used to refer to an absolute weight and an unbearable consequence. It thus refers to deadly sin (Yazır 2016). Indeed, *vebal* means both sin and moral responsibility. Nevertheless, the sense of the term is extremely heavy in both meanings: it amounts to an overwhelming responsibility as well as deadly sin.

10   Imam is a person who leads prayer in the mosques.

11   Couples usually prefer having religious marriage a few days before civil marriage ceremony or just after it. Rarely, they also prefer having religious marriage in the engagement period so that dating can be licit. Yet, definitely, there is no general rule about the order and timing of the marriages.

12   *Hak* means right, justice, law as well as share, due, remuneration and fee. Inspired by Jenny White's translation of the phrase *hakkını helal et*, *hakka girmek* can be loosely translated as 'deriving any unjust profit (which is *haram*) from a relationship with someone' or 'having a reciprocal moral debt to someone for the things s/he has done' (White 1994: 97).

13   In Islamic jurisprudence, there are four types of termination of marriage: '*talaq* [in Arabic], or repudiation of the wife by the husband; *khul and mubarat*, or termination of the marriage contract by mutual consent (initiated by wife and accepted by the husband); *tatliq*, or separation by the decree of the court; and *faskh*, or annulment of the marriage contract' (Mir-Hosseini 2000: 37).

14   It is worthy to note that in Turkey, a substantial number of Muslims consider divorce as an encouraged act, even as a sin; however, what is denounced by sharia is not divorce in a general sense, but *talaq*. The Prophet Muhammed refers to talaq 'as a lawful act which is most hateful to God'. Notwithstanding, this classical Islamic jurisprudence did not seek to restrain it (Mir-Hosseini 2000: 37).

References

Abou-Bakr, O. (2015), 'The Interpretive Legacy of Qiwamah as an Exegical Counstruct', in Z. Mir Hosseini, M. Al-Sharmani and J. Rumminger (eds), *Men in Charge? Rethinking Authority in Muslim Legal Tradition*, London: Oneworld Publications.

Agrama, H. (2010), 'Ethics, Tradition, Authority: Toward and Anthropology of the Fatwa', *American Ethnologist*, 37 (1): 2–18.

Agrama, H. (2012), *Questioning Secularism: Islam, Sovereignty and the Rule of Law in Modern Egypt*, Chicago and London: University of Chicago Press.

Akınerdem, F. (2019), 'Tailored for Marriage, Ready for The State: Frames of the Family Regime on "The Marriage Show"', in J. B. Kay, M. Kennedy and H. Wood (eds), *The Wedding Spectacle Across Contemporary Media and Culture*, London: Routledge.

Ali, K. (2006), *Sexual Ethics and Islam*, Oxford: Oneworld.

De Certeau, M. (1984), *The Practice of Everyday Life Vol. 1*, trans. S. Rendall, Berkeley: University of California Press.

Diyanet (2017), *Fetvalar*, Ankara: Diyanet İşleri Başkanlığı Yayınları.

Donzelot, J. (1979), *The Policing of Families*, trans. R. Hurley, New York: Panteon Books.

Eralp, F. (2018), *Diyanet Protokolleri ve Ailenin Mutlak Bütünlüğü Çerçevesinde Hayatlarımız Nasıl Şekilleniyor?* Available online: https://catlakzemin.com/diyanet-protokolleri-ve-ailenin-mutlak-butunlugu-cercevesinde-hayatlarimiz-nasil-sekilleniyor/?fbclid=IwAR1DYTV-_ktPn2KMnU0ZkoDd7co1ep1XI56I-wW6yOxt34GdHZzfn1lnd_E

Foucault, M. (1982), 'The Subject and Power', *Critical Inquiry*, 8 (4): 777–95.

Foucault, M. (1993), 'About the Beginning of the Hermeneutics of the Self: Two Lectures at Dartmouth', trans. M. Blasius, *Political Theory*, 21 (2): 198–227.

Foucault, M. (1998), 'Ethics: Subjectivity and Truth', trans. R. Hurley et al. in P. Rabinow (ed.), *Essential Works of Foucault, 1954–1984*, Vol. 1, New York: The New Press.

Foucault, M. (2005), *The Hermeneutics of the Subject: Lectures at the College de France, 1981–1982*, trans. G. Burchell, New York: Palgrave Macmillan.

Foucault, M. (2007), *Security, Territory, Population: Lectures at the College de France, 1977–78*, trans. G. Burchell, New York: Palgrave Macmillan.

Hallaq, W. B. (2003–4), 'Juristic Authority vs. State Power: The Legal Crises of Modern Islam', *Journal of Law and Religion*, 19 (2): 243–58.

Hassan, M. (2011), 'Women Preaching for the Secular State: Official Female Preachers (*Bayan Vaizler*) in Contemporary Turkey', *Middle East Studies*, 43 (2011): 451–73.

Mahmood, S. (2005), *Politics of Piety: The Islamic Revival and the Feminist Subject*, Princeton: Princeton University Press.

Mardin, Ş. (1989), *Religion and Social Change in Modern Turkey: The Case of Bediüzzaman Said Nursi*, New York: State University of New York.

Maritato, C. (2015), 'Performing *İrşad*: Female Preachers' (*Vaizeler*'s) Religious Assistance Within the Framework of the Turkish State', *Turkish Studies*, 16 (3): 433–47.

Messick, B. (1986), 'The Mufti, the Text and the World: Legal Interpretation in Yemen', *Royal Anthropological Institute of Great Britain and Ireland*, 21 (1): 104.

Messick, B. (1993), *The Calligraphic State: The Textual Domination and History in a Muslim Society*, London, Berkeley and Los Angeles: University of California Press.

Miller P. and N. Rose (2008), *Governing the Present*, Cambridge: Polity Press.

Mir-Hosseini, Z. (2000), *Marriage on Trial: A Study of Islamic Family Law*, London: I.B. Tauris.

Mir-Hosseini, Z. (2015), 'Muslim Legal Tradition and the Challenge of Gender Equality', in Z. Mir Hosseini, M. L. Al-Sharmani, J. Rumminger (eds), *Men in Charge? Rethinking Authority in Muslim Legal Tradition*, London: Oneworld Publications.

Sirman, N. (2005), 'The Making of Familial Citizenship in Turkey', in F. Keyman and A. İçduygu (eds), *Challenges to Citizenship in a Globalizing World: European Questions and Turkish Experiences*, London: Routledge.

Tucker, J. (1998), *In the House of the Law: Gender and Islamic Law in Ottoman Syria and Palestine*, California: University of California Press.

Tuksal, H. (2018), *Kadın Karşıtı Söylemin İslam Geleneğindeki İzdüşümleri*, Ankara: Otto Yayınları.

Wadud, A. (1999), *The Quran and Woman: Rereading the Sacred Text from a Woman's Perspective*, Oxford: Oxford University Press.

White, J. (1994), *Money Makes us Relatives: Women's Labor in Urban Turkey*, Austin: University of Texas Press.

Yazır, E. H. (2016), *Hak Dini Kur'an Dili*, İstanbul: Hisar Yayınları.

12

Positioning the critical pious self vis-à-vis authoritarian populist body politics: Limits of feminist dissent in pious women columnists' narratives in Turkey

Didem Ünal

Introduction

In the context of rising populism, authoritarianism and neoliberal governance, women's bodies become embattled sites of both suppression and resistance. In Turkey, as the Justice and Development Party (Adalet ve Kalkınma Partisi, AKP), the ruling party since 2002, has shifted towards more authoritarian lines in the post-2011 period,[1] governing of women's bodies and sexualities has come to function as an operating mechanism of the authoritarian-populist rule. In this political climate where neoliberalism, neoconservatism, pro-Islamism, nationalism, populism and antifeminism converge, leading to dramatic shifts in the gender regime, 'woman's body' has assumed various meanings and tasks as a political site of authoritarian-populist governance, as a political metaphor and discursive tool, as a policy instrument and as a field of protest in contemporary feminist struggles.

In reaction to the proliferation of misogynist discourses under the AKP rule, feminist counter-publics have engaged in various attempts to oppose relentless control and surveillance over women's bodies (Aksoy 2018; Cagatay 2018). Especially in secular gender equality activism, woman's body operates as a powerful site of resistance and a critical narrative line in the critique of the antifeminist ethos of the gender regime. Given this, the question of how to incorporate women's diverse bodies – trans, lesbian, Islamic – into contemporary feminist struggles becomes critical in countering the religio-conservative backlash in the gender regime. This question offers a critical vantage point from which to learn about different conceptualizations of women's bodies in public discourse. Moreover, it can expose the demarcation lines that divide women from different ethnic, religious and socio-economic backgrounds on the inclusivity of contemporary feminist struggles.

In the age of democratic backsliding and backlash against women's rights, feminist women are faced with the urgency of responding to the religio-conservative backlash in the gender regime through effective collective action frames and sustainable coalitional ties. In such a context, intersectional feminist politics is key in that it provides a solid ground in collective action for the representation of demands and concerns of different womanhood positions and can lead to greater efficacy in political results (Gökarıksel and Smith 2017). The 'secular-Islamic' bifurcation in the women's movement complicates the prospects of feminist collective action organized through intersectional lenses. In the recent era, this bifurcation has increasingly evolved from dichotomous framings and essentialist fixation of identities to collaborative and dialogic relationships forged in the face of feminist emergencies (Simga and Goker 2017). Yet, it is also worth noting that essentialist elements in both camps that resist deliberation and collaboration might block sustainable political ties and undermine the coalitional spirit (Unal 2019).

In a context where the authoritarian-populist regime defines women's agency as compliant and instrumental and the Sunni Islamic tradition becomes a main pillar in the reshuffling of the gender regime, critical pious agency gains prominence in challenging 'docile' femininity promoted through familial/pronatalist discourses and policies. Recent studies demonstrate that in contemporary Turkey, the performance of critical pious agency is highly dependent on the issue-based cleavages at stake in gender debates; it entails hybrid subject positions especially when it comes to 'controversial' issues such as feminist self-identification, family, women's sexualities and reproductive rights (Kubilay 2014; Aksoy 2018; Özcan 2019; Unal 2019).

Against this background, this chapter aims to investigate how questions regarding the inclusivity and the deliberative potentials of feminist defiance and feminist protest are framed and negotiated in the narratives of pious women actors known as intermediary figures in the public sphere who suggest dialogic ways to read Islam and feminism together. Within this frame, it discusses the issue-based cleavages in pious women columnists' narratives on the intertwining of political agency, women's embodiment and feminist protest, particularly focusing on how they deal with AKP's body politics. Exposing the hybrid and intricate aspects of their narratives, it engages in a comprehensive frame analysis of their newspaper articles and press interviews between 2012 and 2019.

In the post-2011 era, the complexities arising from the highly agonistic political environment have led to flexibilities, temporalities, shifts and instabilities in critical pious subject formation. On the one hand, pious women public figures under consideration here support the AKP's strong stress on familialism, regarding family as the key unit in socialization and frame pro-Islamist politics as the guarantor of veiled women's pious lifestyles in Turkey (Arat 2016). Yet, they simultaneously oppose the utilitarian approach to headscarf in AKP politics and the masculinist opportunism underlying it. Some of them fiercely criticize the authoritarian elements and the masculinist values at stake in the party's gender policy perspective (Aksoy 2018). As such, both commitment to the religio-conservative project of political Islam and feminist/pro-feminist critique of it are part of their complex borderland positions. One should also note that they do not represent a homogenous group. Those who have close ties with the AKP might prefer to adopt a cautious and moderate stance in their pro-feminist critique, while others who declare a firmer commitment to feminist ideals and affirm feminist self-identification critically distance themselves from the authoritarian elements of political Islam.

Considering these complexities, the chapter delves into the intricate aspects of pious women columnists' narratives on three heated gender debates: (i) the abortion debate in 2012, (ii) secular feminist protests on the discursive regulation of maternal body and access to abortion and (iii) the 2019 Feminist Night Walk. It particularly elaborates on the following interpretive schemas and argumentative lines that pious women columnists engage with to conceptualize and discuss women's bodies and sexualities: (i) woman's body as an 'individual property' or as an 'entity entrusted by God', (ii) the regulatory power of discourse on women's bodies, (iii) women's body as a site of protest in feminist political activism and (iv) 'radical' framings in feminist protests.

The chapter will also point out that calling for an inclusive feminist activism that would embrace Islamic conceptualizations of woman's body, pious women columnists initiate a possibility for enacting a constructive dialogue on pressing gender issues. Their call for inclusivity is crucial for unpacking the complexities of coalition-building and collective action frames in contemporary women's activism. Yet, this dialogic potential and the prospects for building coalitional feminist activism in their narratives are severely blocked along the following points: (1) denial of legitimacy to secular feminist protests organized around 'controversial' issues such as women's reproductive capacities, (2) neglecting the implications of the overarching discursive governance of women's bodies and sexualities and (3) past feelings of resentment and stereotypical categorization and marginalization of secular feminist activism.

Within this frame, the chapter concludes that pious women columnists' views on contentious feminist politics and its deliberative qualities fluctuate on an elusive ground, the contours of which are mapped out by their 'in-between' positions on women's bodily autonomy and reproductive rights and the vulnerabilities they face in the current antifeminist, authoritarian-political regime that does not tolerate dissent and opposition. The pro-feminist/feminist character and the dialogic possibilities of their narratives significantly diminish in cases where they ignore the power of discourse on women's bodies and associate feminist defiance and street protest with extremism and vociferousness.

Women's bodies in neoliberal-authoritarian regimes

In authoritarian contexts where every sphere of life is put under ubiquitous surveillance, women's bodies are deeply enmeshed in political struggles, becoming a critical site of power inscription and contestation, oppression and resistance (Sutton 2010; Harcourt 2013; Doğangün 2019). Study of body politics in such contexts reveals linkages between power, ideology and embodied experiences and exposes how women's bodies are perceived as vehicles of radical social and political transformation.

The disciplinary body politics, in Foucauldian sense, relies on a technique of political hegemony enacted upon the body through regulation and manipulation of bodily experiences in gendered ways (McNay 1992). In authoritarian contexts combined with a neoliberal logic that requires subjects to be self-managing and self-enterprising individuals in everyday life, women are exposed to a ubiquitous disciplinary body politics at multiple levels through complex technologies of subjection, knowledge and power. These technologies perceive woman's body as a policy instrument and a discursive tool and utilize it as a free-floating signifier that brings together powerful and often contradictory ideological elements of the political regime under a single rubric, ensuring a coherent narrative order of the hegemonic political discourse. Some scholars use the metaphor of 'political glue' or 'symbolic glue' to explain the narrative function that women's bodies carry out in the ideological patchwork of such regimes (Mayer et al. 2016; Kováts 2017).

Recent feminist scholarship on anti-gender populist movements in Europe and all over the world suggests that women's bodies in a context of rising right-wing populism are utilized as flexible symbols often articulated in reference to the defence of a naturalist gender order, regulation of abortion and reproductive rights and curing the demoralization of society (Köttig et al. 2017; Kuhar and Patternotte 2017). As a result, various ideological elements such as nationalism, familialism, pronatalism, anti-gender ideology and neoliberalism re-engineered and reinforced though the religious ethical frameworks are blended into each other, ensuring the continuation of the political regime. In such contexts, the political rule is reinforced through gendered nationalist discourses backed up by a bold stress put on familial and pronatalist policies, which are further justified with a reference to the neoliberal logic that cuts down on social security benefits, relocates politics of care in the family and puts the burden of familial care on women's shoulders (Akkan 2018; Verloo 2018). In this equation, women's bodies are present at every level of policy and discourse, assuming the role of a polysemic 'political glue'. One could suggest that it is this narrative function and the discursive power attributed to women's bodies that reinforces the authoritarian-neoliberal regulation of women's bodies and renders women's embodied experiences in such regimes more acute and painful.

On the other hand, we should also remember that women's bodies are more than just a site of oppression. In oppressive contexts where women face disciplinary body politics and gendered violence, they become a critical site of resistance and protest (Sutton 2007, 2010; O'Keefe 2014; Butler 2015). There are various ways through which women's bodies can be involved in feminist protests. First, activists can make protests possible through utilizing their bodies as political arguments (Sutton 2007). They can performatively present their bodies as a site of protest and as symbols that convey political meaning. Second, they can make use of the material characteristics, needs or vulnerabilities of their bodies (Sutton 2007). Defining bodily needs and risks as part of activist practices, they may situate the materiality of the body, the needs and vulnerabilities arising from it at the very centre of the protests.

Despite the crackdown on civil society in contemporary Turkey, feminist protesters have organized various street protests in the recent era where they have protested the proliferation of misogynist discourse and policy with colourful banners, flags, music, dance and feminist slogans written on their bodies and T-shirts (*Hurriyet Daily News* 2012, 2013c, 2016, 2017; *DuvarEnglish* 2019). They convey their demands by presenting their bodies as 'text' or 'political argument' and make use of their bodily vulnerabilities in order to underline that women's body is a main locus for feminist activism. This chapter discusses how different conceptualizations of women's bodies and feminist protest might assist/block contemporary feminist struggles in Turkey. It provides a detailed glimpse into the power differentials that underlie different conceptualizations of women's bodies and feminist protest on the secular-Islamic axis and generate different positions on contentious feminist politics.

The case of Turkey

The interweaving of pro-Islamism, neoliberalism, authoritarianism, nationalism, populism and conservatism in contemporary Turkey reinforces disciplinary body politics through a complex patchwork of regulatory narratives on women's sexualities, subjectivities and agencies (Cindoglu and Unal 2017; Güneş-Ayata and Doğangün 2017). With the aim to ensure ubiquitous control on women's bodies and sexualities, the current gender regime mainly regulates three policy areas, namely reproduction, sexuality and family (Acar and Altunok 2013). The following gender agenda frequently comes to the foreground in AKP's conservative gender politics: (1) reification of 'natural differences' between the sexes and reproduction of traditional gender roles, (2) embeddedness of paternal authority in the populist idea of the people that equates the survival of the nation with the protection of family and (3) utilization of the Islamic tradition in the maintenance of the conservative gender regime and operationalization of the Islamic concept of gender complementarity as a 'superior' model to Western feminism.

Attributing sacredness to the unity of family, the populist AKP rule sustains the idea of organic coherence of the nation through an elaborate discourse representing family as the basic societal unit and enforcing it as a major regulative principle in gender performances and in public imagination. This populist appropriation of the idea of family serves as a building block in ensuring the continuity of the masculinist political imaginary and operationalizes hegemonic gender codes to be utilized in the construction of 'ideal' masculinities and femininities. Recent policy attempts and public discourses on women's sexualities and reproductive capacities such as the anti-abortion initiative in 2012 followed by serious restrictions imposed on C-sections and incitement to early marriage have been emblematic of the fact that familialism is further coupled by pronatalism as a major discursive and policy tool in the contemporary political landscape.

On different occasions, AKP politicians urged married women to have at least three children, suggesting that 'strong families lead to strong nations' (*Hurriyet Daily News* 2013a). Moreover, the party defines ideal femininity over women's reproductive choices and capacities and prioritizes women's familial responsibilities over their career choices with the argument that 'childless women are deficient and incomplete' (The *Guardian* 2016). The call on women to have at least three children, coupled with an anti-abortion stance, has generated a discursive ground where surveillance mechanisms on women's sexualities and reproductive capacities and the regulatory public discourse aiming to confine women to familial roles have become ubiquitous (Cindoglu and Unal 2017; Özgüler and Yarar 2017).

Replacing the principle of gender equality with the Islamic idea of *fitrat* (disposition), which presupposes that each gender should act in accordance with the principle of complementarity of genders, AKP's gender politics associates women mainly with motherhood and the familial realm. In 2011, the State Ministry for Women and the Family was replaced by the Ministry of Family and Social Policy, shifting the focus from women's rights to women's roles as mothers, wives and daughters. Hegemonic codes of gender binary in this political discourse are further reinforced through an overtly antifeminist standpoint that labels feminism as extreme, anti-family, anti-motherhood and anti-religion and condemns feminists for the dismay of the family unity in modern society (Unal 2021). On different occasions, feminists are criticized for misunderstanding Islam and for being detached from the society's core norms and values (Tuysuz 2016).

In a nutshell, the utilization of the conceptual metaphor of nation modelled upon the heteronormative family ideal, the pronatalist and anti-abortionist approach to women's reproductive rights, the reproduction of hegemonic gender binary through authoritarian discursive acts and policy frameworks, the ubiquitous control on women's bodies, sexualities and reproductive capacities, definition of ideal femininity over conservative lifestyles and marginalization of feminist goals and ideas as antithetical to society's 'cultural essence' comes to the forefront as the building blocks of the disciplinary body politics in the age of AKP.

Against this background, this chapter asks the following questions: How do pious women columnists known for their feminist/pro-feminist stance narrate, resist and/ or reproduce the ways in which women's bodies are perceived as vehicles of radical social and political transformation in contemporary Turkey? What are the contours of the feminist narratives lines in their accounts that can align with the secular women's movement in articulating a powerful critique of the contemporary gender regime? How do they define feminist activism and street protest against authoritarian-populist body politics?

Methodology

This chapter provides a qualitative analysis of the discourses of four pious women's columnists, namely Hidayet Sefkatli Tuksal, Nihal Bengisu Karaca, Sibel Eraslan and Yıldız Ramazanoğlu, on the following public debates: (i) the abortion debate in 2012, (ii) secular feminist protests on the discursive regulation of maternal body and access to abortion and (iii) the 2019 Feminist Night Walk. It aims to expose the interpretive schemas and argumentative lines that pious women columnists utilize to conceptualize and discuss women's bodies, sexualities and feminist protest. Study of constitutive frames and narrative elements in subjects' discourses is especially useful to expose Janus-faced, in-between positions that may shift on various levels, depending on the power differentials and subjective concerns at stake (Bacchi 2005).

Unlike pious women public figures in the 1970s who played an active role in the public sphere to confront ultra-secularism in the country but did not problematize its gender dynamics, pious women columnists under consideration here are precursor actors in the media field who adopt gender-conscious lenses (Köse 2014; Yılmaz 2016). They actively engage with pressing gender debates from within a borderland position where they attempt to reconcile Islam and feminism through a dialogic approach (Arat 2016).

Pious women columnists' discourses in Turkey are quite heterogeneous in that they entail multiple voices, a broad range of political positions with differing commitments to feminist ideals and various rhetorical strategies to reconcile religio-conservatism and gender-conscious lenses. One should also consider that in the current era where not only secular feminism is marginalized as 'anti-religion and anti-family' but also Muslim feminism is perceived as a threat to the anti-gender, anti-feminist political agenda (Sönmez 2019), feminist/pro-feminist pious women columnists face risks, vulnerabilities and harassment if they choose to articulate a bold feminist critique.[2] The sample used in this study consists of heterogeneous positions with regard to Muslim feminism and the critique of the AKP rule and thus provides a limited vantage point into the limits and possibilities of feminist and pro-feminist pious women columnists' engagement with AKP's body politics. Yet, despite the limitations of the sample size, the chapter provides enough clues to discuss the heterogeneity among pious women columnists and the recent issue-based cleavages in their critique of AKP's body politics. It employs the terms 'feminist' and 'pro-feminist' to capture this heterogeneity and to stay attentive to the fact that some pious women columnists under consideration endorse the feminist label and enact feminist commitments while others adopt a reformist conservative approach that denounces feminist position yet appropriates feminist notions and rhetorical frames in line with the religio-conservative agenda and formulates a woman-friendly policy framework that attempts to advance women's status in society without clashing with AKP's gender complementarity model (Bachetta and Power 2013; Özcan 2019).

Intricacies of pious women columnists' bridge positionality

Situated in a very complex position on the Islamic-secular axis, feminist/pro-feminist pious women public intellectuals articulate multiple critiques in the public sphere: (1) critique of orthodox Kemalist ideology, (2) critique of male hegemony in the Islamic tradition and in Islamist politics and (3) critique of secular feminist rejection of religion and the elitist tendencies in secular women's activism.

Unlike orthodox components of Muslim women's movement that prioritize Islamic precepts in their framing and understanding of gender issues (Cosar and Onbası 2008; Aksoy 2015), reformist pious women have successfully utilized progressive secular feminist principles and ideas in organizations such as The Capital City Women's Platform (BKP), a women's organization founded in 1995 in Ankara. Some pious women columnists under consideration here have significantly contributed to reformist Muslim women's organizations. For example, Hidayet Şefkatli Tuksal, scholar/columnist, has taken up crucial roles in BKP, affirmed her feminist position on different occasions and epitomized the critical pious agency that cultivates an intellectual/activist disposition geared towards improving women's position in society along feminist premises (Rinaldo 2014). On the other hand, Yıldız Ramazanoğlu, columnist/author, has actively engaged both with secular and Muslim feminist circles. Citing affective solidarity and friendship as a key element in feminist activism and thinking, she provides a relational and intersubjective account of feminism beyond the divisiveness of essentialist notions of identity (Unal 2015).

Pious women columnists' feminist/pro-feminist views on pressing gender issues display a 'bridge positionality' through which they practise dual commitment to Islam and progressive feminist ideals and publicly struggle to uphold these seemingly contradictory or oxymoronic positions. On various occasions, they have clearly stated that they value both religion and feminist ideals as integral to their selves (Unal 2015). In trying to reconcile Islam with progressive feminist ideals, they situate themselves in a borderland position where the meaning always fluctuates between religious and secular feminist reference points. They criticize the AKP on various matters such as the instrumental utilization of headscarf as a political symbol and the misogynist policy perspective restricting women's access to reproductive health; yet, they also align with it, affirming the party's family-centred conservative gender politics and its heterosexual family ideal.

Some of the women columnists studied here have significantly contributed to AKP's coming to power and have been involved in the radical transformation of political Islam in Turkey in the last two decades (Arat 2016). As this 'common fate' positions them as close allies of the government, they prefer to adopt a cautious and moderate stance in their pro-feminist critique. On the other hand, those with firm feminist commitments who choose to be more vocal, critical and fierce in discourse and collective action despite the vicissitudes of the authoritarian regime generate a significant potential for the cultivation of coalitional ties in the women's movement.

Discussion

The abortion debate

In 2012, the AKP proposed a draft bill on abortion that would require all abortions to take place within the first six weeks of pregnancy (*Hurriyet Daily News* 2012). Given that abortion in Turkey has been legal until the tenth week of pregnancy since 1983, feminist circles became alarmed about the anti-abortion initiative, articulating a strong critique against a possible backlash on women' reproductive rights. Confronted with severe criticisms from different segments of the society and the European Union, the government dropped the anti-abortion bill. Although it did not become codified, access to abortion at state hospitals has become largely restricted (Güneş-Ayata and Doğangün 2017).

The heated public discussion on abortion in 2012 has generated a significant ground in the women's movement to reflect on the possibilities of building feminist coalitions against AKP's neoliberal-authoritarian body politics. The majority of feminist protests against the recent anti-abortion initiative were organized by secular feminists around the following mottos: 'It is my body, so who are you?', 'my body, my decision', 'abortion is a right, choice belongs to women', 'take your hands off my body' and 'we don't discuss our right to abortion' (*Hürriyet Daily News* 2012). The abortion debate also sparked an online photo campaign initiated by *bianet*, a news portal with a feminist gender agenda, which invited users to submit a photo of themselves wearing T-shirts printed with the motto 'my body, my decision'. The campaign rapidly became a widespread protest movement with the motto 'my body, my decision'. Deploying different activist tools such as protests, meetings and press declarations, the secular women's movement generated a discursive milieu where the proliferation of anti-abortion discourses can be strongly challenged. Yet, this activism could not develop inclusive collective action frames that would also appeal to pious women.

During the public debate on the anti-abortion initiative, a great majority of pious women public figures and activists have unanimously opposed a possible ban on abortion (Kubilay 2014). Yet, they have added that they personally oppose abortion for religious reasons and believe that the foetus is entrusted to the mother by the divine authority. Thus, their critique of the anti-abortion initiative mostly stems from a functionalist perspective where they prioritize women's health and define abortion as a legitimate practice especially when women are vulnerable due to economic difficulties, sexual violence and health emergencies (Kubilay 2014).

Given that their discourses have considerable impact and efficacy in the Islamic circles, their unanimous critique has significantly contributed to the feminist struggle against the anti-abortion initiative. Yet, their critical stance did not turn into a coalitional position where they can successfully align with secular feminists around overlapping collective action frames. Many pious women columnists have argued that secular feminist slogans deployed in the protests against the anti-abortion initiative put the emphasis exclusively on women's bodily autonomy and frame the issue of abortion primarily with respect to 'the right to abortion' (Eraslan 2012b; Ramazanoğlu 2012a, 2012b; Tuksal 2012a, 2012b). They find the categorical secular feminist stress on women's bodily authority quite problematic as it is difficult to reconcile with the Islamic conception of woman's body. According to the Islamic line of thinking, bodily autonomy is not granted to the individual will; rather, the body is entrusted to individuals by the divine authority (Şişman 2007). Criticizing the secular feminist stress on an absolute ownership over the body, Ramazanoğlu (2012b) states:

> Our body does not belong to anybody but is entrusted to us. For me, it is not appropriate to claim an absolute ownership over the body that we did not create; it is equally inappropriate to assume that one can use it as one wishes.

On the other hand, stressing the significance of inclusive collaborative collective action frames in women's activism, Tuksal (2012a) states:

> Unfortunately, I disagree with my feminist friends over the cliché slogans they used... In Turkey, it is impossible to mobilize women through the language they use. How many women attended that protest? Pious women, too, have a lot to say about abortion and contraception.

In line with these critiques, some secular feminists have also pointed out that the individualized notion of the self in the secular feminist discourse of 'the right to abortion' precludes receptivity to different womanhood positionalities (Bora 2012).

One can suggest that in contemporary Turkey, secular and pious activists are confronted with the task to seek for new collective action frames that can include different feminist strategies and womanhood experiences in embodied feminist protests. Scholars of intersectionality note that a dynamic, relational intersectional approach puts different axis of differentiation into a productive dialogue without reducing them to one another or defining them in an additive or hierarchical way (Phoenix and Pattynama 2006; Ferree 2009). Accordingly, a relational intersectional approach avoids juxtaposing the secular feminist discourse on women's access to abortion and the Muslim feminist position on this matter in a binary oppositional relationship; rather, it argues that they can coexist in an inclusive feminist protest.

The remarks quoted above do not necessarily exclude the prospects of finding a relational intersectional language in this regard. Yet, as demonstrated below, in some narratives this dialogic potential can be easily dismissed or abandoned. Thus, the heterogeneity of the narratives in question needs to be carefully contextualized. As the findings suggest, issue-based cleavages such as women's bodies, sexualities and reproductive rights destabilize critical pious agency, leading to ambivalences and multiplicities in the intertwining of Islam and feminism. The promising qualities of pious women columnists' call for an intersectional framing of pro-abortion discourse fade away especially in narratives where Islamic references are prioritized and the feminist critique is toned down to the extent that feminist defiance and street protest are marginalized.

Hybrid narratives on feminist protest and the power of discourse

Pious women have engaged in various forms of contentious politics in the last decades in Turkey. They have performed individual strategies of dissent in higher education, at workplace as well as in the publishing industry, Muslim women's activism and in pro-Islamist politics (Aksoy 2015). The politics of dissent in their life-histories, self-projections and future aspirations is quite heterogeneous and multilayered and must be understood with a focus on individuals' lived religion, self-constitution/self-transformation and the authenticity of double commitment to religion and progressive liberal ideals (Singh 2015; Nyhagen and Halsaa 2016).

The abortion debate in 2012 has exposed that issues such as women's sexuality and reproductive rights dramatically complicate their positions on feminist dissent. Arguing that secular feminist protests against the anti-abortion initiative convey an exclusionary political message, some pious women public figures labelled them 'excessive' and 'unnecessarily vociferous'. They also criticized feminist politics of dissent that expresses political agency by using woman's body as a political argument. Addressing the protestors who took to the streets during the abortion debate, Eraslan (2012a) states:

> Abortion is all about a metal tool's cutting, evacuating your body... Therefore, I cannot understand the festival atmosphere generated for the defense of abortion...
> I am totally irritated by this celebratory mode and acts of undressing.

In June 2012, feminist protesters in various cities in Turkey came together against a possible ban on abortion with colourful, humorous banners, songs, slogans, dance and musical instruments (*Hurriyet Daily News* 2012). Accusing the protesters of adapting a celebratory tone towards abortion, Eraslan implies that secular feminist protesters' use of their bodies as sites of protest is inappropriate not only because of the political message that these bodies embody but also because of the very act of utilizing woman's body as a site of an 'excessive' feminist protest. Eraslan suggests that this form of secular feminist protest with slogans written on bodies about a 'controversial' issue degenerates the gist of the feminist critique.

On the other hand, Karaca finds this form of secular feminist activism unproportionally defiant:

> As if abortion were banned... The PM only wants to open up a discussion about it... Some (secular) women intellectuals have unfortunately gone blind so badly that they label everything as sexist. Of course, no one can tell them not to speak but it is obvious that they speak very loudly and generate a devastating effect on society. We cannot label each and every social project that we don't like as authoritarian. No conservative politician would argue in favor of abortion... To me, the politicians who urge the public to discuss abortion are not authoritarian. They only introduce you a perspective. It is up to you to accept it or not.
>
> Personal interview 2013

During the abortion debate, Karaca has written many newspaper articles where she questions the instrumentalization of abortion for economic means (Karaca 2012b), addresses the perils of the prohibitionist approach for women's health (Karaca 2012a) and severely criticizes the vulgar and provocative language used by AKP politicians in defending the anti-abortion bill (Karaca 2012d). She also criticized the restrictions imposed on C-sections, arguing that 'C-section is a matter of woman's right to reflect on her body' (Karaca 2012a). Yet, the quote above is different from this line of critical thinking in that it demonstrates that Karaca undermines the regulatory power of discourse on women's reproductive freedoms.

Stressing that anti-abortion initiative has not been codified, Karaca regards secular feminist alertness unnecessary and disconcerting in terms of society's 'core' values that she defines along conservative lines. In doing so, Karaca ignores the fact that although the anti-abortion initiative has not been codified, it has led to many de facto limitations regarding women's access to abortion at state hospitals. Her critical stance towards the prohibitionist political approach to abortion and her uncritical justification of AKP's discourse on women's reproductive rights as a typical example of a conservative democratic political vision generate a cacophony of meanings in her narrative and thus blur the pro-feminist tones of her critique.

In a press interview, Tuksal also undermines the power of discourse, ignoring the ways in which single discursive acts may generate regulatory discursive mechanisms operating on women's bodies and reproductive capacities:

> Society is not shaped by discourse. There are social dynamics deeper than this. Of course, I do not affirm what they are saying. But there is no need for exaggeration.
>
> (Arman 2015)

Referring to President Erdogan's remarks that 'birth control is a method of deception' and 'no Muslim family would use contraception' (*BBC Turkce* 2014), Tuksal states that she does not take it seriously when a male politician argues for the banning of contraception (Arman 2015). This line of thinking concludes that misogynist discourse on women's reproductive capacities is alarming only when it is codified. Stating that Erdogan must have meant 'abortion', not contraception, Karaca (2016) also normalizes/justifies AKP's approach to reproductive rights as 'moderate' and defends the contours of an Islamic-oriented approach to reproductive capacities in the political field.

Ferree (2009) reminds us that discursive statements that may seem to be single speech acts are always part of a broader discursive regime where they neatly map out the contours of discourse and conduct on issues at stake. Their efficacy does not just fade away once the heated public debate cools down; rather, their effects might be quite latent and thus not easy to disclose at first glance. Noting this, one could argue that pious women columnists, no matter how reformist their views on the coexistence of Islam and feminism might be, trivialize the power of discourse on women's reproductive capacities and/or translate conservative politicians' prohibitionist approach to women's reproductive freedom into a moderate position on the political spectrum. They also seem to suggest a non-confrontational understanding of politics that undermines secular feminist alertness and vigilance on the power of discourse and turns a blind eye to the significance of the confrontational character of feminist protest.

Discursive regulation of maternal body

In 2013, in a TV program, Tuğrul İnançer, a religious scholar well known in Islamic circles, stated that pregnant women should not wander around in tight clothing, suggesting that their public visibility is immoral and disgraceful:

> Announcing pregnancy with a flourish of trumpets is against our civility. They should not wander on the streets with such bellies... It is not aesthetic... it is disgraceful.
>
> (*Hürriyet Daily News* 2013b)

Upon this remark, pregnant women gathered in Istanbul in Taksim Square and in Kadıköy to protest İnançer's misogynist remarks and chanted slogans such as 'our bodies are ours' and 'resistpregnant' (*Hurriyet Daily News* 2013c). Some of the protesters also wrote this slogan on their bodies. Women protesters' husbands and boyfriends also supported the demonstration by wearing pillows under their T-shirts. Eraslan (2013) criticized this protest for being vulgar and insensitive to İnançer's well-respected scholarly position:

> Mr Tugrul Inancer only reacted to the pornographic display of pregnancy. Those who have always seen motherhood as a backlash started shouting 'resist, pregnant'. Inancer was only talking about past Ramadans where submission and modesty reigned... He speaks from the viewpoint of religious sensitivities.

Karaca (2013) was critical of the misogynist implications of İnançer's remarks in the beginning; yet, she toned down her critique upon the outbreak of secular feminist protests. She argued that these protests stem from an inauthentic threat perception on the secular feminist front:

> They were protesting as if these (İnançer's) remarks resonate in their lives and could threaten them… Who has ever attempted to prevent you from giving birth the way you like or filming your labour and screening it to your friends? Who has ever intervened into your wardrobe that never included a proper maternity gown.

Assuming that secular feminist women are not vulnerable vis-a-vis Inançer's remarks as they are already 'emancipated' and thus are immune to misogynist discourses, Karaca obviously ignores the gist of the feminist politics of transformation that aims for a gender equal society through intersectional awareness, dissent and activism. As Cooke (2001) defines, 'feminism involves political and intellectual awareness of gender discrimination, a rejection of behaviors furthering such discrimination, and the advocacy of activist projects to end discrimination'. Labelling secular feminist alertness on the power of discourse as unnecessary, vociferous and extreme, the statements above underestimate the durability, efficacy and forcefulness of the misogynist discursive regime in contemporary Turkey.

The debate on the 2019 Feminist Night Walk

The heated public debate on the 2019 Feminist Night Walk was another critical instance for pious women columnists to reflect on the idea of feminist defiance in the age of authoritarian-conservative gender politics. Thousands of women gathered in Istanbul on 8 March 2019 for the Feminist Night Walk that has been held annually on Taksim Square since 2003 to celebrate the International Women's Day. Yet, the police forces dispersed the march by firing tear gas, pepper spray and by blocking the march route. Moreover, in an election rally on Sunday following the Feminist Night Walk, President Erdogan showed a video taken during the protest, where women chant slogans while a nearby mosque was reciting the call to prayer. He accused women who took part in the march of disrespecting Islam:

> They disrespected the Azan (Muslim call to prayer) by booing and whistling… These women who gathered in Taksim under the leadership of CHP and HDP were disrespectful to the Azan. They whistled… These are people who also never read the national anthem. (BBC 2019)

These accusations also resonated in the AKP cadres with the claim that the protest of the Azan is ideologically utilized against the nation (Evrensel 2019). Some male Islamist public figures called the marchers 'prostitutes' and argued that such feminist protests aim for 'a genderless society along anti-family and anti-religion precepts' (Dilipak 2019). The majority of pious women public figures known for their gender-conscious lenses recognized the feminist women groups' statement that they did not protest the call for prayer (BBC Türkçe 2019). They argued that the accusations against feminist protesters misrepresent the event and generate antagonistic feelings in society. Karaca (2019) stated on Twitter:

> Some of the banners and codes of conduct in the Feminist Night Walk were too excessive to be acknowledged. But this is not the point. The point is that women's organizations clearly stated that they protested not the Azan but the police barricade. If there was no intention of targeting the Azan, why do you keep accusing them?

Karaca also shared the 17th Feminist Night Walk Initiative's press statement in order to stand in solidarity with the marchers. On the other hand, she labelled the banners used during the march 'excessive', echoing the stereotypical critique that deems feminist protest 'immoral, militant and insulting to women'. In this sense, her narrative is quite hybrid, both rejecting the marginalization of feminist protest and reproducing the accusations against the protesters.

Targeting the banners used during the march, Eraslan (2019a) argued that feminist marchers promote anti-religion discourse, encourage anti-familialism and defend sexual promiscuity:

> As a writer who has been active in various initiatives for more than thirty years working for women's rights, what shattered me most was that they [*marchers*] reduced women's rights to relentless sexuality, limitless alcohol, anti-family stance and transsexual promiscuity… Those drawings of sexual organs and breasts on every banner… What is this, if not a pornographic decline and commodification of women's body? Don't you realize that you are turning woman's body into a commodity?… Pious writers who tried to cover up this disgrace by saying that the marchers did not boo the Azan, seem to have forgotten old days when the azan was forbidden in this country.

According to Ferree (2003), contentious actors choose between 'culturally resonant' and 'radical' collective action frames, depending on their goals. Within this frame, a 'radical' framing aims to restructure hegemonic discourses while 'culturally resonant' frames tend to operate in harmony with hegemonic norms and aim to achieve greater efficacy in political action. For Eraslan (2019a), secular feminists' radical framings of gender issues delegitimize feminist defiance and render feminist protest as a site for marginal acts. Having assumed significant roles in publishing, journalism, women's activism and Islamist politics since the mid-1990s, Eraslan has been known as an 'intermediary' actor in the public sphere reconciling Islam and feminism (Bora and Günal 2002; Unal 2015; Arat 2016). Yet, her failure in the recent era to take a healthy distance from the authoritarian regime and her close ties with the government destabilized her pro-feminist public identity that marked her public persona in the 1990s and the early 2000s. Her account 'purifying' feminist protest from its radical framings and bodily aspects recognizes feminist voices only if they operate through culturally resonant frames. This framing of 'ideal' protest in non-confrontational terms is in line with AKP's idea of docile women's activism.

The critique of radical framings in feminist activism also resonates in Tuksal's recent press interview:

> In contemporary Turkish media, we mostly come across radical feminists' slogans such as 'Damn with your Family' or 'Men kill this many women every day'. I don't find these slogans appropriate. I also disagree with the idea of genderless society with queer sexual identities. These arguments seem to me as a reflection of a shallow youth ideology marked by hedonistic drifting and 'I get whatever I want' mentality used in the name of freedom.
>
> (*GazeteDuvar* 2019)

Culturally resonant collective action frames harmonized with the stress on family and gender complementarity are key in Tuksal's understanding of feminist defiance; yet her narrative differs from Eraslan's and Karaca's narratives in the sense that she does not regard radical feminist framings 'illegitimate', respects the broad spectrum of feminist arguments in the women's movements beyond the Islamic-secular binary and avoids reinforcing them.

Politics of resentment

One might argue that pious women columnists' trivialization of the power of discourse on women's bodies, the critique they pose against recent secular feminist protests and their marginalization of radical feminist slogans as 'excessive' are closely related to their past feelings of resentment that originate from the marginal status of religion in the secular women's movement. The secular feminist movement that was mostly restricted to the concerns and demands of urban, secular, middle-class women in the post-1980 era expanded its scope towards a more inclusive agenda in the 1990s (Diner and Toktaş 2010). Yet, under the political climate of the late 1990s where the state regarded the rise of political Islam as a threat to the secular political order, Muslim women became scapegoats of the contentious politics between Islamist and laicist circles, and the growing ties of empathy and dialogue between secular and pious women activists were mostly restricted to the burning debates on Islamic headscarf at the time (Arat 2004). Although the dialogue between different strands of women's movements further enhanced and channels of dialogue proliferated in collaborative activist platforms in the 2000s, feelings of resentment towards secular feminists remained intact in pious women's discourses (Unal 2015). Tuksal's following remark provides a glimpse into this uneasy relationship:

> The ban on headscarves in this country has affected nearly three generations... The feminist movement never challenged the ban in an effective way... And now pious women, very rightfully, ask how they can trust the women who did not do anything at all for them in those days. Thus, I am expecting an apology and critical self-reflexivity from the secular feminist movement.
>
> (Arman 2015)

Feelings of resentment also resonate in Ramazanoğlu's narratives where she extensively elaborates on the exclusionary treatment she faced in secular feminist circles in the 1980s (personal interview 2013). Resentment can be a valid reaction to injustice (Ahmed 2013). Although usually associated with negative feelings such as lasting bitterness and animosity, expressions of resentment can operate as a call to dialogue to deconstruct the existing power differentials and the hierarchies that they sustain. On the other hand, resentment may also lead subjects to speak from within an emotional geography of meanings, the contours of which are mapped out through strict discursive boundary making and marginalization and essentialist framing of the resented party.

The discussion so far has demonstrated that when issue-based cleavages appear between secular and pious women, especially on issues such as abortion and women's bodily autonomy, and further reify the contours of their ideological positions, politics of resentment in pious women's discourse tends to acquire an essentialist tone. Past feelings of resentment might trigger fixation of secular feminist position through essentialist labels. Marginalizing secular feminist activism by associating it with promiscuous sexuality, anti-family discourse, categorical opposition to the AKP rule, elitism, extremism and vociferousness generates a major blockage point in pious women columnists' narratives and hinders the cultivation of a dialogic, collaborative approach.

Concluding remarks

In contemporary Turkey, especially in the aftermath of the Gezi protests in 2013 and the failed coup d'état in 2016, political protest is heavily marginalized in the political discourse, its deliberative potentials are omitted and it is reduced to its adversarial nature and orientation towards conflict (Mendonca and Ercan 2015). In this political climate, the study of how recent feminist protests are perceived and narrated by different actors in contemporary women's movement is significant in many respects. It hints at the fact that in the face of an unprecedented proliferation of misogynist policy and discourse, pressing gender debates on woman's bodies, sexualities, reproductive capacities and subjectivities lead to issue-based cleavages around contentious feminist politics and its deliberative qualities.

This chapter has demonstrated that at an authoritarian-populist political moment where women's bodies have increasingly become a site of social and political control, different conceptualizations of women's bodies deeply matter in feminist conversations on how to bring together women from different backgrounds in feminist protests. Recent heated debates on women's reproductive capacities and the discursive regulation of their bodies have led pious women columnists to seek for argumentative frameworks through which they can reconcile their commitment to progressive feminist ideals with their Islamic conceptualization of woman's body. Moreover, these issue-based cleavages have complicated their positions on feminist dissent and street protest. Based on the discussions so far, it seems that they frame feminist protest in non-confrontational terms and through culturally resonant frames especially when 'controversial' gender debates are at stake. This chapter has also exposed that the dialogic potential in their narratives is severely blocked along the following points: (1) denial of legitimacy to embodied secular feminist protests where woman's body is used as a site of protest, (2) failure to acknowledge the power of discursive governance of women's bodies and sexualities and (3) essentialist tendencies of past feelings of resentment that evolve into marginalization of secular feminist activism.

Pious women columnists' discourses under consideration here are quite heterogeneous in that they entail multiple voices and a broad range of political positions with differing commitments to feminist ideals. Given the vicissitudes of the current authoritarian-political regime that does not tolerate dissent and opposition, self-formation at the intersection of feminism and Islam has become highly fragmented, multiple and contradictory in contemporary Turkey. Increased risks and vulnerabilities associated with feminist positions might lead some reformist pious women public figures to adopt a cautious and moderate stance in their critique. Moreover, organic ties with the AKP and self-positioning as a close ally of the current political regime can lead to a more dramatic destabilization of Muslim feminist position. This multiplication of voices requires us to make nuanced analyses of the heterogeneity of pious women public figures' discourses. On the other hand, one should acknowledge that those who choose to be vocal, critical and fierce in Muslim feminist discourse and collective action despite the vicissitudes of the authoritarian regime significantly contribute to the cultivation of feminist coalitional politics in the women's movement.

In tumultuous authoritarian-populist contexts where identities are further reified in the amidst of fierce political struggles to delineate the boundaries between 'us' and 'them', subjects might be prone to dismiss the heterogeneity of political positions and to reduce them to pre-packed ideological baggage. To avoid this categorical stance, this chapter does not simply conclude that the limitations and the essentialist tendencies in pious women columnists' narratives abolish altogether the dialogic qualities that might surface in their positions. Rather, it should be seen as an attempt to investigate whether the multiplicity of meanings and intermediary, coalitional narrative frames in their positions can contribute to inclusive, egalitarian and sustainable feminist struggle.

Notes

1   Scholars use different typologies to explain the authoritarian shift in the party rule in the post-2011 period such as 'hybrid' regime (Oniş 2016), 'competitive authoritarianism' (Esen and Gumuscu 2016), 'electoral authoritarianism' (Kaya 2015) or 'authoritarian neoliberalism' (Tansel 2018). Particularly focusing on how the AKP's authoritarian and populist characteristics blend together in its gender politics, this chapter utilizes the term 'authoritarian populism' (Norris and Inglehart 2019). It rests on the idea that the patchwork gender politics in the party rule composed of various ideological elements such as nationalism, conservatism, pro-Islamism and antifeminism treats 'gender' as a 'political glue' to serve both populist and authoritarian traits of the regime.
2   In the aftermath of the heated debates on the 2019 Feminist Night Walk, Berrin Sönmez, a pious women columnist writing for *GazeteDuvar*, an online news portal,

was heavily targeted in the official discourse as well as on social media for her Muslim feminist identity. She had participated in the 2019 Feminist Night Walk in Ankara. For Sönmez (2019), the negative campaign utilizing religion to accuse the marchers of the 2019 Feminist Night Walk not only targets secular feminism but also the rising public visibility of Muslim feminism. In a TV program on 11 September 2019, while Tuksal was explaining that the misogynist interpretations of the Islamic tradition render Islam patriarchal, she was harassed by an orthodox Islamist male speaker who attempted to silence her (*Milliyet* 2019).

References

Acar, F. and G. Altunok (2013), 'The "Politics of Intimate" at the Intersection of Neo liberalism and Neo-conservatism in Contemporary Turkey', *Women's Studies International Forum*, 41: 14–23.

Ahmed, S. (2013), *The Cultural Politics of Emotions*, New York: Routledge.

Akkan, B. (2018), 'The Politics of Care in Turkey: Sacred Familialism in a Changing Political Context', *Social Politics: International Studies in Gender, State & Society*, 25 (1): 72–91.

Aksoy, H. A. (2015), 'Invigorating Democracy in Turkey: The Agency of Organized Islamist Women', *Politics & Gender*, 11 (1): 146–70.

Aksoy, H. A. (2018), 'Gendered Strategies between Democratization and Democratic Reversal: The Curious Case of Turkey', *Politics and Governance*, 6 (3): 101–11.

Arat, Y. (2004), 'Rethinking the Political: A Feminist Journal in Turkey, Pazartesi', *Women's Studies International Forum*, 27: 282–97.

Arat, Y. (2016), 'Islamist Women and Feminist Concerns in Contemporary Turkey: Prospects for Women's Rights and Solidarity', *Frontiers: A Journal of Women's Studies*, 37 (3): 125–50.

Arman, A. (2015), 'Ilahiyatçı yazar Hidayet Sefkatli Tuksal: Cocuk Başına Her Ay 1500 Tl Versinler' [Theology scholar Hidayet Sefkatli Tuksal: Child support allowance should be 1500TL per child]. *Hurriyet*, 11 January. Available online: https://www.hurriyet.com.tr/yazarlar/ayse-arman/ilahiyatci-yazar-hidayet-sefkatli-tuksal-madem-annelik-kariyer-cocuk-basina-her-ay-1500-lira-versinler-27935311 (accessed 28 October 2018).

Bacchi, L. C. (2005), 'Discourse, Discourse Everywhere: Subject "Agency" in Feminist Discourse Methodology', *Nordic Journal of Women Studies*, 13 (3): 198–209.

BBC (2019), 'Erdoğan: Taksim'de Kadınlar Günü için Biraraya Gelen Grup Ezana Terbiyesizlik etti', 10 March. Available online: https://www.bbc.com/turkce/haberler-turkiye-47515663

BBC Turkce (2014), 'Dogum Kontrolü ile Yıllarca Ihanet Ettiler', Available online: https://www.bbc.com/turkce/haberler/2014/12/141222_erdogan_dogum-kontrolu (accessed 28 October 2018).

BBC Türkçe (2019), 'What We Know about the Debate on the Feminist Night Walk', 11 March. Available online: https://www.bbc.com/turkce/haberler-turkiye-47530402.

Bachetta, P. and M. Power, eds (2013), *Right Wing Women: From Conservatives to Extremists around the World*, New York: Routledge.

Bora, A and A. Günal, eds (2002), *90'larda Turkiye'de Feminizm*, Istanbul: Iletisim.

Bora, A. (2012), 'Birlik ve Beraberlige en cok Muhtac, Oldugumuz su Gunlerde Kurtaj Yasagı' (The ban on abortion at a time when we need unity and solidarity most), *Amargi*. Available online: http://www.amargidergi.com/yeni/?p=726 (accessed 28 October 2018).

Butler, J. (2015), *Notes towards a Performative Theory of Assembly*, Cambridge, MA: Harvard University Press.

Cagatay, S. (2018), 'Women's coalitions beyond the Laicism-Islamism Divide in Turkey: Towards an Inclusive Struggle for Gender Equality', *Social Inclusion*, 6 (4): 48–58.

Cindoglu, D. and D. Unal (2017), 'Gender and Sexuality in the Authoritarian Discursive Strategies of New Turkey', *European Journal of Women's Studies*, 24 (1): 39–54.

Cooke, M. (2001), *Women Claim Islam: Creating Islamic Feminism through Literature*, New York: Routledge.

Cosar, S. and F. G. Onbası (2008), 'Women's Movement in Turkey at a Crossroads: From Women's Rights Advocacy to Feminism', *South European Society and Politics*, 13 (3): 325–44.

Dilipak, A. (2019), '8 Mart'ta Ne Oldu?' (What happened on 8 March?), *YeniAkit*, 8 March.

Diner, C. and S. Toktas. (2010), 'Waves of Feminism in Turkey: Kemalist, Islamist and Kurdish Women's Movements in an era of Globalization', *Journal of Balkan and Near Eastern Studies*, 12 (1): 41–57.

Doğangün, G. (2019), 'Gender Climate in Authoritarian Politics: A Comparative Study of Russia and Turkey', *Politics and Gender*, published online.

DuvarEnglish (2019), 'Istanbul Police Disperse Demonstrators Demanding End to Violence against Women', *DuvarEnglish*, 26 November. Available online: https://www.duvarenglish.com/women/2019/11/26/istanbul-police-fire-tear-gas%20plastic-bullets-to-disperse-womens-day-rally/ (accessed 28 October 2018).

Eraslan, S. (2012a), 'Kürtaja Yönelten Sebeplerle Mücadele' (The struggle with factors associated with abortion). *Star*, 12 June. Available online: http://haber.star.com.tr/yazar/Kurtaja_yonelten_sebeplerle_mucadele/yazi%20601678 (accessed 28 October 2018).

Eraslan, S. (2012b), 'Üç Kelimede Kürtaj: Cenin, Cinnet ve Cennet' (Abortion in three words: Fetus, insanity, and heaven). Star, 31 May. Available online: https://www.star.com.tr/yazar/Uc_kelimede_kurtaj_Cenin_cinnet_ve_cennet%20yazi-594575/ (accessed 5 November 2018).

Eraslan, S. (2013), 'Nasibimiz Kalktıysa Tugrul Baba Ne Yapsın', *Star*, 31 July. Available online: https://www.star.com.tr/yazar/nasibimiz-kalktiysa-tugrul-baba-ne-yapsin-yazi-777429/ (accessed 5 November 2018).

Eraslan, S. (2019a). 'Ezani Yuhalamadilarsa Sorun Yok', *Star*, 13 March. Available online: https://www.star.com.tr/yazar/ezani%20yuhalamadilarsa-sorun-yok-yazi-1439367/

Esen, B. and Ş. Gumuşcu (2016), 'Rising Competitive Authoritarianism in Turkey', *Third World Quarterly*, 37 (9): 1581–606.

Evrensel (2019). 'Tum Yonleriyle Taksim'de Ezani Protesto Ettiler Carpitmasi' (Everything on the Fake Claim That They Prostested the Azan on Taksim), *Evrensel*.

Ferree, M. M. (2003), 'Resonance and Radicalism: Feminist Framing in the Abortion Debates of the United States and Germany', *American Journal of Sociology*, 109 (2): 304–44.

Ferree, M. M. (2009), 'Inequality, Intersectionality and Politics of Discourse: Framing Feminist Alliances', in E. Lombardo et al. (eds), *The Discursive Politics of Gender Equality*, 86–104, New York: Routledge.

GazeteDuvar (2019) 'Hidayet Sefkatli Tuksal: Kapitalist Oluyor da Müslüman Feminist Niye Olmasın?', *GazeteDuvar*, 14 December. Available online: https://www.gazeteduvar.com.tr/yazarlar/2019/12/14/824704/ (accessed 15 December 2019).

Gökariksel, B. and S. Smith (2017), 'Intersectional Feminism beyond US Flag Hijab and Pussy Hats in Trump's America', *Gender, Place and Culture*, 24 (5): 628–44.

The Guardian (2016), 'Turkish President Says Childless Women Are Deficient, Incomplete', 6 June. Available online: https://www.theguardian.com/world/2016/jun/06/turkish-president-erdogan-childless-women-deficient-incomplete (accessed 15 December 2019).

Güneş-Ayata, A., and G. Doğangün (2017), 'Gender Politics of the AKP: Restoration of a Religio-conservative Gender Climate', *Journal of Balkan and Near Eastern Studies*, 19 (6): 610–27.

Harcourt, W. (2013), *Body Politics in Development: Critical Debates in Gender and Development*, New York: Zed Books.

Hurriyet (2017), 'Kadiköy'de Kıyafetime Karışma Eylemi' (Protest in Kadıköy dubbed 'don't mess with my outfit'), *Hurriyet daily*. 29 July. Available online: http://www.hurriyet.com.tr/gundem/kadikoydekiyafetme-karisma%20eylemi%2040534870 (accessed 5 November, 2018).

Hurriyet Daily News (2012), 'Turkish Women Protest Abortion Ban with Music and Dance', 4 June. Available online: https://www.hurriyetdailynews.com/turkish-women-protest-abortion-ban-with-music-and-dance–22308 (accessed 5 November, 2018).

Hurriyet Daily News (2013a), 'Turkish PM Reiterates His Call for Three Children'. Available online: https://www.hurriyetdailynews.com/turkish-pm-erdogan-reiterates-his-call-for-three-children-38235 (accessed 28 October 2018).

Hurriyet Daily News (2013b), 'Presence of Pregnant Women in Public Is Disgraceful, Says Turkish Lawyer'. Available online: http://www.hurriyetdailynews.com/presenceofpreg%20antwomeninpublcisdisgracefulsaysturkishlawyer.aspx?pageID=238&nID=513%200&NewsCatID=341 (accessed 5 November 2018).

Hurriyet Daily News (2013c), 'Pregnant Women Gather to Protest Sufi Thinker', 25 July. Available online: https://www.hurriyetdailynews.com/pregnant-women-gather-to-protest-sufi-thinker-who-urged-them-not-to-stroll-in-public-51442 (accessed 5 November, 2018).

Hurriyet Daily News (2016), 'Turkish Government to Revise the Child Abuse Draft after Facing Uproar', 20 November. Available online: http://www.hurriyetdailynews.com/turkish%20government-to-revise-child-abuse-draft-after-facing-uproar-106346 (accessed 5 November 2018).

Hurriyet Daily News (2017), 'Turkish Women March against Rising Intolerance in Istanbul', 30 July. Available online: http://www.hurriyetdailynews.com/turkish-women-march-against%20rising-intolerance-in-istanbul-116102 (accessed 5 November 2018).

Karaca, N. B. (2012a), 'Kürtaj ve Sezaryen' (Abortion and c-section), *Haberturk*, 30 May. Available online: http://www.haberturk.com/yazarlar/nihal-bengisu-karaca/746454-kurtaj%20vesezaryen (accessed 28 October 2018).

Karaca, N. B. (2012b), 'Kürtaj Yasağı, Kimlik ve Ekonomik Büyüme' (Ban on abortion, identity, and economic growth), *Haberturk*, 6 January. Available online: http://www.haberturk.com/yazarlar/nihalbengisu-karaca/747074-kurtaj%20yasagikimlik-ve-ekonomik-buyume (accessed 28 October 2018).

Karaca, N. B. (2012d), 'Doğmus bir Çocuğun "Kürtaj" Sorgusu' (An infant's inquiry about abortion), *Haberturk*, 8 June. Available online: https://www.haberturk.com/yazarlar/nihal-bengisu-karaca/749076-dogmus-bir-cocugun-kurtaj-sorgusu (accessed 29 October 2018).

Karaca, N. B. (2013), 'Hamile Kadınlar ve Tugrul İnançer', *Haberturk*, 2 August. Available online: https://www.haberturk.com/yazarlar/nihal-bengisu-karaca/865825-hamile%20kadinlar-ve-tugrul-inancer.

Karaca, N. B. (2016), 'Müslüman Aileler ve Doğum Kontrolü' (Muslim families and birth control), *Haberturk*, 2 June. Available online: https://www.haberturk.com/yazarlar/

nihal-bengisu-karaca/1247936-musluman-aileler-ve-dogum-kontrolu (accessed 29 October 2018)

Karaca, N. B. (2019), Available online: https://twitter.com/nibenka/status/1104882689394515969.

Kaya, A. (2015), 'Islamisation of Turkey under the AKP Rule: Empowering Family, Faith and Charity', *South European Society and Politics*, 20 (1): 47–69.

Kováts, E. (2017), 'The Emergence of Powerful Anti-Gender Movements in Europe and the Crisis of Liberal Democracy', in M. Köttig et al. (eds), *Gender and Far Right Politics in Europe. Gender and Politics*, London: Palgrave Macmillan.

Köttig, M. et al. (2017), *Gender and Far-right Politics in Europe*, London: Palgrave Macmillan.

Kubilay, Ç. (2014), 'Islami Muhafazakar Kadın Yazarların Perspektifinden Kürtaj Tartışması: Elestirel bir Değerlendirme' (Abortion debate from the perspective of pious women writers: A critical evaluation), *Alternatif Politika*, 6 (3): 387–421.

Kuhar, R. and D. Patternotte. (2017), *Anti-gender Campaigns in Europe: Mobilizing against Equality*, London: Rowman & Littlefield International.

Mayer, S., I. Šori and B. Sauer (2016), 'Gendering "the People": Heteronormativity and "Ethno-Masochism" in Populist Imaginary', in M. Raniere (ed.), *Populism, Media and Education*, London: Routledge.

McNay, L. (1992), 'Foucault and Feminism: Power, Gender and the Self', in C. Ramazanoglu (ed.), *Up Against Foucault: Explorations of Some Tensions between Foucault and Feminism*, London: Routledge.

Mendonca, R. F. and S. A. Ercan (2015), 'Deliberation and Protest: Strange Bedfellows? Revealing the Deliberative Potential of 2013 Protests in Turkey and Brazil', *Policy Studies*, 36 (3): 267–82.

Milliyet (2019), 'Şu kadına haddini bildir', 11 September. Available online: https://www.milliyet.com.tr/milliyet-tv/su-kadina-haddini-bildir-video-3160780.

Norris, P. and R. Inglehart (2019), *Cultural backlash: Trump, Brexit, and authoritarian populism*, Cambridge: Cambridge University Press.

Nyhagen, L. and B. Halsaa (2016), *Religion, Gender and Citizenship: Women of Faith,Gender Equality and Feminism*, New York: Palgrave Macmillan.

O'Keefe, T. (2014), 'My Body Is My Manifesto: Slutwalk, Femen, and Femmenist Protest', *Feminist Review*, 107: 1–19.

Oniş, Z. (2016), 'Turkey's Two Elections: The AKP Comes Back', *Journal of Democracy*, 27 (2): 141–54.

Özcan, E. (2019), *Mainstreaming the Headscarf: Islamist Politics and Women in the Turkish Media*, London: I.B. Tauris.

Özgüler, C. and B. Yarar (2017), 'Neoliberal Body Politics: Feminist Resistance and the Abortion Law in Turkey', in Wendy Harcourt (ed.), *Bodies in Resistance: Gender and Sexual Politics in the Age of Neoliberalism*, 133–61, London: Palgrave Macmillan.

Phoenix, A. and P. Pattynama (2006), 'Intersectionality', *European Journal of Women's Studies*, 13 (3): 187–92.

Ramazanoğlu, Y. (2012a), 'Erkeklerin Kürtajı' (Men's abortion), *T24*, 13 June. Available online: https://t24.com.tr/haber/kurtaj-icin-siddet-uygulayan-erkeklerden-haberiniz-var-mi,206235 (accessed 29 October 2018).

Ramazanoğlu, Y. (2012b), 'Uludere Kırılma Noktamız' [Uludere is our breaking point]. *Radikal*, 3 June. Available online: http://www.radikal.com.tr/turkiye/uludere_kirilma_noktamiz-1089937 (accessed 29 October 2018).

Rinaldo, R. (2014), 'Pious and Critical: Muslim Women Activists and the Question of Agency', *Gender and Society*, 28 (6): 824–46.

Simga, H. and G. Goker (2017), 'Whither Feminist Alliance? Secular Feminists and Islamist Women in Turkey', *Asian Journal of Women's Studies*, 23 (3): 273–93.

Singh, J. (2015), 'Religious Agency and the Limits of Intersectionality', *Hypatia*, 30 (4): 657–74.

Sönmez, B. (2019), 'Islık, Ezan ve Islami Feminizme Saldırı', (Whistle, Azan and assault against Islamic feminism), *GazeteDuvar*, 12 March. Available online: https://www.gazeteduvar.com.tr/yazarlar/2019/03/12/islik-ezan-ve-islami-feminizme-saldiri/

Sutton, B. (2010), *Bodies in Crisis: Culture, Violence and Women's Resistance in Neoliberal Argentina*, NJ: Rutgers University Press.

Sutton, B. (2007), 'Naked Protest: Memories of Bodies and Resistance at the World Social Forum', *Journal of International Women's Studies*, 8 (3): 139–48.

Şişman, N. (2006), *Emanetten Mülke: Kadın-Beden-Siyaset [From Entrustment to Property: Woman-body-politics]*, Istanbul: Iz Yayıncılık.

Tansel, C. B. (2018), 'Authoritarian Neoliberalism and Democratic Backsliding in Turkey: Beyond the Narratives of Progress', *South European Society and Politics*, 23 (2): 197–217.

Tuksal, H. S. (2012a), 'Her Çocuk icin Maaş Verin, Sonra Üç Çocuk İsteyin' (First provide child support, then ask for three children), *Aksam*, 6 June. Available online: http://www.aksam.com.tr/guncel/her-cocuk-icin-maas-verin,-sonra%20ucisteyin%20119841h/haber-119841 (accessed 28 October 2018).

Tuksal, H. S. (2012b), 'Uludere'de Kürtaj yok, Çocuk Cesetleri Var' (Uludere is not about abortion, it is about children's dead bodies), *Radikal*, 6 June. Available online: http://www.radikal.com.tr/turkiye/uluderede_kurtaj_yok_cocuk_cesetleri_var%201090283 (accessed 28 October 2018).

Tüysüz, G. (2016), '7 Times Turkish President "Mansplained" Womanhood', *CNN*, 9 June. Available online: https://edition.cnn.com/2016/06/09/europe/erdogan-turkey-mansplained%20womanhood/index.html (accessed 28 October 2018).

Ünal, D. (2015), 'Vulnerable Identities: Pious Women Columnists' Narratives on Islamic Feminism and Feminist Self-Identification in Contemporary Turkey', *Women's Studies International Forum*, 53: 12–21.

Ünal, D. (2019), 'The Abortion Debate and Profeminist Coalitional Politics in Contemporary Turkey', *Politics & Gender*, 15 (4): 801–25.

Ünal, D. and D. Cindoğdu (2013), 'Reproductive Citizenship in Turkey: Abortion Chronicles', *Women's Studies International Forum*, 38: 21–31.

Ünal, D. (2021), 'The Masculinist Restoration Project in the Rhetoric of Anti-Gender Movements: The Case of Turkey', in O. Hakola et al. (eds), *Culture and Politics of Populist Masculinities*, United States: Lexington Books.

Verloo, M. (2018), *Varieties of Opposition to Gender Equality in Europe*, New York: Routledge.

Index

www.ingramcontent.com/pod-product-compliance
Lightning Source LLC
Chambersburg PA
CBHW060153280326
41932CB00012B/1745